CW01095953

Studies in Regional and Loca

General Editor Jane Whittle

Rethinking Ancient Woodland

The archaeology and history
of woods in Norfolk

Gerry Barnes and Tom Williamson

University of Hertfordshire Press
Studies in Regional and Local History

Volume 13

First published in Great Britain in 2015 by
University of Hertfordshire Press
College Lane
Hatfield
Hertfordshire
AL10 9AB
UK

British Library Cataloguing in Publication Data
A catalogue record for this book is available from the British Library

ISBN 978-1-909291-57-7 hardback
ISBN 978-1-909291-58-4 paperback

Design by Arthouse Publishing Solutions Ltd
Printed in Great Britain by Henry Ling Ltd, Dorset

Contents

Figures

Acknowledgements

A large number of individuals and organisations have helped with this book, by allowing access to archives or sites, or by providing help, advice or information. We would like to thank, in particular: Gilbert Addison; Chris Allhusen; Gavin Alston; Gary Battell; Robin Carver; Peter Clarke; Nick Coleman; Sid Cooper; Brian Cushion; Patsy Dallas; John Ebbage; David Fox; Rob Fuller; Lynn Giles; David Green; Jon Gregory; Lady Rose Hare; Sarah Harrison; Rory Hart; Colin Hitchman; Ben Hogben; Matthew Hutton; Henry Kilvert; Robert Liddiard; Jim Lyon; Sir Rupert Mann; Diana MacMullen; Andrew MacNair; Lawrence Malyon; Colin McDonald; Nicholas Meade; Sam Neal; Colin Palmer; Andrew Rogerson; Steve Scott; Tim Snelling; Annie Sommazzi; Sarah Spooner; Adam Stone; Robert Tamworth, Earl Ferrers; Clive Walker; Henry Walker; Stephen Westover; David White; Lucy Whittle; Anne Wood; Alison Yardy; the staff of the Norfolk Record Office; the Norfolk Wildlife Trust; the Woodland Trust; and numerous undergraduates and MA students who have, over the years, taken Landscape History courses at the University of East Anglia. Figure 9 is reproduced with permission of Andrew MacNair; Figures 18, 27, 28, 30, and 48 courtesy of the Norfolk Record Office.

Lastly, we would like to acknowledge the very generous financial contribution made by the Scarfe Trust towards the costs of publishing this volume.

The owners of the woods we have studied have been remarkably helpful in allowing access to their property, and we would emphasise that, with a handful of exceptions, the places we describe are not open to the general public, and are strictly private.

Abbreviations

CCR   Calendar of Close Rolls
CIPM   Calendar of Inquisitions Post-Mortem
CLR   Calendar of Liberate Rolls
CPR   Calendar of Patent Rolls
HALS   Hertfordshire Archives and Local Studies
NHER   Norfolk Historical Environment Record (Union House, Gressenhall)
NRO   Norfolk Record Office
NWT   Norfolk Wildlife Trust
SSSI   Site of Special Scientific Interest
TNA   The National Archives

Studies in Regional and Local History

General Editor's preface

The nature and role of England's historic woodlands remains a relatively neglected aspect of England's local history, despite extensive discussion by ecologists and archaeologists. It is therefore a great pleasure to be able to introduce Gerry Barnes and Tom Williamson's study of Norfolk woodland as volume 13 of *Studies in Regional and Local History*. Professor Tom Williamson is a leading landscape historian and archaeologist who has published extensively on the development of England's medieval and post-medieval rural landscape. In this volume he joins with Dr Gerry Barnes, the retired former Head of Environment at Norfolk County Council, to present a rich and detailed account of the evolution of Norfolk's woodland from prehistory to the present day.

Oliver Rackham brought a number of seductive theories about the history of English woodland to a wide readership. Perhaps the most important of these was the idea of 'ancient woodland' in the English landscape as largely representing the remnants of prehistoric wildwood, which had survived, albeit subject to significant human management, into the present day. Ecologists have argued that the number and types of plant species found in particular woods are a guide to their antiquity, as many species colonise new ground only very gradually, while the *Ancient Woodland Inventory* launched by the Nature Conservancy Council in 1981 sought to identify and record all woods in England and Wales of 'ancient' origin. In this book Barnes and Williamson gently take issue with these approaches. Drawing conclusions from systematic fieldwork surveys of fifty Norfolk woods, as well as from historic maps and estate documents, they present evidence showing that 'ancient' woods are a largely man-made environment; that many of these woods have originated since the late medieval period, even as recently as the nineteenth century; and that their characteristic vegetation develops much more rapidly than many have previously assumed. Rackham emphasised the importance of coppicing as the traditional form of woodland management: Barnes and Williamson draw attention to other forms of management that existed before, after and alongside coppicing, such as the use of woods as pasture, game reserves, elements in aesthetic landscapes, and in Norfolk's case, as bomb stores during the Second World War.

As well as combining a range of evidence in innovative ways, *Rethinking Ancient Woodland* demonstrates the benefits of viewing woodland within wider trends of rights to property and land management. Rural historians are familiar with the piecemeal enclosure movement of the late medieval and early modern period when small private fields were separated from common farming systems. The history of woodland throws the spotlight on an earlier phase of enclosure, when lords separated and enclosed areas of woodland for their private use, making woods part of the lord's demesne rather than a common resource for tenants. Over the years, changing fashions in lordly leisure from medieval deer parks to the pheasant coverts in the eighteenth and nineteenth centuries have had a significant impact on woodland, together with changing the aesthetic fashions of lords' country-house estates. Trees were not simply elements of the lordly landscape however. Barnes and Williamson suggest tenants' carefully nurtured selected trees on areas of common land, as how else can the survival and replenishment of mature trees on extensively grazed commons be explained?

Rethinking Ancient Woodland brings the history of woodland right up to the present day. The replacement of wood and charcoal with coal as a domestic and industrial fuel reduced the value of woods' main product, but coppicing only gradually fell out of use. Nineteenth century landlords sought to improve woods in the same spirit as they improved agriculture, with schemes for better drainage and replanting with new tree types. It was only in the twentieth century, with the decline of great estates, that wholesale neglect set in: once a most valued resource, woods were now largely redundant of productive uses within the agricultural landscape. The effect of non-management has been just as profound as earlier management systems, altering the dominant tree types and ground flora of woods.

In charting the long history of the rise and decline of woodland management Norfolk is a particularly interesting case study. Norfolk was very densely populated in the medieval period, and the predominance of good agricultural land meant that areas of woodland from the medieval period onwards were relatively sparse. The pressure on woodland as a resource which these circumstances created meant that Norfolk woodlands have been heavily managed since the early medieval period. Yet even in Norfolk a great diversity of woods survived, and continue to display a rich variety of botanical environments to the present day. With its detailed appendix containing an entry on each of the woods Barnes and Williamson have surveyed, *Rethinking Ancient Woodlands* shows clearly how far the history of ancient woodland can be 'read' from its surviving remains, in terms of both archaeological and botanical evidence. At the same time, it reveals the degree to which these 'natural' environments are the product of millennia of varying strategies of human intervention.

Jane Whittle
June 2015

Chapter 1

Studying ancient woodland

This volume is the result of several years of research into the history and archaeology of long-established, semi-natural woodland – 'ancient woodland', as it is often called – in one English county, Norfolk. There have been a number of important studies of woodland over the last few decades, and readers may be wondering why we need another, and especially one which is focused on one particular area of the country. Our answer is that most of those studies, although differing in many of their details, share a broadly similar perspective, mostly emphasising the essentially 'natural' character of 'ancient woodland', or at least its antiquity and stability in the landscape. Many, moreover, are written by individuals with a background that is primarily in ecology or one of the other natural sciences. This book approaches the subject, mainly although not exclusively, from the perspective of the landscape historian and archaeologist, and considers woodland and its development as part of the wider history of the landscape. It re-examines the character of 'ancient woodland', casting some doubt on its long-term stability and antiquity and the extent of its continuity with the natural vegetation. Indeed, it effectively questions the very usefulness of the term itself, while at the same time recognising, and celebrating, the immense importance of old woods in terms of both the natural and the historical environment.

The historiography of ancient woodland

By the middle decades of the nineteenth century it was already widely recognised that there were significant differences in the ecological character of recently planted woodland and older, semi-natural woods, and that some of the latter represented the remains, modified by human exploitation, of the natural forests that had originally covered England (Watkins 1988, 238). By the end of the century botanists such as Clement Reid, and the contributors to the various Victoria County Histories, were suggesting that the particular kinds of plant species found in many woods represented survivors from these primaeval, natural woodlands (Reid 1899; Watkins 1988, 240), and in 1910 Moss, Rankin and Tansley were able to argue that *most* British woods represented the direct 'lineal descendants of primaeval forests' (Moss *et al.* 1910). But it was only in the middle decades of the twentieth century, most notably with the writings of men such as A.G. Tansley and H.L. Edlin, that serious attempts were made to understand how these 'forests' had developed, and how they had then been transformed into the small pockets of woodland surviving in the modern landscape.

As a result, in large measure, of the development in the early twentieth century of palynology – the analysis of ancient pollen preserved in bogs, lake sediments or other anaerobic conditions – it became apparent that, following the end of the last Ice Age, around 11,000 BC, England had gradually been colonised by plants and animals as the climate warmed and as a continued connection with Continental Europe (the English Channel and the southern North Sea were flooded only in the seventh millennium BC) allowed different species to move northwards with relative ease, beginning with pine and birch. The natural vegetation thus developed through a process that ecologists call 'succession'. As the climate warmed up, plants colonised in a more or less predictable sequence, each creating conditions which allowed successors to establish and flourish, leading in time to the development of a climax vegetation of closed-canopy forest which survived intact until the arrival of farming soon after 4000 BC. Following this, most of England was gradually cleared of trees, but if land is abandoned for any length of time succession begins once again, and within a short period grasses and herbs will give way to scrub, and scrub to woodland, as experiments carried out at Rothampsted in Hertfordshire from the 1880s – involving the deliberate abandonment of two small plots of land – demonstrated (Lawes 1895; Brenchley and Adam 1915).

The larger of the abandoned plots at Rothampstead, in Geesecroft Field, came in time to be occupied by mature woodland dominated by oak and ash; and the fact that oak (*Quercus* sp.) was the most common timber tree found in old English woodlands, as well as more widely in the countryside, led to the understandable belief that this had been the most important species in the natural woodlands of the pre-Neolithic period. Tansley concluded in the 1930s that 'native oak forest ... covered very extensive areas' even into the historic period, with pedunculate oak dominant on deeper, damper, heavier soils, and sessile or durmast oak on lighter, drier, more acid formations (Tansley 1949, 246–7). In Edlin's words: 'The two oaks, sessile and pedunculate, are the trees that figure largest in these natural woodlands, and may safely be taken as having formed the largest element in forests of late prehistoric and subsequent historic times' (Edlin 1956, 73). 'Oakwoods of one kind or another are so ubiquitous over Britain, that one can advance, fairly safely, the working hypothesis that mixed oakwood is, or has once been, the normal forest cover on most areas that can carry woodland at all' (Edlin 1956, 74).

Researchers in the mid-twentieth century, it should be noted, also acknowledged that other species had dominated the natural vegetation in particular districts. But, again, this belief was to a large extent based, not unreasonably, on the character of what were perceived to be the surviving, modified 'fragments' of the natural vegetation. Edlin thus suggested that the beechwoods found in the Chiltern Hills and in south-east and south-central England were of 'natural origin'; Tansley argued that their distribution may once have been more widespread, the present occurrence of beech-dominated woodland being the consequence of climatic change and human interference (Tansley 1949, 248–9). Ash, both men thought, and for similar reasons, may also have been locally dominant in the natural forests. But it was only in the north of Britain, in the 'highland zone', that the dominance of oak was thought to have been seriously challenged by other species, especially birch and pine, in the untouched forests of remote prehistory. It must be emphasised that Edlin in particular – a forester by training – was fully aware that the present appearance and vegetational structure of old woodland also owed much to human management over the centuries. But edaphic factors, and the survival of characteristics inherited from the natural woodlands, were given priority in early interpretations.

The belief that oak forest had been the predominant British forest community on most soils, before the first clearances by prehistoric and later farmers gradually fragmented the primaeval woods, was initially supported by the evidence of preserved prehistoric pollen sequences. But as more pollen evidence became available through the middle and later decades of the twentieth century, and better methods for analysing it developed, this perception began to change. It became evident that small-leaved lime (*Tilia cordata*), rather than oak, had been the most important component of the post-glacial vegetation across much of lowland England, accompanied by varying mixtures of oak, hazel, ash and elm, and with pine and birch locally significant. In the north and west lime was less frequent and pollen cores suggested instead the presence of woodlands comprising diverse mixtures of oak, hazel, birch, pine and elm (Bennett 1988, 251; Rackham 2006, 82–90). The dominance of oak as a timber tree in most English woods could now be seen as a consequence of economic rather than natural factors: it made the best timber for the construction of houses and ships, being relatively easy to work when green, but becoming as hard as iron once seasoned. The loss of lime from the landscape, and its absence from no more than a small percentage of English woods, likewise demonstrated the extent to which the latter were not simply the tattered remnants of the original vegetation, but had been quite extensively modified by many centuries of management. It was this subject – how woods had been exploited in the medieval and early post-medieval periods – which became in the last decades of the twentieth century one of the principal concerns of woodland historians, and especially of the most important student of ancient woodland, the individual who brought to currency the term 'ancient woodland' itself, Oliver Rackham.

Rackham was an ecologist by training but was also an effective historian, able to read Latin and deal with medieval palaeography, as well as being an able field archaeologist. His approach to woodland was articulated in a number of erudite, influential and engagingly written publications, most notably *Trees and woodland in the British landscape* (1976), *Ancient woodland* (1980), *The history of the countryside* (1986a) and *Woodlands* (2006). In this series of volumes Rackham discussed in far more detail than his predecessors had done the way in which, from the early Middle Ages, portions of the surviving 'wildwood' – his term for the natural vegetation, unaffected by human settlement and agriculture – had gradually come to be enclosed and managed more intensively by manorial lords as 'coppice with standards'. In this form of management the majority of trees and bushes were cut down to at or near ground level on a rotation of between seven and fifteen years in order to provide a regular crop of 'poles' – that is, straight and relatively narrow pieces of wood suitable for tools, minor parts of buildings and vehicles, fencing and fuel – the plants regenerating vigorously from the stump or 'stool', or suckering from the rootstock. There were relatively few 'standard' trees – ones allowed to grow naturally and harvested for timber – for if these had been numerous their canopy shade would have suppressed the growth of the underwood beneath: woods, that is, were about producing wood more than about producing timber (Rackham 1986a, 65–8). Most standards were felled when relatively young, at 80 to 100 years of age. Coppices were vulnerable to grazing livestock – at least in the early stages of the rotation – and it was primarily for this reason that woods needed to be securely enclosed, with banks, ditches and hedges. Intensive management had become necessary because, as population rose during the early Middle Ages, and the area used for growing crops and grazing livestock increased, the amount of wood and timber that could be derived from less intensively managed woodlands was insufficient for the needs of society:

prices rose, and what we now describe as 'traditional' forms of management thus became economic. Not all woods managed as coppice-with-standards, however, were the direct descendants of the wildwood. Rackham emphasised, to an extent that his predecessors had not, that a significant number of semi-natural woods were 'secondary' in character – that is, they had spontaneously grown up (or had otherwise become established) on land which had been cleared and farmed for a period in the distant past, but which had then been abandoned (Rackham 1976, 18–19). This had sometimes happened in prehistoric or Roman times, sometimes in the later medieval or early post-medieval periods. Rackham researched, and explained, many aspects of woodland ecology and discussed – in a chapter in his 1976 book which has yet to be bettered – the methods of fieldwork, including archaeological fieldwork, which need to be employed in the study of ancient woods (Rackham 1976, 114–42).

Rackham charted, with erudition and clarity, not only the rise of traditional woodmanship but also its decline in the course of the eighteenth and nineteenth centuries, as coal replaced wood as a fuel, as items manufactured from iron replaced those formerly fashioned from wood and as new ideas of forestry – involving the establishment of non-renewable plantations, lacking a coppice understorey and with trees treated as a crop, planted, thinned and then felled – rose to dominance. Traditional forms of management finally came to an end in the course of the twentieth century, when many woods were grubbed out for agriculture or replanted as plantations, often with exotic conifers. Only where woods were managed primarily for the purpose of nature conservation were ancient practices maintained or reinstated.

Rackham's work has been immensely influential among landscape historians and others, and until his recent death he was unquestionably the best-known writer on ancient woodland in Britain. Others, however, have also made important contributions to the subject which – while perhaps less well known outside the natural sciences – have arguably been as important. In particular, George Peterken, during a long career with the Nature Conservancy and subsequently as an independent consultant, published a number of key articles and two major books on woodland: *Woodland conservation and management* (1981) and *Natural woodland: ecology and conservation in northern temperate regions* (1996). In these he discussed the dynamics of woodland ecology in Britain and beyond and also – like Rackham – categorised the various types of semi-natural woodland found in this country, defining a range of distinctive 'stand types' – combinations of particular shrubs and trees – which made up different kinds of woodland and placing them within a wider European context (1981, 118–73). Perhaps his greatest contribution to the study and conservation of woodland was, however, through his involvement in the compilation of the *Ancient Woodland Inventory*, initiated in 1981 by the Nature Conservancy Council (Nature Conservancy Council 1981; Spencer and Kirby 1992, 78). Peterken, while fully acknowledging the role of management in the development of woodland vegetation ('few if any stands qualify as being strictly virgin' (Peterken 1981, 44)), also emphasised the influence of soils and climate in generating the 'forest types of Europe' from which British woodlands had ultimately developed (Peterken 1981, 34–7). He also usefully discussed the complexities inherent in the term 'natural woodland' (Peterken 1996). He emphasised how the pre-Neolithic vegetation of England – in its condition of 'original-naturalness', 'before people became a significant ecological factor' – was different from what it would be in a state of 'present-naturalness', defined as the 'state that would prevail now if people had not become a significant ecological factor', simply because of climatic changes and of other entirely natural influences and process which have operated over the intervening millennia. But more radically different still would be 'future-natural' woodlands, which Peterken defined as those 'which would eventually develop if people's influence were completely and permanently removed'. This is because so many new species have been introduced into the country since prehistoric times, while others have become extinct (Peterken 1996, 13). The 'future-natural' forest that would emerge if nature was somehow to be left to its own devices would thus probably contain a large proportion of sycamore trees.

Ecologists are now, for the most part, fully aware that surviving areas of old-growth forest throughout the world have been radically altered by human exploitation. Little if any 'wildwood', to use Rackham's term for truly virgin forest, survives: 'the very concept of wildwood has shrunk in the face of archaeological and historical discoveries ... Anyone who restricts the term "natural woodland" to woods with no human influence risks creating an empty category' (Rackham 2006, 103). Nevertheless, the idea persists that ancient woods represent, at least in the case of those that are 'primary', a direct link with the natural vegetation, and that variations in composition thus reflect – in part – variations in that of the 'wildwood' itself. The extent to which coppiced woodland represents a 'natural' habitat lies at the heart of this book; but perhaps equally important is the related issue of its antiquity and its stability in the landscape, to which we shall also return repeatedly in the chapters that follow.

Figure 1 'Ancient woodland indicators': a display of bluebells and wood anemones beneath outgrown coppice of ash and hornbeam.

Ancient woods are valued by botanists and ecologists because, as has long been recognised, they contain a number of distinctive plants – around 250 species of flowers, sedges and grasses occur mainly or exclusively within them (Colebourn 1989) – that in turn provide food for a range of important, and often rare or infrequent, invertebrates (Figure 1). But such plants flourish best where woods are subject to regular coppicing. Larger woods were usually felled section by section, in rotation, creating a mosaic of blocks of coppice in different stages of regrowth. Coppicing opens up the floor of the wood to light, yet at the same time leaves the ground flora undisturbed: the resulting growth of woodland herbs is ideal for sustaining a wide range of insects, especially butterflies such as the pearl-bordered fritillary, the high brown fritillary and the Duke of Burgundy. Indeed, the decline of coppicing over the last century or so has been a major factor in the fall in butterfly numbers in England (Warren 1989, 185–96). The abundant supplies of food afforded by such diverse and continually changing environments also attract a wide range of birds and mammals, although the former in particular were also directly encouraged by the structural diversity afforded by traditional management. Bird species display much variation in terms of their preferences for different stages of coppice regrowth, and thus the mosaic of fells serves to increase the scale of diversity (Carter 1990; Fuller and Green 1998).

Even in an unmanaged state ancient woods are beneficial to wildlife, especially in intensively farmed districts where there is little other cover. Large numbers of birds and mammals are attracted to the margins of woods, for 'edge' environments are of critical ecological importance: animals benefit from the opportunities to forage for food in adjacent fields or pastures, but also enjoy the cover, and further sources of food, provided by the wood itself. Woods, occupying ground that has often never been ploughed, may also contain areas of standing water which, once again, may otherwise be rare in intensively farmed districts. But, all this said, there is widespread agreement that the degree of diversity is greatest where woods are actively managed, and that neglected woods, outgrown and shady, are of significantly less conservation value.

Defining ancient woodland: the *Ancient Woodland Inventory*

The *Ancient Woodland Inventory*, with which Peterken was centrally involved in the late 1970s, was created in order to establish the extent and quality of ancient, semi-natural woodland remaining in England and Wales at a time when much had recently been grubbed out for agriculture or damaged by replanting with commercial conifers. It was intended that this document, which was compiled using a methodology first trialled in the county of Norfolk, would provide a baseline against which subsequent changes in the area and condition of ancient woodland could be judged. It would also act as a guide to local authorities and others in the formulation of woodland conservation policies, through, for example, the identification of some woods as Sites of Special Scientific Interest (SSSIs), thus assisting in the preservation of the distinctive flora and fauna associated with this kind of habitat. Replanted sites, or 'Plantations on Ancient Woodland Sites' (PAWS), were also included on the grounds that residual fragments of original vegetation might survive among the conifers (Peterken 1981, 11).

Following terms and concepts first fully articulated by Rackham a few years earlier, the *Inventory* applied the term 'ancient woodland' solely to areas that have been continuously wooded since at least AD 1600, a 'cut-off' date adopted partly in the belief that, prior to this, few woods had been deliberately planted, but also because little reliable cartographic evidence, which could be used to confirm or deny the existence of particular woods, survives from before that date. Such woodland was further subdivided into examples which were of 'primary' and of 'secondary' character (Peterken 1981; Rackham 1976; Spencer and Kirby 1992). Primary ancient woods were defined as those occupying sites which have remained wooded since prehistory. Secondary ancient woods, in contrast, are areas which have been cleared for farming, settlement or industrial use at some time in the past, but which were subsequently abandoned and recolonised by trees, although before the start of the seventeenth century (Peterken 1996, 17; Rackham 2006, 20). Ancient woods of both kinds are characterised by a coppice-with-standards structure, usually still clearly discernable in spite of many decades of neglect; and boast a range of distinctive 'woodland indicator species' (Rose 1999, 241). These, in theory, include a variety of mosses, fungi, bryophytes and lichens, but in practice the emphasis was, and has subsequently been, on a range of vascular plants: herbs, generally slow-colonising species which are shade tolerant or shade-bearing, are often dependent on high levels of humidity, and usually have poor resistance to grazing. Embracing a wide range of species, although varying from district to district, these typically include dog's mercury (*Mercurialis perennis*), bluebell (*Hyacinthoides non-scriptus*), primrose (*Primula vulgaris*), wood anemone (*Anemone nemorosa*), wood spurge (*Euphorbia amygdaloides*), wood melick (*Melica uniflora*), yellow archangel (*Lamiastrum galeobdolon*) and water avens (*Geum rivale*) (Rotherham *et al.* 2008, 36–7). The significance of such plants was noted, in a Norfolk context, as early as 1924 by H.E. Beevor:

> Our original old woods may, I believe, be readily identified, because every wood containing the wild hyacinth I take to be such. Outside the wood, bluebells rarely appear in the hedgerow, if so they proclaim a woodland that has disappeared. (Beevor 1924, 502)

In the case of 'primary' woods, the presence of these 'ancient woodland indicators' was thought to reflect the fact that their current vegetation is the 'direct descendant of original, natural woodland' (Peterken and Game 1984, 156). In the case of secondary woods, in contrast, it was a consequence of longevity and stability of land use, and of location. As the introduction to the *Inventory* suggests:

> Woods which were cleared were often not isolated from the remaining primary sites but were either within or adjacent to them. If woodlands did recolonise the site then the area could rapidly acquire the appropriate species from woods nearby … As both types have been managed under traditional regimes … it is now almost impossible to distinguish between the two. (Nature Conservancy Council 1981, 4)

We will discuss the significance of 'ancient woodland indicators' at some length below. It is important to note here, however, that a number of researchers have suggested that as evidence for the status and antiquity of particular woods they should be used with some caution (Peterken and Game 1984, 155; Rose 1999, 249; Wager 1998). Rose, for example, has emphasised that 'they should be regarded only as a tool, and not as an infallible guide' (Rose 1999, 250), while Rotherham has argued that their use has often been 'too formulaic', and has emphasised the way in which the affinity of 'indicator species' with ancient woodland 'varies tremendously with geology and hence soils and/or drainage, and especially with climate and microclimate' (Rotherham 2011a, 172, 174, 178). He and others have also emphasised that different kinds of plant may have 'indicator' status in different geographical contexts (Rotherham *et al.* 2008, 37). Dog's mercury, for example, appears a reasonable indicator of antiquity in the Midlands, but can be found in some relatively recent woods in parts of East Anglia (Rackham 1986a, 108).

A relatively small proportion of the woods included in the *Inventory* were not of the coppice-with-standards type, but were instead surviving fragments of 'wood-pasture', a form of land use which was common in the Middle Ages but which declined in importance steadily thereafter. Wood-pastures were, like most coppiced woods, thought by those responsible for the *Inventory* to be modified remnants of the 'wildwood', but they comprised areas which were used both for producing wood and timber *and* for grazing livestock. They thus lacked a managed understorey, which would have been damaged and eventually killed off by grazing, and instead the majority of trees were systematically pollarded: that is, cut in the manner of coppice stools but at a height of around two to three metres, raised on a trunk, or 'bolling', out of the reach of browsing animals. Many wood-pastures were to be found on common land – on the manorial 'wastes' (Rackham 1986a, 119–52; Dallas 2010, 23–36). But some were private, in which case they were often deer parks – venison farms and hunting grounds which had been enclosed from the common woods with banks, ditches and fences usually more substantial than those which encircled coppiced woods (Liddiard 2007). Interest in wood-pastures as a distinct habitat has increased markedly in recent decades, in part because of a growing recognition of the importance of veteran trees as a key wildlife habitat.

Relatively few wood-pastures now remain in England. Those areas of common wood-pasture which survived the encroachments of cultivated land or enclosure as coppiced woodland or deer parks were, according to many writers, inherently unstable environments. Their trees were vulnerable to damage from stock, through the stripping of bark, for example, or the compaction of the ground above their root systems. More importantly, once trees died, were blown down or were felled it was difficult to establish replacements in the face of sustained grazing. According to conventional wisdom, fencing off portions of land to protect new trees (or, indeed, for any other purpose) was difficult, if not impossible, as it conflicted with the rights of commoners to freely access and exploit the common (Rackham 1986a, 121–2). Those examples which survived into the post-medieval period were usually destroyed following enclosure in the eighteenth and nineteenth centuries. Private wood-pastures also declined in late medieval times as a consequence of rising costs and changing fashions, and any that survived into the post-medieval period often came to form the settings for country houses, and were thus normally thinned and tidied up in the eighteenth or nineteenth century through conversion to the more open 'landscape parks' associated with Lancelot Brown, Humphry Repton and their contemporaries. Ecologists tend to disagree over whether the term 'ancient woodland' should be reserved for woods of coppice-with-standard type, or should also embrace wood-pastures. While we will, in the pages that follow, pay some attention to wood-pastures, and especially to their surviving remnants within the study area – the county of Norfolk – we will be mainly, although not exclusively, concerned with ancient woods of the coppice-with-standards type.

The implications of ancient woodland

The last three decades of the twentieth century thus saw the emergence of the idea that there is an identifiable, distinct kind of habitat which can usefully be termed 'ancient woodland'; that this has varied origins, but comprises in large part areas of the natural vegetation – Rackham's 'wildwood' – only modified by human management; and that such woodland displays distinctive features of structure and vegetation which distinguish it clearly from woods of more recent, post-sixteenth-century, origin. These distinctive vegetational characteristics were inherited directly from the native vegetation: in Edlin's words, they were 'relics' of the original vegetation, albeit – as he emphasised on a number of occasions – 'modified to a greater or lesser extent by man's purposeful or casual actions over many centuries' (Edlin 1956, 65).

Inherent in this model is the idea of stability: the wildwood had achieved, through natural processes of succession, stable vegetational characteristics which were then preserved in large measure once woods were isolated, enclosed and managed. The distinctive 'ancient woodland indicators' are thus survivors from the wildwood, incapable of colonising new areas of woodland with any speed, so that they fail to occur in recently established woods and plantations. This in turn implies that woods do not come and go from the landscape but – once defined by enclosure and embanking – remained as stable features until destroyed. Rackham thus eloquently described how the Bradfield Woods in west Suffolk

> are well documented back to 1252 and would still instantly be recognised by Abbot Symon of that year. The outline of the woods was virtually unaltered until the 1960s, and is demarcated by a mighty bank which may already have been old in Abbot Simon's time. The woodland is managed almost exactly as it was then … . (Rackham 1986a, 63)

This concept of traditional woodland – stable, ancient and with distinctive botanical characteristics inherited from the natural vegetation – can usefully be viewed as part of a wider paradigm for understanding the history of the English landscape which developed during the last third of the twentieth century. The notion that the range of distinctive 'ancient woodland indicator' plants represents survivals from the natural vegetation, for example, has parallels in ideas about the vegetation of English hedges put forward by Ernest Pollard in the 1960s. Max Hooper, Pollard's colleague at the Monks Wood Research Station in Cambridgeshire, developed the idea that hedges acquired additional shrub species, through processes of natural succession, at a relatively steady rate. Because most hedges had (he thought) been planted with only one species, they could therefore be dated by the number of different kinds of shrub which they contained in a standard length of 30 yards – the famous, or infamous, 'Hooper Hypothesis' which attracted much attention from local and landscape historians in the 1970s and 1980s (Pollard *et al.* 1974, 79–85; Barnes and Williamson 2006, 24–41). Pollard's argument was rather different, although it appeared in the same co-written volume as Hooper's theory, as well as in a number of articles. He distinguished a particular kind of hedge which he termed a 'woodland relic hedge' (Pollard *et al.* 1974, 86–90; Pollard 1973). This was very mixed in composition and contained large quantities of the slow-colonising woodland shrubs, with 'different shrubs dominant for short lengths, including hazel, dogwood, maple, woodland hawthorn, service and spindle' (Pollard 1973, 351). In addition, such hedges featured particular herbs – our familiar 'ancient woodland indicators', such as dog's mercury or bluebells – growing at their base and in the associated ditch. Pollard concluded that these hedges must have originated as assarts in woodland: that is, they had come into existence as fields were cut out of the virgin woodland, as cultivation expanded in early times. Their diversity had not been *acquired*, over time, in the manner that Hooper's approach would suggest. Instead, it had been *retained*, from the time of the hedge's origins. Pollard originally argued that 'there was little doubt' that such hedges were 'relics of old woodland, the former wood-edge vegetation being managed to form a hedge' (Pollard 1973, 351); however, in their 1974 book Hooper and Pollard admitted another possibility – that early colonists had simply improvised hedges around their new plots by gathering shrubs from the adjacent areas of woodland (Pollard *et al.* 1974, 98). Either way, the idea that plant communities descended from the natural vegetation could survive in landscape features of extreme antiquity has obvious parallels with the usual interpretation of the significance of 'Ancient Woodland Indicators' in woodland.

Rackham, as well as coining the term 'ancient woodland', is also responsible for the concept of 'ancient countryside', a broad kind of landscape which he distinguished from what he described as the 'planned countryside' (Rackham 1976, 1–3). The latter predominates across a broad swath of lowland England, running from Yorkshire in the north-east to the south coast. In the medieval period this had been 'champion' countryside, characterised by nucleated villages farming extensive communal open fields. Few hedges had existed, and woodland tended to be concentrated in limited areas, usually royal 'forests' such as Rockingham or Bernwood. Because in most places within this broad zone open fields survived well into the post-medieval period and were then enclosed by large-scale planned reorganisation – often effected by parliamentary enclosures – these areas have a field pattern defined by recent, ruler-straight, species-poor hedges. This, in Rackham's almost poetic words, is:

> The England of big villages, few, busy roads, thin hawthorn hedges, windswept brick farms, and ivied clumps of trees in the corners of fields; a predictable land of wide views, sweeping sameness, and straight lines. (Rackham 1986a, 4–5)

'Ancient countryside', which dominates the areas to the south-east and west of this 'planned' zone, is quite different. Here open fields – if they existed at all – disappeared at an early date; settlement tended to be more dispersed in character, with numerous small hamlets and isolated farms, as well as villages. Hedges here are, in general, older and woodland more abundant. This is:

> The England of hamlets, medieval farms in the hollows of the hills, lonely moats and great barns in the claylands, pollards and ancient trees, cavernous holloways and many footpaths … irregularly-shaped groves and thick hedges colourful with maples, dogwood and spindle …. (Rackham 1986a, 4)

The majority of ancient woodland is to be found in ancient countryside such as this, and Rackham emphasised the antiquity and stability of both, reproducing side-by-side in his great work *The history of the countryside* a map of Earl's Colne in Essex surveyed in 1598, and the same area as shown on the first edition Ordnance Survey six inches : one mile map of 1896, and emphasising that 'almost everything in the modern landscape was already there in 1598 … the wood outline is exactly the same as in 1598' (Rackham 1986a, 16–17).

By the time that *The history of the countryside* was published in 1986 some archaeologists and landscape historians were suggesting that in certain districts the basic fabric of 'ancient countryside' – the pattern of fields and lanes – might have originated long before the earliest maps, like that of Earl's Colne, were surveyed, and long before the Middle Ages: in fact, in late prehistoric or Roman times. It was an idea which Rackham, in his chapter on 'Fields' especially, embraced with some enthusiasm (Rackham 1986a, 156–64). The concept has a long history but was first seriously and convincingly articulated from the late 1970s by Warwick Rodwell and Paul Drury, who noted that in some parts of Essex patterns of fields could be found which, because they shared a common orientation across extensive areas, appeared to have been planned (Drury and Rodwell 1980). These often covered an area significantly larger than the vills or manors of the Middle Ages, implying that they had been laid out in some earlier period, probably the Roman or later Iron Age. They also noted the fact that in a number of places in the same county, as at Little Waltham, Roman military roads appear to slice through the field pattern in a way analogous to a railway line or bypass, leaving awkward corners, in such a manner as to suggest that the fields were earlier, and thus of early Roman or prehistoric date (Rodwell 1978). During the 1980s and 1990s researchers found examples of similar putative 'relict landscapes' elsewhere in England, many of them taking the form of 'co-axial' field patterns of the kind known from dated prehistoric contexts, in the form of earthworks or cropmarks: that is, they were laid out around a number of parallel axes, with few transverse elements running for any distance, so that they resembled in plan rather wavy, irregular brickwork. Most such survivals were in 'ancient countryside' areas, although some examples were also discerned in the furlong patterns shown on early, pre-enclosure maps of townships in 'champion' districts. They are particularly prominent in parts of Norfolk and Suffolk (Williamson 1987; 1998a; Davison 1990, 73–4; Hesse 1992); in western and in south-eastern Cambridgeshire (Oosthuizen 1998; 2003; Harrison 2002); on the dipslope of the Chiltern Hills in Hertfordshire (Rowe and Williamson 2013, 103–11); on the London clay uplands in the south-east of that county (Bryant *et al.* 2005); and in the Arrow valley of Shropshire, around Hergest and Lyonshall (White 2003, 37–47, 73–5). Like those identified by Drury and Rodwell, these ancient 'field systems' were roughly dated by the way that they extended over tracts of land much more extensive than medieval manors or parishes, and in particular by the way that some examples were apparently 'slighted' by Roman military roads.

This is not the place to discuss either the problems with the simple bipartite model of the English landscape – the division into 'woodland' and 'champion', 'planned' and 'ancient' – or the idea that much of the medieval and modern landscape developed directly from patterns of land division established in remote prehistory (Williamson 2013). The point, rather, is that the concept of 'ancient woodland' – descended from a natural 'climax' vegetation, and then remaining largely stable in its composition over an immense period of time – forms part of a wider narrative, one which tends to emphasise the stability and antiquity of the English countryside, rather than dynamism and change.

The challenge to stability: dynamic models

The models for the development of England's natural vegetation formulated by men such as Tansley were firmly tied to the concept of succession: that is, the idea that natural plant communities will gradually progress towards a stable 'climax' – a suite of species in a particular ratio and relationship that will continue unchanged unless disturbed by outside influences, especially climatic ones. While the development of pollen analysis in the middle and later decades of the twentieth century gradually changed our ideas about the precise *composition* of the 'wildwood', it did not challenge the basic idea that England had, before man began to make extensive clearances, been characterised by a stable 'climax' vegetation which almost everywhere comprised closed-canopy woodland. In 1986, however, Oliver Rackham suggested that some areas of more open ground must have existed as part of the country's natural vegetation (Rackham 1986a, 330). Four years later such ideas were taken much further by the Dutch ecologist Frans Vera. He drew attention to the importance of oak and hazel in pre-Neolithic pollen cores, noting that these species do not flourish in closed-canopy conditions. The pollen of various trees and shrubs characteristic more of woodland edges than of continuous woodland was also prominent, including that of blackthorn, hawthorn, rowan, cherry, apple and pear, as was that of wood-edge herbs such as mugwort (*Artemisia vulgaris*), nettle (*Urtica dioica*) and sorrel (*Rumex acetosa*) (Vera 2002a and b). Vera suggested that succession to closed-canopy forest had been checked by the grazing of large herbivores such as auroch (wild cattle) and deer. The 'natural' landscape of north-west Europe had, in fact, been more 'savannah-like' or 'park-like' in character, with areas of open grassland scattered with trees and patches of scrub, and with only sporadic stands of denser woodland. Vera conceded that the pollen evidence superficially indicated a landscape dominated by woodland, rather than by open pasture, but he argued that intensive grazing would have 'limited the flowering of grasses, and thus the pollen emitted by grass into the atmosphere', while the movement of grass and herb pollen, he further speculated, might have been constrained by the fact that the landscape, while essentially open, nevertheless included scattered trees and areas of dense scrub (Vera 2002a, 88). He also noted that oak and lime emit more pollen when growing in open, park-like conditions than when they are crowded together in densely shaded woodland. Our modern ideas about Europe's natural vegetation, he further argued, were largely based on the kinds of environment experienced by early settlers on the east coast of America; on observed patterns of succession on land abandoned in parts of England during the agricultural depression of the early twentieth century (as well as in other contexts, such as on the experimental plots at Rothamsted noted earlier); and on the character of the remaining woods and forests across Europe, which were generally assumed to represent surviving fragments of the 'natural' vegetation. All these supposed analogies were misleading because they came from contexts in which the grazing of large herds of herbivores had long been curtailed.

In addition to all this, Vera suggested that the pre-Neolithic landscape had been more dynamic in character than the conventional concept of the stable, climax 'wildwood' allowed. It included patches of thorny scrub where trees were able to seed and grow, protected from grazing animals. As these reached maturity they eventually shaded out the protective thorns, but by this time they were relatively immune to the herbivores (Vera 2002a, 377–9). Eventually, individual trees grew old, or were out-competed by neighbours, and the area they occupied became open grassland once again: the landscape was thus an ever-changing mosaic. Vera's hypothesis, it must be said, has met with a mixed reception from researchers, one study concluding that the contention that 'the bulk of the lowland landscape was half-open and driven by large herbivores … is not currently supported by the evidence' (Hodder *et al.* 2009, 12). Rackham has cogently argued that the failure of oak to seed and thrive in shade may be the result of the arrival of American oak mildew disease in comparatively recent times, and has pointed out numerous other problems with Vera's model (Rackham 1980, 502–3; Rackham 2006, 92–8). Equally important is the fact that, if the natural environment had been a largely open one, it is difficult to account for the sheer scale of the decline in tree cover, clearly indicated by pollen evidence, in early prehistory. This decline began on a small scale in the Mesolithic (around 5600 BC) and then, after a subsequent period of stability, continued more rapidly with the arrival of farming around 4000 BC. Pollen samples assigned to deciduous woodland on average declined, within the space of a few centuries, from 85 per cent to 65 per cent of total pollen (Woodbridge *et al.* 2012, 7). Nevertheless, some parts of England do appear to have had fairly open landscapes throughout the Holocene: French *et al.*, for example, have suggested that the Allen valley within Cranbourne Chase never had anything other than patchy and variable woodland cover (French *et al.* 2007). The landscape of England before the advent of farming was almost certainly more varied and in places more open than we used to believe but yet, equally certainly, much less open than Vera has argued (Birks 2005; Mitchell 2005).

Vera's 'dynamic forest' is one aspect of a wider shift in ideas about the way that natural plant communities develop, and in particular over whether vegetation, left to its own devices, will inexorably progress towards a stable 'climax'. The concept of succession, as originally formulated by ecologists such as Clements in the early twentieth century, assumes that this development will follow, in effect, a unilinear path to a fixed and predictable end (Clements 1916). In the 1930s and 1940s Tansley and others argued that different plant communities could, in theory, develop in the same environmental circumstances through the influence of minor and random factors – the so-called 'polyclimax theory' (Tansley 1949). But the very idea of an ordered progression to one stable 'climax', or even to several, began to be questioned in the 1970s (William and Nisbet-Drury 1973; Connell and Slatyer 1977). By the end of the twentieth century some ecologists were arguing that natural landscapes are best considered as ever-changing, dynamic systems, comprising habitat 'patches' which are constantly developing, interacting with each other and responding to a myriad of external, especially climatic, influences (Worster 1993, 165). No habitat or ecosystem remains 'stable' for long, and its future development is always essentially unpredictable in character.

There are particular problems with applying the idea of 'succession' to England's early post-glacial vegetation, for, as this was first developing, humans were already beginning to have a significant environmental impact. Levels of predation by post-glacial Mesolithic hunters would have had a significant effect on the large herbivores which Vera believes were the main ecological 'drivers' in the pre-Neolithic landscape. There is certainly evidence that hunting communities had a direct effect on the vegetation by burning substantial tracts, probably in order to concentrate game in particular locations, although the extent of the practice remains unclear (Simmons 1996). More importantly, within a few millennia of the ending of the Ice Age human societies began to have a far more profound impact through the introduction of farming. Thereafter, not only were the natural forests progressively fragmented but – perhaps of equal importance – they were significantly modified by exploitation.

From the 1970s an explosion of archaeological evidence – what Christopher Taylor described as the 'quantitative revolution' in British field archaeology (Taylor 1975) – served, indirectly, to throw light on the probable intensity of such exploitation. Archaeologists had formerly assumed that extensive tracts of England, especially those lying on the heavier clay soils, had been largely unsettled, and their woodlands uncleared, before the Middle Ages. It now became apparent, as a consequence in particular of aerial photography and intensive fieldwalking surveys, that large numbers of prehistoric and Roman settlements could in fact be found in almost all environments, implying wide areas of cleared ground. This emerging recognition had been a major factor in the development, during the 1970s and 1980s, of the ideas about 'relict landscapes' briefly outlined earlier. Population had fallen during the fifth and sixth centuries, in the immediate post-Roman period, implying a degree of woodland regeneration, before recovering again in the middle and later Saxon periods. Pressure on the wooded 'wastes' beyond the cultivated fields thus presumably fluctuated over time, increasing as population rose through later prehistory and into the Roman period, falling during early Saxon times, and then increasing again as population rose to unprecedented levels in the later Saxon and early medieval periods. But in most periods since the Bronze Age the intensity with which woodlands were used must have been considerable in most districts. As we shall see, such exploitation will have involved not only the cutting of wood and timber for fuel and materials but also, crucially, grazing with a variety of livestock. We tend to think of sheep as animals that live off grass but they will happily consume woodland vegetation, being particularly partial to ash, ivy and holly. Cattle will likewise browse off whatever foliage they can reach. As late as the sixteenth century Thomas Tusser advised the cutting of branches from trees to provide feed in winter months, and 'leafy hay' was harvested and stored in parts of England into the twentieth century (Grigson 1984, 74). But in the denser stands of woodland pigs would be pastured, especially on the acorns, beech mast and nuts in autumn.

Some historical ecologists – most notably Ian Rotherham – have argued that before substantial areas of woodland were embanked and enclosed in the twelfth or thirteenth centuries to allow for more intensive management by coppicing, the areas of grazed woodland and 'waste' lying beyond the arable lands of villages, farms and hamlets may have continued to display some of the characteristics of Vera's 'dynamic savannahs'. Grazed now primarily by domestic livestock – exotic species brought from abroad – areas of woodland and open ground nevertheless continued to alternate over time (Rotherham 2011a, 180–1). There are reasons for doubting whether, in Norfolk at least, such a situation continued as late in time as Rotherham suggests. There is, however, little doubt that grazing, and the cutting of wood and the felling of timber, must have maintained some degree of dynamism in the 'wastes' of early and middle Saxon times; and that the wooded ground from which our 'primary' ancient woods were enclosed was already very different, in its vegetational characteristics, from the 'wildwood' – whatever precise form the latter may have taken. The massive reduction in the proportion of small-leaved lime in the landscape between later prehistory and the Middle Ages is one clear indication of this: it almost certainly reflects the fact that lime has poor resistance to grazing, and woods were – by the time of the Norman Conquest – everywhere intensively grazed (Rackham 1986a, 140–1). Moreover, like Rotherham, we would emphasise the fact that woods, once established as enclosed and defined areas, could be less stable features of the landscape than is usually suggested. They could come and go, and they could leave behind some botanical mark of their former presence which, when circumstances changed, could reassert itself as a new area of woodland became established on the same site. This explains a key feature of the approach to woodland history set out in this book: the way in which we examine woods within the contexts not only of the wider landscape and its history but also of the character of neighbouring or proximate environments, rather than as habitats both stable and largely sealed from their surroundings.

It is likely, moreover, that major shifts in ecological character must have occurred once woods were brought under more intensive management as enclosed coppice from which grazing animals were excluded. This is apparent from differences in the ecology of surviving areas of woodland and of wood-pasture. Classic 'woodland indicator' species are not well represented in managed wood-pastures, and were thus presumably relatively rare in the grazed woodlands of early medieval times. Some classic 'ancient woodland indicators' are restricted to ancient woodland because they are able to tolerate large amounts of shade – coming into leaf very early, for example, as does dog's mercury. But others flourish, at least in part, because of aspects of traditional management. Some, such as wood anemone (*Anemone nemorosa*), are well adapted to surviving the periods of shade which occur in the later stages of the coppice cycle, lying dormant until coppicing opens up the floor of the wood to light: but they can do this only if the floor of the wood remains undisturbed (Colebourn 1989, 70). Others (such as water avens (*Geum rivale*) and pignut (*Conoipodium majus*)) are largely restricted to ancient woods simply because they cannot survive grazing pressure well, and woods – unlike wood-pastures, or agricultural land – were places where grazing stock were excluded, or admitted for only limited periods of time (Colebourn 1989, 74).

When these new and intensively managed environments came into existence their biological character must have changed with some rapidity. It was then further altered by variations in management practices over time. As Edlin observed of Tansley, 'I think it is only a fair criticism of his work to assert that, in discussions of particular types of woodland, too little attention is paid to the past, or even the current, influence of man … ' (Edlin 1956, 65). We would argue that such a criticism, while much less true of more recent generations of woodland specialists, still contains, nevertheless, at least a grain of truth. Changes over time in the length of coppice rotations, for example, would have had an impact on the character of the ground flora, as would alterations – consequent upon changes in market conditions – in the relevant importance of timber and coppice within a wood, an increase in the former reducing the vitality of the latter and increasing the degree of shade more generally. It is also possible, perhaps likely, that the systematic selection and encouragement of particular shrub species influenced the composition of the understorey within managed woods, as it certainly did that of their timber component.

It is thus arguable that ancient woods are best considered not as unchanging, stable systems, but rather as dynamic ones, affected by variations in the intensity of exploitation associated with demographic and economic factors, as well as by purely natural processes, including climatic change. And because they were and are dynamic and changing, approaches to woods which place a particular emphasis on their *early* history – as fragments of wildwood, as artefacts of traditional management through coppicing – may fail to explain, and may even misunderstand, key aspects of their present composition and character. This in turn explains another distinctive aspect of the approach adopted in this study, for we consider not only the medieval and early post-medieval management of woods, but also their relatively recent history. We discuss how ancient woodland acquired new uses in the post-medieval period as game reserves, as elements in aesthetic landscapes, as places to hide bomb stores. We discuss new ideas, emerging from the late eighteenth century, about how established woods could be improved through drainage and replanting. We emphasise, in particular, that woods as we see them now – especially in terms of the understorey they contain – have usually been neglected or undermanaged for a century or more, or have only recently been brought back into management. The particular combination of species we find within them is in part, we suggest, an artefact of neglect: the consequence of what happens when a particular suite of plants, created and sustained by human interference, is then left to its own devices.

Conclusion

In the foregoing pages we have set out not a coherent manifesto for how the study of ancient woodland should be approached, but rather an explanation of the particular perspective adopted here: one which employs archaeological and historical, and to an extent botanical, evidence to understand how a sample body of woodland has developed over time, and which seeks to place woodland more generally within a broader historical, environmental and topographic context. Such a perspective is not superior to those adopted by others, nor is it entirely new – having much in common, in particular, with that adopted by Nicola Bannister in Sussex (Bannister 1996) and by Ian Rotherham and his team in Yorkshire, the latter in particular arguing that current approaches to wooded landscapes 'are fundamentally flawed by the absence of an understanding of the historic context of the sites and of their ecologies' (Rotherham 2011b, 161). But, as we shall see, a specifically 'landscape' perspective can throw important new light on our understanding of these important habitats.

Chapter 2

The contexts of ancient woodland

Soils and climate

Many studies of ancient woodland, quite understandably, tend to focus on woods and their particular botanical and archaeological characteristics in isolation – paying some attention, perhaps, to local soils and drainage conditions, but ignoring the wider human landscape of fields and commons, villages and farms (e.g., the otherwise excellent Read and Frater 1999). In reality it is impossible to understand ancient woodland without paying full regard to this more general spatial context. Norfolk is a particularly suitable place to examine woodland in these terms, for it exhibits a remarkable diversity of geological formations and soil types, ranging from light and porous sand and chalk to heavy, poorly draining clay, which in turn gives rise to equally marked variations in settlement patterns and field systems. Some parts of the county were occupied by extensive open fields and commons in the Middle Ages, and in some cases up until the nineteenth century. But elsewhere open arable had disappeared by the late Middle Ages, and in some districts had always been of limited extent. In some districts settlement is clustered in loosely nucleated villages; elsewhere it is highly dispersed across the landscape. While it would be wrong to describe Norfolk as in any way 'typical', in terms of either its natural or its historic environment, it does embrace landscape types which can be found much more widely across lowland England.

The county's climate is, however, rather less representative. It is influenced, above all, by its low relief, its location on the eastern side of the country and its proximity to the Continent. It is thus little affected by the prevalent wet winds from the Atlantic, so rainfall is low and there is a greater daily and yearly temperature range than elsewhere in the UK (Barrow and Hulme 1997). There are, however, appreciable climatic differences within the county, ranging from the drier Fens (which receive less than 600 mm of precipitation in an average year) to the wetter hills of north-west Norfolk or the Holt–Cromer ridge (which receive 700 mm or more). The most hostile climate is that of Breckland, the extensive tract of sandy land in south-west Norfolk and north-west Suffolk, compounding the problems posed to cultivators by acid and infertile soils. Here, frosts have been recorded in every month of the year (Hodge *et al.* 1984, 27–34). On the whole, however, the county's climate is a good one for farmers, especially for those producing cereal crops. Low summer precipitation, in particular, means that these can ripen safely and be harvested dry – circumstances less certain in the west of England, and crucial in the long-term development of Norfolk's society and economy (Barrow and Hulme 1997; Hodge *et al.* 1984, 28–30; Williamson 2013, 107–24). The character of farming over the centuries has, however, also been influenced – and perhaps more fundamentally – by soils, and these in turn by geology.

Like other parts of eastern England, Norfolk has a geology dominated by relatively soft, young rocks. Chalk, laid down in the Upper Cretaceous, comprises the basic

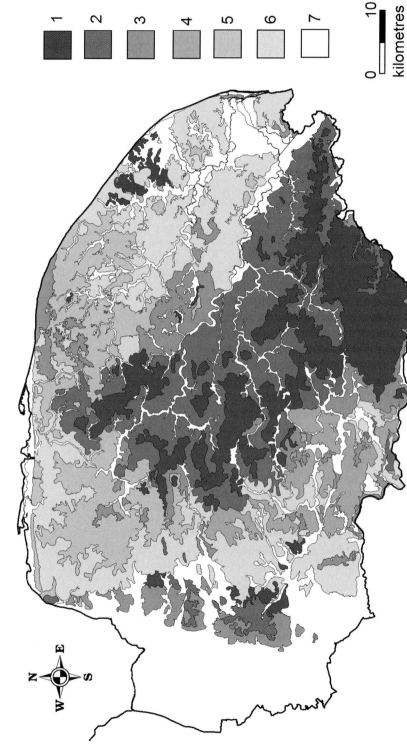

Figure 2 Norfolk: simplified soil map. (1) Beccles Association (heavy, poorly draining clays on level or gently sloping ground); (2) Burlingham and Hanslope Association (lighter clays, mainly on valley sides); (3) Felthorpe, Downham, Newport and Ollerton Associations (sandy, stony and very acid soils, mainly overlying non-calcareous formations, some affected by groundwater); (4) Worlington and Methwold Associations (deep sandy soils); (5) Barrow and Wick 3 Associations (non-calcareous sandy or gravelly loams); (6) Wick 2 and Newmarket Associations (neutral or calcareous loams); (7) peat and alluvium.

underlying geology and, rising gradually in height from east to west, forms the low hills characteristic of north-west Norfolk. Towards the south-east it dips gradually and becomes buried ever deeper beneath younger formations (Chatwin 1961; Funnell 2005). These lie 'unconformably' with the chalk – they were deposited only after the rocks laid down immediately above the latter had been eroded – and are of much later date, the most important being the so-called 'Crag' deposits – a complex sequence of gravels, clays and shelly sands of late Pliocene and early Pleistocene origin (that is, between 3.5 and 1.6 million years ago). For the most part, however, this solid geology of chalk and crag is obscured, to varying degrees, by drift deposits laid down in glacial times, and it is these which form the parent material for most of the county's soils (Boulton *et al.* 1984; Funnell 2005). The most important of these is the chalky boulder clay, which covers large tracts of the centre, south and south-east of the county. It comprises a sticky calcareous clay which, as its name suggests, contains large amounts of chalk as well as varying quantities of flint and (less commonly) fragments of other rocks. The till surface forms a slightly tilted plateau which falls gently to the east, following the dip of the underlying rocks, and which is dissected by stream and river valleys to very varying degrees. In some areas, as around Long Stratton in the centre–south of the county, very extensive tracts of level land occur; elsewhere, as in the far south-east, around Hedenham and Ditchingham, the plateau is so dissected that it scarcely reads as a 'plateau' at all. Other important glacial deposits include the Brown Till of Norwich Brickearth, which is widely distributed across the north-east of the county; the great moraine of sand and gravel, probably of Devensian date, which forms the ridge of high ground between Holt and Cromer in the far north of the county; fluvioglacial sands and gravels, found in particular in the area immediately to the north of Norwich; and a variety of Aeolian or windblown deposits, varying from the loess which covers parts of the east of the county to the extensive sands which are found in Breckland in the south-west.

Such a varied geology has given rise to an even more varied range of soils (Figure 2). The Soil Survey of Great Britain employs two units for analysing and mapping soils: series and associations (Hodge *et al.* 1984, 52–69; Avery 1980; Clayden and Hollis 1984). A 'series' is a distinct type of soil with a particular mineral content, structure and other characteristics. An 'association' is a group of series which are usually found together in close proximity; it is generally named after the dominant series within it. Soils can vary greatly even within small areas, such as a single field, but only a few parts of the county have been mapped at a sufficient level of detail – at the level of the individual series – to represent such complexity. For much of the analysis presented in this book we therefore employ the more general mapping units of the associations.

The more level areas of the boulder clay plateau occupying the central and southern areas of Norfolk are characterised by poorly draining, seasonally waterlogged soils that are difficult to work but essentially fertile in character; these are broadly classified by the Soil Survey as the Beccles 1 Association, a grouping which includes soils of the stagnogley Beccles and Aldeby Series and the pelostagnogley Ragdale Series. These latter soils are particularly poorly drained, in part because they occur on level or only gently sloping ground; they have a Soil Moisture Regime Class of III, meaning that the soil profile is wet within 0.70m of the surface for 90–120 days a year. In the Middle Ages and the early modern period much of this land was occupied by woods and common pastures, although demographic pressure ensured that the majority was probably ploughed: early maps show surprising quantities of open-field arable, even on the heaviest soils, while the gently sinuous boundaries of the enclosed fields suggests that it had once been more extensive. Demesne farms probably had more land under pasture than peasant farms, but even they were only 'moderately well provided with grassland' (Campbell 2005, 48). With the technological improvements of the agricultural revolution and high farming periods in the eighteenth and nineteenth centuries – including land drainage and improved forms of plough – larger areas were brought into cultivation, a development which involved the enclosure of large areas of former common land and, as we shall see, the stubbing out of some areas of ancient woodland. Today, most of the clays are intensively cultivated for cereals, sugar beet and oilseed rape in fields which are often large and prairie-like.

The soils found on the sides of the valleys dissecting the clay plateau, in contrast, which are mostly classified as belonging to the Burlingham 1 and 3 Associations, are sandier and more freely draining in character, partly because they occur on sloping ground but partly because the character of the till is different here, the valleys cutting into deposits laid down by early phases of the Anglian glaciation. Small areas of Hanslope Association soils – heavy but slightly calcareous clays – also occur in some locations in the far south of the county, most notably in the valleys of minor tributaries draining into the river Waveney. Such land, in all periods, was more amenable to cultivation than the heavier soils of the plateau. The claylands, taken as a whole, are a classic area of 'ancient countryside', characterised by a dispersed pattern of settlement (with farms generally scattered around the margins of greens and commons) and by early enclosure. There was, and is, much woodland here, and – in spite of the impact of modern farming – ancient hedges and old pollards still survive in some numbers.

To the north-east the clay plateau is flanked by more freely draining soils. Although areas of sandy drift occur in places, much of north-east Norfolk is characterised by the deep loams of the Wick 2 and 3 Associations, formed in wind-blown silty deposits laid down during the Devensian glaciation over the Norwich Brickearth or over glaciofluvial sands. Such soils are at least moderately fertile, although often prone to drought, and those of the Wick 2 Association, which cover some 500 square kilometres in the area between Sheringham, Yarmouth and Cromer, are among the most easily worked and fertile soils in England (Hodge *et al.* 1984, 346–51). Not surprisingly, this was one of the most densely settled districts in early medieval England, with extensive areas of 'irregular' open fields and, once again, a settlement pattern characterised by farms and cottages scattered around the margins of greens and commons (Campbell 1981). But such was the density of population and the intensity of cultivation that relatively little woodland appears to have existed here by the end of the Middle Ages.

To the south-west of the clay plateau, in the south-western corner of the county and extending into neighbouring Suffolk, lies the region called Breckland. Here light, wind-blown sands were deposited in the Devensian glaciation over boulder clay or, more usually, chalk, ensuring a particularly arid and often acid environment. The dominant soils are those of the sandy and infertile Methwold and Worlington Associations (Hodge *et al.* 1984, 249–53, 368–70). In addition, patches of the even more marginal Newport Association soils, formed in more gravelly deposits, occur around the margins of the district, especially at their junction with the boulder clays to the east. Breckland is also, however, characterised by tracts of more calcareous soils (formed in underlying chalk and 'head') – principally those of the Newmarket 2 and 3 Associations – which generally occur on the lower ground, on the muted escarpment to the west and in the principal river valleys (Hodge *et al.* 1984, 265–9). These latter soils formed core areas of settlement in prehistoric, Roman and early Saxon times, their importance becoming eclipsed only from the later Saxon period as settlement and cultivation expanded on the more fertile but less tractable soils of the claylands to the east. In medieval and early post-medieval times the land was farmed in extensive open fields in which the holdings of individual farmers lay intermingled across wide areas; settlement mainly took the form of nucleated villages located in the principal valleys. The acidic uplands lying between the main valleys, in contrast, were seldom brought into permanent cultivation before the eighteenth century, being exploited for grazing and fuel and largely occupied by rabbit warrens and heaths. Indeed, even at the end of eighteenth century, to judge from the county map published by William Faden in 1797, well over 40 per cent of Breckland was still occupied by heathland of various kinds (Wade Martins and Williamson 1999, 13). Some of these surviving heaths were enclosed and reclaimed during the first half of the nineteenth century, but extensive tracts survived until they were planted up with commercial conifer plantations by the Forestry Commission in the first half of the twentieth. Little ancient woodland can be found in this district, most tree cover having been removed in early historic times: intensive grazing by sheep flocks militated against survival or regeneration. Numerous plantations, however, attest to the prominence of large landed estates in the post-medieval landscape.

To the north of Breckland, in north-west Norfolk, more extensive areas of Newmarket 2 soils, formed in chalk and 'head', occur on sloping ground, but the more level uplands are covered in layers of Aeolian sand, giving rise to the agriculturally poorer soils of the Barrow Association (Hodge *et al.* 1984, 107–11). These sandy deposits are, however, much thinner than in Breckland, and the heaths which occupied them were thus more easily reclaimed in the post-medieval period, few surviving into the nineteenth century – hence the name of 'Good Sands' applied to the district by the eighteenth-century agriculturalist Arthur Young (Young 1804, 10). Settlement tended to take the form of nucleated villages and before the seventeenth and eighteenth centuries the land was cultivated in extensive open fields similar, in many respects, to those found in the Midland counties of England. This was the heartland of Norfolk's 'agricultural revolution', and today the landscape is characterised by straight-sided fields typical of post-medieval enclosure of open fields and commons.

In the area to the north of Norwich, between the boulder clay plateau to the west and the fertile loams to the west, are extensive areas of sands and gravels deposited by the outwash waters of ice sheets during the Anglian or, just possibly, the Devensian glaciations (Boulton *et al.* 1984). Much of the district is dominated by particularly poor soils of the Newport 1 and 4 and Felthorpe Associations, although there are also numerous pockets and ribbons of more loamy soils, mainly of the Wick 3 Association. Other areas of acid, gravelly soil occur further north, along the north coast and especially along the Holt–Cromer ridge. A broad, intermittent band of poor soils, principally those of the Newport 4 Association, thus extends northwards from Norwich, intermittently, to the coast – an area sometimes referred to as the 'Northern heathlands'. This district was less appealing to early farmers than the acid sands of Breckland, in the south-west of the county, in large measure because the underlying geology here comprises crag rather than the chalk which – in the latter district – could be employed to neutralise soil acidity. Settlement was sparse here in all periods, and extensive tracts of heathland remained into the nineteenth century, and sometimes beyond; today, like Breckland, although to a lesser degree, the district boasts a number of Forestry Commission plantations.

Although deposits of glacial origin thus account for the majority of soil parent materials in Norfolk, in some districts post-glacial or Holocene ones are also important, especially in the level reclaimed wetlands of Fenland in the west of the county. Peat occupies extensive areas in the southern part of this district and much also occurs in the far east of the county, within the smaller wetland area known as the Broads. It accumulated when the post-glacial rise in sea level caused freshwater flooding of the shallow Fen basin and the Broadland river valleys (Funnell 1993). Extensive areas of alluvium were also deposited by various phases of marine transgression in the eastern Broads, the northern Fens and along the coast to the west of Weybourne. The principal river valleys in the county likewise contain various combinations of alluvium and peat. In medieval and post-medieval times land use in these areas varied considerably, although the peatlands were usually exploited as common land, being grazed to some extent but also cut for peat, fodder and thatching materials, while the silts comprised rich grazing marsh or – particularly in the northern Fens, or 'Marshland' – was cultivated as arable (Silvester 1988). Some areas of both varieties of wetland, however, were given over to wet woodland dominated by alder, normally referred to locally as 'carr'.

Lastly, in our somewhat simplified account of Norfolk's complex soils and physical geography, we need to mention the deposits pre-dating the chalk, which are exposed on the surface in a narrow band of country running along the margins of the Wash and along the eastern margins of the Fens – Kimmeridge clay, the Sandringham Sands and Gault clay. The clays give rise to soils similar, in general terms, to those associated with the boulder clays in the centre and south of the county; the Sandringham sands, in contrast, are associated with acid, infertile soils which – like those in the areas to the north of Norwich – lack underlying deposits of chalk which might be employed to improve them. These various formations and deposits were interdigitated in complex ways, giving rise to landscapes displaying diverse combinations of nucleated and dispersed settlement.

The human landscape: settlement and farming

As we have emphasised, the character and development over time of Norfolk's ancient woodland can be understood only within the wider context of the history of the landscape, and in the pages that follow we set out, of necessity briefly, some of the broad strands in the development of the local countryside. Analysis of pollen from the sediments at the bottom of a number of the county's natural lakes or 'meres' (Hockham Mere, Sea Mere, Diss Mere, Old Buckenham Mere) and from a smaller number of riverine and coastal locations provides broad information about the impact of man on the Holocene environment, although unfortunately many of these sequences are poorly dated (Sims 1973; Bennett 1983; Peglar *et al.* 1989; Fryer *et al.* 2005). These show that pine and birch woodlands of the early Mesolithic were succeeded, in the period after *c.*6500 BC, by mixed woodland in which lime, together with oak and elm, was generally dominant, although pine continued to be a major component on dry, acid soils, especially in Breckland. Limited modification of the natural vegetation during the Mesolithic was followed, from around 4000 BC, by more extensive but nevertheless localised clearances carried out by Neolithic farmers. Much woodland persisted, especially on high interfluves, into the Bronze Age, but by the Iron Age 'open agricultural landscapes were widespread' in the county (Fryer *et al.* 2005, 11; Rackham 1986b, 162–3). Archaeological fieldwalking, aerial photography and the meticulous recording of chance finds and of objects recovered by metal detectorists leave no doubt that Norfolk, like other areas of lowland England, was already by the time of the Roman Conquest a well-settled district, far beyond the pioneer stage.

Although in Neolithic and Bronze Age times farms and fields had largely been concentrated on the lighter and more calcareous soils, by the end of the Iron Age they were widely scattered on almost all soil types. Pollen cores from Hockham Mere, Old Buckenham Mere and Diss Mere all suggest rapid deforestation of their catchments in the course of the Iron Age (Wiltshire and Murphy 1999). In the Roman period – when an abundance of well-fired pottery ensures that settlements are recovered with relative ease in field surveys – there was an average of between 0.5 and 1.5 settlement sites per square kilometre and, while not all were necessarily occupied at the same time, the majority were probably in use during the second and third centuries (Williamson 1993, 42–7). In David Gurney's words, 'together the evidence points to a landscape mainly cleared and farmed, with numerous settlements and a population of several hundred thousand' (Gurney 2005). This peak was followed, however, as in the rest of England, by an apparent reduction of population in the course of the fifth and sixth centuries, with farms generally retrenching to the lighter, more easily cultivated soils. Settlement became not only sparser but also more mobile than it had been in the Roman period. At Witton, in the north-east of the county, for example, eight Romano-British settlements were discovered through fieldwalking, but only four areas of early Saxon occupation. Selective excavation and intensive surface collection revealed, moreover, that only one of these was in use throughout the fifth and sixth centuries. Of the others, one was occupied in the fifth century and one in the sixth, while the third could not be dated accurately (Wade 1983). Nevertheless, while there is some evidence (most notably from Diss Mere and Staunch Meadow at Brandon) for a measure of woodland regeneration, mainly in the form of increases in the frequency of ash, birch and hazel pollen, elsewhere – as at Scole or Hockham Mere – the evidence suggests landscapes of largely open grassland, albeit with some decline in the frequency of cereal pollen (Fryer *et al.* 2005, 11; Bennett 1983).

Such evidence might be taken to imply that the area of woodland in the county has been limited – comprising discrete parcels, rather than extensive and continuous tracts – since later prehistory. But while the numbers and widespread distribution of early settlements in the county are striking, we should not necessarily assume, as some landscape historians have done, that this was everywhere matched by very extensive and continuous areas of cultivated land. There has been a tendency to assume that all farmsteads recovered by field surveys were involved to some extent in arable production, but a proportion may represent isolated grazing ranches, while some may have been involved in the exploitation of woodlands. Certain later prehistoric sites in the more agriculturally marginal locations, such as that excavated at Park Farm near Wymondham in Norfolk, appear to have been only seasonally occupied (Ashwin 1996). Moreover, while traditional forms of pollen analysis can inform us about *relative* increases or decreases in woodland in the immediate locality of the pollen core (itself usually taken from waterlogged deposits surrounded by an area of light and comparatively fertile soil within a major valley), they have been able to tell us rather less about *absolute* levels of woodland in the wider landscape, on interfluves where soils were more acidic, poorly draining, or both. Nor are they good at distinguishing, for example, a landscape of hedged pasture fields from a thinly timbered wood-pasture. Recent developments in palynology, involving a more quantitative approach to the data, may resolve some of these issues (Twiddle 2012), but existing pollen evidence from the county, while it fails to provide hard evidence for a significant degree of woodland regeneration in the immediate post-Roman period, does not entirely preclude the possibility that substantial quantities of land did indeed revert at this time to grazed woodland or scrub. As we have already noted, some landscape historians have attempted to assess the extent of pre-medieval clearance and cultivation through topographic analysis, arguing that much of the basic framework of the medieval and modern landscape – the layout of roads and the pattern of fields – has, over extensive tracts of ground, late prehistoric or Roman origins. The archaeological evidence from ancient woodland is of some importance in this respect. Where such woodland occurs within an area of 'relict landscape', we might legitimately expect to find a continuation of such field systems, in earthwork form, beneath the woodland. More generally, we might expect to discover – on a fairly regular basis – evidence of prehistoric or Roman settlement or agriculture in such locations, just as we find extensive areas of 'Celtic fields' on the downlands of southern England. But such evidence is, as we shall see, very limited.

Whatever the extent of post-Roman woodland regeneration, there is little doubt that from the seventh and eighth centuries the population began to increase once again, and settlements gradually ceased to migrate around the landscape, instead stabilising, in most parishes, at one or, more rarely, two or three points. The spreads of debris representing such settlements, which are commonly located beside what is now the site of the parish church, usually cover a more extensive area than those associated with the more mobile sites they replaced (in part perhaps because they were usually occupied for a longer period of time), generally covering between 1.5 and 3 hectares. In contrast, later Saxon occupation – dating to the tenth and eleventh centuries – in a parish commonly covers three or four times this area, and in some cases more. Not only did existing middle Saxon sites expand significantly but, from the later tenth century, numerous new sites now appeared, away from parish churches, spreading along roads and around the margins of what were presumably already becoming defined 'greens' and commons. In the parishes of Great and Little Fransham, for example, intensive fieldwalking by Andrew Rogerson revealed that middle Saxon occupation was represented by a single scatter of pottery covering an area of a little over a hectare. Late Saxon settlement, in contrast, was represented by two large sites, each covering a similar or slightly greater area, together with no less than sixteen smaller sites scattered across the parish (Rogerson 1995, 105–8; 123–30; 191). Pollen evidence suggests that the area under cultivation in the county expanded at the expense of pasture, and the heavier clays began to be settled and farmed once again (Bennett 1983; Godwin 1968; Peglar *et al.* 1989; Murphy 1993; Rogerson 2005). To judge from the evidence of Domesday Book some rural districts in Norfolk probably contained more people in 1086 than they did in the nineteenth century. Yet the same source also attests the survival of extensive tracts of uncleared woodland.

The largest wooded areas were located in what Rackham has termed a 'wooded crescent' curving through the centre of the county; a rather less striking concentration formed a north–south band along the edge of the Fen basin and the Wash in the west of the county (Rackham 1986b, 164–5) (Figure 3). Major place-names, mostly coined in the later Saxon period, which contain elements referring to woodland – *leah*, *feld* and the like – have a similar distribution, although with a subsidiary cluster, not really noticeable in Domesday, around the margins of the Norfolk Broads to the east of Norwich (Figure 4). There are good grounds for believing that the overwhelming majority of this late Saxon woodland was grazed wood-pasture, rather than the kind of enclosed and coppiced woodland common in later centuries. As in neighbouring counties, Domesday records woodland in terms of the numbers of swine which it could support, suggesting that one of its primary uses was as swine-pasture, with herds of pigs being driven into woods in the autumn to fatten on acorns and nuts – a practice which would have been difficult or impossible to manage if woodland had been dominated by coppice stools, which were vulnerable to browsing animals. Although Domesday only implies the use of woodland for grazing pigs, other domestic stock, as already noted, will thrive on woodland vegetation, and place-names such as Hardwick ('the herd farm'), located on heavy or otherwise marginal soils within the wooded zones of the county, suggest that some Saxon settlements may have originated as specialised grazing establishment, and that cattle and sheep as well as pigs were fed in the woods.

Settlement continued to expand into the post-Conquest period, its character continuing to diverge from the familiar pattern of nucleated villages and extensive, highly regulated open fields which became usual in Midland counties. In most parts of Norfolk, even those characterised by light and freely draining soils, there were by the twelfth and thirteenth centuries usually some outlying farms and hamlets in addition to the main focus of settlement (Williamson 2013, 154–8). That focus, moreover, was itself often more like a collection of contiguous hamlets than a compact village in the usual sense. Indeed, in parts of Norfolk individual 'villages' might be supplied with two or even three separate parish churches (Rogerson *et al.* 1997). But, in many areas, especially where the soils were heavier, there was no real village nucleus at all. Settlement not only expanded around but shifted wholesale to the margins of greens and commons, forming loose girdles of farms and cottages around the damp, peaty floors of major valleys, poorly draining concavities in the surface of clay plateaux or areas of acidic, gravelly drift (Davison 1990; Addington 1982; Wade-Martins 1980). As a result of this process churches were often left peripheral to the main concentrations of settlement and in many cases still stand quite alone in the midst of the fields (Wade-Martins 1980; Davison 1990).

Such idiosyncracies of settlement were matched by peculiarities in agrarian organisation. Open fields approximating to the familiar Midland pattern – in which holdings were scattered evenly throughout the area of the township, and farming was organised on highly communal lines – could be found in the west of Norfolk, on the narrow strip of heavy clay soils lying on the edge of the Fens, and more generally on the light soils of Breckland and in the north-west of the county (Martin and Satchell 2008, 208–12). In these two latter districts, however, there were significant deviations from Midland practice. Nutrients were rapidly leached from the porous soils and fertility could be maintained only by grazing huge flocks of sheep on the heaths or harvest residues by day and closely folding them on the arable by night, when it lay fallow or before the spring sowing: the flocks were usually under the control of manorial lords, rather than the community, as part of the 'fold course system' which was a particular feature of the poorer soils in East Anglia during the Middle Ages and the early post-medieval period. The flocks were larger, and folding arrangements more systematically organised, than was usual in Midland areas, and grazing was everywhere intense (Bailey 1989; Allison 1957; Postgate 1962; Wade Martins and Williamson 1999, 9–13). Elsewhere in the county, in the centre and east, there were rather greater deviations from Midland practice. Open fields took 'irregular' forms, with holdings of individual farmers clustered in particular parts of the arable, and with often limited degrees of communal regulation. This was especially true on the fertile loams of the Wick 2 Association in the north-east of the county, where communal rights were often restricted to the grazing of the harvest aftermath (Campbell 1981; Martin and Satchell 2008, 208–10). Here, as in the west of the county, the open arable was often extensive, broken only by areas of intensively grazed common land, around which settlement sprawled in chaotic fashion. On the claylands of the south and south-east, however, the open fields were interspersed not only with commons but also with woods, deer parks and hedged fields farmed from an early date in severalty (Wade Martins and Williamson 1999, 21–5). As a result, these were landscapes characterised by a much greater degree of botanical continuity with the primaeval 'wildwood' than were those in the west or the north-east of the county. This was also true, to some extent, of the band of sandy, acid soils running north from Norwich intermittently to the coast, where extensive tracts of common wood-pasture, deer parks and managed woodland survived into the post-medieval period.

In the period between the eleventh and the later thirteenth centuries the countryside of Norfolk thus filled with people and, as arable expanded, areas of non-arable land use were given greater definition. Some of the dwindling areas of grazed woodland continued to be exploited by local peasant populations, but many sections were enclosed, as deer parks or coppiced woods, by manorial lords. It was in this period, to judge from the available evidence, that ancient woods as we now understand them first came into existence. We shall examine this crucial phase, of closer definition and more intensive land management, in more detail in the next chapter. But we will also explore, in more detail than is often the case in studies of this kind, the subsequent fate of the managed woodland; and, once again, some of the key features in the wider development of the landscape during these recent centuries need to be briefly presented.

Perhaps the most important factor was the progress of enclosure – the proliferation of hedged fields at the expense of open fields and common land. In the south and east of the county, where field systems were generally 'irregular' in character, the fifteenth, sixteenth and seventeenth centuries saw much 'piecemeal' enclosure. Numerous private agreements – sales and exchanges – led to the amalgamation, and subsequent hedging, of groups of contiguous open-field strips, a process which tended to preserve, in simplified form, the essential layout of the earlier landscape (Dymond 1990, 143–6). On the claylands in particular this proliferation of enclosed ground was closely associated with the emergence of a more specialised farming

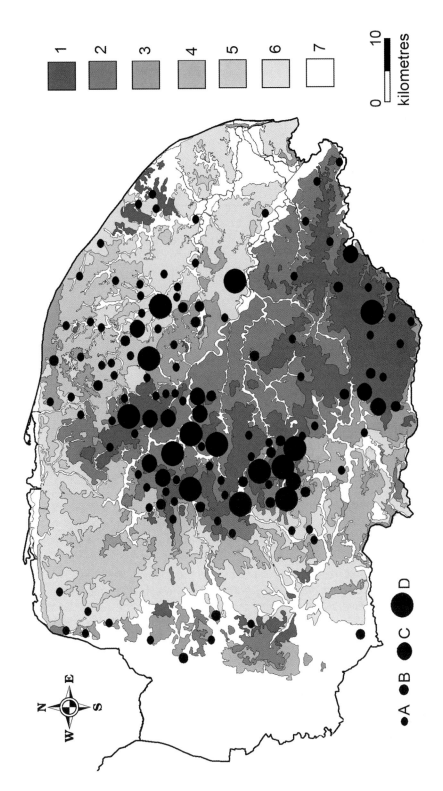

Figure 3 The distribution of Domesday woodland in Norfolk. (A) Vills with woodland for 100–150 swine; (B) vills with woodland for 151–300 swine; (C) vills with woodland for 301–450 swine; (D) vills with woodland for more than 450 swine. For soils key see Figure 2.

economy based around dairying and cattle rearing, in which arable husbandry took a subsidiary role. By *c*.1700 very little open arable remained in the district. In much of the east and north-east of the county, similarly, the area of open fields contracted steadily, again in part as a result of the increasing importance of cattle husbandry (Campbell 1981). But while piecemeal enclosure might serve to extinguish open fields in these two districts, it made little inroads into areas of common grazing land, which generally survived into the early decades of the nineteenth century. They were then finally extinguished by a wave of parliamentary enclosure acts (Turner 2005).

On the light soils in the west and the north of the county, in contrast, where folding flocks were crucial for maintaining fertility and field systems were generally more communal and 'regular' in character, early enclosure by piecemeal methods made much less headway and the majority of open fields still survived at the start of the eighteenth century. Here enclosure was closely associated not with an expansion of livestock farming but with the intensification of arable husbandry (Wade Martins and Williamson 1999, 34–43). This part of Norfolk was at the forefront of the classic 'agricultural revolution': the adoption of new rotations, in which fodder crops such as turnips and clover were alternated with cereal courses, rendered redundant the great nutrient reservoirs of the heaths. Not only the open fields, but also these areas of marginal grazing, were now enclosed and 'improved'. This was achieved in a range of ways but often by parliamentary enclosure acts which, unlike those affecting common land in the south and east of the county, usually embraced all the remaining open land in a parish, arable and grazing alike. Landscapes of open fields and heaths were thus replaced by rectilinear fields defined by species-poor hedges – classic 'planned countryside', to use Rackham's term (Rackham 1986a, 4–6). But not everywhere. In Breckland the extraordinarily marginal character of the soils ensured the survival of much heathland, in part because it could not be economically reclaimed and in part because particularly large flocks of sheep were needed to maintain the arable in good heart.

The south and east of the county, and the north and west, were broadly differentiated not only by differences in enclosure history and in the development of agriculture but also by their social and tenurial structures. Even in the early Middle Ages the latter districts had, in general, been more strongly manorialised than the former (Campbell 2005). By the eighteenth century they were coming to be dominated by particularly large landed estates. Smaller proprietors, unable to invest in the range of improvements required to raise arable productivity on these light lands, were systematically bought out by large ones. In the south and east of the county, in contrast, a more diverse landholding base, inherited from the early Middle Ages, was preserved in part by the development of a cattle-based economy and in part by the character of the local soils. Even in the later eighteenth and nineteenth centuries, when arable tended to expand here once more at the expense of pasture, the accumulation of land in the hands of large landowners was retarded, largely because of the relatively high value of this more fertile land (Wade Martins and Williamson 1999, 76–81). Large estates certainly existed, especially on the clays, but their holdings were often splintered rather than continuous. The north and west of the county thus became increasingly aristocratic in character; the south and east remained more 'peasanty'. Such differences had important environmental implications. By the early nineteenth century many of the largest landscape parks were located in the west, but,

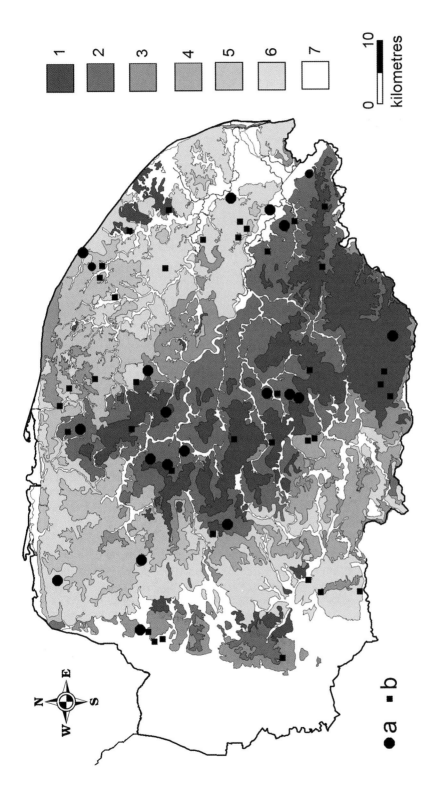

Figure 4 Woodland place-names and soils. (a) Names incorporating the element *leah*, 'a wood or clearing'; (b) names incorporating other woodland elements (*feld, wudu, holt, graf, sceaga, skogr, lundr, hangrs, wald, hris*). For soils key see Figure 2.

1
2
3
4
5
6
7

0   10

kilometres

N
W E
S

● a   ■ b

more importantly, landowners here indulged, from the early eighteenth century, in a sustained campaign of tree-planting.

In such a brief thumbnail sketch we have, inevitably, grossly over-simplified the post-medieval landscape history of Norfolk. There were, for example, some districts in the east of the county, such as the 'Island' of Flegg, in which – as in the west – open fields survived largely intact into the early nineteenth century, although here as a consequence of particularly fertile soils and particularly high land prices, coupled with the limited degree of communal regulation imposed across the open arable (Bacon 2003). Conversely, some districts in the west of the county – especially on the edge of the Wash, to the north of King's Lynn – retained woodland and wood-pasture commons into the post-medieval period in a manner not dissimilar to that seen in the claylands of the south-east. Some of the more misleading of these generalisations will receive a measure of qualification in the chapters that follow. The general distinctions we have outlined do, however, serve to highlight a key difference in what may be termed botanical continuity. For the most part, the light soils in the west and north of the county lost most of their woodland at an early date and, until the eighteenth century, boasted relatively few hedges. Their commons were grazed by sheep and rabbits, and few seem to have retained any significant degree of tree cover far into the post-medieval period. On the claylands of the south and east, and to some extent on the band of sand and gravel running north from Norwich and on the light, fertile soils in the east of the county, more woodland survived into the medieval times, enclosed and managed by manorial lords; larger numbers of hedges appear to have existed throughout the Middle Ages; and, even in the post-medieval period, some commons still carried significant numbers of trees.

Ancient woodland in Norfolk

The county's ancient woodland has been the subject of a considerable amount of attention in the past. The *Ancient Woodland Inventory* was itself based on a methodology first trialled in the county in the 1970s (Spencer and Kirby 1992, 79), and many Norfolk woods have been discussed by Oliver Rackham, who was himself born in the county. Examples of Norfolk woods thus feature fairly regularly in Rackham's *Ancient woodland* (1980) and *Woodlands* (2006); he also presented a general overview of the county's woods in an important article published in the *Transactions of the Norfolk and Norwich Naturalists' Society* in 1986 (Rackham 1986b). In addition, a preliminary survey of the archaeological potential of the county's ancient woods was produced in 2004 by Brian Cushion for Norfolk Landscape Archaeology (Cushion 2004); the history of its deer parks has been considered by David Yaxley, Jonathan Dye and, in particular, Robert Liddiard (Yaxley 2005; Dye 1990; Liddiard 2010); while an important consideration of its common wood-pastures has been published by Patsy Dallas (Dallas 2010). We have drawn extensively on all these studies in the discussions that follow.

The *Ancient Woodland Inventory* lists just over 250 woods in the county: the precise figure depends on whether conjoined but separately named woods are counted as one wood, or as more. The overwhelming majority are of coppice-with-standard form but a few examples with wood-pasture origins, and in which the principal features are ancient pollards rather than coppices, are included in the list: most notably, Felbrigg Great Wood and Hull Wood in Bayfield. The county is characterised by a multiplicity of scattered, small and medium-sized woods rather than by the kinds of extensive and continuous tracts found, for example, in the Chiltern Hills in Buckinghamshire, Oxfordshire and Hertfordshire. Nathaniel Kent reported in the late eighteenth century that the area of woodland 'of old standing' in Norfolk was 'not considerable'; and that 'a single wood, or coppice, was found here and there, but no great tract together' (Kent 1796, 86). The *Inventory* woods range from tiny examples, technically too small for inclusion under the terms stipulated by the *Inventory* itself – such as Sparham Grove (1.7 hectares) – to larger ones such as Hockering (88 hectares) and Foxley (124 hectares). The latter are rare, however, and the majority of the officially recognised ancient woods in the county are in the range of 10 to 25 hectares. Their vegetation is diverse, varying not only between but also within individual woods, often to a marked degree.

A number of methods of classifying the vegetation of ancient woodland exist, most notably those proposed by George Peterken, Oliver Rackham and J.S. Rodwell, in the National Vegetation Classification (NVC) system (devised in the 1980s to categorise the totality of natural and semi-natural plant communities found in Britain) (Peterken 1981; Rackham 1980; Rodwell 1991). These various systems, while to some extent employing similar categories, are by no means identical. The NVC system, based on a combination of dominant tree and herb species, describes nineteen major types of woodland in Great Britain, of which only eight are found in Norfolk: W1 (*Salix cinerea/ Galium palustre*); W2 (*Salix cinera/Betula pubescens/Phragmites australis*); W5 (*Alnus glutinosa/Carex paniculata*); W6 (*Alnus glutinosa/Utrica dioica*); W8 (*Fraxinus excelsior/Acer campestre/Mercurialis perrenis*); W10 (*Quercus robur/Pteridium aquilinum/Rubus fruticosus*); W14 (*Fagus sylvatica/Rubus fruticosus*); and W16 (*Quercus spp/Betula spp/Deschampsia flexuosa*). Of these, four are low-lying wetland communities, which actually account for only a small minority of the woods listed in the *Inventory*. The four remaining categories fail to fully account for a substantial proportion of Norfolk's ancient woods, especially those dominated – sometimes to the almost total exclusion of other species – by hornbeam.

Peterken's system, devised for the Nature Conservancy Council in the 1970s (Peterken 1981), is more useful. It divides semi-natural woodland into twelve main 'stand types' based on the dominant tree/shrub species, some of which are further subdivided: more than one stand type commonly occurs within a single wood. No fewer than 25 of the defined subcategories are present to some extent in Norfolk woods, although often in small quantities: thus, where Type 1 (ash–wych elm woodland) is present, wych elm commonly features as only a handful of stools.[1] The distinctions between many of these stand types are fine, and in practice they often merge almost imperceptibly within the area of individual woods. Type 2 (ash–maple

---

1. Elm continues to survive in significant numbers as a hedge shrub in Norfolk, and in places as coppice, but tends to be infected by Dutch elm disease when it reaches a significant height and acquires a fully developed bark. Where stands of elm have been badly affected by Dutch elm disease, clear felling has often occurred, followed by replanting – usually with deciduous species, as in parts of Hedenham Wood and Round Grove Wood, both in Hedenham. The East Anglian elm, with a narrow pointed leaf, is the only variety usually present, variously termed *Ulmus minor* var. *minor* (Richens 1983, 4) or *Ulmus carpinifolia* (Rackham 1986a, 234–6, 245).

woodland) is thus very common throughout the county and occurs in a wide range of environments, although mainly in poorly drained contexts. Most examples are found within woods featuring hazel–maple–ash coppice under oak, and occasionally ash, standards. The amount of maple can vary widely, from scattered stools to almost complete dominance, although hazel is usually the most common species in the understorey. The closely related stand Type 2Aa (wet ash–maple woodland) is also very common, being found throughout the county on heavy, poorly draining soils, often within what are otherwise hornbeam-dominated woods. The difference between the two types – 2 and 2Aa – largely relates to elements of the associated ground flora, and both are similarly distinguished from Stand Type 2Bc (ash–maple woods on poorly drained light soils) and Stand Type 3 (ash–hazel woods). Also closely related are Stand Type 3Aa, the heavy soil variant of acid pedunculate oak, ash–hazel woods, frequently found in south-east Norfolk, in association with heavy soil stand types such as 9Ab, 2Aa and 10A, where patches of light surface soil exist; and Stand Type 3Ab, the light-soil variant of acid pendunculate oak, ash–hazel woods, also fairly common in such contexts, and in woods growing on light land in north Norfolk, in places where flushed soils – that is, nutrient-enriched soils at the base of slopes – occur.

The various stand types featuring lime (*Tilia cordata*) as a significant component (4a, acid birch–ash–lime woods; 4Ba, the lowland variants of maple–ash–lime woods; 5a, acid pedunculate oak–lime woods; and 5b, acid sessile oak–lime woods) similarly merge almost imperceptibly into each other, responding to minor variations in soil acidity or drainage within the area of individual woods. Several are again usually present in close proximity, and the differences between them are often fine. Type 5a thus features small-leaved lime, oak, downy birch (*Betula pubescens*) and hazel coppice beneath oak standards: *Salix caprea*, *Salix cinerea* and holly can form minor components of the coppice, with a little gean, elder and hawthorn also often present. Type 5b has a coppice which varies from lime, birch and hazel to lime and sessile oak with birch and holly, all under sessile oak standards. Rowan is occasionally found, but no other species. Most of the rest of the county's ancient woods are accounted for by stand Types 6a, 6c, 6d and 6e (all oak woods, distinguished by whether *Quercus petraea* or *Quercus robur* (or both) is present, and by whether hazel or birch is the main sub-dominant); stand Type 7 (various forms of alder wood); stand Type 8 (beech woods); stand Types 9A, 9Ab, 9Ac (varieties of hornbeam wood); and stand Type 10 (suckering elm stands).

Although we do refer to this system of classification at various points in this book, in practice most Norfolk woods, as a result of variations in soil types and past management history, contain such a mixture of stand types that its systematic use would lead to a degree of complexity perhaps unnecessary in what is primarily a historical and archaeological enquiry. More importantly, from a historical perspective, it is clear that the extent or even the presence of particular stand types within individual woods, and their wider regional prominence in a range of neighbouring woods, have changed over time, and are in part artefacts of management or neglect, rather than a simple consequence of purely environmental factors. Detailed classification, useful for botanical recording and analysis, can obscure a simpler reality which might be summarised as follows. The majority of ancient woods in Norfolk, mainly but not exclusively on boulder clay soils, have standards of oak and sometimes ash over a coppiced understorey containing some combination of ash, hazel and maple, with other species usually present only at relatively low frequencies. In the south and south-east of the county, in contrast, but also on clay soils, the coppice is generally dominated by hornbeam, with ash/hazel/maple as subsidiary components, again under oak and ash standards. Rather rarer, and restricted to acid sands and gravels in north Norfolk, are woods which largely boast an understorey of coppiced oak, accompanied by an often limited range of other species. Woods in which lime is a significant component are even rarer, being largely restricted to Hockering Wood and Park Wood in Hockering, in the centre of the county, and to Swanton Novers Great Wood in the north: in the former woods, lime is accompanied by hazel, ash and maple but in Swanton Novers oak coppice also occurs. Elsewhere, while lime can be found, it is a minor or sporadic component, as at Horningtoft Great Wood. Wayland Wood in Watton and a few other woods in the vicinity are characterised by coppice featuring large amounts of bird cherry; Felbrigg Great Wood, uniquely, is dominated by (pollard) beech. In addition, we should note the many woods in the county that contain areas of suckering elm, and the presence of woodland dominated by alder, either growing in patches within damp areas of woods occupying clay plateau sites and mainly dominated by other species, or as 'carrs' or wet woods occupying damp flood-plain sites.

Whatever their precise composition, ancient woods in Norfolk, as elsewhere in England, have usually been unmanaged, or minimally managed, since the early or middle decades of the twentieth century. Some private landowners have, over the last three or four decades, brought portions of particular woods back into regular management, although escalating deer numbers make such endeavours increasingly

Figure 5 Recently cut coppice of bird cherry and ash in Wayland Wood.

Figure 6 Neglected coppice of ash and hornbeam in Wayland Wood.

problematic. More extensive areas are coppiced in woods managed by the Norfolk Wildlife Trust (NWT), such as Wayland Wood or Foxley. At the former, the difference in the character of the vegetation in managed and unmanaged sections is striking (Figures 5 and 6).

Examining ancient woods

In order to obtain a better understanding of the origins, history and character of ancient woodland in Norfolk a systematic survey of fifty woods was carried out by the authors over a number of years: the results of this are presented in the Appendix (Figure 7). All but two of these woods are included in the *Ancient Woodland Inventory*: the exceptions were examples which fully fit the criteria for inclusion but which were, for some reason, omitted when that document was compiled (Round Grove, in Hedenham, and Toombers Wood, on the boundaries of the parishes of Stow Bardolph, Stradsett and Shouldham Thorpe). The sample was chosen so as to be reasonably representative of the ancient woods in the county in terms of stand types, location and size. Woods completely, or very extensively, replanted as plantations in the later twentieth century were not examined. This was not only because of the damage done to the original vegetation but also because any earthworks (other than perimeter banks) were usually levelled, in whole or part, by large-scale replanting: more ephemeral earthworks are, for obvious reasons, particularly susceptible to complete destruction. Historical, topographic and archaeological investigations formed the core of this project, but details of vegetation – stand type, structure, ground flora and the rest – were also recorded.

The principles of woodland archaeology have been discussed in some detail by Oliver Rackham and, more recently, by Ian Rotherham and his colleagues (Rackham 1976; Rotherham and Ardron 2006; Rotherham *et al.* 2008, 107–17). An important distinction can be made between what Rotherham has aptly described as the archaeology *of a wood*, and the archaeology found *in a wood*. The former includes features associated with the management of the wood, such as external boundary banks or saw pits; the latter, found within secondary woodland, comprises those features derived from a previous, non-wooded landscape, such as former field boundaries. As we shall see, this distinction, while useful, is not entirely clear-cut. Such archaeological evidence can tell us much about the history of a wood but in the case of the larger and more densely planted examples accurate surveys can be problematic. Bathe and his colleagues have described the difficulties of 'conducting archaeological surveys amidst thick vegetation, poor light and intrusive tree roots' (Bathe *et al.* 2011, 59): surveying equipment, such as total station theodolites, is difficult to use over long distances, and was thus employed only where particular features, such as moats or enclosures, needed to be recorded in detail. Some of this more detailed survey work was carried out by undergraduate students on field courses, although always under close supervision. More general surveys were undertaken using hand-held GPS devices but these – even the more expensive ones – can give inaccurate readings under heavy canopy. In addition, some woods – especially those characterised by an understorey of ash, hazel and maple, rather than oak or hornbeam – are so overgrown that slighter earthworks may be difficult to locate during transects. For these reasons, for a number of the larger woods ground survey was supplemented by an examination of LIDAR[2] images, although those available often fail to reveal the more subtle of the archaeological features visible on the ground.[3]

Field survey of the sample woods was accompanied by an investigation of the documentary and cartographic evidence relating to each: again, the principal sources and approaches have been discussed in some detail by Rotherham and Rackham (Rotherham and Ardron 2006; Rackham 2006, 164–86). The evidence relating to the sample woods varies greatly in character and quantity. Only a small minority have useful associated documentary evidence relating to the medieval period, and less than a sixth are depicted on maps of pre-eighteenth-century date. Most examples are first shown, with any degree of accuracy, only on the tithe award maps of the late 1830s and 1840s. Much of the detailed evidence relating to their management and character thus comes from the post-medieval centuries but, as already noted, it can be argued that much of the character of ancient woodland was forged in relatively recent periods. In addition to the documentary evidence relating to the sample

---

2 LIDAR – Light Detection and Ranging – is a remote sensing method used to examine the earth's surface and capable of penetrating the tree canopy.

3 Financial constraints ensured that we were obliged to use the data made available, free to academic users, by Geomatics, most of which is at a resolution of one metre, and sometimes as much as two metres.

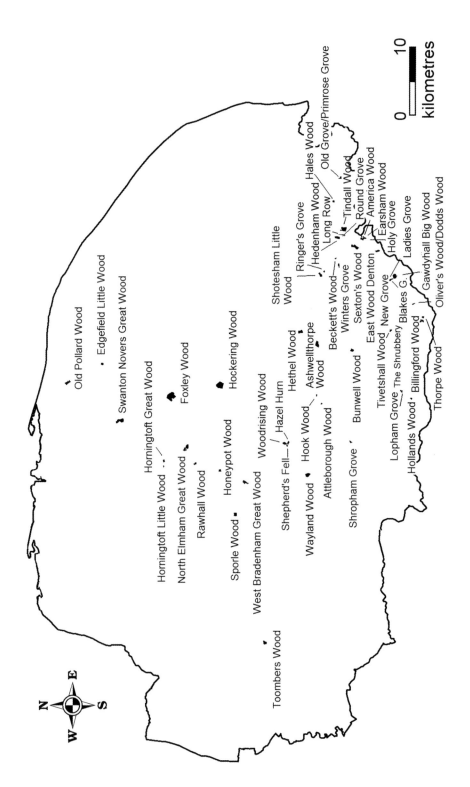

Figure 7 The locations of the sample of fifty woods surveyed.

woods, a wider trawl through the material at the Norfolk Record Office and the National Archives at Kew was undertaken in order to set the sample within a wider context and throw more general light on woodland history in the county. In a similar way, much use was made of such sources as the County Wildlife Site descriptions held by the Norfolk County Wildlife Sites Partnership to obtain both information on the species content and structure of woods not included in the sample, and additional observations relating to woods that were included. In short, while the sample of fifty woods formed the core of this research, our arguments and conclusions are also based on a wider range of evidence, combined with a general consideration of the locational and topographic characteristics of woodland, within the context of the wider historical and archaeological evidence for the long-term development of the county's landscape.

Chapter 3

The origins of coppiced woodland

The evidence of location and distribution

We suggested in the previous chapter that areas of woodland were probably first enclosed and coppiced in Norfolk on a significant scale in the course of the eleventh, twelfth and thirteenth centuries, and that before this time wood and timber had been supplied by rather larger tracts of less intensively managed wood-pasture. Domesday Book implies that most woodland in the county was still being used as swine pasture, and was thus by implication uncoppiced; but, by the middle of the thirteenth century, at places such as Hindolveston, Hedenham and Ditchingham, we have clear documentary evidence for the existence of enclosed and coppiced woods. Rackham has suggested that, in Norfolk, as in other counties in which it records woodland in terms of the numbers of swine that could be fed in it, Domesday may itself hint that the process of enclosure for more intensive management was already under way (Rackham 1976, 55). In a total of 35 vills within the county the number of notional swine which could be fed in the manorial woods fell by a half or more between 1066 and 1086, a phenomenon which has been noted in other counties in eastern England in which Domesday both records woodland in terms of swine and provides details for the resources of manors at the time of the Conquest, as well as at the time of the survey itself. The declines were often considerable – from 1,000 to 500 in the case of North Elmham, for example. Rackham has argued that these reductions reflect the fact that a proportion of the woodland in the places in question was being fenced off and managed as coppice – thus reducing the amount available for pannage (Rackham 1976, 55). There are, however, some problems with this argument, and alternative explanations for these changes can be suggested. The disruptions caused by the upheavals of the Conquest and its aftermath, for example, may have led to under-management, and perhaps to phases of unrestrained felling on the part of the local peasantry (Lennard 1945). It is particularly noteworthy that the reductions are not matched in any systematic manner by declines in the numbers of actual swine kept on demesnes. Unfortunately, it is impossible to throw any light on this issue by examining the distribution of the places affected by reductions because, as with many other matters, those responsible for recording or compiling the information in Domesday were inconsistent. In the centre of the county, for example, 60 per cent of all manors in the hundred of Mitford appear to have experienced a reduction in woodland, but for the adjoining hundred of Eynesford, on broadly similar soils, the figure is only 4 per cent.

Although some areas of woodland were probably enclosed and coppiced in the period before the Conquest, the archaeological evidence for the wider development of the landscape strongly suggests that this was mainly a phenomenon of the twelfth and thirteenth centuries. A key fact here is the location of ancient woods. Of the 252 examples recorded in the county in the *Ancient Woodland Inventory*, around 40 per cent occur on the heavy clay soils of the Beccles Association, which cover just 12

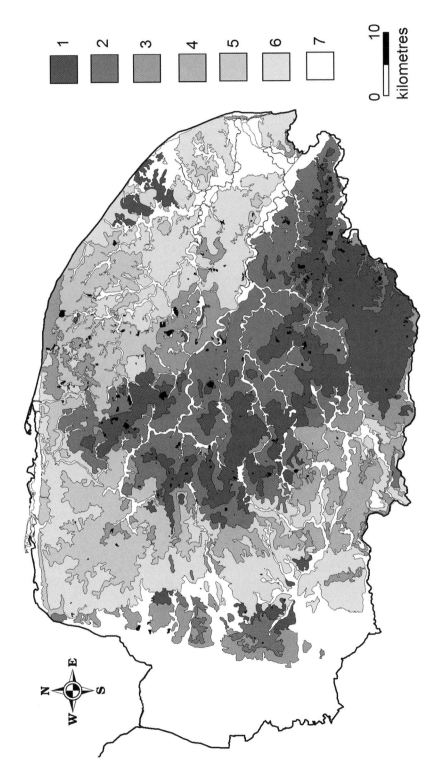

Figure 8 The distribution of woods included in the *Ancient Woodland Inventory*, and soils. For soils key see Figure 2.

per cent of the total land area of Norfolk. A further 10 per cent lie on clay soils of the Burlingham Association, while around 14 per cent occur on the sandy, acidic soils of the Newport Association (Figure 8). In fact, the association of woodland with the most poorly draining and/or most acidic soils is closer than these figures suggest because, as already noted, for most of the county soils have not been mapped at a very high level of resolution, but only at a scale of 1:250,000, and thus on the basis of associations, rather than series. In the few places in the county where more detailed mapping has been carried out we can often see how the location of particular woods is decided by the presence of pockets of particularly difficult soils, such as those of the Newport or Beccles Series, within associations otherwise composed of more congenial series. Many of the woods which the 1:250,000 map shows as occupying sites on Wick 1 and Wick 2 Association soils, for example, are actually located on the Newport Series soils which form a minor component within those associations. It is also noteworthy that almost all of the most extensive areas of woodland in the county included in the *Ancient Woodland Inventory* are largely or entirely located on the more agriculturally marginal soils. It is the smaller examples which occupy better-drained and/or less acidic soils and many of these, as we shall see, are secondary rather than primary in character. Thus of the ten largest areas of woodland in the county listed in the *Inventory* five (Swanton Novers Great Wood, Fulmondeston Severals, Foxley, Hockering and Brooke) occupy Beccles Asssociation soils, while two (Haveringland Great Wood and Felbrigg Great Wood) lie on Newport 4 soils. Of the remainder, both Hindolveston Wood and Tindall Wood, while mapped as falling mainly on Burlingham soils, lie partly on soils of the Beccles Association and occupy level, poorly draining sites, suggesting a dominance within their area of soils of the Beccles Series. Not only are most ancient woods thus located on land that was, at least in the medieval period, relatively marginal in agricultural terms, but most were also located in places which were *spatially* marginal, in the sense that they lay some way from the parish churches which, as we have seen, appear to mark the main foci of middle and later Saxon settlement in the county (above, p. 24).

In general terms, the land occupying such marginal locations does not appear to have been brought into cultivation much before the later decades of the eleventh century, to judge from the fieldwalking surveys carried out at Hales, Loddon and Heckingham by Alan Davison, and in Great and Little Fransham by Andrew Rogerson (Davison 1990; Rogerson 1995). The ploughing up of these areas, at a distance from the primary areas of Saxon settlement on lighter or more fertile soils within the principal valleys, is attested archaeologically by the distribution of stray sherds derived from manuring, and was accompanied (in the manner already described: above, p. 25) by the dispersal of settlement around greens and commons, a process which may have begun as early as the later tenth century but which intensified in the course of the eleventh and twelfth and continued into the thirteenth. As they appear on the earliest maps, the curving, convex/concave outlines of these areas of common land appear to define not so much the commons themselves as the ovoid intakes of farmland lying between them: the greens and commons, that is, are the tattered remnants of once more extensive and continuous areas of 'waste'. What is striking is that many areas of ancient woodland, before the large-scale parliamentary enclosures of the early nineteenth century, abutted directly onto heaths, greens and other commons. William Faden's map of Norfolk, surveyed in the 1790s, is a particularly valuable source in this respect for it shows the whole of the county shortly before this great wave of enclosure. Although there are a number of demonstrable inaccuracies in its depiction of woodland, it is striking that around 40 per cent of examples which we can be reasonably certain were of 'ancient' character (rather than recent plantations) directly adjoined a common – and this was after several centuries during which both commons and woods had undergone a significant degree of attrition (Macnair and Williamson 2010, 195). Both woods and commons thus appear to be descended from the same areas of dwindling wood-pasture 'waste' but, while the latter continued to be exploited in common by local communities (often degenerating over time to treeless heath or green), the former were enclosed, managed and preserved by members of the local manorial elite. It is thus likely that both woods and commons became defined and bounded by earthworks and hedges as part of the same process of settlement expansion in the course of the eleventh, twelfth and early thirteenth centuries, rather than at any earlier date.

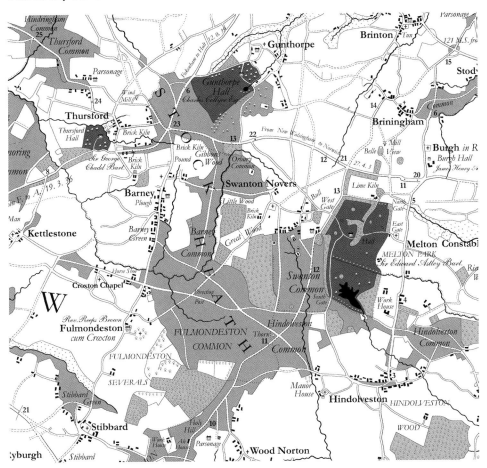

Figure 9 Stock Heath and surrounding area, as shown on William Faden's 1797 map of the county of Norfolk (redrawn by Andrew MacNair). Note how woods, wood-pastures and commons cluster in contiguous blocks, all cut out of the same, once continuous, areas of 'waste'. Melton Constable Park probably originated as a medieval deer park.

What is also striking about Faden's map is that in a number of places it shows marked clusters of woods and commons, sometimes accompanied by what we know from other sources to have been early deer parks. In the area between Hindolveston, Fulmondeston, Melton Constable, Barney, Swanton Novers, Gunthorpe and Thursford, for example, the late eighteenth-century landscape was dominated by the vast, rambling area of Stock Heath and its associated commons – Fulmondeston Common, Hindolveston Common and Orbury Common. Attached to these were a number of areas of ancient woodland – including Swanton Novers Wood – together with an extensive block of private wood-pasture, Fulmondeston Severals, which had probably (like these woods) been severed from the surrounding commons at an early date. On the eastern edge of this block of wooded or formerly wooded land lay the landscape park surrounding Melton Constable Hall (Figure 9). This is one of the few parks in Norfolk designed by Lancelot 'Capability' Brown, but it had much earlier origins, being shown on a map of *c*.1674 (before the present hall was built), and it may have originated as a deer park in the twelfth or thirteenth centuries (NRO Hayes and Storr map 82, M3; Williamson 1998b, 261–3). In a similar way, to the west of the village of North Elmham in central Norfolk, Elmham Heath, Brisley Green, the medieval park at Elmham and Horningtoft Wood must have originally formed one single area of 'waste' which probably included Colkirk Common and Colkirk Wood, a little further to the west; while in the area to the east of East Dereham, Hockering Wood, Norfolk's best example of a lime wood, similarly formed at this time part of a cluster of unploughed land which included Swinnow Wood, Hockering Common, Stiphens Green (shown by Faden as still partly wooded) and various areas of nearby woodland. Hockering Wood, as we shall see, may have originated as a deer park; a second park in the parish, long vanished by the time the map was surveyed, lay a little to the east.

Similar, if less extensive, clusters of woods, commons and wood-pastures can be found elsewhere on Faden's map. Invariably, they occupied land on the interfluves between major river valleys and drainage systems. The Melton Constable cluster thus lay on high ground between the headwaters of the Glaven, Bure, Stiffkey and Wensum; that to the west of Elmham between the Wensum, the Nar and the Panford Beck; and that around Hockering between the Tud and the Wensum. In this context, attention should again be drawn to the distribution of the larger areas of Domesday woodland and to the fact that this is broadly mirrored by that of surviving ancient woods. Both are concentrated, as Rackham has noted, within a 'wooded crescent' running from the north-east of the county, through the centre, and down to the south-east (Rackham 1986b, 165). Norfolk's rivers fall into three groups: short north-flowing rivers; long east-flowing rivers, the lower reaches of which form the Norfolk Broads waterways; and west-flowing rivers which merge with the complex drainage system of the Fens. This arc of wooded countryside corresponds fairly closely to the line of the county's central watershed, which divides watercourses draining east from those flowing north and west (Figure 10).

In part, this relationship between woods and watersheds simply reflects the fact that the higher ground between valleys is generally occupied by heavy clay soils or spreads of acid drift that were particularly difficult or unrewarding to cultivate: the Beccles and Newport Association soils, in particular, dominate in such locations. But to some extent both ancient woods and Domesday woodland tend to cluster on

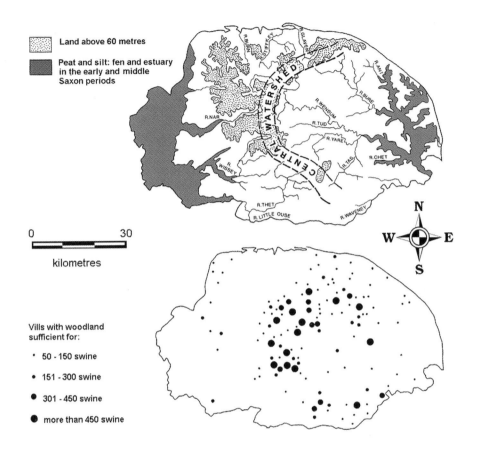

Figure 10 Domesday woodland and drainage basins: the largest areas of woodland recorded tend to cluster on the main watershed running through the county.

interfluves regardless of soil type. This pattern fits in well with the models for early territorial organisation formulated by members of the 'Leicester School' of local and regional historians, most notably Alan Everitt and Charles Phythian Adams (Everitt 1977; Phythian Adams 1987). They have argued that the development of settlement and social territories in England was, over a long period of time, related to basic topographic structures – watersheds and drainage basins – as much as to soils and geology, although the two were, of course, intimately related. Most of the significant settlements in late prehistoric, Roman and early Saxon times were thus located in major valleys (often on gravel terraces) where there was usually a good supply of both water and well-drained and moderately fertile soils suitable for arable cultivation. The higher interfluves, in contrast, were occupied by tracts of woodland and pasture. This was partly because they were often characterised, as is the case in much of Norfolk, by drift deposits giving rise to less fertile or less tractable soils; but it is also because they were *spatially* marginal. This broad distinction, between what is often termed 'river and wold', has been developed by Everitt and Phythian Adams into a general model for understanding not only the development of settlement in England but also that of patterns of territorial organisation. Because the upland 'wolds' between the valleys were areas of grazing and woodland, and at best only sparsely settled, they tended in early times to constitute cut-off points in patterns of human interaction – to form, that is, the margins of social territories. Communities were focused on particular valleys, or valley systems, gradually developing identities distinct from those dwelling on the other side of a watershed. Even when the interfluves came to be more intensively exploited such established patterns of social interaction tended to continue, not least because some of the valley settlements evolved into market centres, with important roles as the social and economic foci for wider communities. Over time, in other words, social territories tended to approximate to drainage basins.

It is perhaps unsurprising, therefore, that the boundaries of the ancient administrative divisions called hundreds – created in their present form in the tenth century, but incorporating in part older and more organic systems of territorial organisation – tend in Norfolk to follow the watersheds between major valleys (Williamson 1993, 128–9). Only as rivers become sufficiently wide in their lower reaches to present a barrier to daily contact did such boundaries leave the high ground to run along these instead. Nor is it surprising that the larger areas of ancient woodland, in particular, often lie close to such boundaries, or that the major clusters of woods, parks and commons just noted generally coincide with places where several hundredal boundaries met. Stock Heath, lying at the centre of the cluster of woods and commons near Melton Constable, is thus located at the point where the hundreds of Eynesford, Gallow, Holt and North Greenhoe converged. These spatial relationships presumably indicate the former existence, in the remote past, of communal woods and grazing grounds lying on the fringes of valley-based territories, the boundaries of which were, to varying degrees, perpetuated in those of medieval hundreds. In a rather similar manner, Higham has noted how in Cheshire 'belts of woodland names' coincide with hundred boundaries: 'the hundreds in their current form were probably formed early in the tenth century, but reflect in part pre-existing divisions' (Higham 1989, 24–5). It might be expected that these relics of particularly extensive tracts of wooded waste should correlate with places where Domesday suggests there were major concentrations of woodland. To some extent they do: that around Melton Constable, for example correlates with the woodland for over 900 swine jointly recorded in the entries for the ten townships which appear to have extended into this area.[4] But while Domesday provides a good *general* indication of the distribution of woodland in the county, in detail it is often a less reliable source owing to the fact that particular manors often possessed outlying portions of woodland, sometimes located several kilometres away. It is only because its ownership was in dispute that Domesday tells us explicitly that an area of woodland in Colkirk belonged to Fakenham, some five kilometres to the north. Similar anomalies can be detected in other Domesday entries (Williamson 1993, 122–3).

While there is thus a broad association of ancient woodland and significant interfluves, it is important to emphasise that in detail the situation is often more

---

4 Barney, Fulmondeston, Gunthorpe, Hindringham, Stibbard, Swanton Novers, Thursford, Wood Norton, Melton Constable and Hindolveston.

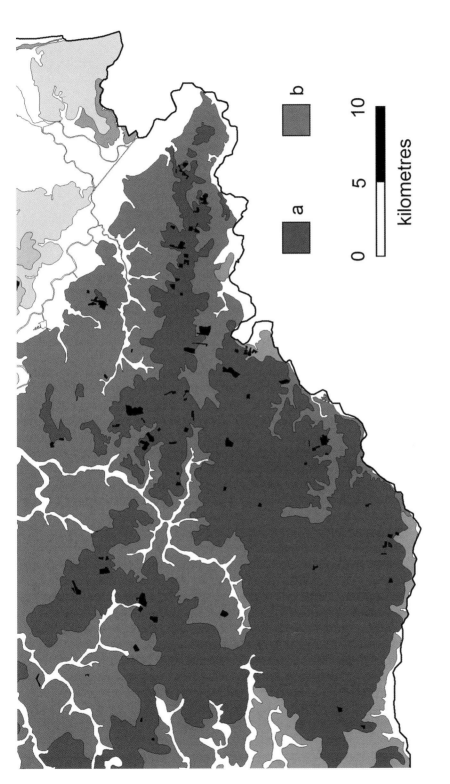

Figure 11 The relationship of ancient woodland to the clay plateau in south Norfolk. As elsewhere in England, woods tend to cluster on the margins of the principal masses of upland clay, rather than being concentrated towards their centres. (a) Beccles Association soils (heavy plateau clays); (b) Burlingham and Hanslope soils (lighter clays on valley sides).

complex, for the woods tend to cluster not on the precise line of the watershed but instead a little way back from it, on the edge of one or other of the valleys it separates. This relationship is most evident in the case of those woods – the majority in the county – associated with the dissected boulder clay plateau. As Figure 11 shows, woods are more likely to be found towards the *margins* of the main masses of boulder clay, on the edges of the valleys dissecting the plateau. They are, in consequence, more frequent where the plateau was most extensively dissected, and correspondingly rare where extensive tracts of level ground occur. Here, before the enclosures in the later eighteenth and nineteenth centuries, areas of common land were to be found instead. This in turn explains why ancient woods are particularly frequent in the dissected countryside in the extreme south-east of the county, especially on the narrow watershed between the Waveney and the Chet and the Broome Beck and the Chet, and contrastingly rare over large parts of central–south Norfolk, on the great level tablelands between the Tas and the Waveney, where their place was taken by large areas of open common, or by ribbons of greens which appear to represent the tattered remnants of once more extensive tracts of common land, as in the area around Shelton. This pattern – of ancient woods clustering on the margins of the areas of agriculturally challenging soils with which they are most closely associated – is rather less noticeable, it should be emphasised, in the case of soils other than those derived from boulder clay, such as those of the Newport 4 Association, although even here it is present to some extent.

Patterns like this have been noted elsewhere. Warner, writing about the medieval landscape of north-east Suffolk, has emphasised how commons tended to occupy the central sections of the boulder clay plateau, with the enclosed woods lying towards their edges (Warner 1987), while Witney has observed how, by late medieval times, most woodland within the Weald of Kent and Sussex survived around the district's periphery rather than, as we might expect, towards its centre (Witney 1998). Witney explained this pattern largely in terms of practical economic factors, in particular access. The twelfth and thirteenth centuries saw a steady decline in the economic importance of the Wealden woods as swine pastures and grazing grounds and a concomitant increase in the demand for, and thus in the value of, wood and timber. Areas of woodland were enclosed, and more intensively managed, in places where their products could be transported to markets with relative ease. In the 'central core of the Weald ... heavy loads were almost undisposable' because of the difficulties involved in moving laden carts in winter time along difficult clay roads (Witney 1998, 20). Colonisation was thus directed into the more remote districts, where the swine-woods were progressively felled and turned to farmland, or else degenerated to open commons: woods survived mainly on the periphery.

Manorial sites and ancient woods

These are convincing arguments, but it is possible that questions of access and management may in some cases have been compounded by patterns of ownership and issues of status. The expansion of settlement from later Saxon times led not only to a proliferation of peasant farms strung out around the margins of commons and the roads leading to them but also to the creation of new manors and sub-manors which were often located at a distance from old settlement foci. In a number of cases, ancient woods and the halls associated with such manors stand in remarkably close proximity: so much so that, in the post-medieval period, some woods have expanded over abandoned manorial sites, incorporating the earthworks of moats and associated enclosures. Two striking examples of this phenomenon occur within the sample of woods examined in this project, both in the well-wooded south and east of the county. The first is Hedenham Wood, first shown cartographically on a map by Thomas Waterman of the Hedenham estate surveyed in 1617 (NRO 1761/1) (see Appendix). The modern Hedenham Hall, which stands some 600 metres to the south of the parish church, represents the medieval manor of Parks: Waterman's map shows the demesne of the main manor, lying some way to the north, a property which was incorporated from the sixteenth century into the neighbouring estate of Ditchingham. A substantial part of this was occupied by Hedenham Wood, within the southern half of which Waterman shows an open clearing marked 'Hell Yards'. This was approached from the east by a road or track, to the south of which was an area – comprising the south-eastern corner of the wood – described as 'Pytle' (the local term for a small field), presumably indicating that it had been added to the area of the wood relatively recently. The open clearing is today occupied by woodland but it contains a complex of earthworks which includes a ditched enclosure bounded on the east by a straight, deep, water-filled linear depression ranged north–south, which is itself flanked to the east, along much of its length, by a substantial bank. The first edition Ordnance Survey six-inch map describes this as a 'moat', but the ditches defining the remainder of the enclosure run uphill and can never have been water-filled. 'Hell Yards' is evidently a corruption of 'Hall Yards', and the earthworks clearly mark the site of a late medieval high-status residence associated with Hedenham manor, featuring a large, probably semi-ornamental, fishpond. In addition, to the south-west of the probable hall site a number of substantial banks and ditches, defining a complex of small enclosures, are buried in woodland. This area was already completely wooded by 1617, but had evidently once been open and had comprised a number of small fields in the vicinity of the hall. Eighty metres to the north of the hall site a substantial bank runs east–west the full width of the wood, evidently representing its original southern boundary (see Appendix entry). To the north of the bank the archaeological evidence suggests that the wood is primary in character, in the sense that it appears to occupy ground never enclosed into fields or cultivated. Evidently, a medieval manorial site lay immediately to the south of an area of primary woodland, which in the course of the fifteenth or sixteenth century expanded over its abandoned site.

The second example, Gawdyhall Big Wood, lies 11 kilometres to the south-east. The wood actually contains two substantial moated enclosures, one in the south and the other in the north-east. The southern moat – the larger of the two – still lay outside the wood when the Ordnance Survey six-inch map was surveyed as late as 1884, and is clearly separated from it by the wood's external boundary bank; its incorporation within the wood occurred only in the course of the twentieth century. The Ordnance Survey shows that the eastern moat already lay within the wood by the 1880s, but an estate map of 1734 (NRO MS 4568) shows that it then occupied a small close lying between the wood and a small roadside green. The manorial history of the parish is confused (see Appendix entry) but both moats, to judge from their substantial size, were manorial. As at Hedenham, both appear to have been intentionally placed on the margins of the wood, and were incorporated within it only following their abandonment.

Norfolk has fewer examples of moats closely related to woods in this manner than the neighbouring counties to the south and south-west – Suffolk, Essex and Hertfordshire. But there are a number of other examples, including the moated site of Tindall Hall, located immediately to the east of Tindall Wood (also in Hedenham; see Appendix); the moated Starston Hall, immediately to the south of Starston Wood; the moated Banyard Hall, beside Banyards or Bunwell Wood (see Appendix entry); and the moated site of Kimberley manor in the parish of Kimberley, over which the adjacent Falstoff's Wood has expanded. In a number of other cases woods and moated manorial sites lie slightly further apart but within 250 metres, thus seemingly in meaningful association, as at Ashwellthorpe and Hethel (see Appendix entries). Rackham has noted this association of woods and moated sites, suggesting that 'moat makers deliberately chose to live next to woods: doubtless they appreciated the shelter and perhaps the concealment' (Rackham 1986a, 363). But it is unlikely that a wood would have provided an effective hiding place and, given that moats can be found to the north and east as well as to the south of woods, shelter may have been a secondary consideration. The convenience of access which more generally appears to have structured the distribution of woodland in the medieval countryside may at these places have been taken to its logical conclusion, so that coppices were placed almost literally on the manorial doorstep, but, in addition, woods, as we have noted, were private property, part of the manorial demesne and may thus – like deer parks – have represented sylvan statements of lordly status. It is noteworthy that where the boundary of Gawdyhall Big Wood passes the southern of the two moats it is raised up higher above the ground outside the wood than anywhere else, accentuating its apparent magnitude when viewed from the moat, perhaps for reasons of display.

These abandoned settlements engulfed in secondary woodland need to be distinguished from two other kinds of high-status site found in ancient woods. One, discussed in more detail below (pp. 57–9), comprises enclosures of a semi-defensive or defensive character which may pre-date the fencing off and management as coppice of the areas of woodland in which they lay or lie. The other consists of specialised enclosures associated with the exploitation of managed woods, but containing other manorial facilities, of which the site within Hethel Wood is the best example. That within Hales Wood might be of similar character, although it is better interpreted, perhaps, as pre-dating the wood.

Ancient woodland, Roman settlement and post-Roman regeneration

Medieval enclosed woods thus tended to be found towards the edges of areas of marginal soil, especially the heavy stagnogleys and pelostagnogleys of the clay plateau in the south and centre of the county. They probably tended to be retained and defined in such locations as the frontiers of cultivation and settlement expanded in the course of the eleventh, twelfth and thirteenth centuries for reasons of access and convenience, but in some cases also, perhaps, for the status they conferred on the manorial sites also established in such locations. As we have seen, the eleventh and twelfth centuries were not the first time that settlement had expanded onto these more marginal soils. Late prehistoric and Roman sites are also found on the clay 'uplands' of the county, while on lighter land clearance and cultivation likewise expanded at some distance from the principal valleys, even if problems of water supply on these more porous geologies often prevented the establishment of actual settlements in such locations. On the fringes of the more marginal soils in the county the frontiers of cultivation thus ebbed and flowed over the centuries, and this in turn raises the possibility that the woods concentrated in these locations may have regenerated over abandoned Roman farmland.

We noted in the previous chapter how debate continues about the extent to which the late prehistoric and Roman landscape was cleared and settled, and that some archaeologists believe that the extent of land use in these periods is indicated in many areas not just by the settlement sites recovered by field surveys but also by the fact that much of the basic fabric of the medieval and modern landscape – the pattern of fields and roads – can be shown to have prehistoric or Roman origins. When, in the 1970s and early 1980s, extensive fieldwalking surveys revealed far higher numbers of Roman and later prehistoric settlements, and on a much greater range of soil types, than archaeologists had hitherto thought might exist, some began to suggest that Roman populations in lowland England may have equalled or even exceeded those achieved by the time of Domesday (Taylor 1975; Fowler 2002, 16–18). But more recently a reaction to such views has set in, among some at least. Glenn Foard, for example, reviewing the evidence for Northamptonshire – a particularly well-studied county – has argued that even if all the Roman sites recovered through fieldwalking had been occupied at the same time, and each occupied by an average of around 20 people, this would still mean a population around half that implied by Domesday Book – assuming, as many researchers have done, that each tenant recorded in the latter source was equivalent to around 5.5 individuals (Brown and Foard 1998, 75).

In Norfolk the same kinds of argument apply. The 22 Roman sites recovered by systematic fieldwalking in the Hales/Loddon/Heckingham area in south-east Norfolk would, assuming that each was occupied at the same time and by an average of 25 people, represent a total population for the surveyed area of around 550. But the combined recorded population of the three places in 1086 was 187, implying a total population of around 935, assuming a very modest multiplier of 5, and of over 1,000 assuming one of 5.5. It is true that Roman settlements can be found virtually everywhere in the county, but not necessarily in the same numbers. In the dissected clayland countryside around Hales, for example, most of the sites discovered by Alan Davison were located on lower ground, close to the main watercourses, or (more rarely) on the margins of the clay plateau, where a perched water table could be accessed via shallow wells. Away from its margins comparatively few sites – no more than two, both small – were located on the clay plateau (Davison 1990, 15, 66). Similarly, Rogerson's survey of Fransham revealed that most Roman settlements were associated with the better-drained clays of the minor valleys, and that away from these, on the more level and poorly draining ground, settlement was sparser (Rogerson 1995). It is, moreover, noticeable that where the boulder clays, acid sands and gravels form particularly extensive and continuous interfluves between major valleys these are generally marked by *lacunae* in the distribution of Roman findspots, including in this case *all* discoveries – stray finds and manuring scatters as well as settlements (see map in Gurney 2005). Some of these correspond with the 'clusters' of woods and commons such as that around Melton Constable that we have already described. The comparatively small number of late prehistoric and Roman sites found

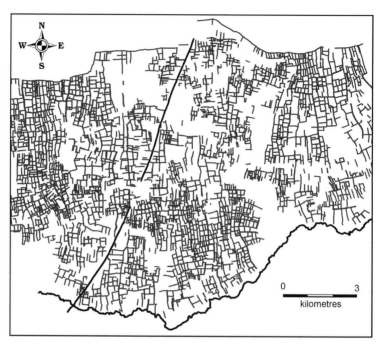

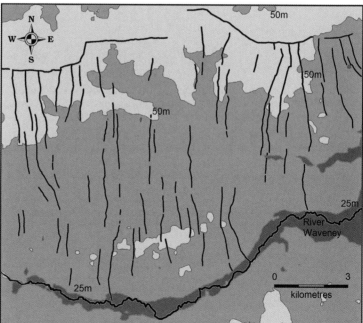

Figure 12 Above: the so-called 'Scole–Dickleburgh field system', a co-axial landscape lying to the north of the Waveney valley in south Norfolk, apparently 'slighted' by a Roman military road, the Pye Road. Drawing based on a wide range of archive maps (Williamson 1987). Below: the principal axes of the 'system' are formed mainly by a network of lanes or former lanes running at right angles to the topography – 'resource-linkage' routes (sensu Harrison 2005, 159–80) which could as easily post-date, as pre-date, the Roman road.

in 'upland' locations in the county, whether on heavy clays or on more freely draining soils, may thus often represent not arable settlements but isolated ranches that exploited upland *wolds* for grazing, pannage, wood and timber.

The evidence for 'relict field systems' surviving within the modern landscape is particularly relevant to this question. Although the idea that much of the fabric of the medieval countryside was of prehistoric or Roman origin has been attacked, or simply ignored, by many archaeologists (Hinton 1997), it enjoys continuing support from some researchers (Rippon *et al.* in press). A number of relict 'co-axial' landscapes have been identified in Norfolk, including the so-called 'Scole–Dickleburgh field system', which extends over more than 30 square kilometres in the south of the county, in the area to the north of the river Waveney, and which is apparently 'slighted' by the Roman road running south from Venta Icenorum (Caistor by Norwich) (Williamson 1987; Hinton 1997; Williamson 1998a) (Figure 12). This, like other examples in the county, has an interesting relationship with parish boundaries, which generally join, leave and rejoin its principal axes in such a manner as to suggest that these, at least, were in place by the eleventh or twelfth centuries, when parishes became fixed in the landscape. What is striking in the present context is that where the larger ancient woods are found within these 'relict landscapes' they often appear to have been superimposed on top of an 'earlier' pattern of fields, superficially suggesting that they have regenerated over areas of abandoned land.

In Norfolk, as elsewhere in England, co-axial field patterns seem invariably to have axes which run at right angles to major watercourses, up the valley sides and on to level interfluves between. A high proportion, although apparently not all, of these axes comprise or originally comprised roads or tracks, features which do not for the most part feature prominently in the accepted prehistoric examples of such landscapes, such as the Dartmoor reaves (Fleming 1988). This recurrent relationship with the broad sweeps of the local topography suggests that the long axes originated as routes for integrating the resources offered by the light valley soils – where, as we have noted, the earliest areas of arable and settlement were located – and the pastures and woods of the uplands. The parallel tracks developed, that is, because there was a recurrent direction of movement between lower and higher ground, as wood and timber were brought from uplands down to valley settlements, and as livestock – including pigs – were repeatedly driven up to the woods and pastures and back again (Williamson 2013, 94–101). Such strongly parallel arrangements of tracks, moreover, do not occur everywhere but only where valleys – or low-lying land close to the sea, in the case of north and west Norfolk – follow a fairly straight alignment. Where they are more sinuous or convoluted, such regular and apparently 'planned' landscapes are replaced by arrangements displaying a rather looser parallelism, the two types merging almost imperceptibly as the character of the topography gradually changes. The patterns of lanes thus arguably came first: the infilling of fields developed later, as settlement and cultivation expanded out of the valleys and on to the more marginal uplands, the orientation of the new boundaries replicating that of the pre-existing routeways around them. The apparent 'superimposition' of Roman roads upon 'earlier' co-axial landscapes, as in the case of the 'Scole–Dickleburgh field system', may thus be illusory. If the original relationship was not between the road and a dense network of fields but rather between the road and a network of widely spaced parallel lanes and boundaries, then the latter could have been imposed on the Roman road just as easily as the other way around, the difference in orientation being explained by differences of purpose. The lanes connected the resources of a local environment, running from river to 'wold', while the Roman road, in contrast, took a direct route from one place of military or civilian importance to another. Differences in their orientation need not necessarily have any chronological implications. This said, it remains possible that, while organic in character, such landscapes do in part have very early origins, and do indeed pre-date the Roman roads that 'slight' them. The relationship between ancient woods and such relict landscapes is thus a matter of some interest. Unless the scale of post-Roman continuity was such that the boundaries of wooded and non-wooded ground remained precisely the same over the centuries, then the pattern of co-axial fields ought to be continued, in earthwork form, within some at least of the larger areas of woodland found within such 'relict landscapes'.

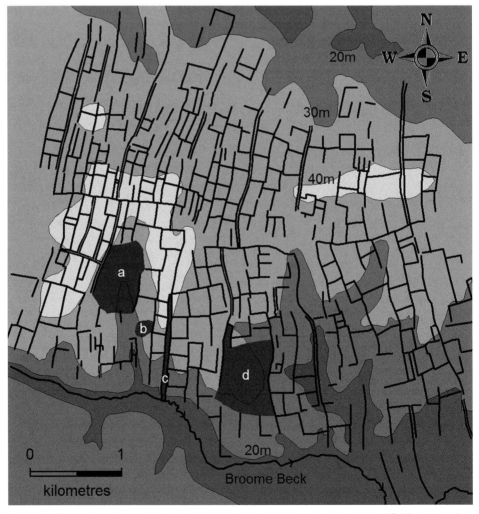

Figure 13 Relationship of the principal areas of ancient woodland and co-axial field patterns in the area around Hedenham and Ditchingham in south Norfolk: (a) Hedenham Wood; (b) Round Grove; (c) Long Row; (d) Tindall Wood.

Figure 13 shows the roughly co-axial networks of lanes and boundaries in the parishes of Ditchingham and Hedenham, one extending south from the valley of the Chet, the other north from the Broome Beck. The main areas of ancient woodland in the area look very much as if they have regenerated over parts of the field 'system', presumably in the post-Roman period. Hedenham Wood and Tindall's Wood are among the largest examples in the county, covering 23 and 44 hectares respectively. Within the southern section of the former lie the earthworks already noted (above, p. 47), representing a late medieval manorial site and associated closes preserved by the southward expansion of the wood. While some of these features share the approximate alignment of the surrounding co-axial 'grid', the original area of the wood, to the north, contains no evidence whatsoever for previous division or cultivation. The much larger Tindall Wood contains no early earthworks at all (see Appendix entry). On the other hand, the *outer* boundaries of both woods appear to be largely defined by axes of the 'field system'. The smaller Round Grove is a secondary wood which has regenerated over an abandoned medieval farm site and associated enclosures, none of which have boundaries which share the orientation of the surrounding grid of fields; while Long Row, with its unusual, attenuated shape, is likewise secondary and contains earthworks which suggest that it originated as a wide drove road that was eventually abandoned and colonised by trees (see Appendix entries). At just over a kilometre in length it forms, in fact, a major axis of the local co-axial landscape, and Waterman's map of Hedenham, surveyed in 1617, shows that it originally continued for a further 0.4 kilometres to the north. All this supports the interpretation of co-axial landscapes advanced above. A framework of sub-parallel tracks and boundaries developed first, at right angles to the principal watercourses. These originally, away from the main valleys, ran through woodland and pasture. In the later Saxon and post-Conquest periods most of the woodland was cleared for cultivation, but manorial lords enclosed some portions located towards the margins of the heaviest upland soils for their own use, the boundaries of which were structured, to a significant extent, by the existing framework of tracks and boundaries.

Close examination of ancient woods which lie within areas of co-axial fields elsewhere in the county tells a similar story. Some contain internal divisions which are roughly orientated with the dominant 'grain' of the local landscape, as at Wood Rising, some of which *may* represent lost elements of early landscapes: but they do not overlie the earthworks of lost co-axial fields. Billingford Wood and Thorpe Wood both lie within the area of the 'Scole–Dickleburgh field system'. The former contains some possible evidence for early agriculture in the form of a linear lynchet created by ploughing (discussed below), but this lies on a different alignment to that of the surrounding 'grid'. Thorpe Wood contains no signs of earlier land use whatsoever.

Archaeological evidence for probable *medieval* settlement and agricultural activity, in the form of earthworks of field boundaries, ridge and furrow, abandoned tofts and the like, is reasonably abundant within ancient woods in Norfolk, indicating – as we shall see – that a significant number have developed, in whole or part, in late medieval or post-medieval times. The areas occupied by such woods may also have been inhabited, divided and farmed in earlier periods, but any above-ground archaeological evidence has been obliterated by medieval activity. Only in a few woods has some slight evidence for possible pre-medieval arable activity been noted, not in the form of the earthworks of field boundaries but rather as lynchets: that is, linear breaks in slope caused by the erosion of soil through ploughing on the downhill side, and its accumulation on the uphill side, of some lost boundary. One example lies within West Bradenham Great Wood. This large area of woodland covers an area of *c.*24 hectares and is ranged roughly south-west–north-east, its boundaries lying conformably with the dominant grain of the neighbouring fields, which display a vaguely sub-parallel pattern, running with the main direction of slope towards the watershed (between the Wissey to the south and the Blackwater to the north). The northern two-thirds of the wood occupies heavy, poorly draining soils of the Beccles Association; the southern section lies on more sloping ground, on soils of the Burlingham Association. This southern section is crossed, from east to west, by a slight but very clear lynchet: it does not appear to be a bank representing a subdivision of the wood or a former external boundary preserved through the wood's expansion. Rather, it appears to be the consequence of agricultural activity pre-dating the wood and, although it cannot be dated with any certainty, is potentially from the prehistoric or Roman periods. Undated lynchets, without ditches but sometimes flanked by low, hardly perceptible banks, have also been noted in Middle or Thorpe Wood in Thorpe Abbots (Figure 14); Hook Wood in Morley St Peter; East Wood, Denton; and Rawhall Wood, although these cannot be closely dated and in some cases – particularly Rawhall – a medieval date is perhaps more likely. To these we should add the evidence from Catfield, in the east of the county, where a number of undated but probably late prehistoric field boundaries

Figure 14 Undated lynchet, flanked by low bank, within Middle Wood, Thorpe Abbots. It is one of three such features within the wood and, whether of medieval or of earlier date, indicates that the southern portion of the wood, at least, is 'secondary' in character.

and trackways are recorded on aerial photographs within the area occupied by Catfield Wood until it was grubbed out in the early nineteenth century (NHER 11669). Unusually, the wood occupied an area of light, freely draining loams of the Wick 3 Association. Even if all the features just noted were, indeed, all of pre-medieval date, this would still constitute a meagre total. In general, the larger ancient woods in the county, those extensive enough to have preserved elements of early field systems rather than to have been slotted into an existing pattern of fields, lack the kind of evidence for prehistoric or Roman farming or settlement discovered, for example, within the Ashridge woods in Hertfordshire by Angus Wainwright (Morris and Wainwright 1995). Sexton's Wood in Denton, extending over nearly 40 hectares, lies entirely on Beccles soils and is devoid of any internal earthworks, while the huge woods at Swanton Novers, Foxley and Hockering, although containing medieval features and a number of enigmatic and probably earlier earthworks, occupy areas which have clearly never been divided into fields and cultivated. Unless the degree of continuity from the Roman to the medieval landscape was on such a scale that precisely the same areas in each period were devoted to woodland then we ought to find within these larger examples, on a fairly regular basis, something analogous to the 'Celtic fields' which occupy many areas of chalk downland in southern England. Yet we do not, and in this respect the evidence from Norfolk contrasts markedly with that from other parts of the country, such as Savernake Forest, where a number of enclosed coppiced woods have been shown to overlie prehistoric arable 'Celtic' fields and Romano-British settlements (Bathe *et al.* 2011). The solitary example of a possible round barrow within Swanton Novers Wood, set in a wood covering more than half a square kilometre and otherwise completely devoid of archaeological features, is a particularly powerful testimony to the extent to which ancient woods in the county generally occupy areas which lay beyond the bounds of cultivation in the pre-medieval period.

Woods as pastures: early pastoral exploitation of woodland

The larger woods, and a significant proportion of the smaller examples, thus appear to occupy areas which have never been cultivated, either in the medieval period or earlier; few appear to have regenerated over abandoned Roman farmland. This does not mean, however, that the areas which they occupy had invariably remained densely wooded up until the time that they were defined and enclosed in the early Middle Ages. In earlier periods the intensity of grazing and other forms of exploitation may have reduced some, at least, to fairly open wood-pastures, especially given the location of many examples, towards the margins of the interfluves and thus comparatively close to long-settled and long-cultivated land. Early pastoral use is suggested by some of the archaeological evidence. Several woods thus contain hollow ways which appear, given the absence of associated field boundaries, to have developed within unenclosed and unploughed landscapes, although it is theoretically possible that the roads ran through abandoned medieval open fields, over which the woods in question have spread or regenerated, as probably in the case of Rawhall. But this seems unlikely in the case of Hazel Hurn Wood in Woodrising, which contains a single short stretch of hollow way; or Shotesham Little Wood, where there are two, separated by some 120 metres and running roughly parallel for a short distance in the western half of the wood. Sporle Wood likewise contains two probable examples. One, ranged east–west and running just inside from the southern boundary, is bounded by a diminutive bank on its northern edge, but the other, ranged roughly north–south near the eastern edge of the wood, is not: it is followed by an intermittent watercourse and may in part be natural. These features may have been formed by droving stock within areas of open pasture, wooded or otherwise. A few of the woods examined contain more enigmatic features which may be related to earlier pastoral use. The southern portion of Hockering Wood occupies sloping ground on fairly well-drained soils, unlike its northern section, which lies on more level clays. A substantial earthwork runs up the slope for some 70 metres. Superficially a hollow way, it is flanked to the west by a wide, denuded bank, the combined effect resembling a linear earthwork perhaps constructed to define the limits of an early grazing ground (although, if so, then its line must have been continued onto the level ground to the north by some other form of barrier, now invisible archaeologically). Of particular interest in this context is Wayland Wood in Watton, which contains no evidence for abandoned field systems, but from which a number of finds of Neolithic, Bronze Age and Iron Age material have been made (NHER 36300). A slight, curving scarp running through the south of the wood may just possibly represent the edge of an enclosure associated with stock management. The rather similar curving bank noted within Horningtoft Great Wood might represent something comparable.

There is some archaeological evidence that a number of areas of what later became enclosed, coppiced woodland were still being managed as part of wider wood-pastures well into the post-Conquest period. Denton Castle first came to archaeological attention in 1850 when Deerhaugh or Darrow Wood, in the remote north-east of Denton parish

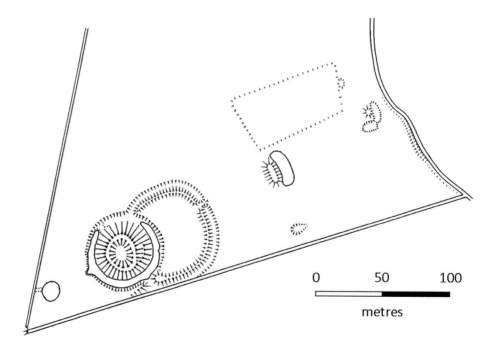

Figure 15 The earthworks of Denton Castle (after Cushion and Davison 2003).

in the south of the county and occupying an area of level, poorly draining boulder clay, was cleared and its area turned over to agriculture (Cushion and Davison 2003, 168–9). The wood had evidently been coppiced, and the remains of a woodbank still survives beside a field boundary to the east of the castle: there is no reason to doubt that, had it survived, Darrow Wood would have been classified as an area of ancient, semi-natural woodland. The castle comprises a diminutive motte and bailey: the former is only *c*.40 metres in diameter, with a surrounding ditch *c*.10 metres wide; the latter – which adjoins it on the east – is a mere 65 metres across (Figure 15). In 1884, when the site was planned and examined by Manning, a roughly trapezoid enclosure defined by a bank with an external ditch lay some 50 metres to the north-east, but this has since been almost entirely levelled (Manning 1884). In contrast to the moated sites at Gawdy, the earthworks of the castle clearly lay *within* the wood, occupying a position nearly 200 metres in from what the tithe award map shows was its external boundary. It is possible that the castle, like the manorial complex in Hedenham Wood, was engulfed by the expansion of a neighbouring area of woodland which had disappeared by the time the earliest maps were surveyed. But the absence of earthworks representing associated fields and closes, of the kind evident around the Hedenham Hall site, strongly suggests that when first built the castle stood within a tract of undivided 'waste'. Most of this was subsequently brought into cultivation, except for the portion around the castle site itself, which was instead – following its abandonment – enclosed and managed as coppice.

Similar in some ways is the unusual complex of earthworks at Horningtoft, in the centre of the county, which was likewise revealed by woodland clearance in the nineteenth century and has again been surveyed by Cushion and Davison (Cushion and Davison 2003, 110–11) (Figure 16). The main feature is an incomplete oval moated enclosure defined by a ditch *c*.7 metres wide, now much mutilated by gravel extraction. This is approached by an entrance roadway flanked by enclosures; further banks and enclosures lay to the north. The whole complex is bounded to the west, at a little distance, by a substantial bank and external ditch running for part of its length along the side of a public road. This formed the western boundary of Horningtoft Great Wood until the middle decades of the nineteenth century. The wood was then progressively reduced in size and now survives as a fragment – still called Great Wood – lying some way to the east. It is possible that, as at Hedenham or Gawdy, a high-status residence was simply placed beside (on the western edge of) an area of ancient woodland, which subsequently expanded across it. But although the oval moat is flanked to the west by some small enclosures, as noted, there is no trace of anything that might be interpreted as a former woodland boundary to the *east*, where there is instead a marked absence of earthworks of any kind: the small ditch shown on Figure 16 is of post-medieval date, marking one of the stages in the contraction of the wood. Here, too, we appear to have evidence of a fortified site placed within what was originally an area of open ground, one part of which later came to be managed as coppiced woodland. Neither of these sites is securely dated, although Denton Castle was probably constructed by the d'Albini family, whose principal *caput* in Norfolk was at New Buckenham: like other minor mottes, it has been plausibly dated to the 'Anarchy' of Stephen's reign (1135–64), and it is possible that it was intended to protect the family's assets in a district close to the great stronghold of their rivals, the Warrennes, at Bungay in Suffolk, some eight kilometres to the east. But what kind of assets? It is unlikely that the site was constructed to defend woodland from attack:

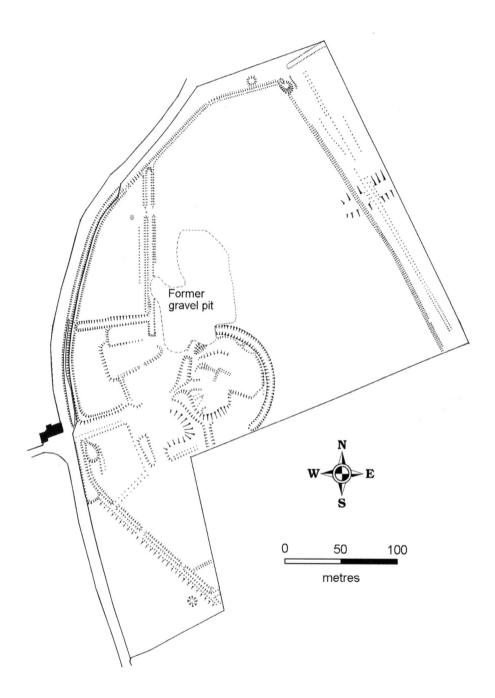

Figure 16 The earthworks at Horningtoft, revealed by the grubbing out of much of Horningtoft Great Wood in the nineteenth century (after Cushion and Davison 2003).

more plausibly, the d'Albinis were concerned to guard herds and flocks in remote grazing grounds from raiding.

A number of high-status medieval settlements discovered within surviving areas of ancient woodland during the course of this research may be of broadly similar character to the sites at Denton and Horningtoft. Those at Hedenham and Gawdy have already been discussed, and evidently represent manorial sites engulfed, following their abandonment, by the expansion of adjacent areas of woodland: others, like those within woods at Hethel, are best interpreted as specialised manorial enclosures associated with the exploitation of woods (the relationship of this substantial earthwork to the outer woodbank suggests that the latter is the earlier feature, but an absence of associated field boundaries makes it clear that the enclosure is not part of a farmed landscape over which the wood has regenerated (see Appendix)). A few examples of such sites may, in contrast, pre-date the enclosure and more intensive management of the woods within which they now lie, and like those at Denton and Horningtoft represent places for the exploitation and protection of demesne herds grazed in open wood-pastures. Hales Wood thus contains an enclosure, evidently medieval and defined by substantial banks, which clearly pre-dates the present medieval woodbank on its northern boundary, and thus perhaps the enclosure and definition of the wood itself. It could well have been used to corral livestock. Hazel Hurn Wood in the parish of Woodrising, one of a complex of three adjacent woods which may have survived as managed wood-pasture well into the post-Conquest period, contains a simple moated site (NHER 8823) which lies some way back from the northern boundary of the wood, which is itself formed on this side by a minor bank and ditch, the consequence of post-medieval contraction. It is flanked to the north by earthwork enclosures but these are too small to represent agricultural fields, and to the south the moat is not, as at Gawdy or Hedenham, divided from the wood by a former boundary bank. Just over 100 metres to the east is another earthwork complex, described in the NHER as a set of fishponds (NHER 25241); but, again without a bank dividing it from the rest of the wood, it might be best interpreted as an enclosure for corralling stock within an open wood-pasture landscape, although in this case the prominent mound lying outside the main enclosure is hard to explain (Figure 17). Another example is the moated site located towards the centre of Hockering Wood, which lies more than 250 metres from wood's boundary and is unassociated with any evidence of hollow ways, field boundaries or the like. In this case, however, the wood itself appears to have developed from a medieval park, and the moat may thus represent the site of a lodge, although it is noteworthy that a short distance to the south-east there is an enigmatic trapezoid enclosure defined by a low bank and external ditch that is broadly similar in size and shape to the now largely levelled example near Denton Castle. All of these sites, like those at Denton and Horningtoft, are to be found in remote 'upland' locations, close to major watersheds, and they may suggest that as late as the mid-twelfth century the areas in which they lie still comprised extensive tracts of unenclosed wood-pasture.

The enclosure of the wastes

The topographical and archaeological evidence briefly discussed above thus suggests that, while the process of enclosing and coppicing woods may have begun in late Saxon times, it was mainly associated with the expansion of settlement onto marginal ground which continued from the eleventh century into the thirteenth. The only

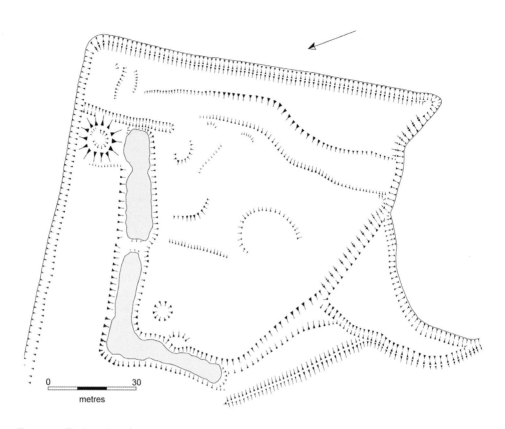

Figure 17 Earthworks of medieval enclosures in Hazel Hurn Wood, Woodrising.

specific documentary reference for the embanking of woodland we have for the county comes from West Bradenham in 1226, which describes how the lord of the manor of Bradenham had 'about the wood … raised one earthwork for the livestock, lest they eat up the younger wood' (Rackham 1986b, 168). Local documents become abundant only from the thirteenth century, and the absence of further references may well suggest that most woods had been embanked by then. The Ely Coucher Book of 1251 names six woods in Norfolk owned by the abbey of Ely, all clearly private property and by implication bounded and coppiced. At Hindolveston in 1277–8 £10 10s was paid for major ditching and fencing works, and in 1297–8 a new woodbank, with hedge, was constructed around both woods at a cost of £10 10s (Rackham 1980, 157–9).

As these references indicate, coppiced woods, in Norfolk as elsewhere, were enclosed by banks that were topped by a hedge or fence and accompanied by an external ditch. Deer parks, in contrast, usually, but not invariably, were surrounded by a bank with an *internal* ditch. The former arrangement was intended to keep livestock out, the latter to keep deer (and sometimes other stock) in. But the sheer size of many external woodbanks – revealed most clearly where they have been isolated within a wood by its later expansion – is noteworthy, and we need to remember the extent to which their accompanying ditches have become silted and filled with leaves and other debris over the centuries. Most woodland boundaries which can, with confidence, be attributed to the twelfth or thirteenth centuries have a total width, including both bank and ditch, of between 5 and 7 metres, and a height above the internal woodland floor ranging from 0.3 metres to as much as 1 metre in rare cases, such as at Foxley (see Appendix). Additions made to a wood later in the medieval period were generally enclosed by noticeably less substantial banks. At Wayland the original 'core' of the wood is surrounded by a bank and ditch around 7 metres wide and 0.5–0.75 metres in height, while the later 'extension' to the east – perhaps of fourteenth- or fifteenth-century date – is enclosed by a boundary no more than 5 metres wide, the bank of which is often hardly visibly above the woodland floor. A similar contrast – between banks defining an original, early medieval, core, and those embracing a late medieval or post-medieval extension – is evident elsewhere, as at Hedenham. To some extent such differences may be due to the fact that the older boundary has had more time to accumulate material dredged from the ditch and placed on the bank during routine maintenance. But the trend is continued with boundaries known or suspected to have originated in the eighteenth or nineteenth centuries, which are usually marked with slight banks and ditches, little more than a metre or two in width: these are still topped in some cases with the remains of hawthorn hedges, and in general terms appear little different from the boundaries surrounding contemporary hedged fields.

If the main purpose of the boundary bank and ditch was to prevent livestock, including deer, from straying into the wood and consuming the coppice stools, which were especially vulnerable during the early stages of the rotation, this gradual decline in magnitude over time is difficult to explain. Nor is it immediately obvious why the earlier medieval banks, and the hedges or fences that surmounted them, needed to be significantly larger than the hedges and hedgebanks surrounding private fields, which fulfilled a similar function. The change could reflect the relative abundance of deer – capable of jumping a hedge of normal height and form – in the early medieval landscape and the decline in their numbers in subsequent centuries. But it may also suggest that we should consider the earlier woodbanks not simply as features analogous to field boundaries but as ones related more to the earthworks raised around other seigniorial possessions in the twelfth and thirteenth centuries, such as deer parks and manorial enclosures, or even to the embankments raised around smaller castles. They were intended, that is, to be expressions of power, status and ownership. Their size may also indicate an expectation that livestock would not simply stray from adjoining pastures, but would be deliberately introduced into woods with human assistance. As we have emphasised, before woodbanks were raised the areas they enclosed had formed part of the common wastes: creating a wood was an act of privatisation and enclosure, and a demonstration of lordly power over customary rights of access. Woodbanks may thus have had a symbolic as much as a practical significance. They were intended to deter trespassers who were keen to exercise ancestral rights as much as to prevent the entry of animals acting of their own volition.

Ecological impacts of enclosure

As we briefly suggested in Chapter 1, once portions of woodland were enclosed and subjected to management by coppicing their botanical character must have begun to change. It is usually argued that the classic 'indicator species' were inherited from the vegetation of the wildwood and remain closely associated with areas of ancient woodland primarily because they find it difficult to colonise beyond them (Peterken and Game 1984). They thrive in conditions of shade and high humidity, and cannot therefore readily tolerate dry or open environments, or are out-competed there by other species. The high phosphate levels found in most agricultural soils are also inimical to them, or, at least, in such circumstances they cannot compete successfully with other species (Helliwell 2006, 134; Wulf 1997). They are, in contrast, tolerant of soils with limited availability of nutrients (Grime 2001). Their failure to colonise recent woods is, however, mainly a consequence of their slow rates of dispersal (Beckett 2009, 51–2; Spencer 1990, 98–102). Dog's mercury, for example, ejects seeds explosively from seed pods, but these are unable to travel much more than 0.3 metres; primrose seeds can merely roll down slopes, or be carried short distances by ants; wood anemone seldom sets viable seed, and spreads vegetatively, by rhizomes. Some of these plants, especially primrose, must once have had some other means of spreading, given their widespread occurrence in the British Isles: possibly they were once carried on the feet or fur of wild animals (Helliwell 2006, 134; Couvreur *et al.* 2004). Such arguments imply that these plants were relatively common in the 'wildwood', but became restricted to its fragmented remains, isolated within farmland, and have been used to explain their close affinity with ancient woodland not only in Britain but more widely across Europe (Hermy *et al.* 1999), including in Germany (Wulf 1997), Poland (Dzwonko 2001) and Sweden (Brunet and Von Oheimb 1998).

It must be emphasised, however, that most 'ancient woodland indicator species' are not characteristic of all kinds of ancient woodland, for they are not well represented in surviving wood-pastures (Colebourn 1989, 65; Rotherham 2012). They were thus presumably also relatively rare in the grazed woodlands which pre-dated the development of coppiced woodland in early medieval times, and possibly in the 'wildwood' which existed before the advent of farming. Moreover, the suggestion that most of these species are found in ancient woods and not in recent ones because they have low dispersion rates and fail to thrive on former agricultural soils is only partly true: for, as we shall see, in the right conditions many can colonise new woods with remarkable rapidity (below, pp. 131–3). As Thompson and colleagues have noted in Somerset, 'there are probably no common species incapable of colonising ... secondary woodland' (Thompson *et al.* 2003, 253). Most 'indicator' plants, it is true, flourish in woodland because they thrive in moist and shady conditions, and can thus outcompete other species less well adapted to these circumstances. Some come into leaf very early, for example, such as dog's mercury. Others, such as herb Paris, primrose, wood anemone or bluebells, can survive long periods of shade, flowering and setting seed when the woodland floor is exposed to light (Helliwell 2006; Valverde and Silvertown 1997; Colebourn 1989; Beckett 2009, 51–2). All may well have increased their frequency significantly once intensive, regular systems of management commenced (Colebourn 1989, 70). But other 'indicators' (such as water avens (*Geum rivale*) and pignut (*Conoipodium majus*) are largely restricted to ancient woods simply because they cannot survive grazing pressure well (Colebourn 1989, 74). Indeed, to judge from their poor representation in wood-pastures and their fate in those ancient woods currently subject to heavy grazing by deer, most characteristic woodland plants, including herb Paris, bluebells and dog's mercury, likewise have relatively low resistance to grazing (Mitchell and Kirby 1990; Dolman *et al.* 2010). Sheep are particularly inimical to them: 'close grazing by sheep proved to be a sure way of eliminating woodland plants' (Beckett 2009, 53). Few of these species, moreover, recover from a sustained period of ground disturbance.

The close association of 'indicator species' with ancient woodland is not, therefore, simply due to the fact that they were characteristic plants of the 'wildwood' which are able to colonise only very slowly beyond its tattered remnants. The highly unnatural systems of management to which such areas have been subjected over long periods of time have allowed these plants to flourish; but of equal or greater importance to some species may have been the fact that coppiced woods were the only areas of the medieval landscape which were neither regularly grazed nor ploughed. 'Ancient woodland indicators', in other words, were almost certainly more common in managed medieval and post-medieval woods, and remain so in their neglected and derelict remnants in the modern landscape, than they would have been in the grazed 'wastes' from which these were enclosed, whatever precise form these may have taken. The recognition that the development of their characteristic flora was to a significant extent a consequence of human management systems places ancient woods alongside grazed downlands and meadows: it serves to move them, as it were, further along the continuum that runs between the completely natural and the entirely human and artificial.

Conclusion

Although there is no doubt that late prehistoric and Romano-British settlement was extensive in Norfolk, occurring on all soil types, the archaeological evidence from, in particular, the larger areas of ancient woodland suggests that farms and settlements were not found to the same extent everywhere. Evidence for pre-medieval field systems and agricultural activity from within ancient woods is meagre, suggesting that these have not in general regenerated over abandoned Roman farmland and that the poorer sands, gravels and clays on which most of the larger examples are located generally survived as undivided or minimally divided tracts of woodland and grazing into the early medieval period. Some woods may have been enclosed and coppiced in later Saxon times but for the most part this appears to have been a development of the post-Conquest period, probably concentrated in the twelfth century but continuing in some places into the thirteenth. The enclosure of woodland was part and parcel of a wider process of enclosure and the allocation of resources that took place as settlement and cultivation expanded onto more marginal land and which also included the definition of areas of common land and the creation of deer parks. The enclosure of woods, like the enclosure of parks, was an act of lordly appropriation, something which may explain the remarkable size of many early woodbanks. Enclosure, and the imposition of coppicing, will have changed the botanical composition of woodland in significant ways, and 'ancient woodland indicator species' were probably much less frequent in the grazed wooded 'wastes' of Saxon times than they became in the managed woods which were enclosed from them. Rather than representing survivors from the 'wildwood', the particular suite of plants characteristic of ancient woods is, in large measure, an artefact of management.

Chapter 4

The character of coppiced woodland

Management

Surviving areas of ancient woodland in Norfolk range in size, as we have already noted, from tiny copses covering less than a hectare to large examples such as Hockering and Foxley, which extend over nearly 90 and nearly 125 hectares respectively. There are grounds for believing that the medieval and, to a lesser extent, the early modern landscape would have featured a higher proportion of small coppiced woods, at least in the old-enclosed parts of the county. At Fransham in the fifteenth and sixteenth centuries there were at least fourteen such diminutive areas of woodland, ranging in size from 0.75 acres to 6 acres, none of which survived into the nineteenth century (NRO MS 13097 40 A4). Small areas of woodland like this might be coppiced at one go but the larger woods were divided into 'fells', usually long-established and with particular names, which were cut in succession. A map of 1815 shows, for example, how Foxley Wood was divided into areas called Foxley Corner Fell, The Great Fell, Alder Carr Fell, First, Second, Third, and Fourth Long Fells, Narrow Fell, Woodhouse Fell and Hazle Hill Fell (NRO NRS 4087) (Figure 18).

It is often suggested that the average length of coppice rotation increased from medieval through post-medieval times, from around seven years in the thirteenth century to around fourteen by the nineteenth (Rackham 1976, 64–6, 82–3; Rackham 1986a, 85, 92). In Norfolk, at least, the evidence for such a development is not entirely clear-cut. A survey of Beeston Priory in the fifteenth century thus described how one 23-acre wood was divided up into six compartments: five acres were under seven years' growth, and not valued, but there were '3 acres of 7 years growth, 3 acres of 8 years growth, 2 acres of 9 years growth 2 acres of 10 years growth and 8 acres of 14 years growth' (Jessop 1887). Conversely, at Gillingham in 1717 the underwood was cut every seven years, as it was at Horningtoft as late as the 1830s (TNA IR 18/6019). Particular circumstances, including the density of standard trees and the species composition of the underwood, as well as the individual financial circumstances of owners and the state of the market for underwood, presumably explain such variations, and while there may have been an overall trend towards longer rotations there were many exceptions.

The value of the income received from coppice in the Middle Ages, in comparison with other forms of land use, is usually difficult to quantify as the area of the woods mentioned in documents and the proportion felled in any one year are often unclear. It is thus difficult to ascertain the significance of the facts that in 1276 at Kenninghall the underwood was worth 40s a year (Blomefield 1805, I, 142); that at Great Plumstead in 1282 37s 4d was received from sales of underwood (Blomefield 1806, IV, 22); while at Winfarthing in 1383 the underwood was worth 12d a year (Blomefield 1805, I, 120). But estimates of the value of the underwood per acre also exist, and these show much variation. At Colkirk in 1332 it was valued at 3s per acre (Blomefield 1807, V, 982),

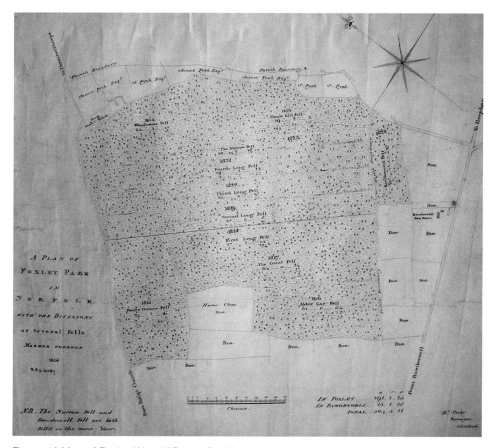

Figure 18 Map of Foxley Wood ('Foxley Park'), 1815, showing the division into 'fells'.

but at Gateley in the same year, and no great distance away, at only 3d (Blomefield 1807, 1002); on the Bigod's estate at Ditchingham in the 1270s it was worth around a shilling per acre per annum (Rackham 1986b, 166–7). As Rackham has pointed out, this is nearly three times the income from arable land in the district. Even at Gateley the value was not much below the average income from arable, and many woods occupied poorly draining or acidic soils where cereal yields would, of course, have been lower than average. Post-medieval valuations tell a similar story, the £3 an acre for the coppice estimated at Sporle in 1745 comparing favourably with the income from local arable land as indicated by rental values, once the length of the coppice rotation (nine years) is taken into account (NRO 20888). Coppiced underwood was thus, throughout the medieval and post-medieval periods, an economically competitive form of land use on the more agriculturally marginal soils where most woods were located, although against such figures for income we need, of course, to set the necessary expenditure involved in protecting and managing such woods. Many medieval woods had a permanent woodward or overseer. One was appointed for the Norwich Cathedral Priory's woods at Hindolveston (Eastwood (123 acres) and Westwood (175 acres)) in the 1270s at an annual salary of £1 7s 5d (Rackham 1986a, 157). North Elmham Great Wood, or Burgrave Wood as it was known in 1454, covered

197 acres and likewise had a permanent keeper: in 1401 payments were made to both him and his 'boy' (Holkham Hall Muniments, compotus no. 2, 1401).

In part, variations in the value of and income from underwood may reflect the relative importance placed on standards, as opposed to coppice, in the management of the wood. If there were too many standard trees, then too much shade would be cast, and the growth of the coppice would be suppressed. The surviving documents sometimes hint at changes in this ratio and its effects. In 1261–2, for example, sales of underwood from the two Norwich Priory woods in Hindolveston brought in £4 per annum. In 1272, however, the priory sold a large quantity of timber for £213 16s 8d. The amount received from underwood sales increased markedly thereafter (to £39 in 1309/10 and averaging £24 *per annum* during the following decade), almost certainly because, by drastically reducing the number of standards, the vigour and value of the underwood was increased (NRO Dean and Chapter Rolls 4739–4793). Later, during the period 1358–89, the annual income declined again, possibly signalling a return to a higher density of standards.

The best evidence for the density of timber trees in a medieval Norfolk wood comes from a survey of Sporle Wood, the property of the Paston family, made in 1472 (Gairdner 1904, V, 167). Today the wood comprises ash–maple–hazel understorey with oak standards. Interestingly, the survey divides the wood into two distinct areas. The document gives the length of the wood's boundaries, suggesting that it was then significantly larger than today, perhaps extending over some 65 acres (c.26 hectares) (today it covers 20 hectares). A perimeter belt twelve feet (3.66 metres) in from the top of the perimeter ditch is recorded separately. This had an area of around two acres, and no less than 220 standards are recorded here, compared with only 436 in the whole of the rest of the wood. There were thus (very roughly) around 110 standards per acre (270 per hectare) in the perimeter strip, but only c.7 per acre (c.17 per hectare) in the interior. The former was thus effectively being treated as high forest (270 standards per hectare is equivalent to a modern semi-mature crop spacing of oak in a high forest system) and any coppice must have been severely over-shadowed by the timber trees. The documents offer no explanation for this arrangement, but it may have been intended to offer a degree of protection from gale damage to the more scattered standards in the main body of the wood. Whether such an arrangement was common practice remains unclear. The lower density of standards within the main body of the wood, of course, was more typical of medieval woodland, the main purpose of which was evidently to provide large amounts of wood rather than timber.

There is some evidence that the density of standards may have increased in many woods during the post-medieval centuries – something which would at least in part explain the suggested extension in the length of the coppice rotation – and in Sporle Wood itself a record of the timber left standing in each fell in the early 1750s suggests that there were by then around 60 an acre – more than eight times the medieval density in the central body of the wood. It is possible, in turn, that this was in part a consequence of legal changes. An act of 1543 – one of several pieces of legislation which attempted to regulate the management of woods and ensure a continuance in the supply of timber – stipulated that when coppice of 24 years of growth or less was felled, 12 young oaks called *standils* or *stores* were to be left per acre (if there were not enough oaks, then elm, ash, beech or, surprisingly, aspen were to be left instead). It is noteworthy that lease agreements for Gressenhall Wood in 1613 and for Wayland

Wood in 1674 insist that 12 new trees per acre were to be left at the end of the lease, in addition to those already growing there (NRO MR 211, 241x 6; NRO WLS LXIX 25). But some lease agreements stipulate much lower numbers – only 8 per acre at Ellingham in 1682, for example (NRO BRA 301/1) – while, in contrast, others stipulate even greater quantities – as many as 20 an acre at Honeypot Wood in Wendling in 1835 (NRO EVL 650/6). As none of the agreements gives us any clear idea of how many standard trees already existed in the woods in question it is impossible to ascertain the overall density of standards per acre, but other sources make it clear that this varied greatly. A parliamentary survey of Toft Wood in East Dereham, made in 1649, recorded 2,860 timber trees on 143 acres, amounting to 20 standards per acre. In contrast, a survey of the Duchy of Lancaster estates carried out in 1609 records a total of 734 trees in 70 acres of woodland in Tunstead, around 10 per acre, while in Southwood, one of the largest woods on the estate, there were fewer than 10 (TNA PRO E178/4988 82482).

In the early Middle Ages woods were, like other demesne assets, usually kept 'in hand' by manorial lords and the information that we have about their appearance and management derives principally from the accounts kept, in particular, by ecclesiastical institutions such as Norwich Cathedral Priory or by large secular estates – such as that of the Bigod earls, who owned the woods around Hedenham and Ditchingham. But from late medieval times direct management of woodland declined, as demesne assets were more generally leased during the economic downturn of the later fourteenth and fifteenth centuries. Over the following centuries, even where woods continued to be retained in hand, aspects of their management and exploitation were often leased out. Sometimes the cutting of the underwood only was rented out, on a yearly basis and to a number of different individuals. An enquiry into Wayland made in 1593 repeatedly asked whether the wood was sold 'by the acre or otherwise' (Norfolk Record Office WLS IV/6/15). Alternatively, a group of people could collectively lease the rights to the underwood, as in 1358 at Hindolveston, where they were let to a syndicate of unfree tenants who appear to have been, in effect, a firm of hurdle makers (Rackham 1980, 157–8). Sometimes it is unclear whether a single individual was bidding for the whole of the underwood or several were so doing. Thus at Sporle Wood in 1469 competitive quotes were obtained from a number of individuals desiring to cut the underwood, and John Paston described how he intended to be in Sporle 'tomorrow or Thursday to see what may be made of the wood, and who will give most for it' (Gairdner 1904, Vol. 5, 63). In other cases one or more individuals rented the entire wood for a term of years, just as they might rent a house or a farm. Usually the timber was reserved for the landlord, but in some cases the lessee contracted to remove a proportion of this as well. The period of the lease might be as short as two years, as at Gressenhall in 1613 (NRO MR 211, 241x 6); or as long as 21 years, as in the case of woods at Fransham in the 1540s and 1550s (NRO MS 13253 40B4); at Bressingham in 1682 the lease was even longer, at 31 years (NRO BRA 301/1). Whatever their precise terms, the agreements drawn up often contain terms and conditions which shed useful light on the details of woodland management. The 1613 lease for the woods at Gressenhall, for example, describes how the lessee could fell 240 timber oaks during the term of the lease, and all the underwood, except 'the old storrells and standells of young oak and ash which heretofore have been maintained and preserved as former felles of the said underwood'. In addition, 12 new *standells* or *storrels* of young oak or ash were to be marked and retained per acre 'in fit and convenient places to stand still and remain for new storrels or standells on and beside the old and former storrels and standells'. Routes for carrying and carting out the material were to be agreed, and permission was given to 'dig and make ... so many pits called saw pits as shall be ... convenient for the sawing, cutting, contriving and converting of the said timber trees'. A further clause forbade the pasturing or feeding within the wood of any of the horses that were to be used to extract the timber or underwood. In addition, the purchasers were, before operations commenced, to 'make a sufficient hedge and fence between the wood ... and the ground' of the lessor (NRO MR 211, 241×6).

Rather similar agreements were drawn up for the leasing of Wayland Wood near Watton in 1674 (NRO WLS LXIX 25); for various woods in Ellingham in 1682 (NRO BRA 301/1); and for Banyards Wood in Bunwell in 1675 (WLS LXIX 25). These similarly laid down the area to be coppiced each year, the number of standard trees to be left and the price to be paid for each acre of underwood cut. Particular attention was paid to the maintenance of stock-proof hedges and ditches so that, in the words of the Banyards Wood agreement, 'the springs thereof are preserved and kepte as they owght'. At Wayland in 1674 the lessees were allowed £3 towards the costs of fencing. The need to prevent damage to the coppice from horses used in forestry operations is also often mentioned – one lease refers to the importance of 'preserving the shoots and slopps of such wood from being bitt by the horses fetching the same', while others refer to the need to keep the horses muzzled. Some agreements are so detailed that it is possible to discern variations in the character of different parts of a wood, related perhaps to earlier management history. The Wayland lease of 1674 thus makes a clear distinction between that part of the wood called The Nabb and the rest. The underwood in the former was worth per acre around two-thirds that in the rest of the wood: there were either fewer stools per acre in The Nabb, or the underwood was of poorer quality (NRO WLS LXIX/25).

The leasing out of woods brought particular problems, especially on large or far-flung estates, so that surveys – including recommendations for future action – were commissioned at intervals. One, carried out for the duke of Lancaster's estates in 1565 by William Humberstone, was to report on

> The number of acres thereof, the nature and kind of soil of the same, what woodes and underwood are growing and being in and upon the same or any part thereof. The quantity and number of acres of the farm woods or underwoods, how the same is beset, which woods and underwoods and with what manner and kind of woodes, how many years growth the same woodes be. And what everyone thereof to be sold is worth to our most wode and commodity. And what waste, fell or destruction have been at any time within this seven years made done or committed in or upon the same woods or underwoods or any of them by whom and by what commanded or appointed and by what value and what money hath been received for the same and by whom and thereupon of your doing and proceeding. (TNA PRO Public Record Office DL 42/97 p. 70)

One complication was that manorial tenants sometimes possessed customary rights to gather wood for household repairs, tools or fencing. At Fulmodeston as late as 1604 a valuation of timber, woods and underwood specifically excluded the common rights to 'housebote, hedgebote, palebote and ploughbote' (TNA PRO DL44/673). At Gimmingham in the early seventeenth century the established custom that tenants could purchase wood from Southwood transmuted at times into a general free-for-all. An inquiry was established in June 1611 into 'the extent of the depredations upon Southwood' and described how a variety of local people, both individually and in concert, had broken down hedges to allow cattle and horses to graze in the wood, severely damaging the coppice (TNA PRO Duchy of Lancaster Special Commission No 873, 8 James I). Further problems were caused by the splitting of use-rights, for, in addition to the frequent division of exploitation between underwood and timber, third parties might have the right to graze sections of the wood once the coppice had regrown. In September 1574 Francis Wyndham complained to his brother-in-law Nathaniel Bacon about how the woods in Hindolveston and Tittleshall, which he was intending to lease, were already covered by two leases: one to a Mr Symonds for the young oaks and 'shreddings and toppings', and one to a Mistress Symonds for the liberty of grazing (Smith *et al.* 1979, 127). By the seventeenth century game was also beginning to be important. A lease of 1682 thus gave the right of 'all liberty of hunting, hawking, fishing and fowling and all game' in the woods at Lopham separately from other rights (NRO BRA 301/1). Such confusions continued into the eighteenth century. In 1751, at Reffley Wood near Kings Lynn, the agent noted that:

> The pasturage … belongs to the inhabitants of certain houses … the timber and underwood … to Mr Folkes. The game … to my Lord Andover who is presumed to be Lord of the Soil … To whom does belong the right to killing … Rabbits? (NRO HOW 612/4)

The features of the wood: boundaries, ponds and settlements

Where woods were directly managed by estates, the maintenance of external banks, ditches, hedges and gates features as a regular expense wherever detailed accounts survive. At North Elmham in 1326, for example, the ditch and bank around the wood were repaired, the gates mended and bolts, locks and keys made for them (NRO Dean and Chapter Muniments 4737), while in 1328–9 the ditch was cleared – a total length of 648 perches. At Hindolveston in 1277–8 £1 10s was paid for major ditching and fencing works, and in 1297–8 a new woodbank, with hedge, was constructed around both woods at a cost of £10 10s (Rackham 1980, 157–9). The maintenance of boundaries, gates and hedges also features prominently in the terms of post-medieval leases, as in the examples quoted above. As noted in the last chapter, woodbanks constructed in the early Middle Ages were often massive features, with bank and ditch commonly seven or more metres across, the top of the bank rising more than a metre and a half above the flanking ditch (Figure 19). Those raised in the post-medieval period, however, were generally smaller, and those of eighteenth- and nineteenth-century date little different from the hedgebanks around enclosed fields. Not all early woods, it should be noted, were so bounded. Where woods lay on sloping ground the boundary might take the form of a distinct scarp or lynchet, without obvious sign of flanking ditch or even bank, as on the western boundary of Little Wood, Edgefield, or along the northern side of East Wood, Denton.

Figure 19 A section of the medieval woodbank at Hockering, marooned within the wood by subsequent expansion.

Documentary evidence sometimes implies that the bank was topped with a fence or a dead hedge, but usually a hedge of normal form appears to have been used. A survey of Sporle Wood, made in 1472, thus describes how:

> As for the fencing of your dykes, … you should fell your bordorys off your wood
> the southside viz towards Pickenham from the Wanges to Walsingham Way is 80
> roode at least, the price of the roode being 3d, digging, plashing and hedging,
> (Gairdner 1904, Vol. 5,167)

None of the ancient woods surveyed is still bounded by a maintained hedge, although outgrown remains of several examples survive, albeit now reduced to disconnected lines of stools. Notable examples include the lines of massive hornbeam and maple stools along the western boundary of the southern section of Tivetshall Wood and the outgrown hornbeam stools on the western boundary of Gawdyhall Big Wood, which still display clear signs of plashing. In a class of its own is the boundary of Edgefield Wood. Here, bounding the lynchet which forms the western edge of the wood, but also continuing along the woodbank which forms the northern and southern boundaries, are the remains of an oak hedge, comprising huge coppice stools, evidently an outgrown medieval feature (Figure 20).

Although, as we noted in the previous chapter, boundary banks, ditches and hedges may initially have served a partly symbolic function, asserting seigniorial rights to appropriate a portion of the common wastes, their primary purpose was to

Figure 20 Massive stools of oak on the woodbank at Edgefield Wood, evidently the remains of a medieval hedge.

prevent stock from straying in and damaging the coppice, and both medieval and post-medieval documents make frequent references to the consequence of poor maintenance. In 1450 James Gresham wrote to John Paston concerning the 'Inquiry made as to the injury of Sporle Wood for lack of hedging. The three years growth of the wood availeth no man' (Gairdner 1904, Vol. 2,159). The farmers renting neighbouring land were often the culprits, as at Castle Rising in 1786, where Mr Beck, 'a very unpleasant tenant':

> Will not keep his cattle out of the wood, though I requested him in the most civil terms to do it. I have now ordered the woodman and Browne to impound the cattle if they are found there, otherwise all the underwood and young wood must be destroyed. (NRO HOW 757/35)

The boundaries of woods were also – for reasons which have never been fully explained – often planted with pollards. Surviving examples tend either to be oak or to replicate the character of the dominant species in the understorey, with fine examples of limes at Hockering, a wood famous for its lime coppice; and massive hornbeams at East Wood, Denton (Figure 21). Some examples are large 'veterans', potentially of medieval date, but the practice of placing pollards on boundaries evidently continued well into the post-medieval period, for examples can be found on straight, slight post-medieval boundary banks, as at East Wood in Denton, Holland's Wood or Hockering

Figure 21 Pollarded hornbeam on the woodbank at East Wood, Denton.

Wood, as much as on ancient, massive ones. Wayland Wood near Watton was expanded to the west some time after 1724: an oak pollard stands on the diminutive boundary bank then established, its girth of 3.5 metres perhaps consistent, in such a location, with an eighteenth-century planting date.

As well as being bounded by boundary banks of various kinds, many woods in Norfolk, as elsewhere, also contain internal banks and ditches. Some of these, as we shall see, mark where woods have been expanded, leaving the original external boundary marooned within the body of the wood, but others represent internal divisions made for a number of reasons in the Middle Ages and later. There is little evidence that these correspond with the individual 'fells' into which the larger areas of woodland were divided, and most seem to relate to patterns of ownership, for sections of particular woods could be sold, or granted to religious houses; or they could, at least before the late twelfth century, be divided by inheritance. What the *Ancient Woodland Inventory* treats as a single wood with a single name, earlier maps, even the first edition Ordnance Survey six-inch maps from the late nineteenth century, will sometimes treat as two or more conjoined woods or as a large wood with individually named subsections. Internal banks often seem to correspond with the boundaries of such divisions. Gawdyhall Big Wood, for example, had sections named Horse Wood, Great Hawker's Wood and Little Hawkers Wood on the first edition Ordnance Survey six-inch map: the latter names identify these sections of the wood with the medieval manor of Hawkers (Blomefield 1806, V, 365). The main internal boundary bank running north–south through the centre of the wood appears to be the shared western boundary of the two latter woods, while another, less imposing, earthwork in the east can similarly be identified with the eastern boundary of Horse Wood. The bank and ditch running north–south through the centre of the *Inventory*'s Blacks Grove in Kirby Cane similarly divides areas described by the Ordnance Survey as Blacks Grove (to the east) and Cook's Close (to the west). Thomas Waterman's map of Hedenham Wood, surveyed in 1617 (NRO MC 1761/2), shows the north-eastern section of the wood without trees (although it is explicitly described as 'wood') because it was in separate ownership. While the bulk of the wood was owned by Phillip Bedingfield, this section was the property of one Robert Rachmen. The two sections of the wood remained in separate ownership until the parliamentary enclosure of 1816, when John Irby, by then the owner of the Rachmen portion, exchanged it with James Bedingfield for land elsewhere in the parish (NRO C/Sca 2/100). The division between the two properties is marked by a slight but well-defined ruler-straight bank which was probably of no great antiquity at the time the map was made. It is possible that some of the internal divisions recorded in woods, in the form of earthwork banks and ditches, indicate the continuing use of some portions for grazing. Many, it must be said, make very little obvious sense, at least in terms of the wood's current shape and boundaries. It is possible that they relate to the subdivision of use or ownership within earlier and more extensive tracts of wooded ground, before the wood in question attained its present dimensions: at Hockering they may mark enclosed coppices within a deer park originally more extensive than the present wood (below, pp. 203–4).

Although there are documentary references to the felling and sawing of timber trees and to charcoal making, neither has left much in the way of clear archaeological evidence, in marked contrast to the situation in other areas where woodland has been surveyed archaeologically, such as the district around Sheffield (Rotherham and

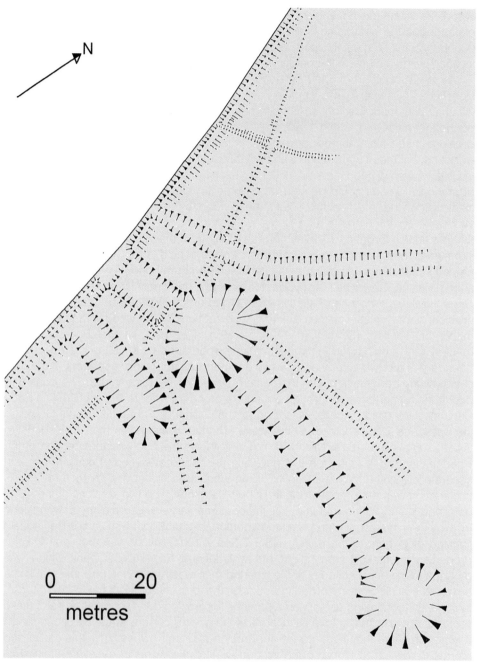

Figure 22 East Wood, Denton: an undated complex of pits, banks and hollow ways on the western boundary.

Ardron 2006, 234–7). A relatively small number of woods, including Foxley and Hook Wood in Morley, contain unequivocal examples of former saw pits, while no certain sites of charcoal kilns have been located. Larger pits are, however, a regular feature of ancient woods in Norfolk and some – as in the northern section of East Wood, Denton – are of significant size. Private woods were convenient and uncontentious places in which to extract clay, sand or gravel, but in some cases it is likely that such features relate to excavations made on open common land across which woods only later expanded. Much of the northern section of Edgefield Little Wood – almost certainly a late medieval addition to the original core made at the expense of open heath – is covered in small, amorphous pits, mainly five to ten metres wide but sometimes smaller, which were presumably dug for the extraction of gravel. In clayland areas such extraction pits rapidly become ponds, although in the case of primary woods many ponds appear to have natural origins, sometimes forming chains which may be the consequence of periglacial activity, as, for example, in Tindall Wood. Whatever their origins, ponds served as a source of water for horses employed in the extraction of wood and timber and for any stock being grazed within the wood at some advanced point in the coppice cycle. In a few cases, as in the western section of East Wood, Denton, a pond is approached along a substantial hollow way which cuts through the external woodbank, perhaps indicating that stock were regularly driven in to water there from the adjacent fields. The hollow way is itself interrupted by a small later pit, with another to the south: slighter hollow ways also fan into the wood, cutting through two phases of woodbank to create a particularly complex and intractable piece of archaeology (Figure 22: see Appendix entry). This second pit is one of many examples which lie actually on the boundaries of the wood. In most such cases, although not in this one, the ditch accompanying the woodbank simply widens into a broader, water-filled area. Such ponds, lying as they do outside the woodbank, must have been intended to provide water for stock in the adjacent fields, although quite why they are such a common feature of woodland boundaries remains unclear. To some extent their prominence may be more apparent than real, arising from the wholesale disappearance of similar ponds associated with field boundaries in the surrounding landscape as a consequence of twentieth-century field amalgamation, but the number present on the margins of some woods seems higher than that in the surrounding landscape as this is depicted on maps dating to before the period of agricultural 'modernisation'.

Woods in the Middle Ages were invariably part of the lord's demesne and, as we have noted, might on occasions be located in close proximity to manorial sites. At least one example, Hethel Wood, appears to contain a high-status settlement *within* its boundaries, which was presumably created to assist in the exploitation of the wood itself. It may have served as the residence of the woodward, and also as a place in which wood and timber harvested from the wood could be processed. But it may also have been used as a convenient place to locate other demesne resources, for it contains what appear to be medieval fishponds and a low mound which might have served as the base for a dovecote. Such sites are hard to distinguish from those high-status complexes, briefly discussed in the previous chapter, which seem to *pre-date* the enclosure of the wood and its management as coppice, and were associated instead with the management and protection of herds in unenclosed wood-pastures: the complex of earthworks in Hazel Hurn Wood, Woodrising, which, like that at Hethel, includes possible fishponds and a prominent mound, could be of either kind. The two classes of site are not theoretically distinct, of course: an embanked site used for corralling stock might have been found new uses once a wood had been enclosed and coppiced, as perhaps at Hales Wood (see Appendix entry).

The stability of woodland

Many writers, as we have seen, have emphasised the essential stability of ancient woods in the landscape since their boundaries first became established in the early Middle Ages (e.g. Rackham 1986a, 62–4; 1976, 113). This characteristic was encouraged by a number of factors, including the physical size of, and scale of investment in, perimeter banks; the general profitability of woods throughout the medieval and for much of the post-medieval periods; and the costs involved in grubbing them out, in whole or part, and converting the area which they occupied to new uses (Rackham 1986a, 88–90). But, as Rackham has also emphasised, woods in fact often expanded or contracted over the centuries in response to economic and demographic fluctuations and the whims of landowners (Rackham 2006, 66–9). Enclosed woods were absolute private property, adjacent land was frequently in the same ownership, and boundaries could thus be altered over time in a way that those of commons, for example, could not.

Such variations in extent are frequently evident from archaeological evidence and/ or topographic observations, but they are also hinted at in the documentary evidence. In general, references to the grubbing out of woods seem to be most common, as we would expect, at times of increasing population – the twelfth and thirteenth centuries, and the sixteenth and early seventeenth – and less frequent in periods of demographic contraction or stability. However, this broad pattern requires some qualification. To begin with, while there are numerous references to 'assarting' in medieval documents from the county many if not most probably refer to the expansion of arable at the expense of wood-pasture, heath and other rough grazing – manorial 'waste' – rather than to the grubbing out of private enclosed woods. The 'assarting' recorded at places such as Feltwell in Breckland in 1252, for example, is more likely to have represented the conversion of open heathland than the clearance of woodland of any kind, given the general paucity of the latter in this district already apparent in Domesday Book (Bailey 1989, 113). Some such references do, however, seem to relate to the clearance of discrete parcels of – presumably – enclosed woodland, such as the 'three woods' which were destroyed between 1272 and 1290 at Carbrooke (TNA Ancient Deeds B6802, B7365, B7383), or the three woods at Forncett which were asserted in the late thirteenth century (Davenport 1906, 26–7). An Inquisition for North Elmham from *c*.1250 describes how Stertesende and Mechelwode in Burgrave had recently been cleared, causing a dispute between the vicar and the prior of Norwich (Carthew 1877, 533); while in Colkirk most of the assarts recorded in manorial documents in the later twelfth and thirteenth centuries were, to judge from their location, at the expense of demesne woods, rather than commons, and especially around the margins of what became Colkirk Wood: one is probably indicated by the Stub Close recorded on a map of 1592 on the wood's northern boundary (Rutledge 1989, 21). We should also note that particular circumstances – the needs or policies of individual owners – might ensure localised *expansion* of coppiced woodland, even in the period before the

Black Death when high food prices made agricultural use of land more profitable, even on relatively marginal soils. In 1307 Roger de Fraxino thus obtained permission to close two public roads, one east and one south of Colkirk Wood, presumably, as Rutledge has suggested (and as the topography strongly implies), in order to enlarge it (Rutledge 1989, 21–2; Carthew 1877, 97–100).

After the Black Death declining grain prices reduced the amount of assarting, while marginal land was less likely to repay the costs of cultivation and might on occasions be allowed to revert to scrub. At Fransham, for example, the area called Pilwood had been cleared and cultivated by 1273, but by 1570 a survey described it as '80 acres, whereof X is run in boschys' (Rogerson 1995, 375). In an adjoining close three out of twelve acres had likewise 'run' to trees or bushes, and two out of sixteen acres had suffered a similar fate in Great Close, although whether such abandonment proceeded to full regeneration is uncertain. By the middle of the sixteenth century, presumably in response to rising grain and livestock prices, the removal of woodland recommenced. Some of the Fransham woods were grubbed up entirely; others were reduced drastically in area. A grove called Kenwaldeshalle, for example, from which wood and underwood were sold in 1442/3, and which was still woodland in 1455 and in 1570, when it was said to cover 30 acres, had been reduced to a mere seven acres by 1595 (NRO MS 13140 40A5; 13048 40A2; 13085 40A3; 13084 40A3). A small wood called Knyghtwood on the parish boundary with Beeston, from which underwood was sold in 1431/2 and 1437/8 (HALS 8185; NRO MS 1303740A1) and which was still described as woodland (*boscus*) in 1577, was said in 1604 to have been 'newly converted from woodgrounde' (NRO MS 13156–7 40A6; MS 13284–5 40C2). Small areas of woodland seem to have been particularly vulnerable to clearance. The rector of Little Fransham was amerced for cutting underwood in 'le grove aput Chownes' in 1432, which, to judge from a survey of 1502, covered a single acre (NRO MS 13097 40A4; 13167 40A7). By 1603, however, when this land was leased out it was described as 'late converted from wood to pasture' (NRO MS 13279 40C2). Nearby Jecks Grove was also converted from wood to pasture in the early seventeenth century, while a one-acre grove called Bullesgrove was again described as 'late converted from wood to pasture' when leased out in 1603 (NRO MS 13159 40A6; MS 13279 40C2). A lease of 1637 describes the 3.25 acres of Annyells grove as 'being of late woodeground and stubbed up' (NRO MS 13326 40C2), while a grove just to the north of Brownsmore Common, covering a mere 1.25 acres, was described in 1677 as 'now converted to pasture' (NRO DN/TER/68/4.1). The fluctuating extent of woodland is particularly well documented in the case of the parishes of Great and Little Fransham, but evidence from elsewhere suggests a similar picture, with some expansion of woodland in the fifteenth and early sixteenth centuries followed by a period of sustained clearance in the mid–late sixteenth and seventeenth centuries. In Whissonsett, for example, an indenture dated 25 August 1655 hints at two sites of recent clearance: ' … a close adjoining [Whissonsett Hal] containing 20 acres of pasture called the Home Wood … and close called Felled Wood containing 40 acres of pasture' (Carthew 1877, 267).

Not surprisingly, individual woods often exhibit complicated sequences of contraction and/or expansion when we consider the archaeological evidence (the character of the external boundaries, and the configuration of any internal woodbanks) alongside the topographic evidence (the relationship of the wood to the surrounding landscape). Such phases can, unfortunately, usually be only very broadly dated.

East Wood, Denton, now extends over an area of 14.3 hectares lying close to, but not on, the eastern boundary of Denton parish, from which its long eastern boundary is separated by a string of relatively narrow fields. As described in more detail in the Appendix entry, the wood originally appears to have extended all the way to the parish boundary, but this section was grubbed out some time in the seventeenth or eighteenth centuries; the south-eastern corner of the wood was subsequently further truncated. On the western side, likewise, the wood appears to have been reduced in stages, firstly in the Middle Ages and subsequently, to the south, in the post-medieval period – again, probably in the seventeenth or eighteenth centuries.

Other large areas of woodland have histories characterised more by progressive expansion rather than contraction. Wayland Wood lies in the south-east of Watton parish and the pattern of boundaries shown on the earliest surviving maps may suggest that, even in its enclosed and coppiced form, it had once been considerably larger. But the archaeological evidence indicates steady growth in its area over the centuries. The curving bank/scarp running through the southern section of the wood hints that at some stage the wood's southern boundary lay some way to the north of its present line (unless, of course, this feature represents some earlier, pre-wood enclosure – prehistoric pottery has been found within it and, as explained in the Appendix entry, the evidence suggests that the wood may have had an early importance as a hundredal meeting place). Subsequent expansion is more clearly indicated. The present boundaries of the wood are marked mainly by a substantial bank and ditch, together around seven metres across, with the top of the bank standing around 0.5–0.75 metres above the interior of the wood. The way in which, on the eastern side, this runs through the interior of the wood shows that the area lying further to the east is a later extension. This covers around 8.5 hectares and is enclosed by a bank forming what is now the eastern and south-eastern boundaries of the wood, which is significantly less substantial than that associated with the original wood, although likewise apparently of medieval date, and perhaps originating in the fourteenth or fifteenth century: this part of the wood was certainly in existence by 1593/4, when Wayland was the subject of a legal dispute (NRO WLS IV/6). In the southern part of this eastern extension is a complex of earthworks of uncertain character but relating to an earlier agricultural landscape which existed before the wood expanded. It should be emphasised, however, that these new areas were not, initially at least, in the same ownership as Wayland. The complex of earthworks in the south of the wood includes an enclosure called Threxton Nabb in sixteenth-century documents and on a map of 1723, which was in the Middle Ages owned by Thompson College; the rest of the eastern side of the wood was called Mounteneys, and was part of the manor of Mounteneys in Threxton (NRO WLS IV/6; WLS/941×6). It was only in the late seventeenth or early eighteenth century that all three woods came to be in the same ownership. The distinction between internal banks marking the expansion of a wood and examples marking property boundaries is thus blurred. Here, and perhaps elsewhere, new areas of woodland may have arisen spontaneously on marginal land beside existing woods, which their owners then enclosed and managed as coppice. A third extension was made to the west of the wood, probably in the post-medieval period as it lacks a proper perimeter bank, although evidently before 1723, when a map (NRO WLS XVII/9 410X6) shows it as part of the wood. A final small extension, to the north, was made after 1723 but before the early nineteenth century. A straight ditch, rather than a woodbank, marks the eastern edge of this last addition to the wood.

Some other large woods in the county appear to include large areas of late medieval expansion at the expense of farmland. Hedenham Wood, as described in the previous chapter, spread southwards across an abandoned manorial site and its fields in the fifteenth or sixteenth centuries: subsequently, in the nineteenth century, much of the western section of the wood was grubbed out. Although the evidence is not completely clear-cut it is likely that the eastern section of Gawdyhall Big Wood, near Harleston – an area of around 11 hectares – is likewise secondary, and probably of late medieval date. Many small woods also have histories of expansion and contraction which, while evidently complex, are now impossible to reconstruct. Hook Wood in Morley is shown with the same outlines as today on a map of 1629, which also suggests that it lay within the area of a former deer park (NRO PD 3/108). It has fairly small woodbanks on its southern, eastern and western sides, but only a straight ditch on the northern: the field immediately beyond is described as 'Stubb'd Wood' on the map. But the wood's earlier boundaries were evidently different again, for a substantial woodbank of typical early medieval form runs east–west through the wood, some 10 to 20 metres to the north of its present southern boundary. This is ditched on the *north*, implying that both the majority of the present wood, and the 'stubbed' section to the north of this, were additions to an original core. Evidently, the area of Hook Wood had been changed on at least two occasions before it was mapped in 1629: the wood was a shifting, fluid thing, not a fixed and stable one. Earsham Great Wood, which has what appears to be a former boundary bank running east–west through its centre, is perhaps a similar case. Even woods which have largely remained within their boundaries since first enclosed can exhibit evidence of minor, piecemeal expansion or contraction. Narrow strips have been appended to Sporle Wood, Hockering Wood and Shotesham Wood, possibly following the piecemeal enclosure of small groups of strips lying within adjacent areas of open field; woods have expanded over hollow ways running along their boundaries, as at The Shrubbery in Tivetshall; and small groups of fields have been incorporated into the north-west of Hockering Wood, the south of Shotesham Little Wood, the east of North Elmham Great Wood and elsewhere.

In addition to woods which have expanded in late medieval or early post-medieval times over areas of adjacent farmland or settlement, a significant number of *Inventory* woods surveyed appear to completely overlie areas which had, in the period before the Black Death, been cleared, enclosed and cultivated; that is, they are entirely secondary in character. The entire area of Tivetshall Wood, for example, appears to have been divided into enclosed fields across which the wood either regenerated or was deliberately planted some time in the late medieval or early post-medieval period. Toomber's Wood appears to have largely if not entirely developed at the expense of farmland, much of it ploughed as ridge and furrow. Beckett's Wood in Woodton likewise overlies an area of former arable land, as well as probable toft sites. Round Grove in Hedenham, covering an area of 2.6 hectares, completely overlies the area of a medieval settlement and its associated enclosures; nearby, Long Row appears to have developed at the expense of a wide drove road or linear common; while Attleborough Wood, the surviving 'rump' of it at least, overlies a hollow way which, bounded by banks, probably ran through a farmed landscape. Rawhall Wood may likewise be secondary, overlying an area of open-field arable crossed by a hollow way, although the evidence here is less clear-cut. Most of these woods are relatively small, it should be noted. It is the larger woods in Norfolk that appear more likely to be entirely, or largely, 'primary' in character. The secondary character of many other small woods, such as Dodd's Wood in Rushall, attested in documentary or cartographic evidence, is obscured archaeologically by the simple fact that, because these often occupy what had formerly been single fields, they fail to contain evidence of former field boundaries.

Management, use and species composition

It might appear obvious that the main use of woods in both the medieval and post-medieval periods was to produce fuel for domestic fires and local industries, and environmental historians have often attempted to calculate England's aggregate fuel supplies largely on the basis of the area covered by coppiced woodland, together with the output of coal mines (Allen 2009, 96; Collins 1996; Warde 2006, 34). In reality, the majority of fuel consumed, in Norfolk as in many other parts of England, probably came from other sources (Warde and Williamson 2014). Peat was dug from low-lying fens throughout the medieval and post-medieval periods and, although the deep excavation in river valleys in the east of the county which created the 'Norfolk Broads' largely came to an end in the fourteenth century, the removal of peat through shallower diggings continued into the nineteenth century, and may even have increased in scale from the later eighteenth (Williamson 1997, 98–103). The county's abundant heathland – still extending over more than 30,000 hectares even at the end of the eighteenth century[5] – grew significant quantities of gorse (or 'furze'), heather ('ling') and other vegetation that was regularly burned as a domestic fuel. Such material was especially useful for oven firing, but was also employed on a more general basis. In the early seventeenth century Thomas Blenerhasset could comment that Horsford Heath was 'to Norwich and the Countrye heare as Newcastle coales are to London' (Barrett-Lennard 1921, 70). Heather, broom and gorse were all used industrially, especially for firing brick kilns. When Blickling Hall in Norfolk was constructed in 1617–21, for example, more than a million bricks were fired in kilns entirely fuelled with gorse and broom faggots brought from the heaths at nearby Cawston and Saxthorpe (NRO MC3/45). The continuing importance into the nineteenth century of peat dug from fens and vegetation cut from heaths is evident from the fact that no fewer than 250 parliamentary enclosure awards in the county set aside portions of such land for the poor to use as 'fuel allotments'. Some were relatively small but others – as at Bridgham or Feltwell – extended over 100 hectares or more (Birtles 2003, 196, 307–9).

Most domestic fuel, however – at least by the seventeenth century – probably came from hedges and from the pollards planted within them. William Marshall noted

---

5   Faden's county map of 1797 describes 16,620 hectares as 'heath' but at least half of the 38,794 hectares described as 'common' probably comprised heathland, given its location, and some heathland vegetation presumably survived the intensive grazing within the 6,042 hectares marked as 'warren'. See Macnair and Williamson 2010.

as late as 1787 how, in north-east Norfolk, the 'old hedges, in general, abound with oak, ash and maple stubs, off which the wood is cut every time the hedge is felled; also with pollards, whose heads are another source of firewood'. The entire supply of wood in the district, he added, 'may be said, with little latitude, to be from hedge-rows' (Marshall 1787, 96). The extreme density of hedges in the sixteenth, seventeenth and eighteenth centuries in many parts of the county may, in part, be explained by their role as a fuel source. A 'Particular of Mr Rodwell's Farm' in the Norfolk parish of Diss, for example, made as late as 1771, describes 21 fields with an average size of less than three acres (NRO NRS 12793 3F F8). This was an extreme case, but maps and surveys nevertheless suggest that, by the early post-medieval period, in all the enclosed areas of the county, hedges formed a dense and intricate web across the landscape. Such hedges contained, moreover, a phenomenal density of trees. Data from nine surveys examined by Rackham, from farms in Essex, Suffolk and Norfolk made between 1650 and 1771, suggest an average of *c.*25 trees per hectare (Rackham 1986a, 218–21); similar figures come from glebe surveys at Newton Flotman in the early eighteenth century (NRO DUN (C) 82); and from a set of detailed maps drawn up in the mid-eighteenth century by Henry Keymer for farms in Norfolk, which record every hedgerow tree on the properties surveyed (NRO WIS 138, 166X3; NRO PD 703/45–6; NRO Accn. 18/3/82 P1888; NRO BCH20). Whatever the precise figure, the overwhelming majority of farmland trees appear to have been pollarded. On a property in Beeston, near Mileham, surveyed by Keymer in 1761, for example, there were 418 pollards but only 113 timber trees: that is, nearly 80 per cent of the trees were pollards (NRO WIS 138, 166X3). Timber surveys from elsewhere suggest very similar ratios, in the 70–80 per cent range: on a farm at Stanfield in *c.*1798 there were 192 pollards to 66 timber trees (74 per cent pollards), while on a farm at nearby Whissonsett at the same time there were 131 pollards and 59 timber trees (70 per cent pollards), and, a few years earlier, 309 to 133 (again, 70 per cent) (NRO PD 703/45–6).

In addition to hedgerow pollards many commons, as we shall see, continued to be managed as wood-pastures well into the post-medieval period. Moreover, early maps of the old-enclosed areas of the county often show strips of pollards along the margins of fields. Documents refer to these as 'rows' or *grovetts*. The 1613 glebe terrier for Denton thus describes 'the Churchyard with a Pightell and a little Grovett above that Close towards the south' and 'Two Closes joineing together Westward called South Crofte – the first Close hath a Grovett above' (NRO PD 136/35). Most, as here, were not individually named and were included in the area of an adjacent field: in 1589 Robert Kemp held a seven-acre close *'cum un grovett'* in Gissing (NRO PD 80/90). The presence of rows and grovetts, as well as the density of hedgerow trees, presumably explains the phenomenal density of pollards recorded at places such as Hindolveston in 1731, where 67 pollards are recorded in a single eight-acre close (NRO DCN 59/21/1).

Coppiced woods were thus not the only or even the main source of fuel in medieval and post-medieval Norfolk; but nor were coppices only or perhaps even mainly used to supply firewood. Documentary sources suggest that, while woods did provide fuel, mainly in the form of faggots, they were also and perhaps mainly regarded as providers of wood for other, and sometimes, specialist, purposes. One important use of coppice poles was for making the hurdles which were employed in vast numbers in the county for folding sheep on the arable land in areas of light, leached land (Allison 1957). Both ash and hazel, the most common component of the understorey in Norfolk woods, especially those located on the boulder clays, were used for this purpose. The lessees of Hindolveston Wood in the late fourteenth century were specifically described as 'hurdle makers' (Rackham 1980, 157–8), while John Skayman described in the early sixteenth century how the woods on the Raynham estate were used to make fencing (Moreton and Rutledge 1997, 115). Both ash and hazel were also employed in hoop-making, another craft mentioned on a number of occasions in relation to woods in the county; and ash was used for such things as tool handles. Coppice wood was also essential in the construction of timber-framed buildings – poles of oak, and sometimes ash and elm, were used as minor elements of the frame, while hazel was a component of the wattle and daub infill. Hazel and ash were also used to make 'broaches' for thatched roofs, and for thatching corn ricks (as at Castle Rising in 1791 (NRO HOW 757/9)).

Coppiced wood was also used to make charcoal, which, lighter and with a higher calorific value than firewood, could be transported economically over longer distances, and especially to fuel-hungry Norwich. It may have become more economically important over time, as the population of the city – and of other towns in the county – grew. An enquiry into the management of Wayland Wood near Watton, made in 1594, records how the underwood was used for hop-poles, poles, hurdles and charcoal (NRO WLS/IV/6/14), while a lease for the woods at Gressenhall drawn up in 1613 allowed the lessees to 'to make and sett within the said wood so many harthes called coal harthes' as they needed to convert as much of the underwood as they wished into charcoal (NRO MR 211, 241×6). In the former case the charcoal was probably made from the hornbeam which occupies the eastern extension of the wood; in the latter from alder, which still dominates much of the understorey. Both these species had other specialised uses. Hornbeam was used for mallets, cog wheels and brake components – it is a phenomenally hard wood, hence its name ('hard beam'). Alder grows straight and rapidly, and is very light: it thus has specialist uses as scaffold poles but also, because it does not rot when wet, for jetties and revetting river banks. Both, however, were probably mainly valued as charcoal-wood.

Other kinds of coppiced understorey, likewise, had particular uses. Lime, found in only a handful of the county's woods, may in the earlier Middle Ages have been used primarily to produce bast for rope making, a process which involved the retting of poles in water prior to the removal of their bark. This may conceivably have been the function of the chains of ponds which survive within Hockering Wood. Much of the wood cut from oak coppice, largely restricted to the poorer soils in the north of the county, was probably used for tanning. Although the bark required for the tanning process was also provided by felled standards, the importance of oak coppice in this regard is perhaps indicated by the fact that early modern references to the industry tend to cluster in this same area. Even on Faden's county map of 1797 the only 'tan offices' marked are all found in the area between Holt and Letheringsett (Barringer 2005, 160–1). Woods may thus have been regarded primarily as sources of wood for a range of specialised purposes, rather than as sources of fuel, not least because in many of them large areas of the underwood were composed of a limited range of species and could thus be graded and sorted with relative ease in a way that material cut from hedges could not. Of course, much of the underwood – especially the offcuts

– was burnt on domestic fires, and the twiggy material was sold for oven firing. But much of the cut material was used in other ways.

The specialised uses to which much underwood was put, together with the relatively limited number of species found in the understorey of most ancient woods, raises the possibility that in some cases particular trees or shrubs may have been encouraged, or discouraged, by woodland managers over time. Such selection is especially likely in the case of secondary woods, occupying land cultivated and settled in the early Middle Ages. The extent to which these may have been deliberately planted, rather than simply arising through natural regeneration, should not be underestimated. Medieval landowners and tenants were, we should note, well used to planting *linear* coppices – hedges – in the landscape, and to selecting individual trees to be managed as timber or pollards at intervals along their length. At Hindolveston in 1312 two men were paid two shillings each for six days' work 'pulling ashes to plant at Hyndringham and Gateli', and one received 25d for thirteen and a half days' work 'planting ashes in the manor' (Rackham 1986a, 224). In Forncett in 1378 men were paid for 'pulling plants of thorn and ash to put on 1 ditch from the south of the manor to the churchyard' (Davenport 1906). Where elm occurs as a component in secondary woods it was presumably planted – the East Anglian elm *Ulmus carpinifolia* does not propagate easily from seed, but only by suckering – unless, of course, it previously existed in hedges or as pollards on the site, as probably at Hedenham Wood and in nearby Round Grove. Documentary references, albeit few in character, make it clear that some woods were deliberately planted in the fifteenth and sixteenth centuries. In 1457 seedlings growing in Anyells Grove in Fransham were destroyed by the trampling of John Balyton's horses, while in 1502 the same grove was described as being 'planted with coppice wood' (NRO MS 13097 40A4; 13155 MS 40A6 and 13167 MS 40A7). And, as early as 1307, as we have already noted, Roger de Fraxino obtained permission to close two public roads, one east and one south of Colkirk Wood, almost certainly in order to enlarge it, an action which is hard to understand unless it involved deliberate planting (Carthew 1877, 97–100). Where the archaeological evidence indicates that particular woods have expanded – presumably in the later Middle Ages – at the expense of farmland or common land, the understorey of the extension sometimes differs from that of the original 'core' to such an extent that it is hard to believe that the former results from the simple spread and expansion of the latter. That within the presumed primary portion of Wayland Wood, for example, is characterised by a mixture of ash, hazel and bird cherry. The understorey within the later 'extension' to the south-east, in contrast, mainly comprises hornbeam and ash. The narrow addition to the western edge of Shotesham Little Wood has an understorey almost entirely composed of coppiced hazel, unlike the rest of the wood, which mainly comprises hornbeam mixed with varying amounts of ash and hazel.

Human choice, planting and encouragement may thus have played a greater role in the formation of the underwood found in ancient woods than we sometimes suppose, and even within primary woods some species may have been deliberately encouraged at the expense of others as part of routine management. A lease for South Hawe Wood in Cawston, drawn up in 1612, thus bound the lessee to plant sallows in cleared spaces following felling (BUL 2/3, 604X7). Hornbeam woods are particularly interesting in this respect. Such woods, generally concentrated on the heavy clay soils in the south and south-east of the county, are among the most numerous in Norfolk. Hornbeam probably only arrived in England during the Neolithic and, while it soon spread rapidly through the country, it clearly failed to colonise many of the districts in which it is now common until the historic period – its appearance in Epping Forest is securely dated to Anglo-Saxon times – and it generally remained a relatively rare tree (Rackham 1980, 221–3). It is noteworthy that, while maple, oak, ash, hazel, lime, beech, alder, yew, birch and willow are all referred to in Old English place-names or appear as boundary markers in early charters, hornbeam does not feature at all (Hooke 2010, 181). Indeed, the earliest English record of a place-name referencing this species – Hornbeamgate in Hatfield, in Hertfordshire – first appears in the documentary record as late as 1366 (TNA E326/4213). The pollen sequence from Diss Mere, which lies within the section of Norfolk in which hornbeam is a major or dominant underwood species, indicates that it was present in the area from only the late Iron Age or Roman periods, and even then only at very low frequencies. It became a significant component of the local vegetation only during the medieval or the post-medieval period, the precise date being uncertain as the pollen sequence is itself not radiometrically dated (Peglar *et al.* 1989). This late appearance is especially striking given that hornbeam produces large amounts of pollen (Rackham 1980, 221), and that Diss Mere lies no more than three kilometres from Billingford Wood and Thorpe Wood, in the underwood of which this species dominates today. We should also note that hornbeam is largely confined to woodland, only rarely featuring as a hedgerow shrub or farmland pollard (Barnes and Williamson 2006, 73–4). Whether entirely the consequence of natural expansion, or partly the result of deliberate encouragement arising from the increasing value of charcoal as a fuel, it is clear that hornbeam-dominated woodland has little direct connection with the natural vegetation existing before woods were defined and enclosed in the early Middle Ages. We might note, in passing, that the two main concentrations of hornbeam woods in England – in south Norfolk/north Suffolk, and south Hertfordshire and south Essex – are close to the country's two largest medieval cities, Norwich and London. As we shall see, there are grounds for believing that hornbeam may have increased its representation in Norfolk woodland still further during the last century or so.

The character of the timber trees found within ancient woods is certainly a consequence of management and selection. Although other species, most notably ash and elm, are mentioned in early documents, the overwhelming majority of standards in Norfolk's woods appear always to have been oaks, planted or selected in preference to other species because of their use in the construction of buildings and ships. The demand for timber may have risen in the course of the fifteenth and sixteenth centuries, as the quality of peasant housing improved and became more commodious and durable in character, possibly leading to an increase in the numbers of timber trees in particular woods. Demand for timber for ships also grew steadily through late medieval and early post-medieval times. Large quantities of timber were needed for both the Royal Navy and for commercial shipping, and Yarmouth, one of the most important ports in England for shipbuilding in the medieval and early modern periods, must have been the destination for a high proportion of the timber felled in Norfolk woods (Malster 1964). In the reign of Edward III the town provided more ships for the state than any other part of the kingdom (Palmer 1856, 107). Even relatively small ships – fifth rate vessels such as the *Sweepstakes*, with 36 close guns and four upper deck guns, which was built by the yard of the Edgar family at Yarmouth in

1665–6 – would have required about 2,000 loads of timber, which equates to about 40 acres of clear-felled woodland at contemporary stocking densities. The beginning of the nineteenth century saw the town at the height of its importance as a shipbuilding port, with production concentrated at Southtown, where Isaac Preston opened the first yard in 1782: during the next 40 years it built 153 vessels (Palmer 1872, 291). While some proportion of the timber used was doubtless sourced from elsewhere, significant quantities must have come from Norfolk woods; and other local ports, including King's Lynn, were also involved in the construction or repair of ships, and thus were potential consumers of local timber.

While there may have been an escalating demand for timber in the course of the sixteenth and seventeenth centuries it is, once again, useful to set managed woods within a wider landscape context, for not all timber came from woodland. Between a fifth and a quarter of hedgerow trees in the county appear to have been standards, rather than pollards, at least by the sixteenth and seventeenth centuries, while others grew in some numbers in pasture fields and parks. Most were oaks: at Langley in the south-east of the county no less than 70 per cent of the timber trees recorded in a mid-seventeenth-century estate survey were of this species, and only 30 per cent ash (NRO NRS 11126); at Buckenham near Blofield in the 1690s 49 per cent were oak and 44 per cent ash, together with 6.6 per cent elm (as well as six poplars and 'young' trees of unspecified species) (NRO Beauchamp-Proctor 334; NRO NRS 11126). The dominance of oak was not universal – on a farm at Beeston surveyed by Henry Keymer in 1761 (NRO WIS 138, 166X3) there were actually more ash than oak trees recorded in the fields and hedges – but it was general. We should also note that timber was often brought into Norfolk from elsewhere in England. One of the major imports into Blakeney, then a small port on the north Norfolk coast, comprised timber from Sussex. On 15 June 1587 the *Henry of Mechinge* arrived from Arundel with 300 ship boards, 3,500 barrel boards, 2,500 inch boards and 1,200 planks. A month earlier, on 17 May, the *Jesu of Brighthempstead* arrived with 1,800 planks and 303 quarters of shipboard (Redstone *et al.* 1936, 21–2). From medieval times, moreover, timber was regularly imported from the Baltic (Quamme 1949, 92; Salzman 1952, 245–6; Carus-Wilson 1962, 191). The hundred rolls for 1243 already show an incredible variety of timber being imported into King's Lynn, most of it already cut (Owen 1984, 43). All this said, woods were a major source of timber, and demand was intense. The replacement of felled trees must often have been through deliberate planting rather than natural regeneration.

Conclusion

Discussions of traditionally managed woods, especially those towards the 'popular' end of the market, tend to emphasise their character as both natural and stable elements in the landscape. Enclosed directly from the 'wild wood', their vegetation is essentially a modified version of that which had developed naturally on the site following the last glaciation. In this and the preceding chapter we have, explicitly or implicitly, questioned such assumptions. Grazing and other forms of exploitation must have significantly changed the botanical character of the 'wastes' even before primary ancient woods were enclosed from them in the early Middle Ages; the exclusion of livestock and the institution of coppicing intensive management brought further changes, probably allowing the classic woodland 'indicators' to flourish as never before. Woodland boundaries have not necessarily remained stable since first established, but have fluctuated over the centuries; many managed woods and portions of managed woods have come and gone from the landscape over time; and a significant proportion of our ancient woods appear to have developed, in whole or part, only in or after the fourteenth century, at the expense of farmland or areas of common grazing. Such secondary woods may have sometimes been deliberately planted, but even in 'primary' woods the character of both timber and underwood may have been altered by selection and other forms of management. Ancient woods, looked at in this way, are perhaps less 'natural' in character than we sometimes suppose.

Chapter 5

Wood-pastures

Introduction

We discussed in the previous chapters the way in which areas of enclosed and coppiced woodland in Norfolk seem to have come into existence as part of a wider process of land-use definition associated with the growth of population and the expansion of settlement and agriculture into areas of marginal land in the course of the eleventh, twelfth and thirteenth centuries. But not all land enclosed by manorial lords from the dwindling tracts of wooded 'waste' was managed in this manner. Some was retained as private wood-pasture, usually, although not invariably, in the form of deer parks. In addition, we should not necessarily assume that population pressure ensured the rapid degeneration to open pasture of that portion of the 'wastes' which escaped enclosure. Wood-pastures, whether on common land or in severalty, remained a prominent feature of the landscape well into the post-medieval period. They produced some timber, but mainly wood, and probably some browse and leaf fodder, cut from pollards of oak, ash and elm – part of a wider tradition of woodland management which extended across Europe and beyond (Slotte 2001; Read 2008; Halstead 1998). It is important to emphasise the prominence of such grazed woodlands in the pre-modern landscape of Norfolk because their wholesale destruction over the last three centuries or so has ensured that we now tend to think of enclosed and coppiced woodland as the only, or at least the principal, form of semi-natural woodland. Up until the fifteenth century, and conceivably until the seventeenth, such woods covered a smaller area of ground, in Norfolk at least, than woodland pastures.

Writers on historical ecology often emphasise that wood-pastures were inherently unstable environments. Their trees were vulnerable to damage from stock through, for example, the stripping of bark or the compaction of the ground above their root systems. It is usually assumed that in common, as opposed to private, wood-pastures there were particular problems in this respect, for once trees were felled, died or were blown down it was difficult to establish replacements because these could not easily be protected from browsing animals, as fencing off portions of a common would conflict with the rights of other commoners to freely access and exploit it (Rackham 1986a, 121–2). However, the fact that an element of wood-pasture management continued on many Norfolk commons well into the post-medieval period suggests that the situation was more complex than this. In part this was probably because, on the more extensive or remote tracts of common land, the pressure of grazing was sometimes insufficient to suppress all growth of naturally seeded or intentionally planted trees and shrubs. But it was also due to the fact that legal mechanisms often existed at a local level which allowed tenants and manorial lords the right to protect new planting.

Wood-pasture heaths

Most of the more extensive areas of common land in Norfolk, at least by the sixteenth and seventeenth centuries, took the form of heathland. Heaths were tracts of land on which, once the tree cover had been removed, the acid character of the soils and underlying geology, coupled with sustained grazing pressure, favoured the development of a characteristic undershrub vegetation dominated by heather (*ling* in East Anglia) (*Calluna vulgaris*), bell heather (*Erica cinerea*), gorse (*furze* in East Anglia) (*Ulex europaeus*) and broom (*Sarothamnus scoparius*). This process was, moreover, associated with the development of soils called *podzols*, in which severe leaching leaves the upper horizon largely depleted of all constituents other than quartz grains, so that a grey upper level, leached of humus and iron, overlies hard layers of humus pan and iron pan where the minerals have been redeposited in the B-horizon (Rackham 1986a, 286–91; Dimbleby 1962; Parry 2003; Webb 1986). Characteristic grasses also thrive in such environments, including sheep's fescue (*Festuca ovina*), wavy hair grass (*Deschampsia flexuosa*) and common bent (*Agrostis tenuis*), while some areas become dominated by bracken.

Although many Norfolk heaths were reclaimed in the course of the Middle Ages and converted to permanent arable, extensive tracts survived through the post-medieval period and into the eighteenth century. Indeed, by the end of the Middle Ages the county could probably boast more heaths than any other in England. Of the 64,756 hectares (160,012 acres) of common 'waste', including rabbit warrens, recorded on William Faden's county map of 1797, 38,794 hectares are described as 'common', 16,620 as 'heath', 6,042 as 'warren', 2,519 as 'green' and 781 as 'moor'. But there is no doubt that many of the areas described as 'common' were, in fact, heath-like in character: Faden tended to simplify local names, and demonstrably preferred the terms 'common' to 'green' and 'moor' or 'heath' (Macnair and Williamson 2010, 105–9; Morley 2003, 26–32). Heaths were widely distributed across the county, a reflection of the fact that most were formed not over acid *solid* formations, but on sands and gravels of glacial origin. As Faden's map makes clear, the greatest concentration, and the largest continuous areas, were to be found in Breckland, in the south-west of the county, where, as we have seen, aeolian sands were laid down during the Devensian glaciation over boulder clay or chalk (Boulton *et al.* 1984). To the north, a second cluster of heaths extended northwards along the edge of the Wash from Mintlyn to Snettisham. This was the only district in the county in which this kind of habitat was associated with solid geology, the heaths in question overlying Greensand and related formations of Cretaceous date. In earlier times there had also been extensive areas of heathland on the higher ground to the west of this belt, in the 'Good Sands' region of north-west Norfolk, but most had been reclaimed during the half-century or so before Faden's map was made by large estates keen to embrace the principles of the 'agricultural revolution'. The geology of the area was broadly similar to that of Breckland, the heaths being associated with layers of sandy drift, but the latter were here thinner and the soils more easily marled and cultivated (Wade Martins and Williamson 1999, 34–43). Further tracts of heathland could, however, be found in the area lying immediately to the north of Norwich and along the north Norfolk coast, on the ridge between Holt and Cromer, where they were associated with outwash sands and gravels, and glacial moraine, respectively. In addition to these concentrations, a scatter of heaths associated with small pockets of glacial sands or gravels existed across the boulder clay plateau in the centre of the county.

It is unlikely that many heaths were truly 'natural' environments. Most, the evidence from local pollen evidence suggests, were originally wooded, and only following the removal of tree cover did large areas of characteristic heathland vegetation, as well as the typical heathland soils, begin to develop. Subsequent exploitation kept them from bushing over once again, for – despite the way in which they were castigated by eighteenth-century 'improvers' – heaths played an important role in the medieval and post-medieval economy. Not only were they grazed, by sheep and in some cases by rabbits, but they were also, as we have already emphasised, regularly cut for gorse, broom and heather, as well as for bracken (mainly used for cattle bedding). In many areas of Norfolk, moreover, some of the heaths were ploughed – either sporadically, or on a long rotation, as outfield 'brecks' (Postgate 1973). Heaths do not, therefore, constitute a stable 'climax' vegetation but are a consequence of particular forms of management, and when in the twentieth century grazing and cutting were reduced, or ceased altogether, they began to change rapidly, becoming invaded by hawthorn, sloe and birch, and eventually by oak (Clarke 1918, 301). It is difficult for trees and bushes to colonise dense stands of heather, but the older, more degenerate stands that develop once grazing is reduced provide more open ground. Once the trees become established they shade out the heather, leading eventually to the development of the *Quercus–Betula–Deschampsia* woodland which is the natural climax vegetation on these poor soils (Rodwell 1991, 377).

It is sometimes assumed that most heaths, in East Anglia as elsewhere, developed in prehistory. Sandy soils, although comparatively infertile, were easy to cultivate and thus attractive to prehistoric farmers equipped with only primitive ploughing equipment. They were thus cleared to make way for cultivated land, and any woodland that remained degenerated at an early date under grazing pressure (Dimbleby 1962). In Norfolk, the evidence certainly suggests that extensive areas of heath developed in the prehistoric period, although mainly towards its end. The pollen found in the soil sealed beneath a Bronze Age round barrow excavated at Bawdsey in the west of the county, for example, shows a surrounding landscape of lime/hazel woodland, and it was some time after the mound's construction that the area became dominated by more open heath (Murphy 1993). The pollen sequence from Hockham Mere implies that the expansion of the Breckland heaths occurred only during the later Iron Age (Bennett 1983), although heathlands must have been locally extensive at a rather earlier date as radiocarbon dating of humus in the B-horizon of buried soils from the first-century elite residential and ceremonial site at Fisons Way indicates that podzolisation was well advanced here, at least, by *c.*850 BC (Macphail 1986). The carbonised plant remains excavated from the site itself included significant quantities of *Ericaceae* and *Calluna vulgaris*.

In fact, many of the county's heaths seem to have developed even later than this, or else were reinvaded by woodland in the post-Roman period, developing anew as population rose again in medieval times. Even in Breckland, pollen diagrams from the Meres at Hockham and Stow Bedon suggest the survival of extensive woods into the post-Roman period, while the concentration of names featuring the element *wald*, usually taken to mean an extensive tract of wild and wooded ground, in the west of the district – Hockwold, Methwold and Northwold – is noteworthy (Bennett 1983). By the end of the Saxon period most of the woodland in Breckland seems to have disappeared, for Domesday records only very small quantities here. But elsewhere, on the more gravelly glacial deposits to the north of Norwich and along the coast between Holt and Cromer, the high woodland totals recorded in the same source suggest that much still survived on acid, heath-forming soils, and only gradually degenerated to more open environments during subsequent centuries. Mousehold Heath is a good example (Rackham 1986a, 299–302). Domesday implies that there was a substantial wood here and the element 'hold' in the place-name derives from *holt*, an Old English term for 'wood'. By the early thirteenth century a more mixed environment was evidently emerging, for in 1236 it was ordered that 'the part of Thorpe Wood covered in oaks should be divided into two equal parts, a half for the bishop, and a half for the prior' (Blomefield 1806, IV, 36). In the course of the thirteenth century the agent of the bishop of Norwich complained that it was proving difficult to restrain the tenant's use of the wood – which was common land – and the trees were disappearing. By the end of the century, documents refer to Mousehold *Heath* (Rackham 1986a, 302).

Mousehold has been written about on a number of occasions but it was by no means unique. A number of medieval and early post-medieval documents relating to the areas of acid sands and gravels lying to the north of Norwich, along the Holt–Cromer ridge, and on the strip of acid sands running north from King's Lynn, seem to describe the presence of grazed woodland in parishes which, by the later eighteenth century, consisted solely of agricultural land (either in open fields or enclosures) and heaths. In 1239, for example, Robert de Hauteyn granted lands to William Lincoln in Taverham, a heathy parish near Norwich, along with 'common of pasture for 8 sheep, 6 beasts, in the woods, except in the park of the said Robert' (Blomefield, 1805, II, 247). In the late sixteenth century the inhabitants of Marsham accused James Brampton of having, among other misdemeanours, 'felleth downe woode growinge uppon the common contrarye to the custome of the mannor' (Smith *et al.* 1983, 242–3). Partly wooded heaths are shown on maps of New Buckenham (1597) (NRO MC 22/11), Haveringland (1600) (NRO MS4521), Castle Rising (early sixteenth century) (NRO BL71) and Appleton (1596) (NRO BRA 2524/6). Indeed, close examination of William Faden's 1797 map of the county of Norfolk indicates, in the form of scattered tree symbols, that a number of residual fragments of wood-pastures remained within areas specifically described as 'heath' (as on Walsham Heath, Hevingham Heath, Necton Heath, Stock Heath, Edgefield Heath and Cawston Heath).

In most cases, as we shall see, such surviving traces were removed when the areas in question were enclosed, usually by parliamentary acts in the two decades or so following the publication of Faden's map. Nevertheless, a field survey undertaken in the course of this project recovered some surviving traces, usually in places where parts of the heaths were planted up as plantations, rather than being brought into cultivation, following enclosure – whether by parliamentary act, or otherwise. The most striking example is on the Bayfield estate, on the glacial moraine of the Holt–Cromer ridge in the north of the county, where more than 70 ancient, pollarded oaks – some pedunculate *Quercus robur*, some sessile *Q. petraea* – survive on dry, leached soils of the Newport 4 and Barrow Associations. Some are found to the west

Figure 23 The 'Bayfield Oak', probably more than 700 years old, is one of several ancient pollards preserved within the woodland around Bayfield Park in north Norfolk, the remnants of once extensive heathland wood-pastures.

of the river Glaven, rather more on the steep slopes of the valley sides to the east. The youngest examples are almost certainly less than 300 years in age – indeed, the majority have girths of less than five metres – although on such poor soils, and growing close together, it is likely that oaks put on girth significantly more slowly than in other contexts and many of the trees may be considerably older than they seem. The largest, the so-called 'Bayfield Oak', has a girth of 9.2 metres and may be as much as 700 years old (Figure 23). Most are found within estate woodland that had been planted before the end of the eighteenth century, presumably on heathland enclosed in the seventeenth century as a consequence of the parish's tenurial character – it was in single ownership by the sixteenth century and all common rights were thus in the hands of the Jermy family, who could therefore enclose the commons at will. Some, however, occupy areas which were still denoted as heathland on the Glandford tithe award map of 1842 (NRO DN/TA 186) and, in some cases, even on the second edition Ordnance Survey six-inch map of 1906. Similar concentrations of oak pollards are found on the Letheringsett estate, some 1.5 kilometres to the east, again buried within an eighteenth-century plantation ('Pereer's Hills'), and a kilometre to the south, within an eighteenth-century plantation called Sand Hill on the parish boundary between Saxlingham and Thornage, in which are concealed no fewer than 50 oak pollards. Here, again, the trees are not large – almost all less than five metres in circumference, and a number less than three metres – but once again we should note that the poor, acidic and well-drained soils, and the densely spaced character of the planting, may well have militated against normal rates of growth. It is noticeable that the majority of the pollards in all three cases are found on sloping ground, perhaps suggesting that they survived better here because the intensity of grazing was less and sporadic cultivation of the heaths impossible. It is also perhaps worth noting that all these groups of trees occur within four kilometres of the town of Holt, a town whose name, shared with the hundred in which it lies, simply means 'wood' and may, perhaps, represent an ancient name for a well-wooded district.

In the far west of the county, on the Greensand ridge to the north of Kings Lynn, another concentration of early pollards survives – once again, buried within eighteenth- and nineteenth-century woodland – at Ken Hill near Snettisham (centred on TF 679349). Here, surrounding an area of surviving heath, there are a number of pollarded oaks with girths of between *c.*4.5 and 5.5 metres. The area is shown as 'Caen Wood' on Faden's map of 1797 but at the time of the parliamentary enclosure of the parish in 1766 was partly used as a rabbit warren (NRO Le Strange OB2; NRO BO1). Further examples of relict wood-pastures can be found on the islands of former heathland scattered across the clay plateau in the centre and south of the county. Numbers of ancient pollards, again all oaks, thus exist within Thursford Wood, a nature reserve managed by the NWT (TF 978332); at The Lings, three kilometres to the south-east, where they survive among later planting; and in Little Heath Plantation, some *c.*2 kilometres to the north-east (TF 993346). All occupy sandy and gravelly soils and the last mentioned, before enclosure in the early nineteenth century, formed the northern section of Stock Heath, the extensive tract of common land, lying at the point where four hundreds converged, briefly discussed in Chapter 3 (above, p. 42). Here, again, few of the trees are large: all but 2 of the 30 recorded have girths of less than five metres. Large trees are better represented at Thursford, however, with one particularly massive example of 7.7 metres, but even here around three-quarters of the 30 specimens have girths of less than five metres. The trees in these various woods were singled out for particular comment by Grigor in 1841, who described how 'some hundreds of acres are here thickly strewed with thorns and holly of most magnificent growth, and ever and anon an old and gnarled oak contrasts and enlivens the scenery' (Grigor 1841, 233).

Although, as we have noted, the sandy district called Breckland had probably lost most of its tree cover at an early date, along its fringes some traces of relict wood-pastures can be found. Broom Covert in Quidenham (TM 025865) is a small L-shaped plantation presumably planted in the eighteenth century and already shown on Faden's county map of 1797. Within it, growing in two main groups, are 30 pollarded oaks with girths of between 2.5 and 5 metres, averaging 3.9 metres. The wood contains earthworks of boundary banks and a hollow way, possibly suggesting that this was an area of private rather than common wood-pasture. Once again the small size of the trees is noteworthy: here it is likely that their growth has been impaired by competition with the dense vegetation around and above them (many, indeed, are now dead or dying), as well as by the poor quality of the soils. Small groups of pollards surviving within Grenadier Plantation in Garboldisham (TL

996825), and in the woods forming the western edge of Merton Park (TL 904970), may similarly represent the remains of wood-pastures rather than former hedgerow trees, but more striking is the concentration of sixteen old pollards in the woods and scrubland around Stow Bedon Mere (TL 950963), an area which was still open heathland when Faden's county map was surveyed in the 1790s. Two-thirds have girths of less than 5 metres, but the others include one magnificent 'champion' tree with a circumference of around 8 metres.

It is noteworthy that these Breckland sites are found towards the margins of the region, on acid soils of the Newport 4 or Ollerton Associations – soils formed in gravels as well as sands, and in the case of the latter affected to some extent by a seasonally high water table. The relict wood-pastures found elsewhere in heathland contexts, around Holt, at Ken Hill and in the Thursford area, and also those which are referred to in medieval and post-medieval documents, likewise occur on Newport Association soils. These are rather different from the much sandier soils, overlying chalk, that occur towards the centre of, and account for most of the area of, Breckland – those of the Methwold and Worlington Associations. There may be an early and important distinction here in the way that heathland developed over time. The Methwold and Worlington soils were more attractive to early agriculturalists than those of the Newport, Ollerton or similar associations. They are interspersed with more calcareous soils in the principal valleys, and themselves overlie chalk, often at no very great depth: the practice of 'marling' (excavating calcareous subsoil and spreading it on the sandy surface to reduce acidity) has been known in this area since at least the thirteenth century (Prince 1964). Some of the heathland in the Breckland district, lying beyond the main areas of arable on the valley soils, was thus cultivated as outfield 'brecks' in the Middle Ages and later. In addition, large flocks of sheep were grazed on the nearby heaths and folded regularly on the arable in order to maintain the fertility of these easily leached soils (Postgate 1973; Bailey 1989). All this would have militated against the long-term survival or regeneration of trees. In addition, where the Breckland sands are deeper and less easy to cultivate large areas were, from late medieval times, given over to commercial rabbit warrens, further discouraging regeneration (Bailey 1989). In contrast, in the other districts of Norfolk where heaths were a prominent feature of the landscape – in the strip of countryside to the north of King's Lynn, in the area to the north of Norwich and along the coast between Holt and Cromer – conditions were rather different. Not only are the Newport soils found in these locations often gravelly, rather than sandy, in character, but instead of overlying chalk they have beneath them, earlier, less calcareous formations, ensuring that opportunities to improve the quality of the soil through marling, and thus to bring it into at least temporary cultivation, were limited. Many of these areas, moreover, also had a relatively high water table, discouraging both sporadic cultivation *and* the establishment on a large scale of rabbit warrens. Heaths were evidently more varied environments than we often assume, with very varied origins, and this may call into question the 'one-size-fits-all' approach implicit in current heathland restoration policies, which often involve the systematic removal of all existing tree cover on the sites in question (Barnes *et al.* 2007).

One particular and curious example of a heathland wood-pasture in Norfolk needs to be mentioned. In and immediately around Felbrigg Great Wood, on acid gravelly soils near the north coast, are significant numbers of old pollarded beeches. It has been suggested that they are among the most northerly indigenous examples of this species to be found in England (Rackham 1980, 326; Rackham 2011, 363). The soils in the area would normally have given rise to a landscape of heaths, and a sketch map of 1777 denotes the area occupied by one of the main concentrations of the trees specifically as 'heath' (NRO C/Sce 2 Road Order Box no. 21). Eighty-one of the beeches recorded have girths of between 4 and 4.9 metres, not large by the standards of this species and – to judge from dated examples elsewhere in the county – are probably of later eighteenth- or nineteenth-century date. A further 50 have girths of between 5 and 5.9 metres, but again – on analogy with other dated examples – there is little reason to believe that these are any older than the middle decades of the eighteenth century. Eleven are more substantial, with girths of 6 metres or more, but only three, with girths of 6.9, 7.4 and 8.9 metres, are larger than examples of 6.8 metres growing in an avenue at Houghton, in the west of the county, known to have been planted in the early 1730s (Barnes and Williamson 2011, 110–12). It is thus possible that none of the Felbrigg trees was planted before the later seventeenth century. This, of course, is no more than a reflection of the relatively short life span of trees of this species, and does not preclude that these examples represent the oldest surviving members of an ancient population. There are certainly records of heathland wood-pastures in the area in the Middle Ages. In the 1490s William Hamund was granted the right to take 'all the underwood and lop all the trees that grow on the land of the said cottage and upon the separate common (*communam separalem*) opposite' at Felbrigg (NRO WKC2/115). On the other hand, it is just possible that the Felbrigg beeches are a relatively recent addition to the landscape, for William Windham of Felbrigg Hall began a sustained forestry campaign in and around Felbrigg park in *c.*1676, and the beeches could conceivably represent one aspect of his estate planting, using trees brought from elsewhere in England. It is certainly remarkable that, while James Grigor provided a detailed description of the trees at Felbrigg in his *Eastern Arboretum* of 1841, he failed to mention any beech trees of significant antiquity here, a surprising omission which may suggest that those he saw were then no more than 175 years old (Grigor 1841, 122–8). It is thus possible that the oldest surviving examples may be the first planted in the area, and had no predecessors. The planting of new wood-pastures on common land by manorial lords, while unusual in post-medieval England, is not without possible parallels. Anne Rowe has recently suggested that hornbeams were widely planted and then cropped by major landowners on the commons of south Hertfordshire in the seventeenth century, although here the market for fuel from nearby London provided them with a particularly strong incentive (Rowe in press).

The situation is not clear-cut, however, for although few if any ancient beeches can now be found beyond the bounds of the Felbrigg estate, on the acid soils in neighbouring parishes stray documentary records attest their presence in the seventeenth and early eighteenth centuries. Beech standards were apparently growing in Edgefield Great Wood, some ten kilometres to the south-west of Felbrigg, in the 1670s (Rackham 1980, 326), while a 1756 timber survey from the Blickling estate, some 12 kilometres to the south-west of Felbrigg, refers obliquely to the existence of beech pollards on the estate when it notes how the total value of the timber given is 'exclusive of all trees under 6 inches Girth and also of all Firrs *Beech Pollards* and all the Plantations in the Park and elsewhere' (our italics) (NRO MC3 252).[6] Such references suggest that beech was more widespread in the local landscape in earlier centuries than it is today, supporting the idea that the Felbrigg examples are the remains of an indigenous population. Unfortunately, there are no pollen records from the north-east of the county, but beech pollen was recorded, albeit at low frequencies, in late prehistoric levels of the cores taken from Diss Mere in the south (Peglar *et al.* 1989).

Sustaining planting on commons

Heaths not only comprised, by the eighteenth century at least, the majority of commons in the county but were also, for the most part, the most extensive individual areas of common land. The 62 'heaths' specifically named as such on Faden's county map of 1797 thus range in size from 9.7 to 2,168 hectares, with an average size of 268 hectares: the 128 'greens', in contrast, the vast majority of which were located on heavy clay soils of the Beccles Association, range from 0.8 to 190 hectares, with an average area of 19.7 hectares. The average 'heath', in other words, was over 13 times the size of the average 'green' (the 465 areas described simply as 'common', as we might expect from Faden's rather general usage of the term, fall in between these extremes, with an average size of 83.4 hectares and a range of 0.8 to 1,957 hectares). In addition, we should note that a high proportion of heaths – just under 40 per cent – are shown on Faden's map without any farms or cottages clustered around their margins, compared with only 4 per cent of 'greens' (areas described as 'common' once again fall in between these extremes, with around 27 per cent lacking any associated dwellings). Houses were also clustered more densely around 'greens' or, to put it another way, if we were to divide up the surface area of the common between the houses that Faden shows surrounding it, those fronting 'greens' would each receive a much smaller area of land than those fronting on 'heaths', the figures being 2.2 hectares per house for greens and 31.5 for heaths (the figure for commons is 8.3) (Macnair and Williamson 2010, 200–8). Heaths were thus not only, in general, significantly larger than greens and other forms of common land in the county, but were also more remote from settlements. Heaths, or parts of them, were thus probably grazed less intensely than most other areas of common land in the county, especially the smaller greens, and this presumably accounts in part for the survival on many of areas of wood-pasture well into the post-medieval period, at least in areas away from Breckland and some parts of north-west Norfolk, where, as we have noted, vast flocks of sheep were retained in order to keep the arable land in good heart.

Nevertheless, there is good evidence that some measure of tree cover was also retained, well into the post-medieval period, on many 'greens' and similar areas of

---

6 Two examples of pollarded beech trees survive today on the estate, although neither is likely to date back to the early eighteenth century. One, in the northern part of Hercules Wood, stands on a low earthwork marking the former boundary of Bucks Common (TG 16577 328430) and has a girth of just over 5.2 metres; the other, in Bucks Common Plantation, may originally have grown in a hedge bordering the side of the old Aylsham–Saxthorpe Road before this was diverted along its present course in the eighteenth century.

common land, despite their being smaller in size and with margins often densely occupied by farms and cottages. Even Faden's county map of 1797 shows some of these smaller areas, mostly located on clay soils, as partly tree-covered: examples include Hoe Common, Podmore Green in Scarning, Stiphens Green in Hockering, Shelton Common, Pulham Common and Fritton Common. Once again, a few traces of these wooded commons still survive in the modern landscape. Fritton, one of relatively few medium-sized clayland commons in the county to escape parliamentary enclosure in the early nineteenth century, is still ringed (in customary fashion) by a girdle of ancient farms and cottages and boasts no less than 20 pollarded trees, many hidden away among the scrub and woodland which has regenerated in relatively recent times owing to a decline in regular grazing. The pollards are concentrated towards the edges of the common, for the most part, near to where the houses stand. Most are oaks, with girths in the range 2.3–5.4 metres, but there are six examples of ash (2.3–3.4 metres) and, somewhat surprisingly, a sycamore (4.1 metres). Most thus appear to be of no great antiquity: many must have been planted and first cropped in the nineteenth century, and some were probably cut regularly into the twentieth. A similar collection of trees survives on Old Buckenham Common. Here, too, the pollards are all relatively young and ash is well represented (in this case comprising the majority of the trees), while the unusual sycamore at Fritton here has its parallel in a pollarded sweet chestnut.

The late survival of wood-pastures, or fragments of wood-pasture, on these rather smaller areas of common land, with settled margins, is superficially surprising. But, as Patsy Dallas has shown, in spite of what is often suggested or implied about the inherent instability of common wood-pastures, in some places at least management systems existed which allowed or encouraged the replacement of lost trees (Dallas 2010). Custom, that is, permitted commoners to plant new trees on commons, and to protect them while young. During a legal dispute in the late sixteenth century concerning the commons at Pulham in south Norfolk, for example, it was stated that 'The tenants of the said manor have used to make benefitt of the trees growing upon the common near their houses which were planted by themselves and their predecessors' (NRO NAS II/17). A survey of the manor of Gressenhall, drawn up in 1579, describes how tenants admitted to holdings received one or more 'planting' (NRO MR61 241X1); a map drawn up in 1624 shows that these were areas of scattered trees growing on the various commons of the parish, in places so dense that the areas in question were effectively wooded. Each planting was associated by name with the various owners close to whose homes, once again, they were located (NRO Hayes and Storr 72). Similar customs are recorded by the county historian Francis Blomefield in his *Topographic History of the County of Norfolk* of 1739. The tenants of his home parish of Fersfield thus had:

> Liberty to cut down timber on their copyholds, without licence and also to plant and cut down all manner of wood and timber on all the commons and wastes against their own lands, by the name of an outrun. (Blomefield 1805, 1, 739, 95)

As at Pulham, the trees being established by the commoners were close to their 'own lands', and in this context it is noteworthy that old trees surviving on the smaller greens and commons tend, as at Fritton, to be concentrated towards their margins. It

Figure 24 Oak pollards on the south-western edge of Fritton Common in south Norfolk: the trees grow in clear lines, indicating that they were carefully planted.

is also worth noting that a number of pollards on the western side of Fritton Common appear to be growing in straight lines in a manner clearly indicative of deliberate planting (Figure 24). Blomefield describes similar customs at other places in the south of the county, including Kenninghall, Diss and Garboldisham (Blomefield 1805, 1, 220, 263). In the long term such rules would not prevent the eventual erosion of woodland – Faden's map suggests that the commons at Fersfield, Diss, Kenninghall and Garboldisham were effectively treeless by the end of the eighteenth century – but they evidently served to retard it.

Private wood-pastures

The other kind of managed wood-pasture which existed in medieval and early post-medieval Norfolk was the deer park, enclosed and private in character. 'Park' is a complex term which has changed its meaning over the centuries but the earliest parks were, as we have already explained, enclosures made from the dwindling 'wastes' in the early Middle Ages in order to provide manorial lords with a source of wood and timber, but mainly with a place to keep deer and other stock (Liddiard 2007; Mileson 2009; Fletcher 2011). Some deer parks existed in England at the time of Domesday – in Norfolk, examples are listed at Holt and Costessey – and it is possible that they were already a common feature of the landscape in late Saxon times: it has been suggested that the *hagas* which are mentioned in the boundary clauses of charters in many parts of the country, a term often taken to mean simply 'hedge' or 'enclosure', had the more specialised meaning of 'fences for concentrating or corralling deer', or even of 'enclosures in which deer were kept'. They may have been, in some cases at least, similar or identical to deer parks (Hooke 2011, 165–71; Liddiard 2003). Norfolk can boast only one certain example – *Schieteshaga* in Hempnall, a property without resources or population listed by Domesday within the vill of Hempnall. Either way, parks were private wood-pastures which functioned as venison farms and hunting grounds but also, as Liddiard has emphasised, had a range of other functions.

Parks were a common feature of the medieval landscape of Norfolk – more than 90 examples are known, or suspected, at various places in the county, although many of these were small or short-lived (Yaxley 2005). Some examples, like that at New Buckenham, seem to have formed part of the 'landscapes of lordship' laid out around the residences of the feudal elite – castles and palaces. They were displays of status which complemented the appearance of a noble residence (Liddiard 2000). But the majority of early medieval parks lay in relatively remote places, some way from the homes of their owners, largely because they had been enclosed, in the manner already described, from the residual areas of woodland surviving towards the edges of cleared and cultivated land. Many contained a 'lodge', sometimes moated, which served as permanent accommodation for the keeper charged with maintaining the park and its deer, and as temporary accommodation for hunting parties (Liddiard 2007). Surrounded by a substantial earthwork bank and fence, parks were, even more than woods, powerful symbols of lordly appropriation of the remaining areas of wild land. In Norfolk, as elsewhere, they were a particular feature of the more marginal soils, where significant tracts of woodland had survived into the Middle Ages.

As Rotherham has noted, such early parks 'took in, and retained, more of the earlier wilderness, waste and associated ecology' than managed woods of coppice-with-standards type (Rotherham 2012, 4). But, as he has also emphasised, 'ecological research often fails to differentiate between contrasting parkland origins and histories, and for many ecologists a park is a park' (Rotherham 2012, 4). Not all medieval parks were enclosed at an early date from tracts of wooded waste, and those that were have not often survived as parkland landscapes to the present. There was, in fact, a marked lack of continuity between parks which survive in the landscape today, as the setting for great houses, and the hunting parks of early medieval times. Such discontinuities are the consequence of both economic and cultural factors. From the late fourteenth century deer parks began to decline in numbers, largely for economic reasons: it was difficult to maintain the deer-proof 'pale' and cover costs more generally at a time of economic depression and straightened seigniorial revenues. Many parks were ploughed up or converted to open pastures or coppiced woodland by their owners. But at the same time new parks were appearing, and the role and function of the park began to subtly change. It became more normal for parks to be located in the immediate vicinity of great houses, rather than at a distance from them, and to become less densely wooded and more carefully designed in character, although they were still essentially wood-pastures, with a significant number of pollarded trees. Many existing deer parks were thus gradually abandoned in the course of the fifteenth, sixteenth and seventeenth centuries, and new ones created next to the owner's home, usually at the expense of farmed land. In addition to changes in role and location, parks anyway tended to disappear from the landscape as, over the centuries, the fortunes of particular estates and families waned. This process of attrition was, however, very extended, and many of the most extensive of the county's *early* medieval parks, including those at Lopham, Kenninghall and Acle, survived well into the seventeenth century (Dye 1990).

There was, moreover, little direct continuity between any of these medieval parks – early or otherwise – and the ornamental parks which still survive in significant numbers around country houses in Norfolk. A few medieval parks did develop into landscape parks in the eighteenth and nineteenth centuries – such as that at Hunstanton – but these were invariably *late* medieval creations, made at the expense of previously cleared ground. Even these were few in number, and many apparent examples of continuity – where a park is known to have existed in a certain parish both in the Middle Ages and in the eighteenth century, and where the same family has owned an estate in the place in question throughout this time – turn out to be illusory. A good example is Kimberley. The medieval mansion of Wodehouse Towers stood on a moated site within a deer park, created in the fifteenth century, in Kimberley parish, some way to the west of the present Kimberley Hall – which actually stands on the eastern side of the river Tiffey, in Wymondham. This latter mansion was erected in the early eighteenth century by Sir John Wodehouse, 4th Baronet, and set within a new deer park. There was no continuity at all with the medieval park: the two parks lay in different places and their areas did not overlap until the subsequent expansion of the new park in the eighteenth and nineteenth centuries (Taigel and Williamson 1991, 69–71). With the possible exception of Melton Constable park, in the centre of the county, landscape parks in Norfolk did not, therefore, develop directly from deer parks established in the course of the twelfth and thirteenth centuries and thus do not, in general, represent a direct link with the wooded tracts of remote times (Dye 1990; Williamson 1998b, 40–6). Here, as elsewhere in England, Rotherham's warnings about the dangers of confusing and conflating different kinds of 'park' are amply justified.

The distribution of medieval parks within the county has been plotted by Robert Liddiard on the basis of a wide range of documentary and cartographic evidence (Liddiard 2010) (Figure 25). When those examples which are probably, or certainly, of fourteenth-century or later date are removed it is clear that 'early' parks, enclosed before the Black Death, tend to be concentrated in particular locations: on the arc of clayland running through the centre and south of the county; on the poor heathy soils to the north of Norwich; in the areas of similar soils on the north coast, between Holt and Cromer; and to the east and north of King's Lynn, in the far west of the county. Such a pattern is enhanced further if we discount those parks identified on the basis of single documentary references or on the basis of field names alone: that is, small, possibly late and probably short-lived examples (Figure 26). This distribution is, not surprisingly, similar to that exhibited by surviving areas of ancient woodland, as well as to that of Domesday woodland and known wood-pasture commons, especially heaths. Parks were thus concentrated on the poor, heathy sand to the north of Norwich (on soils of the Newport 4 and Felthorpe Associations) – where the examples at Cawston, Hevingham, Haveringland and Horsford were all to be found; and on the Holt–Cromer ridge – where the parks at Thornage, Baconsthorpe and Bayfield (the latter probably the site of the park which Domesday mentions in the entry for nearby Holt) all cluster. The string of parks in west Norfolk – Middleton, Gaywood, Castle Rising, Sandringham and Wormegay – are also, for the most part, associated

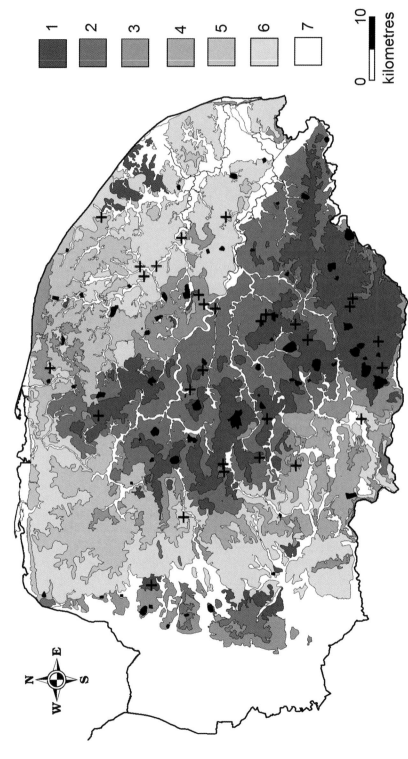

Figure 25 The distribution of all known deer parks in Norfolk established before c.1600. Soils: (1) Beccles Association (heavy, poorly draining clays on level or gently sloping ground); (2) Burlingham and Hanslope Association (lighter clays, mainly on valley sides); (3) Felthorpe, Downham, Newport and Ollerton Associations (sandy, stony and very acid soils, mainly overlying non-calcareous formations, some affected by groundwater); (4) Worlington and Methwold Associations (deep sandy soils); (5) Barrow and Wick 3 Associations (non-calcareous sandy or gravelly loams); (6) Wick 2 and Newmarket Associations (neutral or calcareous loams); (7) peat and alluvium.

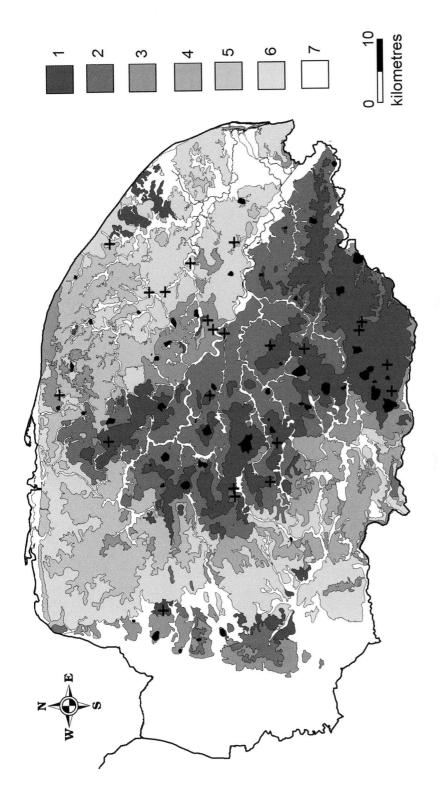

Figure 26 The distribution of deer parks in Norfolk, excluding those probably established after *c.*1350 and/or of short duration. For soils key see Figure 25.

with sandy soils and were evidently enclosed from heathland wood-pastures in an area in which Domesday shows moderate amounts of woodland, and later maps and documents again suggest the presence of wooded commons. It is possible that the castles at Wormegay, Castle Rising, Middleton and Horsford were placed in these areas, in part, because of hunting afforded by their wooded heaths.

Most of the larger and long-lived parks, however, were associated not with sandy and gravelly soils but – like most surviving areas of ancient woodland – with soils formed in boulder clay, and especially with those of the Beccles Association. Most, although not all, were located towards the centres of the clay masses in the centre and south of the county rather than – as is often the case with ancient woods – towards their peripheries. In locational terms, that is, early deer parks were more akin to commons than to woodland, and this presumably explains why the area of the claylands which boasts the highest density of ancient woods – the south-eastern termination of the till plateau, the dissected countryside forming the narrow watershed between the Chet and the Waveney – is noticeably deficient in deer parks. The distinction, while admittedly not entirely clear-cut and more of a tendency than a rule, is explicable in two ways. Parks, although generally well-wooded, were not primarily created with the production of wood and timber in mind, so their owners were perhaps less concerned to place them in accessible positions than would be the case with coppiced woods. But, perhaps more importantly, parks generally covered much greater areas of ground than woods. Some small examples are recorded in the county – the smallest being that mentioned at Hethersett in 1361, covering a mere three acres, which presumably served as a breeding enclosure or something similar (Liddiard 2010, 24). But most were considerably larger. Whereas only four surviving ancient woods in the county extend over an area of more than 0.75 square kilometres, at least 25 early deer parks did so – the real number may well be higher, given the problems involved in identifying the likely boundaries of many examples. What is even more striking is the fact that all four of the ancient woods concerned – Foxley, Hockering, Haveringland Great Wood and Horsford – appear to have developed from deer parks in the later Middle Ages. Their open launds were either planted up as woods, or regenerated naturally to woodland, when they were disparked.

The size of many parks suggests that correspondingly large areas of unused ground must have existed when they were first created, for there is no sign that settlements were moved to make way for them, to judge from such evidence as the chance finds logged in the Norfolk Historic Environment Record and Alan Davison's fieldwalking survey at Loddon, which showed that the area formerly occupied by the medieval park at Hales was quite devoid of evidence of earlier settlement or agriculture (Davison 1990, 30–2). This helps further explain why parks in general occupied areas more remote than woods, away from the main zones of early settlement within the principal valleys.

As Liddiard has emphasised (Liddiard 2010, 3–5), the documentary evidence for the chronology of park-making is both sparse and misleading. As already noted, Domesday records two deer parks in the county – at Holt and Costessey – together with one *haga*, the *Schieteshaga* at Hempnall. Holt was a major royal manor and the centre of the eponymous hundred; Costessey, where a 'park for beasts of the chase' is explicitly described as having been in existence *before* the Conquest, was the *caput* of the great landowner Gyrth, and had probably been an important central place since middle Saxon times (Williamson 1993, 96–100). These examples aside, all the other parks in the county – with the exception of that at New Buckenham, which charter evidence shows was in place by 1146 (around the time that the castle here was nearing completion) – first appear in official documents only in the thirteenth or even the fourteenth century, including those at Castle Rising, Mileham, Wormegay and Horsford, which, as Liddiard notes, were almost certainly, like that at New Buckenham, laid out when the castles with which they were associated were constructed in the twelfth century (Liddiard 2010, 5). The parks at Holt and Costessey themselves only reappear in the documentary record in 1324 and 1302 respectively. As Liddiard has emphasised, 'The records of royal government, which represent the principal sources for confirming the existence of parks, only survive consistently from *c.*1200; thus the majority of parks are first encountered in the historical record after this time' (Liddiard 2010, 3). The misleading character of official documentation is nowhere better illustrated than in the case of the park at Acle, the first documentary record of which – in 1364 – refers to a lost charter which confirmed rights to turbaries which had been enclosed within it by Roger Bigod some time before his death in 1189 (CPR, 1361–1364, 506). The fact that parks generally cover large areas of land itself suggests that they were mainly created in the twelfth rather than the thirteenth century, by which time the landscape was filling up with people, green-edge settlements were appearing in the most remote locations and lords would have found it hard to find extensive, continuous tracts of untenanted ground.

Indeed, in the case of some parks the area of ground covered and the location hint that Holt and Costessey may not have been the only examples in existence by the time of Domesday. In particular, some of the larger parks on the claylands in the south and centre of the county are not restricted to the heavier Beccles Association soils of the level plateau but instead extended down into major river valleys, so that much of their area occupied the kinds of lighter clay soil which the archaeological evidence clearly suggests had, by the twelfth century, largely been brought into cultivation. Silfield or Wymondham park, for example, covered over three square kilometres but largely occupied relatively light Burlingham Association soils in the valley of the river Tiffey, its northern extremity lying a mere 1.6 kilometres from the centre of the medieval town of Wymondham. Earsham, to judge from its depiction on post-medieval maps, extended over an area of 2.3 square kilometres on mixed Beccles, Burlingham and Newport soils, mainly within the valley of the river Waveney, and lay only 1.3 kilometres from the parish church, the probable focus of middle and late Saxon settlement in the parish. The park at Lopham, covering no less than *c.*3.7 square kilometres, occupied an area of mixed Beccles and Burlingham soils extending down into the Little Ouse valley. Its eastern boundary lay only *c.*0.6 kilometres from the parish church and less than 0.4 from the houses of the medieval village. Such circumstances suggest that these large parks were enclosed before the significant expansion of settlement which appears to have occurred in the county from the eleventh century (above, p. 25). It is noticeable that all three of these places were probable middle Saxon estate centres, and remained important and populous places at the time of Domesday, Earsham with a recorded population of 69, Lopham with 48 and Wymondham with no fewer than 371. Earsham gave its name to the hundred in which it lay, was held by Archbishop Stigand in 1066 and had, almost certainly, formerly been the centre of a royal estate. Wymondham, likewise held by Stigand in 1066, was also a place of pre-Conquest importance. It was the largest medieval parish in the county and this, together with the fact that the town became the site of a priory in 1107, probably indicates its former status as a minster territory, and thus again, by implication, an early royal estate centre (Williamson 1993, 92–104). In both cases, the parallels with Holt and Costessey are clear.

Parks were primarily intended as places in which to keep deer, both for the hunt and for the table, and deer are referred to in a number of accounts of park-breaking incidents, as well as in other contexts: the first mention of the park at Gimmingham, for example, comes in an order to the Sheriff in 1240 to take bucks from it (CLR 1226–40, 492). There are fewer references to actual hunting, not perhaps surprisingly given the nature of the surviving documents, although deer coursing appears to have been taking place in the park at Burgh-next-Aylsham in 1311 (CPR 1327–30, 66–7). In physical terms the most important defining feature of a park was its perimeter boundary or 'pale': an Inquisition Post Mortem refers to the 'old ditch of the park' and 'the ditch nearest to the pasture of Gersinghe by which the park is enclosed' at Attleborough in 1297 (Cal IPM, vol. 3, 279). Few convincing traces of perimeter banks survive, however, in this intensively arable county. Part of the southern boundary of Hevingham Park remains on the southern edges of what is now Hevingham Wood; a section of the boundary of the park at Gressenhall may survive as an earthwork bank, now incorporated within the churchyard which has expanded over it; and what may be a section of the eastern boundary of Lopham park is represented by a substantial ditch and bank which runs to the south of Lopham Grove (in 1339 tenants of the manor were fined for 'cutting down trees and carrying away the soil of Fersfield manor, under the pretence of clearing the great ditch round the park') (Liddiard 2010, 31). Park boundaries, unlike those of woods, were in Norfolk as elsewhere normally surmounted by fences rather than hedges. The park at Burgh Next Aylsham is first recorded in 1287 (CCR 12279–1288, 459), when 40 oaks were ordered for enclosing it, while a report of a park-breaking incident at Hevingham specifically mentions the destruction of paling (Liddiard 2010, 25). An unfinished map by Thomas Waterman of Kenninghall park, surveyed in 1621 (Arundel Castle Archives, P5/6), shows a wooden pale and two gates, one described as 'oak gate'.

In Norfolk, as in other parts of the country, parks seem to have varied not only in extent but also in function and appearance. Some were evidently densely wooded: in 1292 the park at Attleborough was said to contain a wood of 469 acres, while that at Tibenham was described in 1309 as 'a wood called "le Park", containing in circuit a league and a half' (Cal IPM, vol. 4, 259). Many clearly contained large numbers of timber trees, to judge from reports of fellings during park-breaking incidents and the frequent references to the value of their 'great timber'. But the majority of parks included a significant proportion of open ground, in order to allow space for hunting. Most, that is, comprised a mixture of wood-pasture and more open pastures, which were here as elsewhere usually called 'laundes', to judge from the occurrence of the field name 'lawn' within the area of former parks. Some also contained embanked coppices from which the deer were excluded during the early stages of coppice growth. The parks at Mileham, Buckenham and Kenninghall all contained such areas, to judge from the valuations made of the herbage *and underwood* (Liddiard 2010), but the most explicit description of this form of management comes from a grant made to John Lowyk in 1391 of:

The underwood in the park of Foxle[y], co. Norfolk ... on condition that of the said underwood sufficient cover be reserved for the king's deer within that park, that he suitably enclose at his own expense from time to time that coppice whereof he takes the underwood, and that the underwood is taken in season. (CPR 1388–92, 486)

The separately named woods sometimes described within parks, such as the wood called 'Burghgrave' which lay within North Elmham park in 1382 (CPR, 1381–5, 167), may likewise represent embanked coppice, although some may simply have been areas of denser wood-pasture which contrasted with the more open laundes. Ancient woods found within the area of former parks may represent such areas of embanked coppice, as at Holland's Wood in North Lopham, although, as the case of Hook Wood in Morley St Peter shows, their present boundaries may be rather different to those established in the Middle Ages (see Appendix entry, Hook Wood, Morley).

As well as deer, other high-status foodstuffs were protected within parks. Several contained fishponds, and some housed a range of game kept in what sound like separate enclosures. It was reported in 1360, for example, that the various 'evil doers' who had broken into the parks at Shipdham and East Dereham had 'entered the warrens there, hunted in these, felled trees, trod down and depastured with cattle the grass there and carried away the said trees from the park and hares, conies, pheasants and partridges from the warrens' (Cal. Pat. Rolls 1358–61, 403). Some parks were also used agriculturally – the earliest reference to the park at North Elmham, for example, from 1205, concerns the provision of grazing for cattle – and parts of parks might even be put to the plough, as at Buckenham, where there were 29½ acres and 4½ perches of arable land lying 'within the park gates' (there was also a 'mowable meadow' here) (Dodwell 1974, no. 171; Liddiard 2010, 15–16). In some cases it seems likely that the line between park and normal demesne land was thus a fine one, and there is a reference to 'closes or pasture called Blofield Park' in 1356 (CPR 1354–58, 335–6). But most medieval parks were clearly a mixture of coppiced woodland, wood-pasture and open pasture, and a map of Lopham park made by Thomas Waterman in 1612 (Arundel Castle Archives P5/1), although surveyed at a relatively late date, probably gives a good impression of their appearance. A lodge stood near the centre of the park (its site now marked by Lodge Farm) and was surrounded by an extensive open laund, sparsely scattered with trees, which was in turn flanked by areas of wood-pasture. There were three large blocks of apparently enclosed and coppiced woodland towards the northern periphery of the park – North Haugh, Lither Haugh and Elme – while other areas of woodland, Little Chimbroke and Poule Chimbroke, are shown in the south-east. In the east of the park Brake Hill is also depicted as woodland. An area described as Chimbroke meadow and crossed by a stream is also noted.

Such a balance of habitats was probably typical, and has implications for the botanical character of those large areas of ancient woodland – such as Foxley or Hockering – which developed from early parks. In Rotherham's words, 'Park landscapes had unimproved grassland across much of the grazed area ... The typical plants of ancient woodland (such as dog's mercury, wood anemone, primrose and bluebell) would have been restricted' in their distribution, mainly to the enclosed coppices (Rotherham 2012, 5).

Conclusion

Neither deer parks nor wooded commons have left much trace in the modern landscape, and it is largely for this reason that we tend to think of medieval woods primarily in terms of areas enclosed and managed as coppice-with-standards. But well into the post-medieval period wooded commons and parks collectively covered much more ground than enclosed woods. They may also have preserved more of the biological character of the wooded 'wastes' than ancient woods of coppiced type. The latter have proved more durable in the landscape, but, as we have suggested, the character and intensity of their management must have ensured a less direct link, in biological terms, with the lost woods of remote antiquity.

As already noted, all of the largest areas of ancient woodland in Norfolk – Hockering, Foxley, Haveringland and Horsford – appear to have evolved directly from deer parks, that at Foxley certainly of 'compartmentalised' type. A number of the smaller woods included in the *Inventory*, such as Hook Wood in Morley, may originally have formed embanked coppices within deer parks, while several medium-sized examples, including Blickling Great Wood, Felbrigg Great Wood and Cley Park, represent more extensive portions of medieval parks, although the first two of these were probably created only in the fifteenth century or later, albeit perhaps at the expense of wooded heath, while virtually nothing is known of that at Cley. Both Haveringland and Horsford were almost entirely replanted with commercial conifers in the course of the twentieth century – they are technically 'plantations on ancient woodland sites', in the terms of the *Ancient Woodland Inventory*. Although Hockering and Foxley have also suffered to some extent in this respect, most of their area is still occupied by coppice and their internal earthworks survive in good condition. Some of the otherwise inexplicable boundary banks within Hockering Wood probably represent former coppice compartments, as may some of the more meagre remains within Foxley Wood. What is striking is that while much or most of the areas now contained within both woods must presumably, and for an extended period, have comprised well-grazed and perhaps fairly open pasture, in botanical terms there is no trace of this. The probable former coppices at Hockering have a ground cover no different from that found within what were presumably the open laundes; both woods contain, throughout their area, a range of 'ancient woodland indicator species' no different to that found in other local woods on similar soils. Other ancient woods may, as we have already hypothesised, have gone through a similar process in the remote past: they too may have lost much of their underwood and perhaps a proportion of their timber, and had their ground flora drastically affected by grazing, in the period before they were enclosed and more intensively managed.

Chapter 6

Ancient woodland in the eighteenth and nineteenth centuries

Studies of ancient woodland usually skip rapidly through the eighteenth and nineteenth centuries before bemoaning the ravages wrought by the large-scale replantings and grubbings-out of the twentieth (see, e.g., Rackham 1986a, 92–7). Yet in some ways this neglect of recent history is a mistake. If woods, as we have emphasised, are best understood as dynamic environments, constantly changing, then much of their present character is arguably the consequence of relatively recent developments, rather than simply representing the survival, untouched through the centuries, of an ancient habitat.

The background

In the period after 1700 the landscape, and the place of woodland within it, was shaped by four main developments, all interconnected in complex ways. Perhaps the most important was the transition to a coal-based economy, something which was essential for a take-off into a modern industrial society: as Wrigley has observed, if coal had not existed England would, by 1815, have required at least six million hectares of managed woodland to meet its energy requirements – nearly half its total land area (Wrigley 1988, 54–5). In national terms this transition may have occurred as early as the seventeenth century, in the sense that this was the time when coal began to provide more thermal energy than organic fuels. But at a regional or local level the picture was much more diverse. Coal was a bulky commodity, valuable but expensive to transport, and its gradual adoption as the principal source of heat and energy throughout England would have been impossible without major improvements in transport infrastructure. From the late seventeenth century major roads in England began to be improved through the institution of 'turnpike trusts', bodies – created by acts of parliament – which would adopt sections of road, erect toll gates, charge tolls and use the proceeds (after a suitable cut had been taken as profit) to keep the route in adequate repair (Albert 1972; Langford 1989, 391–408). More important were the progressive improvements made to navigable rivers and, from the 1750s, the creation of a national canal network. Although canals were few and far between in Norfolk itself, their construction on the coalfields of the north made transport easier and coal cheaper. This said, the impact of 'navigations' within the county should not be underestimated. The Little Ouse was improved as far upriver as Thetford as a result of an act of 1669–70; improvements were made to the Nar in 1759, ensuring that it was navigable to West Acre (Davison 2005; Boyes and Russel 1977); and the Waveney was made navigable between Beccles and Bungay in the 1660s. In the 1770s the Aylsham Navigation extended navigation on the Bure for some 15 kilometres above Coltishall, as far as the town of Aylsham (Spooner 2012), while in the 1820s the construction of the North Walsham and Dilham Canal increased the navigable extent of the river Ant by some 14 kilometres. Coal was the main commodity transported on these waterways (Spooner 2012, 120–3), and it finally penetrated almost every corner of Norfolk, and of England, with the spread of the rail network in the middle decades of the nineteenth century, the first line into the county being constructed in the 1840s. As a consequence of these developments, the consumption of all traditional fuels – peat, gorse and heather as well as wood – seems to have declined, gradually but steadily, from the later eighteenth century (Warde and Williamson 2014, 77–8).

One indication of this decline is provided by the history of fuel allotments. As noted earlier (above, p. 80), in recognition of the way that the local poor had come to rely on gorse, peat and other material cut from commons for fuel, parliamentary enclosure commissioners often allotted an area of land which could be used to provide them with domestic firing – often low-lying peatland or gorse-covered heath. No fewer than 250 parishes in the county had such fuel allotments, some relatively small but others – as at Bridgham or Feltwell – extending over more than 100 hectares (Birtles 2003, 307–9). Yet, right from the start, many were not, in fact, directly exploited but instead rented out by the committees that controlled them, and the proceeds used to buy coal for the indigent; and the proportion so managed increased rapidly through the nineteenth century. No less than 55 per cent of allotment land was already being used in this way by 1833; by 1845 the figure had risen to 60 per cent; by 1883 it had reached 81 per cent; and by 1896, 92 per cent (Birtles 2003, 205). The cutting of traditional fuels on most surviving commons in the county also appears to have come to an end in the middle decades of the nineteenth century: extraction from Whitwell Low Common had thus ceased by the 1870s because 'the houses and fireplaces of the commoners are unusable for the burning of turf' (Birtles 2003, 206). The decline in the use of wood for domestic firing was much more gradual, but significant nevertheless. There was growing hostility, from the later eighteenth century, to pollarding, especially on the part of large landowners and their land agents; in addition, hedges seem to have been cut less systematically for fuelwood and, from the middle of the century, new hedges were generally planted solely with hawthorn, rather than with species more suitable for burning (Warde and Williamson 2014). Insofar as coppiced woods had been regarded as a source of fuel, their exploitation for this purpose likewise declined in the face of the increasing availability of coal, especially from the later nineteenth century. But of equal importance was the fact that, with the progress of industrialisation and continued improvements in transport systems, manufactured items, often made partly of cast iron, could be substituted for those previously constructed from the poles cut from coppices. In fact, the story is rather more complex than this, as we shall see, but overall the economic value of underwood tended to decline, gradually but steadily, in the period after the mid–late eighteenth century.

A second key development in this period, again of critical importance for the development of woodland, was the spread of enclosure. As we noted earlier, large areas of open field had existed in medieval Norfolk, alongside extensive tracts of heath and other common 'waste'. Much open arable was enclosed by informal, piecemeal methods in the course of the fifteenth, sixteenth and seventeenth centuries, but extensive areas remained, in the north and the west of the county especially. Piecemeal enclosure had, moreover, little impact on areas of common land, in which use rights were shared rather than properties intermingled, and large tracts thus survived into the nineteenth century throughout the county. New agricultural methods, rising food prices and the declining importance of heaths and other commons as sources of fuel ensured that they were then progressively enclosed, usually by parliamentary acts, and especially during and immediately after the Napoleonic Wars (Turner 2005; Wade Martins and Williamson 1999). Much land, formerly exploited and managed in common, was thus now privatised, and could either be turned over to agricultural use or exploited in new ways by its owners – one of which was as woodland.

Enclosure had other, more direct effects on particular types of existing woodland. As we have emphasised, although wood-pastures declined steadily through the sixteenth, seventeenth and eighteenth centuries, many still survived on commons at the end of the eighteenth century, if only in vestigial form. Parliamentary enclosure invariably led to the final destruction of such survivals. Many enclosure awards include references to trees growing on common land and contain claims submitted in anticipation of their destruction. The award for the enclosure of Pulham St Mary Magdalen, for example, describes how the Reverend Jeremy Day claimed for 'thirty-eight poplar trees growing on the waste contiguous to the lands of the said estate, and planted, reared and protected by a late proprietor thereof' (NRO PD510/19). The statement of claims for the mid-Norfolk parish of Shipdham similarly record that many of the claimants had the rights to a 'planting' of trees on the common: John Platfoot, for example, held three commonable messuages with rights to common pasture, to cut flags and furze for fuel, and to excavate clay for repairs, and also claimed 'the planting of trees standing upon the said common pasture, opposite and adjoining the said premises respectively' (NRO BR90/14/2, p. 4). Many people in the parish made similar claims: John Mendham thus requested compensation for four trees 'standing and being on the said common, in front of the said messuage'. This particular award is especially informative in that it makes it clear that the majority of trees were, as we would expect, pollards rather than standards. The earl of Leicester, lord of the manor, thus claimed in respect of five messuages the value of:

> All trees, and all bushes and thorns planted or set by him or his predecessors, or his or their tenants, upon the said commons and waste grounds, contiguous or near to any of his said messuages or farms, which have been usually lopped, topped, pruned, or cut by him or his predecessors, or his or their tenants. (NRO BR90/14/2, p.17)

Lucas Strudwick, lord of the three other manors in the parish, similarly claimed compensation for:

> All trees (not being timber trees), and all bushes and thorns planted or set by him or his predecessors upon the said commons and waste grounds contiguous or near any of his said messuages or cottages, which have been usually lopped, [etc.]

Most such trees were, to judge from the available evidence, felled soon after enclosure. Some commons, such as Fritton in the south of the county, escaped enclosure and here pollarding seems to have continued, albeit perhaps on a declining scale. But on the whole parliamentary enclosure saw the final destruction of the county's remaining common wood-pastures.

Among the principal beneficiaries of enclosure were the larger landowners, and in a wider sense the increasing concentration of land into larger and more continuous blocks of property was the third key development affecting the county's landscape in this period. Landed estates comprised extensive and continuous or near-continuous areas owned by particular individuals as absolute private property. At their heart lay a mansion and its grounds, usually accompanied by a 'home farm' which was retained 'in hand'; beyond lay farms which were leased to tenants, together with a scatter of woods, plantations and game coverts which were, like the home farm, usually retained under the owner's direct control (Clemenson 1982; Rawding 1992; Williamson 2007). By the nineteenth century aristocratic properties might extend over 5,000 acres (*c.*2,000 hectares) or more; Holkham covered, at its peak, no less than 43,000 acres (17,400 hectares) (Bateman 1873). The estates of the local gentry embraced a parish or two and ranged from perhaps 500 to 5,000 acres (200 to 2,000 hectares) (Clemenson 1982, 7–99). While often described as a 'relic of the feudal age', the landed estate was a specifically modern form, for its distinguishing feature was untrammelled power over extensive tracts of countryside. In the Middle Ages, in Norfolk as elsewhere, estates had seldom comprised continuous, unitary blocks and rights over land had been complex, for while customary tenants owed rents and services to a local lord, farms passed by inheritance within peasant families and customary land could often be bought and sold, the rents and obligations attached to it simply passing to the new proprietor. Only the demesne of the manorial lord was his absolute property in the modern sense, and even parts of this – as we have seen in the case of woodland – might be subject to some common rights.

The landed estate began to emerge in the course of the fifteenth and sixteenth centuries, alongside modern concepts of ownership – complex developments which cannot be discussed in detail here. In many districts, lords managed to convert customary tenancies into forms of tenure – particular types of 'copyhold' – which meant, in effect, that they were the freehold owners of the property in question, and their tenants were tenants in the modern sense. In Norfolk, however, customary tenancies usually developed into relatively secure forms of copyhold 'by inheritance', so that such land could usually be acquired only through purchase. Large landowners also systematically bought up any small freehold properties which came on the market in the neighbourhood, as well as any available lordships in the locality. In 1813 the agent of the Blickling estate typically described how various pieces of land had been purchased over the previous years 'some of which are so situated as to have been an eye sore from the Mansion house till Lord Suffield became possessed of them' (NRO MC3/592). As an earlier steward put it in 1773, 'If I hear of any uncultivated land or otherwise if adjoining part of your Lordship's Estate to dispose of I will apply after it and acquaint your Lordship of it immediately' (NRO NRS 14625). The growth of large properties was encouraged by the dissolution of the monasteries in 1539, and in the later seventeenth century by legal changes – the development of the entail and the strict settlement, which made the owner of a property in effect a tenant for life, tied by a legal agreement which prevented sales of land so that the estate passed undivided to his heir (Clemenson 1982, 15–18). It was also assisted by the simple fact that, following the Civil War and the Glorious Revolution of 1688, royal power was limited, political authority resided in a parliament of the propertied and estates were thus unlikely to be broken up because their owners had fallen from royal favour or supported the losing side in dynastic or religious struggles. Lastly, large landowners benefited from the enclosure of common land, receiving their own allotment in lieu of manorial rights but also often purchasing many of the diminutive parcels allotted to the smaller freeholders (Beckett 1986). The development of landed estates is central to any understanding of the history of woodland, firstly because most ancient woods, being traditionally part of the demesne land of a manor, came to form part of a landed estate; and secondly because the consolidation of ownership in the hands of large proprietors, together with the spread of enclosure, encouraged a marked upsurge in the planting of new woods and plantations.

The 'Great Replanting'

In Norfolk – as in many other parts of England – the area under tree cover appears to have increased significantly in the period after *c*.1660, with the greatest expansion coming, perhaps not surprisingly, in those districts in which there had previously been little woodland: that is, on the light soils in the north and the west of the county. William Faden's county map of 1797 does not distinguish systematically between ancient, semi-natural woods and more recent plantings, although the latter are sometimes indicated by nomenclature, with 22 examples named as 'plantations' and 'fir plantations' (totalling 177 hectares), four as 'fox coverts' (9.1 hectares), one as a 'nursery' (3 hectares) and three as 'clumps of firs' (41.2 hectares) (Macnair and Williamson 2010, 119–22). But, by using the *Ancient Woodland Inventory*, early estate maps and other sources, it is possible to suggest that around 7,000 hectares of the woodland existing in the county at this date had probably been planted since *c*.1660. This is approaching twice the area of woodland which we can be sure was of 'ancient' status, although much of the *c*.2,000 hectares of woodland on the map with uncertain origins was probably of 'ancient' character.

Most if not all of this new planting was carried out by large landed estates; Thomas Coke of Holkham, for example, planted around two million trees between 1782 and 1805 (Prince 1987). Landowners planted for profit, often using agriculturally marginal land which had, prior to enclosure, been exploited as common grazing. But their enthusiasm was also fired by the writings of men such as John Evelyn, whose 1664 book *Sylva, or a Discourse on Forest Trees* was followed by a rash of similar texts, including Stephen Switzer's *Ichnographica Rustica* (1718). Planting was a patriotic duty, for there was widespread concern that there was a general timber shortage which had implications for the nation's naval power, as writers such as Phillip Miller (1731), James Wheeler (1747), Edmund Wade (1755) and William Hanbury (1758) all warned. In a more general sense the planting of trees demonstrated confidence in the new political dispensation brought about by the restoration of the monarchy and the Glorious Revolution of 1688 (Daniels 1988). It likewise expressed confidence in the continuity of ownership on the part of local dynasties. But planting was also carried out to beautify estates, to demonstrate their extent and, above all, perhaps, to provide game cover.

In the course of the eighteenth and early nineteenth centuries progressive improvements in gun technology – culminating in the 1850s with the development of the breech-loading shotgun – made it easier to shoot game in the air, rather than on the ground. At the same time, enclosure and the consolidation of land into larger and more continuous properties allowed game to be more carefully preserved (Munsche 1981, 8–27). Shooting steadily became more competitive, with shoots involving larger numbers of participants, a process which culminated in the early nineteenth century with the emergence of the *battue*, in which large numbers of birds were driven towards the waiting guns: a practice pioneered, in particular, on the Holkham estate. This growing sophistication and scale of shooting led to the more systematic management and encouragement of game, and to an increasing focus on the pheasant as the principal quarry of sportsmen in lowland areas such as Norfolk. It occupied relatively small territories, could thus be raised in large numbers, and was easily scared into flight (Hopkins 1985, 68). But because it is a woodland bird, large areas of new woods needed to be planted to provide it with a congenial environment (Delabere Blaine 1838, 854; Hill and Robertson 1988, 38–45).

The upsurge in estate planting was associated with the rise of a new form of woodland, the plantation, planted only with timber trees and lacking any coppiced understorey. Deciduous species – particularly oak, sweet chestnut and beech – were mixed with a rather larger number of 'nurses', most of which were conifers. In the words of the agricultural writer Nathaniel Kent, plantations in Norfolk consisted of 'Great bodies of firs, intermixed with a lesser number of forest trees' (Kent 1796, 87). Because it was difficult to deal with the weeds which competed with the young trees, and also to some extent because significant losses were anticipated from drought and the depredations of rabbits and other animals, the trees were often planted more closely than would be usual today, often at a density of around two trees per square metre. They were then progressively thinned, and the fact that the extracted material is often referred to in estate accounts as 'poles' signifies, clearly enough, that it was used in a similar way to the produce of coppices (Williamson 1998b, 183–6). In a typical account, Nathaniel Kent described the great plantation belt around the park at Holkham as comprising 'four hundred and eighty acres of different kinds of plant, two thirds of which are meant to be thinned and cut down for *underwood*, so as to leave the oak, Spanish chestnut, and beech, only as timber' (Kent 1796, 90: our italics). In many cases, the final timber crop was itself only thinned, leaving the plantations to provide shelter and cover for game or to beautify the countryside. When first planted most plantations would have provided good game cover, but as the trees matured and were thinned underplanting was required, often using box, snowberry, Portugal laurel or rhododendron *ponticum* from south-west Asia, 'the crowning plant for game cover' (Forsyth 1946, 251).

Managing ancient woodland in the eighteenth and nineteenth centuries

It might be expected that the fashionable interest in the 'new forestry', coupled with the declining value of underwood, would have led to the neglect of traditional woodland. Indeed, it is noteworthy that Nathaniel Kent's book on the agriculture of Norfolk, published in 1796, devotes 319 lines to plantations (together with an appendix which discusses those composed of sweet chestnut) but just 19 to woodland in the traditional sense (Kent 1796). Many smaller areas of coppiced woodland – and some larger ones, such as Catfield Wood, in the east of the county – were indeed grubbed out altogether in the eighteenth and nineteenth centuries, and a number of larger ones were drastically reduced in size. Improvements in soil quality, through marling and, in particular, improved forms of land drainage, now made possible the cultivation of the poor sites they often occupied (Wade Martins and Williamson 1999, 61–7). Sporle Wood, Foxley Wood, Long Row in Hedenham and probably Gawdyhall Big Wood were all significantly reduced in area in the course of the seventeenth or eighteenth centuries; Beckett's Wood, Hales Wood, Middle Wood in Thorpe Abbots, Hethel Wood and East Wood in Denton very probably so; while almost the whole of the vast Pulham Big Wood was grubbed out. Reductions in area are, because of the greater availability of maps, easier to establish from the later eighteenth century. Hedenham lost around a third of its area, Horningtoft Great Wood more than two-thirds and Rawhall Wood over a quarter in the early part of the nineteenth century; while between *c.*1840 and 1880 Ashwellthorpe Wood, Banyards Wood in Bunwell, Billingford Wood, Horningtoft Great and Horningtoft Little Woods, Old Pollard Wood in Holt, North Elmham Great Wood and Shropham Grove were all significantly reduced in size. All in all, of the woods in the sample which appear to be genuinely 'ancient' in character (in the sense that they originated before 1600), around 60 per cent experienced significant reductions in area in the course of the post-medieval period.

It is easy to see this as a clear sign that the story of traditional woodland was coming to an end, and contemporary forestry writers advocated the conversion of coppiced woods to plantations, either through wholesale replanting or by 'singling' the underwood, where this included species capable of growing into standard trees. James Brown in 1861 thus argued that 'No proprietor of woods is called upon to grow any sort of wood-produce for his neighbours, and sell it to them at a cheap rate, while he can, by altering his system of wood management, sell his produce to a greater advantage at some other place, and in another form' (Brown 1861, 25). But closer inspection suggests a more complex picture. The numerous new areas of woodland established in the later eighteenth and nineteenth centuries were not all plantations: many new coppiced woods, as we shall see, were also planted. To an extent, woods were simply displaying the spatial dynamism we have noted in earlier centuries, but now the greater availability of both large and small-scale maps allows us to see this more clearly. Moreover, it is clear that existing areas of ancient woodland, far from being shunned and neglected by landowners, were now themselves the subject of new fads in forestry. One sign of this was the widespread installation of systems of surface drains within them.

Such drains typically take the form of ditches less than 0.4 metres in depth and between 1 and 2 metres in width, usually but not invariably without accompanying banks. The majority are straight, rather than irregular or serpentine; they often fit in well with the network of rides within a wood; and, when their stratigraphic relationship with other earthworks in woods can be examined, they always appear to be more recent. Such drains eventually feed into the wood's external ditch – frequently cutting through the external woodbank to do so – or, on occasions, into internal ponds. They may make use of earlier banks and ditches subdividing the wood, sometimes – as at Gawdyhall Big Wood or Hethel Wood – obscuring and confusing the true nature of these features. The precise layout, numbers and spacing of drains take a variety of forms. At Foxley Wood much of the ground surface is covered by a highly regular pattern of parallel drains running north-west to south-east, with smaller numbers ranged at right angles to these. At Shotesham, in contrast, and at Billingford there is a much looser pattern of straight drains, dividing the wood's area into wide, irregular squares and polygons. Horningtoft Great Wood is different again, having three dense meshes of parallel drains ranged at different angles. Sometimes, rather than having a dense and regular network, woods contain a sparser pattern, as at Hales Wood or Honeypot Wood. Elsewhere only limited sections of the wood were drained. Thus in Sporle Wood and Lopham Grove small areas are served with shallow gripes arranged in dense 'herringbone' pattern. Many other woods, such as Earsham, only have single drains, or small numbers, dealing with particularly damp areas. Most drainage ditches are ruler-straight but some, as in Gawdyhall Big Wood, are more meandering in character.

Rotherham and Ardron (2006, 237–8) have suggested that the drainage ditches found in south Yorkshire woods are of eighteenth- and nineteenth-century date, and it is likely that most Norfolk examples post-date 1800: the earliest possible indication of the presence of drains, from Foxley Wood, dates to 1815 (see Appendix entry). There are few if any references to drainage in the eighteenth-century literature on forestry, but the topic is often discussed in mid- and late nineteenth-century texts. Brown in 1861 thought that the systematic drainage of woods and plantations had begun only 'from about the year 1830' (Brown 1861, 5). It might be thought that drainage was principally intended to make it easier to work in woods during the wet winter months, for it seems doubtful that it would, to any significant extent, improve the growth of either timber trees or underwood. Contemporary forestry writers, however, were clearly under the impression that it would improve productivity, Brown urging in 1861, for example, that 'a properly executed system of drainage will result in heavier and more profitable tree-crops being yielded' (Brown 1861, 531). Curtis described how drainage:

> Gives a depth of soil capable of storing plant food. It allows, as the water percolates, the free circulation of air, which assists the oxidation of the ingredients in the soil. It increases the capacity for the storage of heat, by enabling land to absorb the sun's rays, thereby enabling the soil to maintain tree life and vigour well into the winter … . (Curtis 1890, 18)

In reality, it is likely that such writers, and the managers and owners of woods and plantations, were mainly influenced by the rage for the underdrainage of arable land which had begun in the eighteenth century and continued into the nineteenth. This involved cutting drains beneath the surface of the soil which removed water first downwards, beyond the root zone, and then laterally, away from the field. It was first carried out employing bush drains (filled with poles cut from pollards or coppices) and latterly using various forms of tile pipe (Williamson 2002, 85–91; Harvey 1980, 72–3; Phillips 1999). Having witnessed the very real benefits that this improvement brought to cereal crops it is perhaps understandable that people expected similar advantages to accrue in woodland. As James put it in 1861, 'Where they have been properly applied to agricultural land, drainage and soil preparation have been the means of improving its productive capacity to an extent which formerly could perhaps hardly have been credited' (Brown 1861, 532).

There were, however, significant differences between the drains laid in these different contexts. In woodland, whether long-existing or newly planted, open drains were used rather than ones buried 0.6–1.0 metres beneath the surface, as was usual on arable land. Brown described in 1861 how

> drains made on arable fields are properly covered up and hidden, both in order to keep the material of which they are made from accident, and to secure all the breadth of land possible for farm cropping; while those made on woodlands are with equal propriety left open, as they would, generally speaking, be gradually rendered inoperative by the descent of the roots of the trees into them in search for nutrients. (Brown 1861, 135)

There were also important differences in spacing. Arthur Young described how field drains in Norfolk were normally laid at intervals of around 12 yards, a distance also mentioned in, for example, the farming diary kept by Randall Burroughes of Wymondham in the 1780s and 1790s (Wade Martins and Williamson 1995, 27; Young 1804, 389–93). The open drains in woodland, in contrast, were in general much more widely spaced, even where they formed a regular mesh or grid covering the whole surface of the wood. In Foxley Wood, for example, they were ranged at intervals of around 100 metres, although in places additional shallow drains were added to the network, probably at a later date; in Shotesham Wood the looser, more irregular grid was for the most part similarly spaced; while the drains in Horningtoft Great Wood were ranged at intervals of around 18 metres: all considerably greater than the maximum spacing of 50 feet – 15 metres – recommended by Brown in 1861. Only the small network of parallel drains occupying part of Sporle Wood is spaced – at just over 11 metres – within the range he recommended, and roughly replicating that usual with field drains.

The fact that the drains were usually dug ruler-straight – no easy task in a wood containing numerous coppice stools and sporadic timber trees with extensive root systems – betrays the hand of faddish, 'scientific' improvement. Yet, while it would thus appear to be true that woodland drainage was, in Rotherham and Aadron's words, 'part of an obsession with land improvement by drainage' (Rotherham and Ardron 2006, 237), it is evident that drainage systems were not installed in Norfolk woods regardless of soil conditions. Of the three woods surveyed which were entirely covered by patterns of surface drains – Foxley, Shotesham and Horningtoft – all lie entirely on particularly poorly draining soils of the Beccles Association, as do three others with extensive, but less dense or regular, systems of drainage – Gawdyhall Big Wood, Rawhall and Hethel. Other woods, containing only a few drains or in which the drains are restricted to certain parts of the wood, are likewise (as with Honeypot Wood or Lopham Grove) mainly on Beccles Association soils, although there are exceptions, such as Sporle, which is mapped by the Soil Survey as entirely overlying Burlingham Association soils, although in most cases the drains are clearly associated with patches of particularly damp ground coinciding with soils of the Beccles Series.

The installation of drains certainly suggests a continuing interest on the part of landowners in traditionally managed woodland. Yet it is noteworthy that the tithe files – surveys of parish agriculture and land use drawn up in the late 1830s prior to the commutation of tithes – often refer to the poor quality of the coppice in Norfolk woods. At North Creake, Gunthorpe, Hanworth, Irstead and Swanton Novers it was described as 'inferior' or 'very inferior', while at Buckenham it was said to be 'but of little value'

(TNA: IR 18/5867; IR 18/5959; IR 18/5966; IR 18/6037; IR 18/6303; IR 18/5816). No less than 52 per cent of comments on the quality of coppice in Norfolk describe it as 'poor', compared with 30 per cent that refer to it as 'good' and 18 per cent that make no judgement either way. Particularly interesting are the few comments explaining *why* the coppice was poor. At Congham it was said to be 'much injured by the timber'; at Hedenham there were 'many old timbers in parts of the woods which reduce the value of the underwood'; while at Fulmodeston the coppice would have been 'much better if timber was thinner' (TNA: IR 18/5861; IR 18/5981; IR 18/5937). In some places it would thus appear that landowners were increasing the density of timber to the detriment of the coppice, presumably because the price of timber held up better than that of underwood but also, perhaps, because of the increasing value of oak bark resulting from the sharp growth of the leather industry from the late eighteenth century (Rackham 1986a, 92). An increase in the density of timber trees would in turn help explain the growth in the average length of coppice rotations in the post-medieval period which has been suggested by some historians, although, as we have seen, the evidence for this, in Norfolk at least, is not entirely clear-cut. Indeed, eighteenth- and nineteenth-century sources suggest a wide range of rotations, presumably related, as in earlier periods, to the composition of the underwood and the purpose for which it was cut. The tithe files, for example, record rotations of 7 years (Horningtoft), 8 years (Woodton), 8 to 10 years (Hedenham and Hockering), 10 years (Denton, Elmham, Gawdyhall Big Wood in Redenhall and Foxley) but only one – 14 years, at Necton – longer than this (TNA IR 18/6019; IR 18/6416; IR 18/5981; IR 18/6005; IR 18/5878; IR 18/5905; IR 18/6188; IR 18/5928).[7] Leases show a similar range. An indenture from 1740 concerning Hockering implies a rotation length of 14 years (NRO BER 336 291/7), a figure apparently confirmed by a map of 1805 (NRO 21428 Box F) and a lease agreement for 1828 (NRO BER 336); an agreement for Sporle Wood, drawn up in 1745, implies 9 years (NRO 20888); another, for Ashwellthorpe in the early eighteenth century, implies 10 years (NRO KNY 571, 372X3); one concerning Attleborough Wood, from 1801, stipulates 10 years (NRO MEA 7/4); while a lease of 1835 for Honeypot Wood in Wendling specifies a 7-year cycle (NRO EVL 650/6).

The density of timber may well have increased in many Norfolk woods, to the detriment of the understorey, but the available sources indicate, in general, a continued interest in coppicing. In many districts of southern England, as Ted Collins has argued, coppicing remained an important economic activity right through until the end of the nineteenth century (Collins 1989): the economic advantages of coppices at this late date was described in articles in the *Journal of the Royal Agricultural Society of England* (Tallant 1880) and around 19 per cent of English woods were still being actively managed by coppicing as late as 1949 (Forestry Commission 1949, 45).

Whatever the situation in earlier centuries, by the eighteenth and nineteenth centuries underwood seems, in Norfolk at least, to have been valued primarily for its specialised uses, especially as raw material for making hurdles, rather than as a source of fuel. In 1730 Edmund Rolfe, the lessee of a large estate in Sedgeford,

---

7   The figure of ten years for Foxley is confirmed by the evidence of a plan of 1815, showing the dates at which the various 'fells' were to be cut (NRO NRS 4087 (123)).

asked his landlord for permission to plant 40 acres of the worst land on the estate with underwood of sallow, hazel and willow, arguing that such wood was 'being continually wanted by the occupiers of the said estate for hurdles for sheep of which there are great flocks' (NRO DCN 59/30/12). A little later Thomas Hale, who probably came from Norfolk, listed the benefits that coppice brought to the farmer in terms of building repairs and 'implements' above those which were bestowed on 'his Chimney' (Hale 1756, 137). In 1796 Kent described how the underwood from coppiced woods was used for sheep hurdles, thatching, hoops and general repairs (Kent 1796, 86), while in 1851 the agent for the Merton estate, Henry Wood, described how larger poles cut from Wayland Wood were used to make hurdles, fencing or bins for storing hay or straw on the home farm, how other material was cut as splints about six feet long for building repairs, and how the smaller material went for thatching broaches and sways and for pea sticks for gardens. Only the residue appears to have been destined for fuel, the smaller brush faggots being sold to bakers and cottagers for 'oven wood' and off-cuts of all products being sold for cottage firing (NRO WLS XVIII/7/1). It may be significant that the few references made in the tithe files to the uses of coppiced wood fail to make any mention of firewood. At Denton the woods were 'cut into hurdles'; at Wreningham the wood was 'most of it hazel and is used for making hurdles'; at Hales it was 'fit for hurdles and roofing'; at Hedenham it was used 'principally for hurdles and thatching stuff'; at Hockering it was 'used for sheep hurdles and thatching and daubing materials'; and at Horningtoft the coppice was described as 'excellent hurdle wood' (TNA IR 18/6019). There were also new uses for coppice poles, for the bush drains now being installed in vast numbers in the arable fields were filled not only with hedge cuttings and poles cut from pollards but also with those cut from coppices in woods. Randall Burroughes of Wymondham, for example, described in the January and February of 1796 how his men were sent 'to a wood at Ashwellthorpe for faggots for underdraining' (the same wood also provided hurdles, however, as Burroughes notes in January 1796 and February 1799) (Wade Martins and Williamson 1995, 75–6, 119). Even where estate accounts refer specifically to the production of 'faggots' we should not necessarily assume that these were destined for burning: account books for the Earsham estate in south Norfolk in the 1830s refer to payments for 'cutting 1,140 faggots for fencing' (NRO WCK 5/260). It is possible that a further decline in the importance of underwood as a fuel source, yet its continued importance for other purposes, may have led to some shift in the character of the underwood towards species best suited for specific uses, such as hurdle making. The tithe files, for instance, describe how there were 35 acres of coppice wood in Buckenham, 'part of which has been newly planted with hazel' (IR 29/5816).

New uses for old woods

One good reason why coppices continued to be cut right through the nineteenth century and into the twentieth was that they provided good game cover, something that has not, perhaps, been sufficiently acknowledged in earlier research. Whereas plantations, as they thinned and matured, needed to be underplanted with rhododendron or other shrubs, the larger coppice woods, cut on rotation, always had significant parts that were suitable for roosting birds. As Miche put it in 1888, 'the principal reason for maintaining old woods near the mansion' was that there was 'never at any one time … so much wood cut down as to cause serious blanks or openings' (Miche 1888, 105). Lord Walsingham and Ralph Payne-Gallwey, describing at the end of the century how Wayland Wood was beaten, commented that 'in about four years after felling, the condition of the undergrowth will be most suitable for this purpose ... In some portions of a large wood, the undergrowth will be from five to ten years old, and much of this will be difficult to beat through and more difficult to shoot in where paths or rides are cut' (Walsingham and Payne-Gallwey 1893, 220). The cover provided by regularly managed ancient woods meant that there was often little need to plant the kinds of ground cover, such as rhododendron, that were widely established in plantations as they matured. Limited areas might be so treated – the concentration of this plant on the moat within Hockering Wood, for example, may indicate its use as a release area. This said, there is some evidence that conifers were established on occasions within ancient woods to provide additional cover. Indeed, around a quarter of the examples shown on the first edition Ordnance Survey six-inch maps of the 1880s and 1890s contain either widely scattered conifer symbols or small areas of more systematic replanting. While these trees may represent additions made to established woods for commercial or aesthetic reasons, which were always intended to grow into timber trees, it is probable that many were initially planted primarily as cover. Many, perhaps, were always intended to serve both purposes, the one when young, the other when mature. Sales particulars from the early twentieth century often suggest that ancient woods contained a significant coniferous element. Hockering in 1923, for example, contained – in addition to oak standards and a mixed coppiced understorey – quantities of larch, Scots pine and Douglas fir. Yet it is noteworthy how ephemeral these alien intrusions often appear to have been. Many woods shown with scattered conifers on the first edition Ordnance Survey maps from the 1880s and 1890s are depicted as entirely deciduous on twentieth-century revisions, and while this may represent differences in the quality of cartography, many woods now entirely composed of deciduous species – such as Tindall Wood in Ditchingham – appear to have had a significant coniferous element in the 1880s.

The networks of rides which had appeared in most woods of any size by the end of the nineteenth century, although in part intended to facilitate forestry operations, were mainly intended to provide opportunities for the sportsman, especially the wide examples cut through the centres of woods such as Hedenham or Brooke (Buxton 1902, 181). It is in fact difficult to know when they first originated. Seventeenth- and early eighteenth-century maps, where they exist, generally fail to show them: the only exception to this is an early eighteenth-century map of Hethel Wood, but here the rides appear to have been part of an aesthetic scheme, a large formal landscape centred on the hall. So far as the evidence goes, woodland rides seem to have developed from the second half of the eighteenth century, but mainly during the nineteenth, and an association with shooting seems clear. Once established, their number often increased over time, as, for example, at Hockering, where the tithe map of 1838 (DN/TA 63) shows less than a third the length depicted on the Ordnance Survey six-inch maps from the 1880s (although here, as always, the schematic nature of the tithe maps when compared with the Ordnance Survey maps should be borne in mind).

The growing importance of woods as game coverts probably explains why they were increasingly retained 'in hand' as the eighteenth century progressed (Marshall 1818, 315–24). The number of lease agreements of the kind discussed in the previous chapter declines markedly in the period after *c.*1760. Where woods were leased to contractors there was obvious potential for a clash of interests: forestry operations and game preservation can easily come into conflict. In 1813 a petition was thus presented in Chancery concerning work undertaken at Helhoughton, the plaintiff arguing that 'William Withers ... caused the whole of the underwood which was growing ... to be cut ... which was very predjudicial to the game' (NRO BUL 11/436).

In addition to being used as game reserves, ancient woods were – like existing farmland trees (Rackham 2004) – often incorporated into the designed landscapes laid out around great houses. How they were treated varied over time, with changing fashions in landscape design. Until the early or even middle decades of the eighteenth century parks and gardens were generally laid out in a formal, geometric manner and avenues focused on the mansion frequently ran out across the surrounding landscape. Gardens often featured areas of ornamental shrubbery/woodland called 'wildernesses', dissected by paths which were initially straight and hedged, later more curvilinear and open (Jacques and Van der Horst 1988, 154–68; Langley 1728, 199– 203; Taigel and Williamson 1991, 11). Ancient woods lying close to major residences might be treated in a similar manner, the underwood providing a solid mass of vegetation which could frame the paths, as, for example, at St Paul's Waldenbury in Hertfordshire (Pevsner and Cherry 1977, 330), but the only certain example of anything like this from Norfolk is Hethel Wood. This is first depicted on an undated early eighteenth-century map which shows the hall, flanked by formal gardens, set within a diminutive deer park, with the wood immediately to the south-west (NRO uncatalogued) (Figure 27: the map is orientated with north at the bottom, so the wood

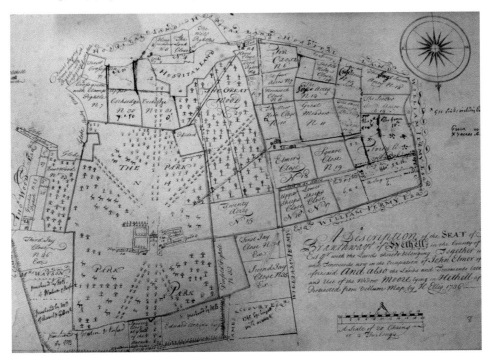

Figure 27 Hethel Park, as depicted on an undated eighteenth-century map: Hethel Wood, on the western edge of the deer park, is dissected by a complex pattern of rides, several focused on the site of the hall and evidently, at least in part, of an aesthetic character.

is shown top centre). A complex pattern of geometric rides was laid out within it, their aesthetic character indicated by the fact that some were aligned on the site of the hall (since demolished). Some can still be traced in archaeological form (see Appendix entry) and the pattern is still shown, with almost no changes (other than the removal of the north-eastern portion of the wood itself) on the Ordnance Survey six-inch maps as late as the 1950s. Elsewhere, woods lying at some distance from a great house might be cut by a single avenue or used to frame a geometric vista towards and away from it. At Raynham, in the west of the county, an avenue that extended for more than two kilometres north-east from the hall cut through the pre-existing Model Wood; at Haveringland maps of 1738 and 1777 show that Great Wood was cut by an avenue focused on the east facade of the hall (NRO MF/RO 97/3; NRO NRS 21403A); while at Blickling Corbridge's map of 1729 shows four avenues extending west, from a small deer park around the mansion, for some 1.5 kilometres across the fields to Great Wood, through which they were continued as open rides (Blickling Hall archives).

From the middle decades of the eighteenth century more informal, 'naturalistic' forms of design became fashionable, following the lead set by Lancelot 'Capability' Brown and his 'imitators' (Jacques 1983; Stroud 1965; Turner 1985). Formal features were removed and mansions were set within open landscapes of grass and scattered timber, often ornamented with clumps of trees and enclosed, in whole or part, by perimeter belts. Where ancient woods lay at a convenient distance from a mansion they might be used as part of the perimeter belt, the disposition of woodland in the landscape thus helping to determine the extent of the park. At Hethel the avenues were removed from the deer park in the later eighteenth century and Hethel Wood became, in effect, part of the belt; at Haveringland the formal landscape was transformed into a naturalistic park, with the Great Wood as its eastern boundary (NRO MS 7723 19B Haveringland Box A); part of Langley Wood was incorporated into the belt of Langley Park (NRO DS 157); while Pond Wood and Hammonds Wood were used to define the northern and western boundaries respectively of Barningham Park (NRO RQG 127, 488X5; Taigel and Williamson 1991, 47–50). The history of Blickling Park in the early eighteenth century was in part determined by a desire on the part of the earls of Buckinghamshire to extend the parkland westwards in stages from the small sixteenth-century core around the mansion as far as Great Wood: this finally became the north-western boundary of the park, part of an extensive perimeter belt, in the 1750s (NRO MC3 252). Other examples of ancient woods which came to form the boundaries of eighteenth- or early nineteenth-century parkland landscapes include the Grove, to the south of Morningthorpe Manor, and Tolshill Wood, which became the north-western boundary of Rackheath Park. Perhaps the most interesting example, however, is Gawdy Hall. The house and its surroundings are first shown on an estate map of 1734: the hall was then flanked by enclosed courts, some presumably containing gardens, and an avenue ran across the fields to the east, but there was as yet no park here, although the substantial and ancient Gawdyhall Big Wood lay to the south (NRO 4568 Cab III). By 1789, when a second map was surveyed, a park of 58 hectares had been laid out around the hall and new areas of woodland planted to the north and west (see Appendix entry), while to the south the park was bounded by the great mass of Big Wood (NRO 4567 Cab II). The main drive to the hall ran from an entrance on the road to the south, taking a slightly winding course through the middle of the wood. It is noticeable today that the standard oak trees lying close to the drive have much larger girths than those found elsewhere in the wood: evidently, they were regarded in primarily aesthetic rather than economic terms.

The way that the drive at Gawdy was deliberately laid out through the middle of an ancient wood may reflect the growing enthusiasm for the 'picturesque' among the landowning class from the later eighteenth century. This was apparent in other ways, most notably in a growing interest in and reverence for ancient trees – something which may always have existed, at all levels of society, but which now took particular forms. One manifestation was the book by James Grigor, published in 1841, entitled *The Eastern Arboretum, or Register of Remarkable Trees … in the County of Norfolk* (Grigor 1841). In this Grigor, a nurseryman by profession, recorded a large number of trees of particular rarity, beauty, size – or antiquity – in the county. These included such veterans as the great Winfarthing oak, a tree renowned well beyond Norfolk's borders (it is mentioned both in Loudon's *Arboretum Britannicum* of 1838 and in Samuel Taylor's *Arboretum et Fruticetem Britannicum* of 1836 (Grigor 1841, 354; Amyot 1874)). It was a massive, picturesquely decaying specimen that had originally grown within the medieval park of Winfarthing, and possibly in the unenclosed wastes from which this had been cut in the twelfth or thirteenth centuries. Many of the ancient trees that Grigor describes, such as Kett's Oak in Ryston (Grigor 1841, 348), had been incorporated within landscape parks, having grown in earlier pastures and hedgerows, and even today around half of the very largest oak trees in the county, with girths in excess of six metres, are to be found within the county's parks and gardens (Barnes and Williamson 2011, 131–7). In the present context, of particular note is the way that fragments of wood-pasture heaths, otherwise rapidly being swept away through the eighteenth and early nineteenth centuries as marginal land was brought into cultivation or otherwise 'improved', sometimes survived on the margins of eighteenth-century parkland. The great concentrations of pollards at Bayfield, for example, are to be found on the rising ground to the east and west of Bayfield Park and, by the nineteenth century, were accessed by drives leading from the hall; and the Felbrigg beeches – if, indeed, they represent fragments of ancient wood-pastures – must owe their survival to the fact that they lay on the northern edge of Felbrigg Park. One of the most interesting examples of the reuse of ancient woodland in landscape designs comes from Holt, in the north of the county. A new hall was built here in 1860 by one Walter Hamilton Pemberton, a few hundred metres to the east of an earlier manor house (Pevsner and Wilson 2002, 556). The tithe award map of 1839 shows that the entire area now occupied by the park was then woodland, out of which the grounds of the new hall were effectively sculpted (NRO DN/TA 494). They remained densely planted, with only limited areas of open grassland that were separated from the still-wooded parts of the site by low banks not dissimilar to early post-medieval woodbanks (see Appendix entry).

New uses were thus being found for ancient woods in the estate landscapes of the eighteenth and nineteenth centuries, uses which might encourage the continued management of ancient woods on traditional lines, even as the economic value of underwood gradually declined. Regular cutting of coppices was essential where woods were being used as game cover, or to provide a massed and solid block of planting to frame or terminate a view in a designed landscape.

'Pseudo-ancient woodland'

Given the abundant evidence for the extensive planting of new woods in the course of the eighteenth and nineteenth centuries, and for the continuing importance of management by coppice-with-standards, it is perhaps unsurprising that a significant number of woods included in the *Ancient Woodland Inventory* for Norfolk turn out, on closer inspection, to have been established long after the official cut-off date for 'ancientness' of 1600. As already noted, the *Inventory* was trialled in this county (in the 1970s, by the then Nature Conservancy Council) and, because its main aim was to quickly establish the extent and quality of ancient woodland remaining at a time when much had recently been grubbed out for agriculture or damaged by replanting with conifers, was initially compiled employing a 'desk top' methodology (Spencer and Kirby 1992, 79). Using the evidence of Ordnance Survey maps, principally the first edition one-inch:one mile published in the 1840s and the six-inch first edition of *c.*1877–92, woods of potentially 'ancient' status were identified according to a range of criteria, including name, position within the landscape and shape (Goodfellow and Peterken 1981, 179; Spencer and Kirby 1992, 80). Suffixes such as 'wood', 'holt' and 'grove' were considered indicative of antiquity, while ones such as 'covert' and 'plantation', for obvious reasons, were not. An irregular shape and location beside a parish boundary suggested antiquity, a geometric form and position (say) close to a country house did not. Such a system of rapid identification avoided detailed cartographic or documentary investigations. In Goodfellow and Peterken's words:

> Ancient woods can be identified by detailed historical research. However, the effort required is considerable and a substitute was therefore needed which yielded reasonably reliable results at a fraction of the cost. (Goodfellow and Peterken 1981, 178)

This initial stage was nevertheless regarded as 'preliminary', the authors of the *Inventory* emphasising that field survey on the ground provided 'the most valuable evidence in determining a woodland's origin' (Nature Conservancy Council 1981, 10; Goldberg *et al.* 2011). But pressure on resources has ensured that such supplementary surveys were not always carried out in detail, or at all. An estimated 32 per cent of records in the *Inventory* were thus based on the interpretation of map evidence alone (Spencer and Kirby 1992, 81), and it is therefore not surprising that at an early stage of the work undertaken for this volume it became apparent that a number of the woods examined, while included in the *Inventory*, did not in fact fulfil the basic criteria for inclusion for the simple reason that they had come into existence in the period after *c.*1600.

The Gawdy Hall estate in south Norfolk, for example, includes three small *Inventory* woods – New Grove, Blake's Grove and Ladies' Grove – that lie scattered around the margins of Gawdy Park (TM 247854), in addition to the magnificent and extensive Gawdyhall Big Wood, an unquestionably 'ancient' SSSI, on its southern edge. All are shown on an estate map of 1783 (NRO MS 4567 Cab II), but not on an earlier one of 1734 (NRO MS 4568) (see Appendix, Blake's Grove). In the nearby parish of Earsham three neighbouring areas of woodland, all of which are included in the *Inventory*, were examined: Great Wood, Holy or Holey Grove and America Wood. Great Wood is shown on an estate map of *c.*1720, although it was then rather smaller than it is today (NRO MEA 3/362). It had been extended to the west, to the present

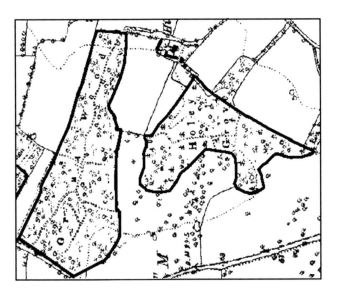

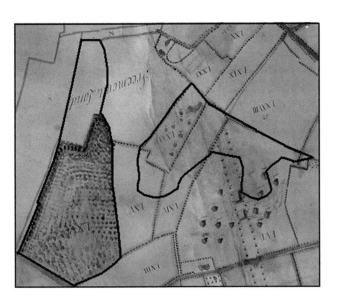

Figure 28 Great Wood (to the north) and Holy or Holey Grove (to the south), Earsham. Left: as depicted on an estate map of c.1720. Right: as shown on the first edition Ordnance Survey map at a scale of six inches: one mile, with the *Ancient Woodland Inventory* area superimposed.

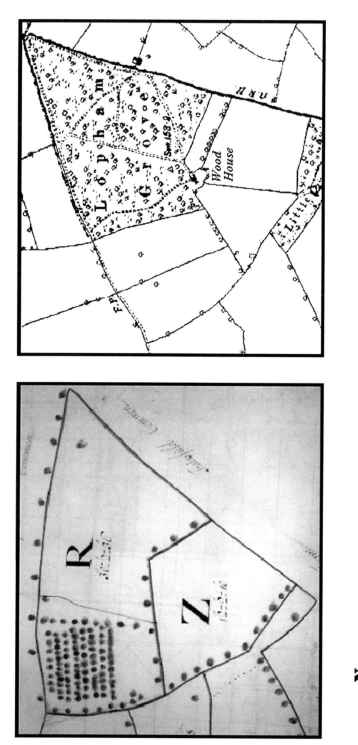

Figure 29 Lopham Grove, North Lopham, Norfolk. Although the entire area of the wood is included in the *Ancient Woodland Inventory* (right, as shown on the first edition Ordnance Survey six inches: one mile map), a map of 1725 (left) shows that it did not then exist.

Inventory boundaries, by the time the next surviving estate map was surveyed in c.1770 (NRO MEA 3/631). Holy Grove, to the south, in contrast, did not exist at all in c.1720, although its northern section included what appears to have been a pasture field scattered with free-standing trees (Figure 28). This area had been planted up as a wood by c.1770, but the majority of the *Inventory* area became wooded only in the course of the nineteenth century. The third of the woods, America Wood, lay outside the Earsham estate in 1720 and is thus absent from the map of that date, but the *Inventory* area appears to have been almost entirely agricultural land as late as 1839 (see Appendix entry).

One of the most striking examples is Lopham Grove, in the south of the county. This is depicted, much as it is today, on the first edition Ordnance Survey six-inch map of 1884 and on the South Lopham tithe award map of 1840 (DN/TA 928), pressed up against the parish boundary between North Lopham and Fersfield, a typical location for an ancient wood. Both maps show a small farm – Wood Farm – on the southern edge of the wood, and the layout of the surrounding field boundaries hints that this may represent a holding carved out of an originally larger wood at some point in the post-medieval period. Field survey revealed (as explained in more detail below) that the wood comprises coppice of hazel, ash, maple and hornbeam, with standards of oak. Its north-western and eastern sides are defined by a fairly diffuse but substantial bank c.4.5 metres wide and 0.5–0.75 metres high; the southern margin has a much sharper, more distinct bank of post-medieval appearance, 3 metres wide and c.0.7 metres high, but nevertheless with a substantial hornbeam pollard growing upon it. The eastern edge is marked only by a ditch. On first examination, this appears to be a 'genuine' ancient wood, the differences in the character of its boundaries perhaps confirming the hypothesis of gradual contraction in the course of the post-medieval period. In reality, the 'woodbank' is an earthwork raised to mark the parish boundary between Lopham and Fersfield, with which this side of the wood coincides, and a map of 1720 shows the entire site as completely unwooded and described as 'Ole Elmere' (Arundel Castle Archives 5H3 18), although it had earlier formed part of Lopham deer park and appears to have been at least partly wooded on a map of 1612 (Arundel archives P5/1) (Figure 29).

A more straightforward example of an 'erroneous' inclusion is what the *Inventory* refers to as Dodd's Wood, but which the Ordnance Survey six-inch map of 1884 describes as two conjoined woods, Oliver's Wood and Dodd's Wood. These, again, lie in the south of the county, on boulder clay soils in the parish of Rushall (TM 205818). No wood appears here on Faden's county map of 1797, but both woods are depicted on Bryant's county map of 1826. Their total area is small (around four hectares in all) and they could easily have been missed from Faden's map, which is, anyway, as we have already emphasised, not entirely reliable in its depiction of woods. But ground inspection reveals that the woods sit neatly within the surrounding field pattern, and the low banks which surround them – and which carry in places the remnants of hedges – are simply continuations of adjacent field boundaries. Evidently, in this case absence from Faden's map *is* to be taken at face value: the two woods represent fields which were planted up as coppice in the later eighteenth or early nineteenth centuries. The conjoined woods named Old Grove and Primrose Grove in Gillingham are likewise of relatively recent origin (TM 412940). Both sites were completely unwooded at the time of the tithe award map, with only a narrow

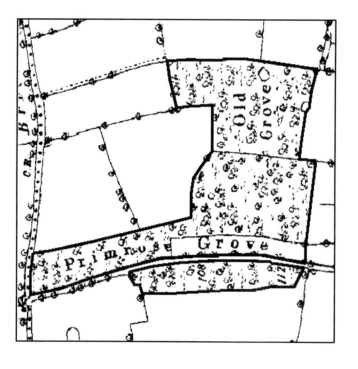

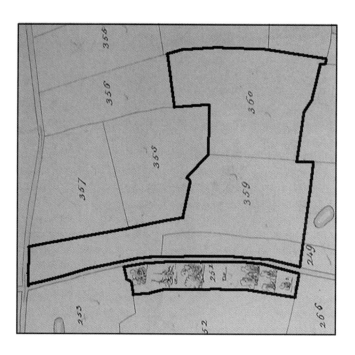

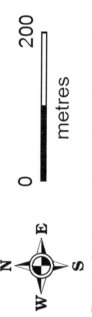

Figure 30 Old Grove and Primrose Grove, Gillingham, Norfolk. Left: as depicted on the tithe award map of 1840. Right: the woods as shown on the first edition Ordnance Survey six inches: one mile map, with the *Ancient Woodland Inventory* area superimposed.

sliver of the *Inventory* area, actually lying outside the named woods and separated from them by a public road, being shown as wooded (Figure 30). This area, moreover, has a shape and location within the field pattern which strongly suggests that it had been planted on land enclosed piecemeal from open fields, presumably in the early post-medieval period (NRO BR 276/1/248). Lastly, map evidence shows that Ringer's Grove in Shotesham was planted after 1650.

Of the 48 *Inventory* woods examined in the sample, no fewer than nine – nearly a fifth – thus appear to post-date, in their entirety, the official cut-off date of *c*.1600. In order to ascertain whether this figure provides a reliable impression of the extent to which such recent woods have been included in the *Inventory* as a whole a brief examination was undertaken into the cartographic evidence relating to *all* the *Inventory* woods in the county. This revealed that a significant proportion were, indeed, first established in the eighteenth or nineteenth century. One example, Brickiln Farm Wood near Billingford in south Norfolk (TM 171806), did not exist even as late as *c*.1890, when the first edition Ordnance Survey six-inch map was surveyed: it is likewise conspicuous by its absence from the tithe map of 1837 (NRO DN/TA 15). A number of others, while depicted on the Ordnance Survey six-inch maps of the 1880s or 1890s, are nevertheless absent from the tithe award maps (surveyed *c*.1840) and were clearly planted in the middle or later nineteenth century: examples include Hagg's Wood, in Salhouse (TG 299149; NRO DN/TA 716), and Common Hill Wood, to the south-west of Holt (NRO DN/TA 494). The *Inventory* area of Privet Wood in Woodton, on the south Norfolk boulder clays, comprises what earlier maps treat as two separate, conjoined woods. One, a narrow strip running north-west from the main body of the wood, is called 'Hermitage Plantation' on the first edition Ordnance Survey six-inch map, and formed the north belt of what had been the landscape park laid out around Woodton Hall. The hall itself had been demolished by the time the Ordnance Survey map was made, and its site is marked within the main body of Privet Wood. The tithe award map, however, shows the hall still standing, and most of the area now occupied by Privet Wood then comprised gardens and pleasure grounds. Only the eastern strip is shown as wooded, and this clearly formed a continuation of Hermitage Plantation, functioning as a perimeter belt to the park and – in part – as a screen to the kitchen garden.It is thus very unlikely to pre-date the eighteenth century. The same is true, to judge from its name, of Mileplain Plantation in Attlebridge (TF 144168).

Most Norfolk parishes have a tithe award map, surveyed in the years around 1840, and such maps – because they record basic land use – are particularly useful in charting the presence, or absence, of particular *Inventory* woods. The existence of particular woods can also be established across most of the county during the immediately preceding decades, but with less confidence, by examining the draft two-inch Ordnance Survey drawings, held at the British Library, which in Norfolk were surveyed at various times between 1813 and 1836. These show, for example, that Frizzleton Wood, north of Houghton Park in west Norfolk (TF 801307) had not yet been planted (BL OSD 246); nor Catlane Wood near Heacham (TF 704388; BL OSD 246); nor Sheringham Wood on the north coast (TG 138416; BL OSD 243). In all these cases, the failure of the woods to appear on the drawings serves to confirm their absence from William Faden's county map of 1797. Faden can, however, provide some useful information. Great Wood in Buxton, on the acid sands north of Norwich (TG 174226), is thus shown as an island of wooded ground in the middle of an extensive tract of warren and heath and is helpfully labelled 'Fir Plantation', strongly suggesting a recent origin. The large Hare Wood in Docking, in the north-west of the county (TF 777358), is likewise labelled 'Plantation', while Bulmer Coppice, on the edge of Rackheath Park to the north-east of Norwich (TG 27411), is shown as part of Mousehold Heath, and was evidently planted up only following enclosure in 1810.

There are no large-scale surveys of the county accurate enough to be used to establish the existence of woodland on particular sites earlier than Faden's county map of 1797, and only a small minority of the parishes in the county have smaller-scale surveys dating to the period before 1800. Many of these, moreover, depict only relatively small areas, usually the estates of particular individuals. Where such evidence is available, however, it reveals further erroneous inclusions in the *Inventory*. Birch Wood in Merton, on the edge of Breckland (TL 917976), had thus not yet been planted in the 1730s, when its area formed part of Merton Common, and even in 1788 a map suggests that it was still a field (WLS XVII/9, 410X6; NRO Mf/Ro 90/2). Neither Popes Wood nor D'Oyly's Grove in the south Norfolk parish of Hempnall (TM 229954 and 228954) appear on Faden's map, and the reality of this omission is confirmed by an estate map of 1767, which shows that neither had then been established (NRO MC 607/1). Watchers Wood in Gayton, in the west of the county (TF 715194), is likewise absent from Faden, and did not exist when an estate map was surveyed in 1726 (NRO BL 41/4), while Hanworth Wood (TG 219345) appears to have been planted as part of the west belt of Gunton Park, a suspicion confirmed by a map of 1754, which shows that it had not then come into existence (private collection).

Although, as we have seen, some ancient woods were incorporated into eighteenth- and nineteenth-century landscape designs, it remains true that *Inventory* woods lying within, or on the edges of, landscape parks should be regarded with particular suspicion, as the example just described, and those at Gawdy and Rackheath, testify. What the *Inventory* refers to as Blyth's Wood on the edge of Taverham park (TG 141128) is depicted, more or less with its current boundaries, on the first edition Ordnance Survey six-inch map. Its area was, however, mostly occupied by farmland when an estate map was surveyed in 1807, albeit a thin section of woodland existed along its north-western edge (NRO BR 276/1/1030). An earlier map of 1740 shows no woodland here at all (NRO CHC 11915): the area was then common land, to judge from a clearer but unfortunately undated map of *c*.1780, which likewise fails to show any woodland here (NRO BR 276/1/1048). The *Inventory* includes another wood labelled as 'Blyth's', lying a little to the east of that just described (TG 149129). This is shown as wooded on the first edition Ordnance Survey six-inch map, but the 1807 survey shows a more complex pattern. Although most of the *Inventory* area was then open ground, it also included three small areas of woodland. Two of these were clumps, planted in 1793 according to information provided on the 1807 map itself. Only the third, covering some 15 per cent of the total *Inventory* area, is a possible candidate for 'ancient' status, as it is described as 'The Woodyard' on the map of 1740 (NRO CHC 11915).

Where eighteenth-century maps are lacking, documentary sources can sometimes suggest a recent origin for particular woods, or groups of woods, included in the *Inventory*. Sheringham Wood, on the Sheringham estate on the north coast, was planted some time in the first half of the nineteenth century, as we have noted, but the two neighbouring *Inventory* woods, Oak Wood and Park Wood, are evidently older, as they are shown on Faden's map of 1797. Armstrong's *History and Antiquities of the County of Norfolk* of 1781 helpfully describes how:

> Upper Sheringham is beautifully adorned by the extensive woods of Mr Cooke Flower, the summit only of the hills are planted, while their bottoms and the rich valleys that divide them are variegated with unenclosed arable land ... Mr Flower has great merit in these plantations as it would at first sight appear impracticable to raise trees in a situation exposed to the keenest sea breezes, but by planting young trees among the furze and ling, they are so sheltered they are so sheltered that after a few years they become able to brave the north-east wind. (Armstrong 1781, Vol. III, p. 101)

Of the four *Inventory* woods on the Blickling estate near Aylsham, in north-east Norfolk, only one – Great Wood (TG 164296) – appears to be genuinely 'ancient' in the sense that it probably pre-dates *c.*1600, although in origin it was perhaps a deer park, rather than a coppiced wood. Of the others, that called the Leaselands (TG 158269) is not listed in a detailed estate survey of 1756 which pays particular attention to the earl of Buckinghamshire's timber and woods (NRO MC3/252). It may have been planted soon after 1771, when the agent – Robert Copeman – wrote to the earl explaining that the new planting there would be delayed until the following year. The reason given – that the timber and pollards already standing needed to be felled first, and the furze cut – may suggest a wood-pasture origin, but more probably indicates the presence of hedges containing standards and pollards around a field (NRO NRS 14625, Feb 28 1771). Jack Bell's Grove (TG 160282) likewise fails to appear in the 1756 survey and, while it may have been included within the adjacent Hercules Grove (which is mentioned, although it does not feature in the *Inventory*) its eastern portion, at least, must post-date 1729, when an estate survey shows an open common here (Blickling Hall archive). The same map shows unequivocally that the site of the Tollands (TG 190293), the fourth of the *Inventory* woods on the Blickling estate, was then occupied by arable fields.

Moving back before 1700 our evidence becomes much sparser. Few detailed seventeenth-century estate maps survive, but those that do, and which show areas that include *Inventory* woods, reinforce the impression that a significant proportion of these, in Norfolk at least, must post-date 1600. Railway Wood, in the east of Melton Constable parish in north-central Norfolk (TG 046313), is absent from Faden, although the neighbouring Redland Wood, to the east, is depicted. The fact that this is described as 'Hatchet Plantation' on the first edition Ordnance Survey six-inch map raises some suspicions about its antiquity, however, and, indeed, neither wood is shown on an estate map of 1676 (surviving as a copy of 1732: NRO Hayes and Storr maps 82 and 83). A map of North Creake surveyed by William Haward in 1600, which likewise survives only as an eighteenth-century copy, shows that Ringate Wood (TF 840378) had not as yet been planted. Its area formed part of the open fields of the parish and was divided into strips entirely under arable cultivation (NRO DN/ADR 10/1). Perhaps the most striking example is Warby's Grove in Gressenhall, which early maps make clear is the truncated remains of a more extensive area of woodland, 'Dentford Hill': one of these maps, from the start of the eighteenth century, helpfully informs us that its entire area was 'sown for a wood 1698 & 1699' (NRO MR 235).

Many of the woods included in the *Inventory* were thus evidently established, on previously unwooded sites, only in the course of the seventeenth, eighteenth and nineteenth centuries. But, in addition, a number of others, while they contain within their boundaries fragments of early woodland, *mainly* comprise relatively recent estate planting. Green Farm Grove near Shotesham in south-east Norfolk (TM 264979), for example, more or less doubled in size between 1842, when the tithe award map (NRO DN/TA 558) was surveyed, and 1880, when the Ordnance Survey six-inch map was produced; and around a third of the *Inventory* area of the wood called Gillingham Thicks, near Gillingham in the south-east of the county, did not exist in the 1840s (TM 218935) (NRO DN/TA 829). Only the southern half of Racknell's Covert in Guist, in central Norfolk (TG 019262), appears to have been planted when the Ordnance Survey two-inch drawings were prepared around 1815 (BL OSD 239): the wood's name strongly suggests that even this small core originated as an eighteenth-century game covert. Snake Wood or Snakes Wood, another of the Taverham estate woods (TG 149139), is shown with the same shape and area on both the first edition Ordnance Survey map and on an estate map of 1807. Maps of 1740 and 1807, however, show less than half of the *Inventory* area as wooded, although the name of the wooded section, which then extended some way to the south of the *Inventory* area – 'Prior's Wood' – clearly suggests a medieval origin (NRO BR 276/1/1030; NRO CHC 11915). Sometimes the relationship between a genuinely 'ancient' core and later additions is even more complicated, as in the case of two *Inventory* woods on the margins of Langley Park in south-east Norfolk, 'The Thicks' and 'Helsmere Hole'. The former (TG 348009) appears entirely wooded on the first edition Ordnance Survey six-inch map but only partly so on a parish map of 1816, when much of its area comprised open parkland (NRO DS 157(39)). The south-western section of the *Inventory* area was wooded at this date, while the north-eastern part, although partly open parkland, also included five clumps. An undated seventeenth-century map shows that much, although not all, of this latter area was then occupied by 'Langley Wood', almost certainly ancient, from which most, although not all, of the parkland clumps were apparently carved. The rest of the *Inventory* wood, however – the majority of the area – did not yet exist (NRO NRS 21407). Nearby 'Helsmere Hole', or 'Hazelmere', as it appears on the modern Ordnance Survey, existed in its present form when the first edition Ordnance Survey six-inch map was surveyed in the 1880s (TG 355019). Its site is not included on the 1816 map, but the seventeenth-century estate map depicts it partly as an area of open-field arable and partly as a scatter of trees – possibly a small area of wood-pasture – around the margins of the pond or 'mere' itself.

Leaving aside these and other cases where *Inventory* woods embrace within their boundaries much post-medieval planting while also including an earlier, pre-1600 'core', we are left nevertheless with a substantial proportion which are evidently, in their entirety, of seventeenth-century or (more usually) later date – around a sixth of the total number of woods included in the *Inventory* for Norfolk. But this figure clearly represents a serious underestimate, given that only a minority of parishes in the county have maps surviving from the eighteenth or seventeenth centuries from which *termini post quem* for the woods within them might be established. The true figure may thus be nearer a fifth of the total, quite possibly more. In highlighting this fact our intention is, however, emphatically *not* to criticise the manner in which the *Ancient Woodland Inventory* was compiled, nor to diminish its value as a tool for conservation management. A 'failsafe' approach was understandably and wisely adopted, whereby a wood was assumed to be 'ancient' unless it was positively proven to be otherwise (Goodfellow and Peterken 1981, 179; Spencer and Kirby 1992, 83). In the majority of cases the woods so identified were, indeed, genuinely 'ancient' in the terms defined by the *Inventory*. Current work on updating the *Inventory*, so far carried out only in south-east England, will doubtless correct some of the 'erroneous' inclusions (McKernan and Goldberg 2011). Much more interesting is the fact that a significant proportion of these woods, when examined on the ground, display many of the features usually associated with ancient woodland.

It might be thought that these relatively recent woods could be distinguished fairly easily from 'genuine' ancient woods on the basis of fieldwork. Being recent, they ought to take the form of plantations or, if coppice, to boast an understorey composed largely or exclusively of a single species, such as hazel or sweet chestnut. They ought to lack much in the way of significant perimetre banks. And, above all, they ought not to include in their ground flora 'ancient woodland indicators' such as dog's mercury or wood anemone. What is surprising is that several of these recent woods, examined as part of this project, were found to display some, and in a few cases all, of these features (Stone and Williamson 2013). Not only do most exhibit relict coppice but some have significant earthworks on their boundaries and boast abundant quantities of 'ancient

Figure 31 Blake's Grove near Gawdy Hall, Redenhall-with-Harleston, is a classic example of 'pseudo-ancient' woodland. In spite of the presence of a massive bank along its western side, coppice-with-standards structure, and an abundance of dog's mercury, the wood was only established some time between 1734 and 1789.

woodland indicators'. Holy Grove in Earsham, for example, which did not exist when an estate map was surveyed in 1720, thus features a coppiced understorey featuring varying proportions of hazel and hornbeam beneath standards of oak and ash, just like the genuinely ancient woods in the immediate area. The floor is carpeted with dog's mercury, and there are scattered examples of water avens and primrose. The western edge of the wood is bounded by what at first sight appears to be a woodbank, and only cartographic evidence confirms that it is in reality a substantial field boundary of medieval or early post-medieval date. There are a number of ancient oaks in the northern section of the wood, but these are former field boundary trees. Lopham Grove, a wood which is unquestionably of eighteenth-century origins, is even more striking in this regard. It boasts a mixed coppice of ash, hazel, field maple and some hornbeam under standards of oak (*Quercus robur*) with some ash and the occasional sweet chestnut. The ground flora contains no fewer than six 'ancient woodland indicators': dog's mercury, wood spurge (*Euphorbia amygdaloides*), wood sedge (*Carex sylvatica*), primrose, bluebells (*Hyacinthoides non-scripta*) and early purple orchid (*Orchis mascula*). As already noted, a substantial bank running around the north-western and eastern sides of the wood, which marks the parish boundary between Lopham and Fersfield (with which this side of the wood coincides), has all the appearance of a medieval woodbank. There is little here to alert the researcher to the fact that this is, in reality, an area of relatively recent woodland. Primrose Grove and Old Grove in Gillingham – conjoined areas of ancient woodland – are in many ways similar. Planted some time after 1840, much of the original ash, hazel and hornbeam coppice survives; the ground flora includes, in addition to dog's mercury and primrose, a range of other plants often used as 'indicators', including dog-violet (*Viola reichenbachiana*), hard shield fern (*Polystichum aculeatum*) and wood speedwell (*Veronica montana*).[8] Other examples of recent secondary woods within the sample surveyed do not display quite such a range of features but nevertheless bear a more than superficial resemblance to genuinely ancient woods. Blake's Grove and Ladies' Grove at Gawdy, for example, comprise oak standards over mixed coppice of ash, hornbeam and maple, and have a dense ground cover of dog's mercury (Figure 31: see Appendix entry); the western boundary of the former has a massive bank, which in fact represents the edge of an adjacent area of roadside common. Dodd's Wood in Rushall comprises mixed hornbeam and maple coppice, with a rather sparser cover of dog's mercury.

   Information included in Norfolk County Wildlife Site Partnership's List of County Wildlife Sites allows a less detailed examination of the structural and botanical characteristics of those recent secondary woods that were not included in the

---

8   The sample also included, as we have noted, some woods which – while not included in the *Ancient Woodland Inventory* – appeared ancient because of their name, shape or location. Toombers Wood, on the borders of Crimplesham, Stow Bardolph and Stradsett, is one example. When examined it proved to be a late medieval or post-medieval secondary wood, much of it overlying ridge and furrow (rare in Norfolk except in this far western part of the county): it is very probably of seventeenth-century or perhaps even later origin. Nevertheless, it has an understorey of coppiced hazel beneath standards of ash and oak, and its ground flora includes primrose (*Primula vulgaris*), remote sedge (*Carex remota*) and wood sedge (*Carex sylvatica*).

sample, and which were not therefore surveyed on the ground. From this source we learn, for example, that Pope's Wood in Hempnall, which was established only in the later eighteenth century, comprises mixed hornbeam and hazel coppice under oak standards, with more limited areas of coppiced birch, sallow and field maple. The ground flora is dominated by dog's mercury, but other plants often employed as 'ancient woodland indicators' are also present, including barren strawberry (*Potentilla sterilis*). Nearby D'Oyly's Grove, likewise planted some time after 1767, comprises oak and ash standards over mixed hazel, hornbeam and ash coppice: the ground flora includes dog's mercury, early purple orchid, remote sedge (*Carex remota*), yellow archangel (*Lamiastrum galeobdolon*), wood sedge, pignut and even the nationally scarce herb Paris (*Paris quadrifolia*). The post-medieval extensions to Green Farm Wood in Shotesham are characterised, as is the original 'core', by hazel and maple coppice; and, while the ground cover is largely restricted to dog's mercury, the wood is enclosed 'by prominent boundary banks which support old coppice stools'. All these examples are found on the rich, damp clays of the Beccles or Burlingham Associations in the south or centre of the county, as are those with similar characteristics examined in the main sample. On the drier soils in the north such woods do not usually include the same range of 'indicator species', and often display a plantation structure rather than taking the form of coppice-with-standards, although this is sometimes as a consequence of later replanting. A number, nevertheless, fall firmly within our category of 'pseudo-ancient woodland'. Sheringham Wood, planted in the early nineteenth century, thus includes some relic hazel coppice and a ground flora featuring wood sorrel (*Oxalis acetosella*) and bluebell. Nearby Oak Wood, almost certainly planted in its entirety in the later eighteenth century, has a ground flora which includes bluebell, dog's mercury and wood false-brome (*Brachypodium sylvaticum*), again with small areas of relict hazel coppice.

Conclusion

Although the history of ancient woodland in the eighteenth and nineteenth centuries is often neglected, close inspection reveals that it has much to tell us about the character of such woods today. It was probably only in this period that many of the grazed woodlands which had once been a prominent feature of the landscape of the county finally disappeared, leaving only those woods managed as coppice-with-standards. Some of these were also destroyed, largely as a consequence of agricultural intensification on the heavier soils in the county, but what remained continued to be managed rigorously, in spite of the rise of the new forms of forestry. Indeed, as we have shown, a number of entirely new areas of coppiced woodland were established in this period, in part perhaps because of the contemporary enthusiasm for game shooting. What is of particular interest is that many of these have since acquired an impressive range of 'ancient woodland indicators', so that they are hard, and occasionally impossible, to distinguish from 'genuine' ancient woods. The distinction between 'ancient' and 'recent' woodland is thus, we would argue, rather more blurred than is often assumed, an issue to which we shall return in greater detail in the final chapter. First we need to look briefly at the development of coppiced woods in the relatively recent past – in the period since the late nineteenth century – and at what this can contribute to our understanding of 'ancient woodland' more generally.

Chapter 7

The recent history of ancient woodland

If the eighteenth and nineteenth centuries are usually neglected in discussions of ancient woodland, this is even more true of the period since 1900. Not only, however, do the present appearance and structure of surviving woods derive in large part from developments since the late nineteenth century but, in addition, some of their more basic characteristics, such as the stand types they contain, may have been crucially affected by comparatively recent changes, and may sometimes be rather less old than we usually assume. Events and processes in recent decades have shaped woods in other important but often neglected ways, contributing to some, for example, a final layer of recent, yet significant, archaeology. For all these reasons, it is necessary to look briefly at ancient woodland in the modern world.

Depression and the great estates

As we have emphasised throughout this study, the history of woodland is inextricably linked with wider social and economic developments, and one key feature of the period after *c.*1880 was the changing character of the agricultural economy. Most ancient woods were the property of landed estates, and the continuation of coppicing into the later nineteenth century may have owed as much to inertia, tradition and the needs of game shooting as it did to any real economic benefits that this form of management conveyed. In Norfolk, as in most other parts of England, the majority of large landowners obtained a significant proportion of their income from agriculture: directly from the profits of their home farm but also, more importantly, from farm rents. For most of the period after *c.*1750 farming remained profitable. But from the late 1870s a serious agricultural depression set in as a consequence of globalisation. Imports of grains from north America, and subsequently of frozen meat from south America and the Antipodes, began to flood the home market, and the scale of the former was no longer limited by the Corn Laws, which had been repealed in 1846. The 'Great Depression' continued, albeit with periods of recovery – most notably, during the First World War – until the outbreak of the Second World War in 1939 (Perry 1974; Brown 1987). In addition to these challenges, landowners in Norfolk, as elsewhere, were also assailed by Death Duties, introduced in 1894 and raised to 15 per cent by Lloyd George and, subsequently, in 1919, to 40 per cent on estates valued at more than £200,000 (Thompson 1963, 325, 330). Their dominance of local politics, moreover, was eroded by the Local Government Acts of 1888 and 1894, which vested power in elected County, District and Parish Councils rather than in the various unelected offices formerly monopolised by the gentry. In many ways, the great age of the landed estate, with which the later history of ancient woodland had been inextricably linked, was over.

Nevertheless, it is important to emphasise that the impact of these changes on patterns of land ownership was more gradual, and less pervasive, than is sometimes suggested. Large estates did not entirely disappear from Norfolk, or anywhere else in England, in the twentieth century: significant numbers remain to this day. It is certainly true that the waning fortunes of agriculture had a direct and immediate effect upon Norfolk landowners, for farm rents declined precipitously from the 1880s (Wade Martins and Williamson 2008, 73–6). The rental income from the Blickling estate, for example, fell from £11,685 in 1877 to £9,893 in 1892, and a major recalculation of rents in 1894 resulted in a further reduction to £6,018 (NRO MC3). But a family's insolvency did not immediately lead to the break-up of an estate. Initially, as landowners fell into financial difficulties, many responded by selling off outlying farms, and if whole estates were placed on the market they often passed, largely or even entirely intact, to new owners who had made their money in commerce or industry – an intensification of a long-established pattern. Almost all of Norfolk's landed estates in fact survived, if reduced in size, at least up until the outbreak of the First World War (Wade Martins and Williamson 2008, 76–80). Ancient woodland on large estates, moreover, continued to be managed relatively intensively, in part because of a marked expansion in game shooting that took place in the later nineteenth and early twentieth centuries. This was partly a consequence of the fashion set by Prince Edward on his Norfolk estate at Sandringham, and partly because game became, in some places, a form of economic diversification, with shoots being run on commercial lines, businessmen and others paying for the privilege of a season's shooting in elegant company (Tapper 1992). There was certainly some large-scale felling of timber trees as hard-pressed landowners capitalised on their assets, and this may have affected managed woods as much as the wider farmland. In 1902 Rider Haggard, witnessing the cutting down of oak in the area between Whissonset and Wendling, commented: 'I think that 'ere long this timber will be scarce in England' (Rider Haggard 1902, II, 506). But on the whole, so far as the evidence goes, most ancient woods continued to be managed on traditional, sustainable lines well into the twentieth century, even if they were no longer making much real money.

From *c*.1920, however, rather than passing intact to new owners or shrinking through the sale of outlying properties, increasing numbers of estates were simply broken up and sold in parcels, often to the farmers who had formerly tenanted them, and this did have implications for woodland management (Barnes 1993; Wade Martins and Williamson 2008, 76–80). What Butcher said of the woods in north Suffolk would doubtless have been true of many to the north of the Waveney: they were 'entirely neglected except for an occasional coppicing when the undergrowth becomes too thick or the owner runs short of hazel sticks or faggots'. Woods were now owned by 'farmers who know little and care less for forestry' (Butcher 1941, 361). Even where estates remained intact, regular coppicing now became uneconomic, given the continuing decline in the market for coppice poles, the challenged condition of estate finances and gradual increases in rural wages. Traditional management had, in most contexts, become an expensive luxury. Large-scale fellings of timber trees also intensified in the inter-war years, both in ancient woods and in more recent plantations. Lilias Rider Haggard, writing in the 1930s, thought that the 'wholesale cutting of timber all over the country is a sad sight, but often the owner's last desperate bid to enable him to cling to the family acres' (Rider Haggard and Williamson 1943, 73). Timber was also felled by the new owners of portions of estates in order to recoup some of the purchase price. Following the break-up of the Morton Hall estate in 1923, for example, large areas of Hockering Wood were immediately clear-felled by the new owner: the wood was sold for £12,050, or £54 per acre, considerably more than the average of £18 an acre paid for the various tenant farms, presumably a reflection of the value of the standing timber (Natural England archives, Peterborough). Large-scale fellings produced some curious features of the Norfolk landscape. On the outwash gravels to the north-east of Norwich the extensive woodlands planted by the Costessey estate in the eighteenth and nineteenth century, mainly consisting of beech, chestnut, oak and larch standards, were largely felled following the sale and break-up of the estate in 1918. 'The despoliation of these woods was carried out without any thought for the future, and in consequence, the greater part of the area is now coppice or a thicket of high shoots which have grown from the old stumps of the stately trees which once adorned the landscape' (Mosby 1938,175). These outgrown pseudo-coppices are still a striking feature of the woods in the area. In reality, of course, the picture is complicated. On some estates, such as Wolterton in north Norfolk, woods were still being actively coppiced into the 1940s (Wolterton archives, WOLT 3/1/16–19). The market for underwood produce, moreover, was not entirely wiped out by coal and the availability of items manufactured in iron. As late as 1923 hurdles and wattles were still being made at Melton Constable, and particular local industries still provided a market, especially brush-makers such as S.D. Page and Britons, both based at Wymondham – although even they, in the inter-war period, gradually came to rely more and more on beech imported from France and Belgium and birch brought from Norway (Clark 1996, 14; Briton Brush Co. 1935, 6–7). But, for the most part, in the middle decades of the twentieth century Norfolk's woods gradually slid into a state of dereliction.

The long agricultural depression, coupled with other changes, had important effects on some of the other environments, historically related to woodland, mentioned in this book. Surviving areas of heath and other rough grazing – mostly common land or poors' allotments – were no longer systematically cut for fuel or for animal bedding. They were also less intensively grazed than in the past, partly because of a reduction in the numbers of sheep being kept locally in the inter-war years, partly because their rough herbage was unsuited to modern breeds and partly because of the problems posed by increasing volumes of motor traffic using the roads which usually crossed them, and the failure of motorists to close behind them the gates placed at the entrances (Wade Martins and Williamson 2008, 133–8). Both bracken and gorse increased at the expense of other heathland plants; Clarke described in 1908 how on several heaths in Breckland the former had 'usurped the position which heather occupied some 20 years ago. Bracken lacks its former economic importance' (Clarke 1908, 567). By the 1940s many heaths and other commons were reverting to woodland. The same fate befell areas of wetland in the county, which were no longer mown for hay, bedding or thatching materials, and by 1950 there was probably more alder carr in Norfolk than there had been since the early Middle Ages (Wade Martins and Williamson 2008, 138–40; Boardman 1939, 14).

The impact of the Forestry Commission

The increasingly derelict condition of marginal grazing land was not unique to Norfolk, and its final shift into woodland was often the consequence not of natural regeneration but of deliberate replanting with commercial conifers under state direction. This was the culmination of a long period of concern about the state of English woodlands the origins of which, as we have seen, lay in the eighteenth century (above, pp. 111–12). The Royal Forestry Society was founded in 1882, and a Select Committee was appointed in 1885 to 'consider whether, by the establishment of a forest school or otherwise, our woodlands could be rendered remunerative' (Simpson 1909, 89). Another was set up in 1889 to 'enquire into the administration of the department of Woods and Forests and Land revenues of the Crown' (Report on the Select Committee on the Woods, Forests and Land Revenues of the Crown, 1890). The Indian Engineering College at Egham in Surrey began forestry courses in 1885 and in 1897 H.C. Hill, who had been a Conservator of Forests in India, wrote a working plan for Crown forests with the stated aim of introducing 'a more scientific system of forest cultivation … also to establish such a system of management as may serve those who desire to study forestry … with a practical object-lesson, such as at the present time they have to go to France or Germany to find' (Annual Report of the Commission of Woods and Forests, 1897). In 1909 John Simpson likewise urged, in an influential book, large-scale afforestation following German models of management, and with the assistance if not the direction of the State (Simpson 1909); in the same year, a Royal Commission recommended large-scale afforestation in the country (Royal Commission on Coastal Erosion and Afforestation, 1909), in part as a means of alleviating unemployment. Also in 1909, Lloyd George introduced development grants to allow both the establishment of schools of forestry and the acquisition of land for planting, and three years later a further Advisory Committee on Forestry was appointed (Ryle 1969). But in 1914 the United Kingdom was still importing about 400 million cubic feet of timber a year, and the experience of the subsequent war revealed dramatically the strategic implications of this dependence on foreign sources, especially in terms of a shortage of pit props which threatened the output of the coal mines, and thus the war effort itself (Schlich 1915).

In 1916 a Forestry Sub-Committee of the Reconstruction Committee was appointed. This committee, which produced the Acland Report, set the tone for Forestry Policy in Britain for much of the twentieth century (Ryle 1969; Ministry of Reconstruction – Forestry Sub-Committee, 1918). Its main recommendation was for the strategic afforestation of marginal land, especially heath and moor, suggesting that no less than five million acres (*c.*two million hectares) of rough grazing could be given over to growing timber, in part to alleviate unemployment. In August 1919 the Forestry Act received royal assent and the Forestry Commission was established. One happy coincidence for the new authority was that many of the exotic conifers which had been trialled in estate plantations in the nineteenth century – Norway spruce, Sitka spruce, grand fir, Douglas fir, western red cedar, larch and so on – were now mature, and their suitability for cultivation in this country thus demonstrated. Influenced by continental practice, and by the kinds of land being targeted for planting, it was a range of coniferous and in part alien species which the Commission mainly employed; in lowland areas in general, and Norfolk in particular, the majority of early plantings were of Scots pine, increasingly accompanied by Corsican pine from the 1930s. By the end of 1929 the Forestry Commission had established 140,000 acres (*c.*57,000 hectares) of plantation in Britain, and a further 75,000 acres (*c.*30,000 hectares) had been planted between 1918 and 1929 by others, including local authorities as well as private landowners (Forestry Commission 1929).

In Norfolk the main areas afforested were on the poor soils of Breckland, where much arable land had actually passed out of cultivation during the previous decades as a consequence of the agricultural depression (Wade Martins and Williamson 2008, 119–22; Mosby 1938, 181). In 1922 the Commission made its first land purchases here, beginning with a small area near Swaffham and followed, soon afterwards, by 3,149 acres (1,275 hectares) of the Elveden estate. The following years saw the acquisition of a series of substantial properties: the Downham Hall estate (4,944 acres) in 1923; the Lynford estate (6,208 acres, *c.*2,500 hectares) and part of the Beechamwell estate (822 acres, *c.*330 hectares) in 1924; and 1,570 acres (635 hectares) of the Ministry of Agriculture's short-lived demonstration farm at Methwold (Skipper and Williamson 1997, 19–20; Forestry Commission Acquisition Files, Santon Downham; TNA FC 54386/2; FC 374/24). The Cockley Cley estate, and parts of the Croxton and Didlington estates, followed in 1925; the Weeting estate in 1926; further portions of the Didlington and Croxton estates in 1927; and another 4,299 hectares of the Croxton Hall estate (much of it already leased by the Commission) in 1928; while the 3,000-acre (1,245-hectare) West Harling estate, a further portion of Lynford and 2,025 acres (820 hectares) of the Hockham Hall estate were acquired in 1930 (Skipper and Williamson 1997, 18–20). Only in 1931, in the face of mounting economic crisis, were significant cuts made to the Commission's budget, bringing acquisitions to an end. Subsequent land purchases were concentrated elsewhere in the country, with only small quantities of land being bought in Norfolk (FC archives, Acquisition Files; TNA FC L3/3, Vol.1; L3/3/15; L3/3/9; L 3/1/1).

Most of the land acquired for planting was derelict or semi-derelict heathland or arable: the report drawn up when Croxton was purchased, for example, was typical in describing the estate as 'partly heath and partly low grade light arable or pasture land which has passed, or is about to pass, out of cultivation'. The prices paid were low – £2 4s 8d per acre for the Downham Hall estate in 1923, £3 10s for Weeting in 1926 and just over £3 per acre for Croxton in 1929 (FC archives, Acquisition Files; TNA FC L3/3, Vol.1; L3/3/15; L3/1/1). The numbers of trees planted grew steadily through the 1920s, peaking in 1927, when no fewer than eight million trees were established on 3,700 acres in the main area of Breckland, with a further 700 acres being planted on the Commission's land further north, around Swaffham. Between 1924 and 1929 an average of 2,226 acres (909 hectares) of plantation was established annually. After 1931 there was a gradual decline in planting as the amount of new land being acquired in Norfolk dwindled and as the available acreage was planted up, with attention turning to the expanding forests in Suffolk – in the southern parts of Breckland and on the coastal heaths (Skipper and Williamson 1997, 22).

Initially, as noted, the Scots pine was the main tree planted, but Corsican pine was also employed in certain locations, and began to be used in preference to Scots pines from the 1930s. Small areas of Douglas fir, European larch, silver fir, western red cedar, western hemlock, maritime and lodgepole pines were also established. Substantial number of indigenous hardwood trees – principally oak and beech – were likewise planted; indeed, more than the present make-up of the East Anglian forests would suggest. In 1935, as many as 428 acres of hardwood trees were planted in Breckland alongside 1,186 acres (480 hectares) of conifers. The main problem with both oak and beech was their vulnerability to the sharp spring frosts to which the district was prone, and to the browsing of deer, the numbers of which rose sharply as planting progressed. Deciduous trees also grew more slowly than pines. Not surprisingly, the numbers planted declined markedly after 1935. Most of those that were established were placed along the sides of the principal roads, in part as a fire prevention measure and in part to assuage growing public opposition to the 'serried rows of conifers' that were transforming the formerly open landscape of heaths and 'brecks' (Skipper and Williamson 1997, 65–7; Tennyson 1939, 76–7).

Although most of the Commission's activities were directed towards the poor soils of Breckland, other areas of the county were also affected. Extensive plantings, for example, were made on the outwash gravels to the north of Norwich and in the area around Swanton Novers in the 1920s. And, in addition to their direct involvement in planting, the Commission also encouraged private owners to restock woodland felled during the First World War and to plant new areas of woodland. Grants were made for each acre planted, with higher rates for deciduous trees than for conifers (Ryle 1969, 265–6). A number of landowners took advantage: on the Quidenham estate in Norfolk, for example, 5,500 Scots pine, 3,000 larch and 3,000 oak were planted under the scheme (Wade Martins and Williamson 2008, 105). Most private owners, in spite of the differential payments offered by the Dedication Scheme, clearly concentrated their attention (as did the Commission itself) on relatively fast-growing coniferous species, in contrast to eighteenth- and nineteenth-century landowners, whose main focus had been on deciduous hardwoods. The extent to which they began to replant within now often semi-derelict areas of ancient woodland – rather than establishing new plantations on new sites, or restocking existing plantations – during the inter-war years is uncertain, but a close examination of the successive revisions of the six-inch Ordnance Survey maps and the RAF vertical air photographs of 1946 suggests that at least until the Second World War most ancient woods in Norfolk contained at most only a scatter of conifers, probably intended (as already noted) for game cover rather than for timber. The western and possibly the northern sections of Edgefield Little Wood had evidently been replanted with conifers by 1946, and large parts of Foxley Wood also appear to have been coniferised; but there are few other certain examples, although none of these sources is entirely reliable or (in the case of the RAF photographs) always easy to interpret. Sometimes a measure of replanting with aliens and conifers occurred after woods were sold by large estates and clear-felled by new owners, as at Hockering, where, the oak timber having been largely removed following the break-up of the Morton Hall estate in 1923, large areas were restocked soon after 1930 with Douglas fir, larch, Scots pine, red oak and Turkey oak (Natural England archives, Peterborough).

Woodland in wartime

The Second World War brought the long period of agricultural depression to an end and stimulated a massive drive to increase agricultural production. Warren, writing about the Essex countryside, described how in the early years of hostilities 'spruce copse and oak wood alike have been felled; and even village commons have been ploughed and planted' (Warren 1943, ix). While the 1946 RAF aerial photographs suggest much large-scale recent felling, few if any of Norfolk's ancient woodlands appear to have been grubbed out in this period to make way for farmland, although at least one – Spring Wood in Hempnall – was partly removed to make space for an airfield. More important was the fact that wartime provided a new role for many of the county's ancient woods, especially as places where munitions dumps and some of the facilities associated with airfields could be conveniently hidden from aerial attack. By 1942, as a consequence of the 'expansion' initiative, there were 37 functioning airfields in Norfolk, occupying around 7.5 per cent of the county's land area (TNA MAF38/574), used by fighters and bombers of both the RAF and the USAAF. It is thus unsurprising, perhaps, that of the 50 woods studied in the sample, 5 contained significant evidence for wartime use – Hethel Wood, Hockering Wood, Honeypot Wood, Billingford Wood and Thorpe Wood – while Earsham Wood and Sexton's Wood in Hedenham contained more limited traces.

The most extensive remains, and in many ways the most intriguing, are those within Hockering Wood. The wood was requisitioned by the Air Ministry in January 1943 and functioned as a centralised repository which serviced a number of bases in the district (TNA AIR 29/1065). The Air Ministry faced continual problems in finding sufficient storage space for the six months' reserve of munitions deemed necessary to replenish stocks kept on the airfields themselves. In 1943 the system of 'Air Ammunition Parks' was overhauled and the two existing facilities in eastern England – at Barnham in Suffolk and Lord's Bridge in Cambridge – were augmented with new sites at Hockering in Norfolk and South Witham in Lincolnshire, and all were now renamed as 'Forward Ammunition Depots' (Falconer 1998). Both of the new sites were located within woodland, as Barnham had partly been. A wooded site, augmented with camouflage nets, provided a measure of concealment, and it was also thought that the trees would help to contain the blast from any accidental explosions. The concealment from the air provided by the trees was clearly a key consideration, for it is apparent from the 1946 RAF vertical air photographs that the storage facilities in Hockering Wood, and especially those for the high explosive bombs, were concentrated in the most wooded areas. In parts where timber had been extensively removed over the previous decades, in contrast, the archaeological traces of wartime use tend to be sparse. Three months after the site was opened an inspection recommended that further measures should be taken to conceal it from the air: the concrete tracks laid out within the wood, evidently too visible, were to be tarmaced and chipped (TNA AIR 29/1065).

Hockering Wood offered additional advantages. It was fairly remote from any significant centre of population, an important consideration considering the combined explosive power of the munitions stored there (on 27 November 1944 4,000 tons of bombs exploded at the depot at Fauld, Staffordshire, creating a crater half a mile long and 140 feet deep and killing 90 people) (McCamley 2004, 92–6). Hockering was also well placed to serve Norfolk air bases, there being no fewer than 15 within a radius of 25 miles (Bowyer 1979). Proximity to the RAF (later USAAF) base at Attlebridge airfield may also have been a consideration in the choice of site, for it provided some of the accommodation for the crew serving the store. The main consideration, however, must have been the sheer size of the wood – at 89 hectares it was the third largest in the county. Bombs and ammunition were brought to the site by lorry from East Dereham railway station, some eight kilometres to the west (TNA AIR 29/1065).

The archaeological remains of this phase of the wood's history are complex and intriguing, and their character illuminated, although not always fully explained, by plans and descriptions preserved in the RAF archives at Hendon and Kew (TNA AIR

29/1065). Many of the existing rides were converted into wide concrete roads nine feet (*c.*three metres) wide, with a main approach road 18 feet (*c.*six metres) wide; these still exist, with widenings at storage areas to allow lorries to be unloaded. Some new concrete roads, unrelated to the earlier ride pattern, were also constructed. Small arms ammunition, fuses and pyrotechnics were all stored in Nissen huts. One of these survives, relocated, at the present north entrance to the wood, and the wall of another still stands near the south-western corner of the wood; but otherwise only their concrete bases remain, now covered in soil on which dog's mercury thrives. The high explosive bombs, in contrast, were stored on wooden pallets in rows 412 feet long, comprising eight 20-foot storage spaces ranged at intervals of 36 feet. Each row was laid out along one of the concrete tracks and, following rules for storage laid out by the Ministry, was separated by a minimum of 120 yards from the next. In order to maximise the use of space, one section of a row was sometimes ranged along a short spur running at an angle off the main track (Air Ministry 1954, 257; TNA AIR 29/1065).

The storage spaces, almost all of which still remain intact, comprise square concrete hard standings bounded on three sides by low earthwork banks around 0.4 metres in height, and with the fourth side open to the road. There are gaps in the corners where the banks meet (Figure 32). The precise purpose of the earthworks, and especially of the corner gaps, remains unclear and is not made explicit in the surviving documents. The banks are too small to have served any useful function in terms of blast containment and they may have been intended simply to better define the storage areas, perhaps in an attempt to ensure that the regulations concerning the safe spacing of the bomb stores were adhered to. Each standing could hold, according to the surviving documents, 50 tons of high explosive, amounting to 400 tons in each row.

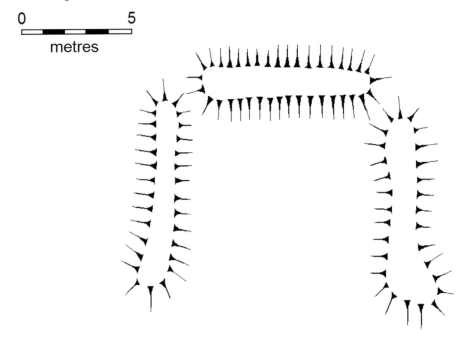

Figure 32 Hockering Wood. One of many low, sub-rectangular earthworks created to store munitions during the Second World War. The banks are less than a metre in height.

As there are 21 separate runs of standings within the wood, the total storage capacity in terms of high explosive alone must have been in the order of 8,400 tons. The site was gradually run down after the cessation of hostilities and finally decommissioned in 1956 (TNA AIR 29/15625; NRO C/P 8/1/166). The earth banks surrounding the storage areas have been colonised by hazel and small-leaved lime, and – like their concrete bases, now buried in soil – carry abundant growths of dog's mercury.

The United States Airforce took over several of the airfields that were supplied by Hockering during 1942 and 1943, at which point they began to be provided with munitions by the Americans' own supply network (Freeman 2001,140, 257). Their forward supply depot, at Earsham, was also associated with woodland, although this time with a number of neighbouring or connected areas of woodland on the estate of Earsham Hall, in the grounds of which the main headquarters campsite was established. Great Wood, Sexton's Wood and America Wood – all areas of ancient woodland – together with the more recent Beech Wood, Park Wood and New Plantation – were all used for storage, and a siding and marshalling yard were constructed to the east of Earsham railway station, on the LNER Waveney valley line, specifically for the unloading of bombs and fuel (Norfolk Federation of Women's Institutes 1999, 74). Concrete roads nine feet (c.three metres) wide were laid out in Earsham Great Wood and Sexton's Wood, as well as in Beech Wood, and still survive there. Remains of Nissen huts and hard standings also survive within Great Wood but, apart from the concreted rides, Sexton's Wood contains few other archaeological traces of this phase of its history. Bombs were also stored elsewhere in the locality, on hard standings beside public roads and along green lanes (TNA AIR 29/1558, plans 3040/52, 3041/52, 3042/52).

The forward ammunition depots, as noted, supplied munitions to individual airfields, all of which themselves needed to find storage to maintain a working reserve calculated to last four days. Although there is no evidence that the presence of woodland acted as a significant consideration in the choice of airfield site – the need for a relatively level location appears to have been paramount – where woods lay close to airfields they might be used to hide ammunition and sometimes other facilities. Honeypot Wood in Wendling lies on what was the south-eastern edge of Wendling airfield, built for the RAF but taken over by the USAAF in 1942 (Freeman 2001, 285, 313). Here, the high explosive bombs were kept within open bays, arranged in groups of four and surrounded by earthwork banks which are much more substantial than those at Hockering. They now boast fine displays of primrose and wood anemone. There was a network of concrete roads, much of which still remains. Here, bombs were rolled from the lorries, down ramps and into the storage bays, on the other side of which another concrete road provided access for the trolleys which took the bombs to the planes. The remains of further storage facilities exist outside and to the south of the wood. There are a number of brick-built buildings, some of which, used for storing pyrotechnics and incendiary bombs, were also placed within enclosures defined by substantial earth banks.

In other cases woods were used not to conceal munitions storage areas but as places to locate other facilities. Hethel Wood lay immediately to the east of Hethel airfield, which, like Wendling, was originally built for the RAF but was transferred to the US Eighth Air Force in 1942 (Freeman 2001, 285, 308). Various communal services and accommodation were located within the wood, technical facilities and

Figure 33 Billingford Wood. Outgrown hornbeam coppice, now grown to canopy level, has suppressed almost all other vegetation over large areas of the wood. In the distance is one of the buildings erected during the Second World War, when the wood was used to house facilities for the adjacent airfield.

headquarters buildings on its western edge. Most of these structures have been demolished, although three small brick buildings still stand on the eastern edge of the wood, piles of concrete mark the sites of others, and one of the rides running east–west through the middle of the wood is concreted. Rather more survives within and around Thorpe Wood and Billingford Wood, which lay immediately to the south of Thorpe Abbots, yet another RAF airfield transferred to the USAAF in 1942. Here the sick quarters were located within Billingford Wood and a variety of technical sites in Thorpe Wood (Freeman 2001, 283). A number of brick-built buildings remain, but their purpose is unclear; there are also concrete bases of further buildings (Figure 33). A roughly triangular-shaped pond is divided in two by a north–south bank which is continued as a low brick wall: it may have been intended to hold water for fire-fighting. Other ancient woods, not surveyed in the sample, were used as part of airfields: the surviving portion of Spring Wood in Hempnall, for example, was used to house dispersal areas for aircraft associated with the adjacent Shelton airfield.

These various piece of wartime archaeology were not recorded or analysed in as much detail as they perhaps ought to have been in the course of this survey not because they are unimportant but rather because they have only a tangential relevance to the main themes of this book. It is, however, striking how rapidly woodland vegetation has recolonised the sites of wartime facilities, with plants such as wood anemone, bluebell and dog's mercury happily growing on the bases of Nissen huts and on blast banks raised around former bomb stores. In some cases there are more dramatic examples of such recolonisation, with quite extensive

143

areas of ground which 1946 aerial photographs show as cleared and occupied by buildings now impossible to distinguish from other areas of the woodland in terms of both ground flora and underwood. These relatively recent archaeological remains also provide opportunities to test some of the methods for roughly dating trees from their waist-height girth measurements that have been formulated by arboriculturalists such as Alan Mitchell and John White (Mitchell 1974, 25; White 1998). One of the blast banks within Honeypot Wood thus provides an accurate *terminus post quem* for the large ash tree growing on top of it, which must certainly be later than its construction in 1943, and possibly several years later if we assume that the site, when occupied, would have been kept clear of encroaching vegetation. It has a girth of 2.7 metres, suggesting a date – according to these methods, and allowing for a degree of uncertainty regarding the density of vegetation around it at various stages of its growth – of between 100 and 200 years, rather greater than the 68 years which was, at the time it was measured, its maximum real age.

The effects of dereliction

While the war effort had an impact on a number of ancient woods in Norfolk, a far greater influence on their current structure and character was their progressive decline into dereliction, something which the war did little to reverse, and which continued into the post-war period. The number of timber trees was often reduced by further opportunistic fellings, but at the same time uncut coppice continued to grow, often to canopy height. The consequent shading, denser than in traditionally managed woods and now uninterrupted by regular cutting, steadily reduced floristic diversity, significantly affecting the characteristic woodland flora in a manner which has been described and documented by a number of researchers (Rackham 2006, 532; Kirby *et al.* 2005). In heavily shaded woods dog's mercury often continues to flourish, although to the exclusion of other 'woodland indicator species'; but in the most heavily shaded examples the ground flora disappears altogether across large areas of the woodland floor. What has received less attention from ecologists is the effects that neglect may also have had upon the shrubs and trees in the understorey, altering them in ways that ensure that the present composition of some woods – their constituent 'stand types' – differs from what would have been found a century earlier, when regular coppicing was still continuing.

We noted in Chapter 3 how hornbeam appears to have increased in importance in the environment of southern and eastern England during the early medieval period, possibly in part encouraged by woodsmen because it made excellent charcoal (above, p. 000). There are grounds for believing that, within those ancient woods in which the species formed a component of the understorey, its prominence increased still further through the twentieth century as woods became increasingly outgrown and derelict. Many ancient woods in the south of the county, as we have noted, are now composed almost entirely of outgrown hornbeam coppice, or contain large sections which are. Hedenham Wood, for example, has extensive areas with almost no other species; more than 75 per cent of nearby Sexton's Wood is now almost pure hornbeam; in East Wood, Denton, three kilometres to the south, the dominance is even greater. Such woods are particularly easy to survey archaeologically because the dense shade cast by the high canopy suppresses the growth of the ground flora to a greater extent than that cast by other species of outgrown underwood. But it is possible that hornbeam has also suppressed the growth of other underwood species in what were formerly more mixed coppices, and that the modern 'stand type' found in such woodland is thus largely recent, and an artefact of neglect.

One clear indication of this is the way in which, within such woods, the understorey tends to be more diverse – with a higher proportion of hazel, maple and ash in particular – beside the principal rides, especially where these are wide: a pattern noticeable, in particular, within Hedenham Wood. The County Wildlife Sites citations note this phenomenon in a number of places, as within Billingford Wood, where the understorey is said to comprise almost pure hornbeam 'except near to the paths which cross the site', where hazel and elder also occur. Ash would be suppressed over time by the density of shade; hazel is more shade-tolerant but would nevertheless eventually be outcompeted by hornbeam in neglected coppice. Rackham (1980) has noted how hornbeam becomes dominant in the understorey of managed woods where coppicing is carried out on a long rotation. If woods are cropped at intervals of less than *c*.15 years, and hornbeam standards are lacking, then hazel, which can fruit on a shorter cycle, may gain an advantage. Conversely, abandonment of coppice would encourage the growth of hornbeam over hazel, leading to the development of ever purer stands (Peterken 1981, 30) (Figure 33).

The pollen sequence from Diss Mere, which lies within the area of south-eastern Norfolk characterised by hornbeam woods, appears to indicate a substantial increase in the proportion of hornbeam in the locality in the course of the nineteenth and twentieth centuries, although the sequence is not closely dated (Peglar *et al.* 1989). Unfortunately, we lack any detailed early descriptions of the underwood of particular woods within this hornbeam zone that could be compared with what is growing there today, but there are some intriguing hints that in the nineteenth century other species were more prominent, and hornbeam less so. The tithe files for Denton thus describe how the main wood in the parish, which can hardly be other than East Wood, 'cuts into hurdles', strongly suggesting that hazel was then more important than it is today (TNA IR 18/5878): hornbeam is almost impossible to use for this purpose because it does not split or 'reave' easily. In a similar way, Hedenham Wood was described in the same source as producing 'hurdles and thatching stuff', while the late nineteenth-century owner described how a period of neglect had ensured that the coppice could not be used for 'hurdle wood', likewise implying that hazel was then a more prominent component than hornbeam (NRO MC 166/238). It is in fact possible that in this particular wood the dominance of hornbeam has continued to increase through recent decades. Rackham's plot of the tree communities present here, made in 1975, appears to show a much more diverse wood than exists today (Rackham 1976, 174). Some of the areas which he mapped as 'mixed hazel', such as that lying immediately to the north of the abandoned manorial site (above, p. 47), now seem to contain stands of pure hornbeam. Conversely, one area of this wood, and a part of nearby Sexton's Wood, have been brought back into coppice management during the last few decades and already appear to have a more diverse species structure than the rest of the wood, as well as having a more diverse ground flora. How far the balance of understorey species in other kinds of woodland – those now dominated by oak coppice in the north of the county, for example, or those containing varying combinations of ash, hazel and maple, which characterise the clays of central Norfolk

– have also changed in the course of the twentieth century is unclear, but it is possible that they, too, have to some extent been altered by progressive dereliction.

Post-War attrition, destruction and survival

Changes in the demand for coppice wood, and the challenged character of estate finances, were not the only factors encouraging the decline of traditional forms of woodland management in the middle decades of the twentieth century. The advent of the Forestry Commission, and of its Advisory Service in particular, saw the final triumph of 'plantation' silviculture, and there are signs that a number of landowners attempted – where the underwood was of an appropriate species – to convert coppice into high forest. Hockering Wood is a particularly interesting example. It was purchased in 1956 by one Captain Hutton following a chequered history in the first half of the century which included large-scale felling of timber in the 1920s, partial restocking with conifers and ornamental oaks in the 1930s and spontaneous regeneration of birch, as well as the wartime use already described (Natural England archive, Peterborough). Around two-thirds of the wood still retained mixed coppice of small-leaved lime and hazel, however, when Hutton purchased it, and over large areas he singled the lime stools, which soon overtopped the hazel and suppressed their growth. Even where singling was not attempted, the growth of the lime seems to have naturally reduced the proportion of hazel in many places. It may be significant that the 1837 tithe file for Hockering describes the underwood as 'principally used for sheep hurdles and thatching and daubing materials', clearly indicating that hazel was then a more prominent feature of this now largely lime-dominated wood (TNA 18/6005). Here, again, the modern 'stand type' provides only a partial indication of the wood's earlier composition.

A much more serious threat to ancient woodland was the large-scale replanting with modern conifers that was encouraged by the Commission through their Dedication scheme, with the support of grants, from the late 1940s: around 21 hectares of Hockering, for example, were planted with Douglas fir, larch, western red cedar and grand fir in 1957/8 (Natural England archive, Peterborough). In many cases, the quality of the timber produced by the replanting of such sites was poor, either because unsuitable species were used (a particular problem in woods located on damp, heavy clays) or because of poor subsequent management. Many landowners often failed to adequately thin the new stands of trees, in part perhaps because their main motivation in replanting had been adequate cover for game birds, rather than the provision of timber. The conversion of ancient woods to 'plantations on ancient woodland sites' affected not only small and medium-sized woods in the county but also some of the largest examples, including Brooke Wood (60 hectares), Haveringland Great Wood (92 hectares) and Hevingham Park (63 hectares). In several other cases, fortunately, replanting affected only a proportion of the wood, leaving most of the area relatively undisturbed, as at Hockering, where much of the coniferised area had been cleared during the war. In a few examples, as at Toombers Wood, rather larger areas were replanted but a significant portion of the old coppiced wood nevertheless remained untouched. Replanting usually had a disastrous affect not only on the wood's flora but also on its archaeology, for it was often accompanied by large-scale levelling and, on heavier land, by the installation of new drainage systems, usually (as at Toombers Wood) consisting of ditches considerably wider and deeper than those employed in nineteenth-century drainage schemes. External woodbanks might survive this onslaught reasonably well, as in the case of Brooke Wood, and some of the larger internal banks could remain if bulldozing was kept to a minimum, as within the coniferised sections of Hockering Wood, but the more ephemeral archaeology was usually obliterated. Many ancient woods were thus drastically modified in the middle and later decades of the twentieth century, but the post-war drive to increase agricultural production, at almost any environmental cost, meant also that government grants were available for converting woods to arable land, although this mainly affected the smaller copses. All in all, between 1945 and 1973 nearly half the ancient woods that remained in Norfolk were either coniferised or grubbed out completely (Spencer and Kirby 1992).

From the 1970s, however, the rate of destruction slowed markedly in Norfolk, as in other English counties. A few woods were badly affected by Dutch elm disease, which arrived in the late 1960s, in part because it stimulated systematic but sometimes inappropriate replanting by some enthusiastic landowners: but elm was relatively rare as a standard in Norfolk woods, and even as a coppice only very localised. By the 1980s concern about the state of Britain's broadleaved woodlands was becoming intense, and 1985 was in many ways a turning point in the history of British woodlands. In July of that year a new policy for forestry, aimed at encouraging the positive and sympathetic management of broadleaved woodlands, was announced (Aldous 1988). Since then, management as coppice-with-standards has been looked on more sympathetically by government agencies, land agents and landowners, and coppicing has been reinstated within sections of a number of woods: of those studied in the sample, Hedenham Wood, Sexton's Wood in Hedenham, Sporle Wood and Tivetshall Wood are all now partly managed on traditional lines. More extensive reinstatement of traditional management has occurred within woods that have been acquired by conservation bodies, and are thus managed primarily for the benefit of wildlife.

Norfolk was, in fact, at the forefront of the movement to establish nature reserves, something which began to be advocated by individuals such as Charles Rothschilde – who was responsible for the foundation of the Society for the Promotion of Nature Reserves in 1912 – in the last years of the nineteenth and first decades of the twentieth century (Evans 1992, 45). While wildlife conservation was not the main concern of the National Trust (established in 1895), its first property, Wicken Fen in Cambridgeshire, a gift from Rothschilde himself, was a site of natural rather than cultural importance, and it was followed by the acquisition of the 1,335 acres (540 hectares) of salt marsh at Blakeney Point in Norfolk – purchased by public subscription and donated to the Trust in 1912 – and by the 1,821 acres (737 hectares) of Scolt Head in 1923 (Evans 1992, 46–7). The first of the County Wildlife Trusts was established in Norfolk in 1926 in order to save the coastal marshes at Cley from being drained for agriculture. But while a number of further reserves were established by this body over the following decades – at Martham in 1928, Alderfen Broad in 1930, Wretham Heath in 1938 and Weeting in 1942 (Gay 1944) – it was not until some time after the Second World War that it began to acquire areas of ancient woodland, beginning with Wayland Wood in Watton in 1975. Honeypot Wood in Wendling followed in 1980, Lower Wood at Ashwellthorpe in 1990, and Foxley Wood in 1998. In addition, Thursford Wood – a former tract of relict wood-pasture embedded in eighteenth- and nineteenth-century estate planting – was received in 1957. Wayland, Foxley, Honeypot and Ashwellthorpe Lower Wood have, to varying degrees, been brought back into coppice management, most extensively in the case of Wayland. A significant number of other woods in the county are classified as Sites of Special Scientific Interest, including Tindall Wood in Ditchingham and Gawdyhall Big Wood; and many more are designated County Wildlife Site – the Norfolk term for what are nationally known as 'Local Sites': locations of 'substantive nature conservation or geological conservation value' which are included in formal planning and development control processes.[9]

The majority of ancient woods in Norfolk are now seemingly safe from large-scale replanting and coniferisation, although occasional losses have occurred in relatively recent times, with the centre of Bunwell Wood, for example, being replanted as an arboretum as late as the 1970s. Most ancient woods are now managed primarily as game cover, for shooting continues to be a major feature of rural life in the county. But we should not be too sanguine about the future. Relatively few examples in the county are managed on traditional lines; many continue to be dense and shady, with a ground cover either sparse or dominated by dog's mercury. Attempts at coppicing are hindered, and the condition of woodland generally adversely affected, by the phenomenal increase in the county's deer population that took place in the course of the twentieth century. Lists of wild mammals published in the *Transactions of the Norfolk and Norwich Naturalists' Society* for 1879 and 1884 do not list deer at all: they were restricted to the various landscape parks of the region, including Holkham, Houghton, Kimberley and Didlington, and were regarded as semi-domesticated (Norgate 1878, 458–70; Clarke 1897, 301). Their numbers took off partly as a result of the large-scale afforestation in Breckland, partly as a consequence of deliberate encouragement for shooting and partly owing to the increasingly undisturbed character of the rural landscape as the mechanisation of farming proceeded apace (Simmons 2001, 252–3; Rackham 1986a, 49–50; 2006, 537–42; Chapman and Whitta 1996). New threats to woods continue to emerge, moreover, including, above all, ash *chalara*: Ashwellthorpe Lower Wood was one of the places where the disease was first noted in the country. It remains to be seen how serious its impact will be, but already landowners are being advised not to coppice ash stools, as young growth is particularly vulnerable to the disease.

Conclusion

The recent history of ancient woodland is generally treated briefly in published works, and in entirely negative terms. But developments since the start of the twentieth

---

9   Paragraph 119 of the National Planning Policy Framework requires that local planning policies should 'identify and map components of ecological networks, including the hierarchy of international, national and locally designated sites of importance for biodiversity, wildlife corridors and stepping stones that connect them …'. In Norfolk, County Wildlife Sites are recognised in all existing and emerging local plans. Most woods included in the Ancient Woodland Inventory are, or should have been, designated as County Wildlife Sites.

century have clearly had an important influence on the present character of woods and may sometimes have obscured the nature of their earlier composition. As in earlier centuries, the story of woodland was enmeshed, in complex ways, with that of the surrounding countryside, and with wider developments in society. Traditional management often continued into the twentieth century but the declining value of coppice products, together with the decline in the fortunes of large landed estates, led to its general abandonment in the middle decades of the century, while the advent of the Forestry Commission ensured that even in the inter-war period some replanting with conifers was taking place, something which accelerated in the post-War years. The Second World War found new uses for a number of the county's woods, adding some important new layers to their archaeology, but did nothing to arrest their continued decline into dereliction, something which may have served not merely to reduce the diversity of the ground flora but also, in some cases, to change the species composition of the underwood. In a number of places coppicing has been reinstated since the 1970s, but most of the county's woods remain in an unmanaged condition and are increasingly threatened by the depredations of deer, by emergent tree diseases and, more locally, by development pressures.

Chapter 8

Conclusion: the nature of woodland

The research presented in this volume, as we emphasised at the outset, is primarily archaeological and historical in character, and focused on one relatively limited area of lowland England. We believe, however, that our conclusions have wider *ecological* implications, for they raise important questions about the way we understand 'ancient woodland' as a distinct kind of habitat. Throughout, our emphasis – perhaps over-emphasis – has been on the essentially *unnatural* character of such woodland, and on the importance of understanding individual woods within wider spatial and social contexts. It is sometimes assumed, or at least implied, that ancient woods represent a direct link with the 'natural' vegetation of England, as this existed before the Neolithic clearances. But even if we reject the arguments of Frans Vera that the natural landscape largely comprised open savannah, with only limited and impermanent stands of woodland, it is probable that later prehistoric, Roman and early medieval settlement in Norfolk was on such scale that woodland vegetation would have been extensively modified, primarily by grazing, but also by exploitation for wood and timber. When woods were enclosed and managed as coppices, moreover, further changes occurred, not least because of the exclusion of grazing stock; and subsequent developments in the management of what were, in essence, valuable pieces of private property will have led to further alterations in botanical character.

Coppiced woods were enclosed, so far as the evidence goes, in the course of the eleventh, twelfth and thirteenth centuries. The fact that woods and commons were (before the widespread enclosures of the latter in the early nineteenth century) often contiguous attests their common origins, and their divergence in environmental terms was a direct consequence of patterns of ownership. The enclosure of woodland was an act of unilateral lordly privatisation, and this may explain the massive size of many early woodbanks, far larger than would be required merely to prevent the accidental straying of stock from surrounding land. The areas so treated were not randomly selected. They tended, in particular, to be located towards the margins of areas of heavy clay in order to reduce the distance that wood and timber needed to be transported along unsurfaced tracks. The location of woodland, that is, was the consequence for the most part of rational economic choice. But there are also, in addition, indications that woods were, where possible, retained close to manorial residences, and here we may see the influence of social and aesthetic factors, associated with the display of status.

In those areas of 'waste' which were not subject to seigniorial enclosure, and which were not converted during the period of rapid early medieval population growth to enclosed pastures or arable fields, underwood must have become sparse but tree cover clearly survived for much longer than is sometimes assumed. Wood-pastures, particularly those on common land, are inherently unstable environments but, as we have explained, customs often existed which permitted commoners and lords to establish and protect new plantings; and thus, on many commons, large numbers of pollarded trees survived into the eighteenth or even nineteenth centuries. Private wood-pastures, principally deer parks, enclosed from the common wastes exhibited less longevity. Many disappeared in the course of the fifteenth, sixteenth and seventeenth centuries – some, such as Hockering or Foxley, becoming coppiced woodland – and there was little continuity between them and the parks widely created as the settings for elite residences in the later post-medieval period. While the latter often do contain some very ancient trees, these were generally incorporated from the hedgerows which surrounded the fields removed when the parks were created. This said, the evidence makes it clear that in Norfolk at least the extent of wood-pastures, both private and common, in the medieval and early post-medieval landscape has been underestimated. Before the later seventeenth century grazed woodland of these kinds would have collectively covered a much greater area of ground than the enclosed, coppiced woods which we now usually think of as 'ancient' or 'semi-natural' woodland.

Not all woods of the latter type, we have also emphasised, originated in the early Middle Ages. Some, such as Tivetshall Wood or Beckett's Wood in Woodton, evidently overlie areas which were farmed or settled during the Middle Ages, and which were abandoned, and became occupied by trees once again, during or after the fifteenth century. Many existing 'primary' woods also expanded over formerly open areas in this period. While we usually assume that such secondary woodland regenerated naturally, there are some indications that a proportion may have been deliberately planted, with timber and coppice, as early as the fifteenth century. Where such woods originated, as they often seem to have done, as late as the eighteenth or nineteenth century, it is hard to see how else they may have arisen. The possibility that a significant proportion of ancient woods were deliberately planted has obvious implications for how far we view them as 'natural' or 'semi-natural' habitats.

The later history of ancient woodland is often neglected in studies of woodland history, but, as we have argued, this is a mistake. Woods were dynamic rather than stable environments and much of their present character derives from relatively recent developments. Traditional woodland management continued right through the sixteenth, seventeenth, eighteenth and nineteenth centuries, although perhaps with minor changes in the relative importance of wood and timber and possibly some extension in the length of the coppice rotation, although the evidence for this is not, in Norfolk at least, entirely clear-cut. In spite of the rise of modern forestry during the eighteenth century, landowners continued to establish new areas of coppice as late as the 1850s or 1860s. The later history of ancient woods was closely tied to that of large landed estates, something which ensured that they acquired a number of new uses. Their role as game coverts probably ensured that coppicing continued into the early twentieth century on a greater scale than the economic value of underwood alone, progressively eroded by industrialisation, would have merited. The rapid decline in traditional management in the middle decades of the century was thus intimately associated with the distress, and often the demise, of large landed properties as much as with the declining value of underwood compared with competitor fuels and raw materials.

In innumerable ways the history of semi-natural woods was thus connected to wider currents of agricultural, social and economic history, and the extent of their human as opposed to 'natural' character is obvious from even a cursory examination of their current composition. The complete absence of small-leaved lime from most ancient woods in the county is remarkable, given its prominence in the prehistoric landscape. Its representation was probably reduced by the use of the wooded 'wastes' as grazing grounds long before coppiced woods became common. Oak was the dominant standard tree in most, if not all, of the latter throughout the medieval and post-medieval periods not because it had been the most common tree in the wildwood, or even in the grazed woodlands of early medieval times, but because it provided the most useful and durable timber. Although direct evidence is lacking, it would be surprising if economic and practical pressures had not also had a similar impact on the composition of underwood, for it is hard to believe that this was not to some extent 'weeded' of unwanted shrubs by medieval and early post-medieval managers, and perhaps at times replanted, as it evidently was in some places in the nineteenth century (above, p. 117). As we have seen, much if not most domestic fuel in Norfolk, by late medieval times, came from sources other than managed woods. Firewood was cut from hedges and from pollards in farmland and on commons; gorse and heather were harvested from heaths; and peat was dug from wetlands. Woods were certainly major producers of fuel but this was probably a secondary function: the admittedly meagre evidence suggests that most underwood was used for, in particular, making charcoal, hoops or hurdles. Such specialised uses may have become more important from the later eighteenth century, as coal gradually became the main domestic fuel in the county, but may always have been there, encouraging deliberate modification of the underwood to ensure the presence or dominance of the necessary species. We have suggested, albeit tentatively, that the prevalence of hornbeam in managed woods – much greater than in the woodlands of prehistory – may be due in part to its suitability for making charcoal, a commodity required in large quantities by the inhabitants of England's second city, Norwich. The phase of neglect and decline in woodland management which began in the early twentieth century itself further altered the botanical character of ancient woods. Increased shading reduced the diversity of the herb layer and may also have changed the character of the understorey, especially where this included a significant hornbeam component. Many of the woods now dominated by this species may have had a more diverse shrub layer when regularly managed.

Many of the above conclusions are based on qualitative rather than quantitative evidence; some, we freely admit, are speculative in character. But a detailed survey of the kind discussed here also allows less impressionistic analysis, and two observations in particular stand out as being of particular importance. One is that the archaeology of ancient woodland in Norfolk is overwhelmingly medieval and post-medieval in character. The most ubiquitous earthworks associated with woods are medieval and post-medieval woodbanks, internal boundaries and drainage ditches, together with extraction pits and high-status enclosures and settlements; woodland of a secondary character also contains field boundaries and the sites of former farmsteads of fifteenth-century and later date. The evidence for prehistoric and Roman activity within the current area of ancient woods is, in contrast, comparatively sparse, although not entirely absent. Woods in Norfolk do not, in general, contain evidence for prehistoric field systems, something which throws important light on the true character of the 'relict field systems' – supposedly planned landscapes of prehistoric or Roman date surviving as modern field patterns – which sometimes exist around them. Many of the largest ancient woods, such as Tindall Wood in Ditchingham or Sexton's Wood in Hedenham, contain absolutely no evidence that their area was formerly farmed, at least in the form of above-ground archaeology; and where such evidence is forthcoming it often suggests pastoral exploitation of unenclosed or minimally enclosed landscapes, rather than arable activity. There are, it is true, examples of possible prehistoric lynchets within woods but none are securely dated and some, at least, may indicate that the woods in question overlie areas of medieval rather than earlier farmland that were cultivated as open fields without hedged boundaries: the absence across most of East Anglia of a distinctive signature for open-field cultivation in the form of ridge and furrow is an obvious problem here. The dearth of prehistoric and Roman earthworks from what are now the only areas in Norfolk to have remained unploughed since pre-medieval times is an important indication of the real extent and intensity of early settlement in the county.

The second observation, perhaps of greater interest to most readers of this book, relates to the antiquity of ancient woodland and its stability in the landscape. While some authorities have emphasised the permanence and continuity of woodland boundaries – and, by implication, the character of woods as refuges for species once frequent in the 'wildwood' but rendered uncommon by its contraction and fragmentation through the expansion of farmland – our studies suggest, for Norfolk at least, a more complex pattern. Only a handful of the woods examined retain in their entirety the boundaries established when they were first sundered from the 'wastes' and subjected to management by coppicing in the early Middle Ages. Around three-quarters of the genuinely ancient woods in the sample – that is, woods established before the start of the seventeenth century – display significant evidence for contraction. Some (such as Pulham Big Wood, Horningtoft Great Wood or Horningtoft Little Wood) represent no more than vestigial rumps of their original areas. Conversely, the extent to which existing woods expanded over neighbouring fields, roads or settlements in the late medieval or post-medieval periods is striking. In some cases such additions are substantial, as at Hedenham, Wayland and probably Gawdyhall Big Wood, although elsewhere they have taken the form of minor intakes of small strips of land, as, for example, in the cases of The Shrubbery in Tivetshall, Sporle Wood or Shotesham Little Wood. Some medieval or later expansion of the original core, as at Edgefield or Foxley, also appears to have been at the expense of adjoining areas of common land; elsewhere, as at Hook Wood, Morley St Peter it perhaps occurred over private pasture or wood-pasture. Woods which appear to retain their original bounds unchanged can thus be counted on a single hand – Honeypot Wood in Wendling, Sexton's Wood in Hedenham, Swanton Novers Great Wood, Tindall Wood and perhaps West Bradenham Great Wood – although even these could be queried by a purist: Tindall Wood, for example, has had a separately named area of woodland (Cooper's Grove) added to its north-western corner; part of West Bradenham was grubbed and farmed for a while in the nineteenth century, before being returned to woodland; even Sexton's Wood has a tiny post-medieval addition to its area. Some Norfolk woods, such as Earsham Great Wood, exhibit particularly complex histories of expansion and contraction. The medieval woodbank running east–west through its centre, the smaller bank on its northern boundary and a complete absence of a woodbank on its southern side suggest that the whole wood had shifted northwards before it was first mapped in *c.*1720. Since then expansion eastwards has increased its area by around 30 per cent. The histories of Hedenham Wood, and of Hook Wood in Morley, suggest similar degrees of shifting instability.

Aside from the many sections of woods that have plainly come and gone over the centuries, the large number of Norfolk woods that appear to be entirely secondary in character is also noteworthy. Well over a third (around 36 per cent) of the woods in the sample seem to have been planted on, or regenerated over, areas of farmland or settlement during or after the late Middle Ages; a figure which falls, but only to 33 per cent, when only woods actually included in the *Inventory* are considered. It is important to emphasise that these are generally the smaller examples. The average size of woods in the sample which appear entirely secondary in character is around 6 hectares, while that of predominantly primary ones is more than three times this. In passing, it is worth noting the high proportion of secondary woods – over half – which are named 'Grove', compared with only 3 per cent of those which are predominantly primary in character; this presumably reflects the fact that this term was in general used for smaller rather than larger woods in the county.

The contrast between 'small' secondary woods and 'large' primary examples should not, however, be overplayed. The comparison is not an entirely meaningful one, given the fact that many of the latter include within their present bounds a significant area of 'secondary' woodland. But, in addition, and more importantly, 'primary' remains a poorly defined and problematic term. Leaving aside the ambiguous, uncertain evidence – the enigmatic lynchets in West Bradenham Great Wood and elsewhere – that some portions of these woods may have been cultivated in prehistoric or Roman times, it is clear that a number of ancient woods occupy areas which, while not formerly cultivated, were probably heavily grazed, as pasture or wood-pasture, before they were enclosed and managed as coppice. Foxley Wood, for example, was originally a compartmentalised deer park, which probably contained open laundes as well as closely grazed wood-pasture; Hockering may have been similar; the three woods at Woodrising appear to have been managed as wood-pastures well into the Middle Ages; and there are hints of a similar history at Swanton Novers. Indeed, as we have emphasised throughout, *all* primary woods must occupy land that was, with varying intensities, subject to grazing before it was enclosed and managed as coppice. The ecology of the areas in question must have been significantly different to that which we now associate with 'ancient woodland', and, in particular, many of the species now considered as 'ancient woodland indicators', with poor resistance to grazing, must have been comparatively rare.

This, in turn, brings us the crucial question of the speed with which ancient woods can acquire their distinctive botanical characteristics. The results of this survey leave little doubt that this can happen much more rapidly than is often assumed. Day (1993), in his study of Sidlings Copse in Oxfordshire, emphasised the extent to which secondary woodland can acquire 'woodland indicators' in the form of vascular plants, but this wood appears to have regenerated over formerly open land in the early Middle Ages, so would qualify as 'ancient' in terms of the *Ancient Woodland Inventory*, having been present in the landscape since *c*.1600. What our results indicate is that a significant number of woods in Norfolk which are accepted as 'ancient' (in the sense that they are included on the *Ancient Woodland Inventory*) unquestionably originated long after 1600, the official cut-off date for 'ancientness'; and that most of these now appear similar, if not identical, to woods of genuinely 'ancient' character.

Not only do these 'pseudo-ancient woods' boast a coppiced understorey but they have also acquired a ground flora which features an often impressive array of 'ancient woodland indicators': fewer than in the case of Sidlings Copse, perhaps, but enough to pass muster as a wood of 'ancient' status. Over a sixth of the *Inventory* woods in the sample studied fall into this category, a figure supported by a wider examination of *Inventory* woods in the county (above, pp. 127–9), but as argued earlier, this is clearly an underestimate: such woods can usually be identified with confidence only on the basis of cartographic evidence, and the majority of parishes in Norfolk lack detailed maps pre-dating 1800, suggesting that the true figure must be nearer a fifth, or possibly more. This is not to say, however, that a fifth of officially recognised ancient woodland in the county *by area* originated in the period after 1600 because, as we have just explained, secondary woods of all types tend to cover, on average, a significantly smaller area than those which are wholly or largely 'primary' in character.

Rather than considering these seventeenth-, eighteenth- and nineteenth-century inclusions in the *Inventory* simply as 'mistakes' which future revision might rectify, it is more useful to consider what they might tell us more generally about the character of English woodland. Although wood anemone, water avens, bluebells and the like are often thought to be useful indicators of a wood's antiquity – of its 'ancient' status – a number of researchers, in addition to Day, have emphasised that they should be approached with a measure of caution (Peterken and Game 1984, 155; Rose 1999, 249; Wager 1998). We have already noted how Rose has emphasised that 'they should be regarded only as a tool, and not as an infallible guide' (Rose 1999, 250), and how Rotherham has argued that their use has often been 'too formulaic' in the past, and emphasised the way in which their affinity with ancient woodland 'varies tremendously with geology and hence soils and/or drainage, and especially with climate and microclimate' (Rotherham 2011a, 172, 178). Of equal importance here, however, is the history of the local landscape. As we have emphasised, most of these plants are relatively slow colonisers, survive best in relatively humid and shaded conditions and often exhibit poor resistance to grazing; many are well suited to the regular cycles of light and shade provided by coppicing. The districts of Norfolk in which pseudo-ancient woods are found – the claylands in the south and centre of the county – contained numerous areas of managed woodland. But, perhaps more importantly, they boasted large numbers of *hedges*. Open fields developed only to a limited extent in these areas and had begun to disappear by the fifteenth century. The bulky, mixed-species hedges of medieval and early post-medieval times, accompanied by deep ditches, provided an environment within which such plants could thrive and a network through which they could spread. Their shrub vegetation and ditches gave a measure of protection from grazing, while regular management, by coppicing or 'laying', provided an environment analogous to that of managed woodland (Barnes and Williamson 2006, 67–9).

Although the landscape thus contained numerous reservoirs of woodland plants, it might be thought that their dispersal into newly planted woods would in most cases be slow. But the very existence of 'pseudo-ancient woods' shows that this is true only up to a point, and that the slow rate of dispersal of some of these plants has certainly been exaggerated. In parts of south and central Norfolk dog's mercury, for example, grows freely even in some nineteenth-century hedges, especially where these were planted at the enclosure of open commons (Barnes and Williamson 2006, 84–94). In such circumstances, moreover, its rate of progress along the new hedge from a boundary on the edge of the common where it had long been present can be easily measured. In many cases dog's mercury has progressed 40 metres or more since the early nineteenth century; in one roadside hedge, planted at the enclosure of Wymondham Common in 1806, it has achieved a distance of no less than 115 metres (Barnes and Williamson 2006, 85). Bluebells and primroses have also spread with some alacrity along many hedges planted in the nineteenth century across former commons, the former in some cases by as much as 100 metres (Barnes and Williamson 2006, 88–90). Given the fact that almost all secondary ancient woods in Norfolk cover less than ten hectares, and that many have high perimeter-to-area ratios because of their attenuated shape or indented outlines, it is easy to see how most could acquire a ground cover featuring many of these more common 'indicators' within a relatively short time. There are 18 woods in the sample which are likely to be entirely 'secondary' in character, including both those which are 'genuinely' ancient and those post-dating 1600. Shape and size ensure that 14 of these have no part of their area more than 100 metres from their outer boundaries, which, in most if not all cases, were formerly those of the field or fields within which they were planted. Several, such as America Wood in Earsham or Old Grove in Gillingham, also incorporate *within* their area the remains of field boundaries from which woodland plants would have dispersed. If the speed with which dog's mercury, primrose and bluebells spread along Norfolk hedges is any guide to the rate of their dispersal in woodland, most parts of such woods would be colonised within two centuries or so. These plants would take longer, it is true, to spread through the four larger secondary woods in the sample: but not that much longer, given that none is so large that any part lies more than 180 metres from the outer margins. All four, we would emphasise, are 'genuinely' ancient woods, of pre-1600 vintage, rather than ones of 'pseudo-ancient' type, giving ample time for thorough colonisation.

It is true that the speed of dispersal of less common 'indicators' cannot be studied in a non-woodland context so easily as can that of dog's mercury, bluebells or primrose, and it is likely that some, at least, colonise hedges and woods much more slowly. In Attleborough Wood bluebell and dog's mercury seem to be widely scattered but wood anemone and yellow archangel tend to occur towards the margins. This said, the presence of wood sedge and early purple orchid in Lopham Grove, planted since 1720, and water avens in Holy Grove, largely post-1770 and entirely post-1720 in origin, is noteworthy. Remote sedge (*Carex remota*) and early purple orchid even occur, alongside dog's mercury and primrose, in Old Grove in Gillingham, which was planted only in the middle or later decades of the nineteenth century, although here the wood overlies a particularly dense mesh of former field boundaries.

Where woods which are mainly primary in character also have a significant 'secondary' component similar arguments apply, although here colonisation needs to be considered in terms of distance from the existing wood as well as from pre-existing hedges on or near the margins of the new addition; and, once again, the likelihood that plants spread from hedges incorporated within the wood by its expansion needs to be noted. Hedenham Wood, for example, expanded southwards by a distance of nearly 300 metres in the sixteenth and seventeenth centuries and the dense network of former field boundaries now preserved in earthwork form within the wood presumably provided the supply of woodland plants which ensured that today the primary 'core' and the secondary addition are botanically indistinguishable. The defining characteristics of what we call 'ancient woodland', often seen as a simple consequence of age, thus appear to be contingent also on location and context: on the character of the local landscape.

To some extent our observations on these matters may have been affected by the somewhat atypical character of the study area. Most of the ancient woodland investigated and almost all of the 'pseudo-ancient' woods identified lie within the old-enclosed 'woodland' parts of the county. Most landscapes of this type in England as a whole boasted, throughout the medieval and post-medieval periods, rather higher densities of woodland than did these areas of Norfolk, and there was thus rather less incentive for owners to establish new areas of coppice that could acquire 'ancient' characteristics in the manner suggested. This said, our conclusions on these matters accord well with the results of recent research by Ian Rotherham and his associates in Yorkshire, which has emphasised how the botanical 'ghosts' of lost woods can continue as residual populations of characteristic woodland plants in areas of relatively undisturbed ground, as, for example, on moorland (Ardron 2013; Alder 2013; Rotherham 2012): such 'woodland specialists' (Kirby *et al.* 2012, 69) might then flourish and spread if woodland conditions returned. The presence of indicator species within a particular wood thus has less to do with its antiquity than with the extent of local botanical continuity, and Rotherham has recently posed the question: 'Are we really talking about "species associated with environmental continuity" or an "index of ecological continuity" rather than indicators of ancient woodland?' (Rotherham 2012, 8). Such contrasts have an obvious regional dimension. In lowland districts there is a broad difference in the degree of potential survival of woodland plants – that is, in the continuity of woodland vegetation – between 'champion' and 'woodland' areas. In the former, wooded landscapes were largely replaced by environments of arable open fields, with few hedges, in the early Middle Ages, in which woodland specialists would have had difficulty surviving. Most hedges, and the majority of woods, in such districts were established following post-medieval (and often eighteenth- or nineteenth-century) enclosure. In 'woodland' districts in the west and the south-east of the country, in contrast – as in south and central Norfolk – not only did more woodland survive through the Middle Ages but the development of open fields was limited, so that the farmed landscape appears always to have been characterised by significant numbers of hedges. It is thus hardly surprising that dog's mercury is a reasonably good indicator of ancient hedges in the 'champion' east Midlands but a less reliable one in old-enclosed central and southern East Anglia (Pollard *et al.* 1974, 91–2, 101–2), and a good indicator of a wood's antiquity in Midland areas but not necessarily elsewhere (Rackham 1986a, 108).

Some researchers, aware of the deficiencies of the *Inventory* and other official or quasi-official lists of ancient woods, are currently seeking to develop a 'robust and evidence-based methodology for assessing and defining ancient woodland', as set out, for example, in the *Ancient Woodland Manual* developed by Ian Rotherham and his colleagues (Rotherham 2012, 8; Rotherham and Wright 2011; Rotherham *et al.* 2008). But the evidence and arguments presented here suggest that we should be wary of seeing 'ancient woodland' as a distinct, definable category – as much of Rotherham's own recent work, with its emphasis on 'ghost' woodland, likewise implies. The Norfolk evidence not only suggests that a 'cut-off date' of *c.*1600 is somewhat arbitrary;

more importantly, it raises the question of whether the term 'ancient woodland', with its implication that biological character is principally dependent upon age, is entirely appropriate or useful. These, again, are not entirely new observations. Graham Bathe and his colleagues, discussing the abundant evidence for the secondary character of most woodland in the Savernake Forest, have recently argued that:

> The success of ancient woodland, as a concept, derives in part from its branding. It conforms to recognised principles evoking a vivid image through its name, conveying the impression of unique characteristics, and appealing to psychological motivations involving beliefs and attitudes ... Who would dare suggest that ancient woodlands were a bad thing? (Bathe *et al.* 2011, 56)

There are, however, obvious dangers in such arguments, at a time when increasing development pressures place many areas of ancient woodland, especially in the south and east of England, under severe threat. The Woodland Trust has recently emphasised the weakness of existing planning policy, noting that no fewer than 111 ancient woodland sites were destroyed in England between 2002 and 2012 (Ryan and the Woodland Trust 2012); and the current trend in government policy is for protection to be weakened, with a presumption in favour of development. The National Planning Policy Framework currently states that 'planning permission should be refused for development resulting in the loss or deterioration of irreplaceable habitats, including ancient woodland and the loss of aged or veteran trees found outside ancient woodland, unless the need for, and benefits of the development in that location, clearly outweigh the loss' (Department for Communities and Local Government 2012). Similar strong recommendations for conserving ancient woods have recently been issued by the Forestry Commission and Natural England (Forestry Commission and Natural England 2014). But in 2013 the government set out plans for a 'biodiversity offsetting' scheme as a green paper consultation, arguing that loss of a particular habitat is acceptable if a similar one can be created, or restored, elsewhere (DEFRA 2013a). If woods widely recognised as 'ancient' are not necessarily ancient at all, and if their supposedly special characteristics can be acquired with some rapidity, as this volume has suggested, then it might well be argued that they are not 'irreplaceable'. They might quite justifiably be removed to make way for roads, housing or some other public good, so long as an equivalent area of woodland was established in their place, on some other more convenient site.

Yet while it may be true that many of the more obvious characteristics of ancient woods are acquired relatively quickly, much further research – carried out by people more knowledgeable than us in the more arcane aspects of biology and ecology – is needed to establish whether this is also the case with less obvious aspects of their flora and fauna. Moreover, terms such as 'quickly' and 'rapidly' are relative. While we have suggested that some 'ancient' woods are not as old as we usually think, this does not mean that any are actually 'young', in terms of human lives or experience, still less that they can be recreated instantly. Even the 'pseudo-ancient' woods discussed in this volume have been in existence for more than a century and a half, usually for more than two centuries. Indeed, blurring the neat distinction usually posited between 'ancient' and 'recent' woodland does not so much reduce the importance of the former as raise the potential status of the latter. If the features we value in ancient woods can be found in some recent ones, then we should value these in a similar way. The clear implication of the *Ancient Woodland Inventory* that woods not included in it are of little conservation value is arguably the real problem here. Moreover, ancient woods have not just a biological but also an archaeological value and a cultural significance, as Rackham in particular has taught us: they preserve direct physical links with the past that cannot be reconstituted, once destroyed, by replanting elsewhere (Council for British Archaeology 2014). Even quite recent woods which lack 'ancient' characteristics may have a historical and cultural significance, as elements in eighteenth-century estate landscapes for example, and certainly contribute to local distinctiveness and our 'sense of place'. We would not apply a simple chronological yardstick, of the kind embedded in the concept of 'ancient woodland', when conserving the built environment: we would not happily condone the uncontrolled demolition of buildings simply because they had been erected after 1600, or 1700, or even 1900.

Woodland in England requires more, not less, protection. Development should be kept as far as possible from ancient woods, and carefully and appropriately buffered (Comey *et al.* 2008). But what is actually needed is more woodland, and more woodland of a diverse character: and this can be achieved only by planting new woods in environmentally appropriate areas at the same time as we fight to retain those we already have, in all their rich variety. The social, economic and environmental arguments for this, even at a time of mounting pressure on land, are overwhelming. Woodland makes up such a minor part of our countryside that small losses, even of relatively recent stands, have a significant environmental and cultural impact. And, in a wider sense, numerous studies and reports have over the last few years detailed the many benefits accruing from woodland of all kinds. The economic value of woods to the six counties in the East of England (Norfolk, Suffolk, Cambridgeshire, Hertfordshire, Essex, Bedfordshire), for example, was estimated in 2010 at £1.3 billion per year: this includes the value of timber and wood products, but also that arising from less tangible things, such as improvements in air quality and water management, enhanced biodiversity, tourism and recreation, health and well-being, carbon sequestration and education (Forestry Commission 2010). The wide range of benefits provided by woodland is indeed accepted in current government policy (DEFRA 2013b): but these are dangerous times. The arguments set out in this book, far from suggesting that 'ancient woodland' is dispensable or replaceable, imply instead that all our woods have a greater value and importance than is currently suggested by our emphasis on this one particular variety.

Appendix

Sites discussed in the text

America Wood, Earsham
TM 31329057

The *Inventory* area of America Wood covers some 7.4 hectares on soils of the Beccles Association. This area excludes the south-eastern corner of the wood but includes the northern section of 'America Lane', effectively a separate wood which lies some way to the east, but which is connected by a narrow strip of woodland. America Lane had not yet been planted up when the first edition Ordnance Survey map was surveyed in 1884 and is not shown on Figure 34; America Wood itself was also, in part, unplanted at this time, the map showing two separate woods here – 'America Wood' to the north and 'Sallow Plantation' to the south (area (a), and areas (b) and (c), on Figure 34)

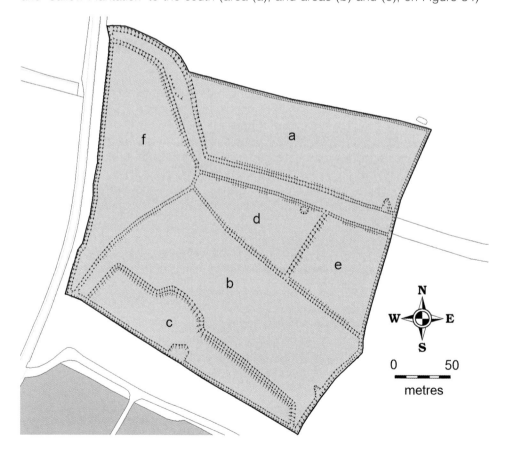

Figure 34 America Wood, Earsham: principal earthwork features (for key see text).

which were separated by farmland (areas (d) and (e)). The western section of the wood (f) was also, at this time, unplanted. The tithe award map, surveyed in 1839 (NRO DN/TA 564), shows that the area of America Wood (a) was then in existence and was bounded to the south and west by a lane; it is also detailed as woodland on a map of the Earsham estate dated 1770 (NRO MEA 3/632). Only the southern strip of Sallow Plantation (area (c)) was wooded in 1839, however, and even this was unwooded in 1770.

The wood is bounded by ditches, mainly still functioning, which are accompanied by only slight banks. Its interior is dissected by deep ditches of similar character, all of which can be correlated with boundaries shown on the tithe award map, including those bounding the lane running along the edges of, and absorbed during the course of the nineteenth century within the area of, America Wood (a). The only earthwork of a different character runs along the northern boundary of area (c): this resembles a diminutive woodbank, around 5 metres wide including flanking ditch, in spite of the fact that the areas it divided were both unwooded in 1770.

The varied histories of the different sections of the wood are reflected in their vegetation, although this has to some extent been obscured by the fact that large areas of the wood have been opened up in recent years as grassy rides. Areas (d), (e) and (f) – which were planted only since the 1880s – contain much sycamore, together with varying amounts of hazel and some ash coppice, and oak and ash standards: the ground is almost entirely covered with dog's mercury. Area (b), planted between 1839 and 1884, has a more intact coppice structure, mainly featuring hazel, but with some maple and occasional hornbeam, under oak standards: the woodland floor is more shaded and the ground flora poorer, including much bramble and nettles as well as dog's mercury. The older sections of the wood – the north (a) and the south (c) – are, in contrast, characterised by hornbeam coppice, together with some hazel, under oak and some hornbeam standards, the latter evidently singled from coppice: curiously, these areas boast less dog's mercury. Some fine hornbeam pollards grow along the southern boundary of (c).

This is largely, if not entirely, a wood of 'pseudo-ancient' type. The northern section – America Wood *sensu stricto* – although present by 1770, is almost certainly of post-1600 origin, lacking as it does obvious woodbanks. The vast majority of the wood was planted, in stages, after *c*.1770. In spite of this, all parts of the wood contain quantities of dog's mercury, while other 'indicators' – primrose, remote sedge and wood sedge – are also present.

Ashwellthorpe Lower Wood
TM 13909803

This 34-hectare wood is owned by the NWT and occupies a level or slightly sloping site on soils of the Beccles Association. It lies immediately to the north of the village of Ashwellthorpe, being separated from the houses by a line of small fields. Its northern edge corresponds with the parish boundary between Ashwellthorpe and Wreningham. Ashwellthorpe Upper Wood lies just over 100 metres to the west, separated from Lower Wood by a narrow pasture field (Figure 35). The enclosure map of 1811 (NRO C/Sca 2/126) and the tithe map of 1842 (NRO DN/TA 621) show Upper Wood as much larger than it is today, extending north as far as the parish boundary and south to

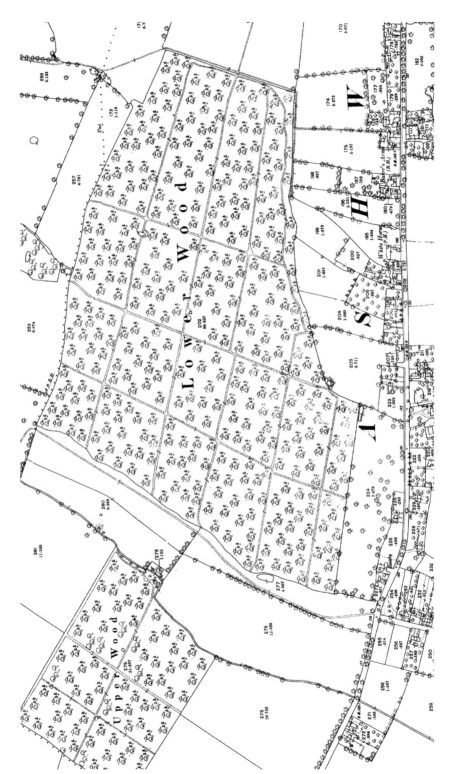

Figure 35 Ashwellthorpe Lower and Upper Woods, as depicted on the second edition Ordnance Survey six-inch map of 1907.

the road leading from Ashwellthorpe to Wymondham. Lower Wood was also larger at this time, extending further to the south-west, almost as far as the same road, from which it was separated by only a line of houses and gardens. These maps thus show, in effect, one large wood separated by a narrow north–south clearing, and William Faden's map of 1797 treats them as a single wood. They had been truncated to their present limits by 1882, when the Ordnance Survey 25 inches : one mile map was surveyed. The large combined wood, it should be noted, was until 1814 bounded to the south-west by Ashwellthorpe Common, one of several large and medium-sized commons which Faden shows along the watershed between the Tiffey (to the west) and the Tas (to the east). Records of timber and underwood sales from Ashwellthorpe dating from the late seventeenth and early eighteenth centuries refer to 16 acres being felled each year, and occasionally 30 acres. As the combined area of Lower and Upper Wood in 1811 was *c.*164 acres, this implies a rotation length of ten years (NRO KNY 571, 372X3).

The composition of Lower Wood is varied, with standards of oak and ash over varying mixtures of hornbeam, ash and hazel coppice, and scattered examples of holly and aspen. The ground flora is particularly rich, with extensive spreads of dog's mercury, bluebells and wild garlic, and with examples of wood anemone, wood spurge, woodruff, herb Paris, twayblade and early purple orchid. There do not appear to be any earthworks within the wood, other than a number of straight drainage gripes, some of which are laid out on a different alignment to the pattern of rides shown on the first edition Ordnance Survey 25-inch map. The straight south-western boundary, where the wood was truncated in the nineteenth century, is marked by a deep ditch accompanied by irregular piles of earth which were dug from it sufficiently long ago to have been colonised by dog's mercury. The other boundaries vary in precise form but are generally of normal medieval type: a substantial bank, rising *c.*0.5 metres above the woodland floor, accompanied by an external ditch, the whole around 6–7 metres in width. Only the western boundary is different. This has a much lower (and in places imperceptible) bank, presumably reflecting the fact that Lower and Upper Woods were severed in the late medieval or post-medieval period by the creation of the north–south 'clearing' already described. There are a number of ponds on the wood's boundary, and traces of a hedge – of outgrown hornbeam and maple – on the eastern side.

Lower and Upper Woods thus appear to have originated as a single wood, 'primary' in character and enclosed from a more extensive tract of common 'waste', fragments of which survived as common land immediately to the south-west into the nineteenth century. The two woods were probably severed after the early eighteenth century; they were further reduced in size between 1842 and 1882.

Attleborough Wood, Attleborough
TM 04209730

Attleborough Wood occupies an area of *c.*2.5 hectares on soils of the Beccles 1 Association, a little to the north of the town of Attleborough. The tithe award map (1839: NRO DN/TA 84 40) and the first edition Ordnance Survey six-inch map (1883) show the wood extending much further to the west and south, covering an area of nearly seven hectares. It is shown with the same outlines on the second edition Ordnance Survey

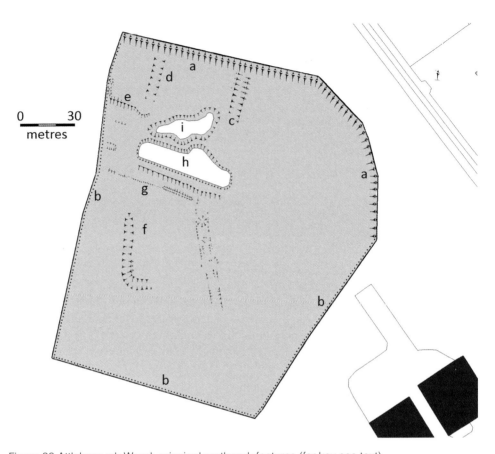

0 _____ 30
metres

Figure 36 Attleborough Wood: principal earthwork features (for key see text).

map of 1907, but had been truncated to its present limits by the time the 1946 RAF aerial photographs were taken. There are no earlier maps and the only documentary evidence so far discovered is a lease agreement from 1801, which stipulates a rotation length of ten years (NRO MEA 7/4). The wood has been used for a variety of purposes over recent years – most recently as a 'Forest School' – and includes a training circuit for the local boxing club. It has also been employed as a dumping ground for rubble and agricultural waste over a long period of time. All this makes interpretation of the earthwork features, in particular, highly problematic: Figure 36 should be treated with a measure of caution, the various banks and scarps in part extrapolated from a ground surface which is generally uneven and covered in amorphous undulations which we have not attempted to map in detail. There is no available LIDAR data.

The vegetation comprises outgrown and neglected ash and hazel coppice with sporadic oak, sycamore, elm and both black and white poplar. The remains of a neglected and abandoned orchard of apple and pear trees exist in the north-east corner, close to the entrance from Wood Farm. The ground flora includes large amounts of dog's mercury together with a number of other ancient woodland indicators, including wood anemone, bluebell and yellow archangel, all of which occur throughout the wood but are more common towards the margins. The interior of the wood is dominated by nettle (*Urtica diocia*), probably a reflection of raised nutrient levels resulting from relatively recent dumping.

The wood is enclosed to the north and east by a woodbank about 0.5 metres high and 3.5 metres wide, flanked by an external ditch 3 metres wide and 1.5 metres deep ((a) on Figure 37). The southern and western boundaries (b) have a small bank, about 0.2 metres high and 1 metre wide, without a ditch, marking where the wood was truncated in the early twentieth century. A marked hollow way (c), about 1 metre deep and around 10 metres in width, runs in from the northern edge of the wood. It is bounded by a slight bank, apparently the remains of a hedge bank, on its eastern side; there is a less distinct bank on the west. It disappears in deep vegetation before the pond (h) is reached, but its line can be picked out, with some optimism, among later undulations to the south of the pond, sweeping in an arc towards the south-east of the wood. Another hollow way (d) runs for a short distance in the north-western corner of the wood, but this is shallower (*c*.0.5 metres) and narrower (*c*.8 metres) and lacks flanking banks. Immediately to the south-west is a bank (e) 3 metres wide and 0.5 metres high, with a steeper face towards the south: the ground to the south is around 0.75 metres below that to the north, suggesting plough erosion along a field boundary: it bulges to the south where it meets the hollow way, probably as a consequence of later dumping. A third linear feature (f), more linear pit than hollow way, 1 metre deep and without flanking banks, occurs in the south-west of the wood. It may be of recent origin, and has certainly been modified in recent years. To the north (g) is a much vaguer and intermittent feature which may represent a former field boundary, although much modified by later dumping, while (h) and (i) are ponds, probably recent.

Given the extent to which earthworks have been obscured by later dumping it is difficult to say much about the origins of this wood, but the hollow way with its flanking bank (c) and the probable field boundary and lynchet (e) leave little doubt that this is a late medieval secondary rather than a primary wood. The concentration of 'ancient woodland indicators' towards the periphery of the wood is interesting in this context.

Beckett's Wood, Woodton
TM 27939491

Beckett's Wood covers an area of 2.6 hectares on Beccles 1 Association soils in the parish of Woodton. It is bounded to the east by a road and to the south by a public footpath. It mainly comprises outgrown hornbeam, ash and maple coppice, with some hazel, under oak standards that are densest to the west. Scattered examples of elm, privet, hawthorn, spindle and guelder rose are also present. Parts of the centre of the wood have been replanted with western red cedar, oak and ash. The ground flora, which is densest towards the centre and east of the wood, includes a number of 'ancient woodland indicators': dog's mercury, false brome (*Brachypodium sylvaticum*), wood sedge (*Carex sylvatica*), hairy St John's wort (*Hypericum hirsutum*) and primrose. The wood is shown, with a similar but not identical outline to today, on the Woodton tithe award map of 1841 (DN/TA 476), the difference being that it then extended slightly further to the south and south-west. This narrow strip of woodland was lost by the time the first edition Ordnance Survey six-inch map was made in the 1880s.

The wood is enclosed to the north by a substantial woodbank, generally around 6 metres in width, including its external ditch ((a) on Figure 37), and to the east by a

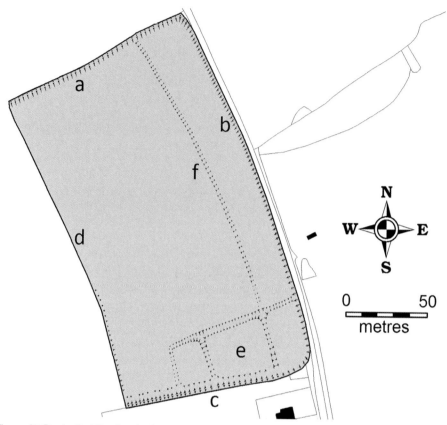

Figure 37 Beckett's Wood: principal earthwork features (for key see text).

similar but slightly narrower bank (b). The southern boundary (c) has a still narrower, and rather sharper and higher, bank which is flanked for much of its length by an internal as well as an external ditch. The western side of the wood (d) has a very slight, hardly discernible bank, no higher than 0.1 metres, which fades out entirely towards the north, suggesting relatively recent truncation or realignment of the boundary here. An oak pollard (with a girth of 3 metres) grows on this western boundary bank, and a large pollarded maple on the northern boundary.

In the south of the wood there are three rectangular enclosures (e), almost moat-like in character, defined by ditches which are between 3 and 6 metres in width and of very varying depth – in part perhaps as a consequence of deliberate infilling. There are no significant accompanying banks. The alignment of the western boundary of the most easterly of these enclosures is continued right through the length of the wood as a linear feature (f) comprising a slight (*c*.0.2 metres high) east-facing scarp flanked by a shallow and intermittent ditch. This runs more or less parallel to the eastern boundary of the wood. The character of these various internal earthworks is unclear. The enclosures are perhaps best interpreted as the remains of abandoned tofts, and the long scarp as the boundary of a field or, perhaps, an open-field strip. The 'tofts' would have fronted on the footpath running along the southern edge of the wood, which was presumably, in origin, a lane. Boundary (c) would be consistent with the edge of a minor lane running on the line of the present footpath, across which the wood extended before being truncated to its present southern boundary some time between 1839 and the 1880s.

This appears to be an area of secondary woodland, the character of the northern and eastern boundaries being consistent with a late medieval origin. The western and southern boundaries were realigned in the eighteenth or nineteenth centuries, the former change perhaps associated with a reduction in the wood's extent on this side.

Big Wood, Pulham St Mary Magdelen
TM 20518959

Big Wood, which is now owned and managed by the Woodland Trust, forms one of a series of interconnected woods lying around the parish boundary between Stratton St Mary and Pulham St Mary Magdelen, although it is the only one included in the *Ancient Woodland Inventory*. The others are New Plantation to the south and Tyrrel's Wood to the north, which the first edition Ordnance Survey six-inch map of 1884 shows as divided into three named sections: Crow Green to the west and Dale Plantation and Low Wood to the east (Figure 38). Crow Green was one of the commons of Stratton St Mary and was still open ground when Faden's county map was surveyed in the 1790s. The first detailed maps of the area – the 1839 tithe maps for the two parishes (DN/TA 492 and DN/TA 12) – show that all the woods were by then within their present boundaries, and that Crow Green was already wooded.

Big Wood covers an area of 4.7 hectares and, together with the adjacent areas of woodland, overlies Beccles Association soils, here generally acidic in character to judge from the character of the vegetation. The wood comprises a central area occupied by hazel coppice and much birch under oak standards, with scattered holly, rowan and young sycamore; and strips to the east and west that are dominated by outgrown stools of hornbeam. The south-eastern section is dominated by birch. The impression is of an ancient wood, heavily felled and invaded by birch at some point in the relatively recent past. The ground cover is sparse: virtually non-existent beneath the hornbeam and dominated by bramble and bracken elsewhere, but there are sporadic areas of dog's mercury and bluebell. The wood is bounded to the south, east and west by straight boundaries marked by ditches without banks, evidently of eighteenth- or nineteenth-century date. On the north, however, where the limit of the wood coincides with the parish boundary between Pulham St Mary Magdelen and Stratton St Mary, there is a particularly substantial woodbank with a slight inner ditch and an outer ditch which carries a small stream, the whole more than 9 metres across. There are some irregular drainage gripes in the northern section of the wood and an area of amorphous disturbances lying just inside the north bank, but no other earthworks.

The manor of Pulham was held by the bishop of Ely in the Middle Ages and the Ely Coucher Book of 1251 describes a wood called Grishaw covering 100 acres (Blomefield 1805, V, 400). Big Wood almost certainly represents its truncated remnants. Not only are the boundaries of the wood (other than that to the north) dead straight, but so too are the neighbouring field boundaries across an area of around 115 acres (46 hectares) bounded to the south by the suggestively named Wood Lane, to the west by a boundary curving, in a long uninterrupted sweep, from Wood Farm to the parish boundary, to the east by the irregular boundary beyond Bales Plantation,

Figure 38 Big Wood, Pulham, as depicted on the second edition Ordnance Survey six-inch map (1907). The shaded area is the suggested extent of the wood before most was grubbed out during the seventeenth and/or eighteenth centuries.

and to the north by the parish boundary (see areas shaded on Figure 38). This wood was presumably stubbed out to create Wood Farm. The wood appears to have still been in existence in the late sixteenth century (NRO 82482), but had disappeared by the time that Faden's map was surveyed in the 1790s.

The adjoining areas of woodland make an interesting comparison with Big Wood. New Plantation, entirely surrounded by straight ditches without banks, may be another remnant of the original wood, in spite of its name: its vegetation is similar to that of Big Wood, with oak standards, coppiced hazel and scattered examples of rowan and sycamore, and a sparse ground flora including scattered dog's mercury. But it is also possible that the area it occupies was completely cleared and then replanted in the eighteenth or nineteenth century: the tithe award describes it as 'coppice' yet calls it 'Furze Covert'. Dale Plantation, to the north of the parish boundary, is unlikely to be ancient – it is bounded on the south by a sharp, narrow bank (on the opposite side of the stream to the woodbank of Big Wood) and by ditches alone on its other boundaries, except the northern section of the eastern boundary, which has a rather diffuse, spread and irregular bank. Its southern section is described as 'plantation' in the tithe schedule. Yet its vegetation is, again, very similar to that within Big Wood, with hornbeam coppice along the eastern side and oak standards over hazel coppice, mixed with much birch, sycamore, scattered alder and holly, elsewhere. Three slight scarps/ditches spaced at intervals of around 7 metres run in from the eastern edge for *c*.30 metres: they probably represent drainage gripes but could relate to earlier agricultural use of the site. Low Wood is more problematic. It, too, has a strip of hornbeam coppice down the eastern side and oak standards over hazel coppice, with birch and some sycamore, in the central and western sections. It is divided by a ditch without a bank from Dale Plantation, but the other sides have a slight, wide but diffuse bank in places, and the northern section of the eastern boundary is marked by a very large, apparently medieval, woodbank. The shape of the northern boundary, however – gently curving and with a marked short dog's-leg – suggests that it was formed from the piecemeal enclosure of open-field arable, and on balance the wood is probably secondary, of late medieval or early post-medieval date. Both Dale Plantation and Low Wood have a very impoverished ground flora, with bluebells and dog's mercury on the boundaries, but only sporadically within the body of the wood.

Crow Green – the most recent of the woods – is rather different in character. It has a central section comprising oak standards with scattered hornbeam and birch, and a ground flora mainly composed of brambles; but its northern and southern sections contain varying combinations of oak, coppiced hazel and outgrown coppiced ash, with some birch and sycamore. Here the ground flora is more varied, especially towards the margins or where dominated by ash, and includes larger amounts of dog's mercury and bluebell than can be found within Big Wood itself.

In the absence of early maps it is not possible to reconstruct, with any confidence, the complex history of contraction and expansion displayed by woodland in this area, but it is striking how the relative antiquity of the surviving areas would be hard to deduce from their structure or vegetation. The *Inventory* area of Big Wood is presumably 'primary' in character, a fragment – as we have argued – of a much larger area of woodland.

Billingford Wood, Billingford
TM 17758039

Billingford Wood lies on the southern edge of the south Norfolk boulder clay plateau entirely on soils of the Beccles 1 Association. In 1884, when the first edition Ordnance Survey six-inch map was surveyed, it covered *c*.18 hectares, but this was reduced by the clearance of a central east–west strip some 100–120 metres in width some time in the late twentieth century. The majority of the wood – the northern section – occupies a level plateau; the southern part lies on slightly sloping ground which forms the edge of the Waveney valley, and here the soils include some Burlingham Series. The early history of the wood, which is now part of the Mann estate based at Thelveton Hall, is poorly documented. The tithe award map (NRO DN/TA 527) shows that in 1839 the wood covered *c*.23 hectares, extending slightly further to the east than today, as far as the straight road shown on Figure 39, Wood Lane, and also further to the north,

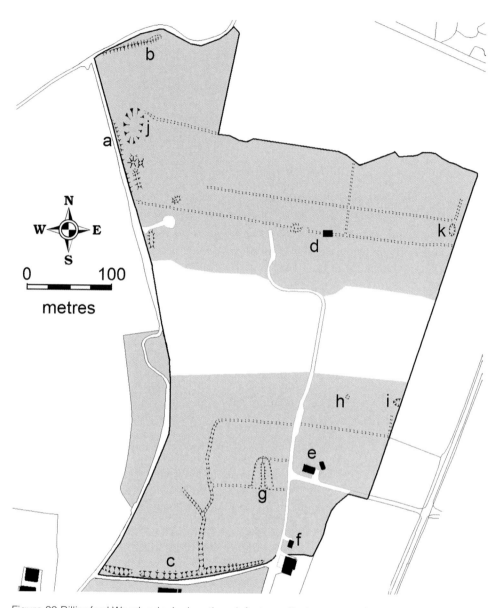

Figure 39 Billingford Wood: principal earthwork features (for key see text).

the present north-western projection of the wood showing its original extent in this direction. The only cartographic depiction earlier than the tithe award map is provided by Faden's map of Norfolk of 1797, which, in so far as its schematic representation tells us anything, suggests that the wood then had a similar outline to that shown in 1839.

The wood mainly comprises outgrown hornbeam coppice with scattered oak standards, although other species are sporadically present in the understorey, including hawthorn, maple and, to the north, hazel. Scattered examples of birch, mainly associated with areas of wartime activity, are also present: the wood was used to house various buildings and structures associated with Thorpe Abbots airfield (built for the RAF in 1942, transferred to the USAAF in 1943), which lies immediately to the east. The ground flora, as often in dense hornbeam woods, is sparse, but includes water avens and dog's mercury. Sections of medieval woodbank survive along the northern end of the western perimeter ((a) on Figure 39); the rest of the western boundary is probably medieval, the woodbank here having been levelled when the wartime track along the margins of the wood was created. Another short section of medieval woodbank runs through the northern projection of the wood (b), a little to the south of the wood's present boundary: its eastern end has been truncated by a wartime track. The deep ditch along the southern edge of the wood (c) (accompanied by a minor bank, or no bank at all) may also be medieval, but all the other boundaries appear post-medieval, each marked by only a small bank and ditch or by a ditch alone. Most were created by the reduction in the wood's area in the nineteenth century. Internally, the wood is criss-crossed by an irregular grid of generally shallow (*c*.0.2 metres) and narrow (less than a metre) drainage ditches. These probably date from the nineteenth century but are often closely associated with wartime features, so may in part be related to this phase of the wood's history.

The wartime remains – which extend to the south, beyond the area of the wood proper, into areas of secondary woodland and scrub (Freeman 2001, 283) – include buildings (d, e and f), the former representing part of the base's sick quarters; amorphous piles of earth and rubble; and concrete bases for buildings, as well as concrete tracks. The most intriguing feature is a roughly triangular-shaped pond (g), divided in two by a north–south bank which is continued as a low brick wall: the sides of the pond are revetted in places.

The only other earthworks within the wood are a slight 'scrape' pond around 5 metres across, perhaps of no great antiquity (h), and three more substantial depressions, dry when visited but probably ponds rather than pits (i, j and k). The last two of these are located, characteristically, on the margins of the wood. In several places the ground surface within the wood has a very gently undulating appearance, suggesting (together with the absence of early earthworks) that the wood is 'primary' in character, and that its area has never been cultivated.

This is a genuinely medieval and apparently 'primary' wood which was truncated along its northern and eastern sides in the nineteenth century and much damaged by wartime activity; it is now neglected and shaded by outgrown hornbeam coppice. In the course of the twentieth century it has expanded to both south and west, across adjacent fields.

Blake's Grove, Ladies' Grove and New Grove; Gawdy Hall, Harleston
TM 24418570; TM 28598544; TM 24868603

The histories of these three areas of *Inventory* woodland are most conveniently treated together. All lie around the northern and western edges of Gawdy Hall Park, an area of eighteenth-century parkland which still survives in good condition despite the demolition of Gawdy Hall itself in 1939 (Kenworthy-Brown *et al.* 1981, 116) (Figure 40). Much of the area mapped by English Nature as New Grove – 1.7 hectares – in fact comprises a modern area of planting immediately to the north of the real wood

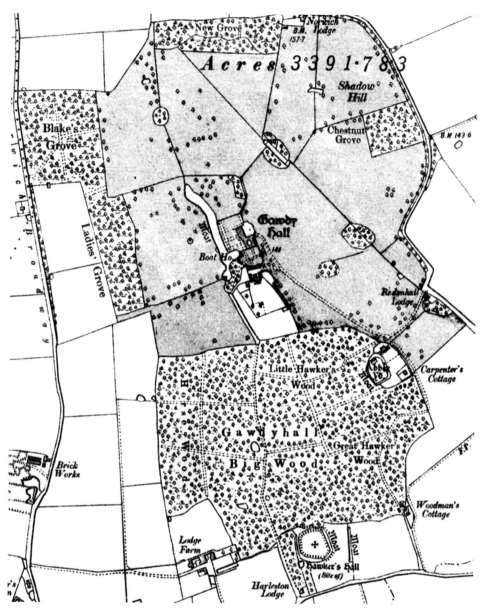

Figure 40 The four areas of ancient woodland in the vicinity of Gawdy Hall in Redenhall-with-Harleston: to the south, Gawdyhall Big Wood; to the north, New Grove; to the west, Blake's Grove and Ladies' Grove.

with this name, originally covering 2.7 hectares, the southern part of which is actually excluded from the *Inventory* area. Blake's Grove covers 4.9 hectares and Ladies' Grove 2.8 hectares. All three woods occupy relatively level ground on Beccles 1 Association soils.

All three woods are shown with the same outlines as today on the first edition Ordnance Survey six-inch map of 1884 and on the Harleston tithe award map of 1839

(NRO DN/TA 222). They are also depicted, with apparently the same outlines, on an estate map of 1789 (NRO Ms 4567), which shows the hall set within a small landscape park. An earlier map of 1734 (NRO Ms 4568), however, which shows the hall standing within a moat and surrounded by walled gardens and enclosed fields, suggests that they had not yet been established. The area of New Grove is marked as 'Dove House Close' and Ladies' Grove as 'Nether Bushy Close', while Blake's Grove formed the western section of 'Nether Bushy Close'. The outline of the latter wood is shown filled with trees, but these are unquestionably later additions, made in pencil. All three woods were presumably planted when the park around Gawdy Hall was laid out in the second half of the eighteenth century.

Much of the area of New Grove was replanted when the adjacent area to the north was afforested, and comprises young ash and some oak standards, with some older oaks and a few sycamore; the ground cover features large amounts of nettles and sporadic dog's mercury. The un-replanted southern strip consists of oak and hornbeam standards, some at least of the latter apparently singled from coppice, very scattered stools of hazel and some sycamore, over a ground cover of dog's mercury. The wood is separated from the parkland to the south by a very slight bank and ditch. Ladies' Grove and Blake's Grove more closely resemble genuine ancient woods. Both contain a mixed coppice of hornbeam, accompanied by ash and hazel and with scattered examples of field maple beneath oak and some ash standards (the latter mainly outgrown coppice). They also contain large amounts of dog's mercury, except where the canopy shade is dense, and here the woodland floor is bare: this is generally where hornbeam predominates.

Blake's Grove is bounded on the east and north by slight banks, generally around 2.5–3.0 metres across and 0.2 metres high, with functioning external ditches; and on the south by a functioning ditch which has no accompanying bank along its western and central sections and a low bank external to the ditch towards its eastern end. All appear post-medieval in character, little more than field boundaries, but the western boundary of the wood is very different. It comprises a substantial bank *c*.3.5 metres wide and 0.25 metres high with a shallow external ditch, beyond which is a level strip of land *c*.4 metres wide lying at a slightly lower level. This in turn is bounded by a minor bank *c*.1.8 metres wide, flanked by a ditch; beyond this lies a public road. This arrangement – a narrow strip of ground bounded to the west by a minor bank and to the east by a massive one and running parallel with the road – continues all along the western side of the wood, except that the inner bank makes a right-angle turn near its northern end, the strip between the two banks here widening into a broader rectangle. At first sight the inner bank appears to be a medieval woodbank, but the narrow strip of land defined by the two earthworks continues to the south of Blake's Grove as a strip of woodland running beside the public road. This is likewise defined by the narrow bank to the west, but to the east by a ditch alone, the large accompanying bank presumably having been removed at some stage in the past – the land to the east is under cultivation. Rather than a woodbank, the large bank thus appears to represent the edge of a narrow roadside green, and is indeed shown as such on the 1734 map. It was made narrower at some point in the eighteenth or nineteenth centuries and planted with trees – the northern section absorbed into Blake's Grove, the southern creating the narrow roadside strip of woodland which today continues south from it.

The boundaries of Ladies' Grove are more straightforward. That to the north is formed by a ditch *c*.3 metres wide flanked by low banks *c*.2 metres wide; that on the west by a low bank 2.5 metres wide and 0.2 metres high, with a hedge on the edge of an external functioning ditch; and that to the south by a similar but rather sharper bank, again with an external ditch. To the east, where the wood abuts the parkland around Gawdy Hall, it is bounded by a low, spread bank *c*.3 metres in width, accompanied by traces of an infilled external ditch.

All three of these woods appear to have been planted in the eighteenth century, and Blake's Grove and Ladies' Grove are classic examples of 'pseudo-ancient' woodland. The western boundary of Blake's Grove seems almost designed to give a misleading impression of the wood's antiquity.

Bunwell Wood or Banyard's Wood
TM 12949218

Bunwell Wood – or Banyard's Wood, as it was referred to until the eighteenth century (NRO ANW/S 6/8–13) – occupies 17 hectares on Burlingham Association soils on a site that slopes slightly towards the south, some nine kilometres to the south of Wymondham. The moated Banyard's Hall lies less than 200 metres from its eastern boundary: in the nineteenth century it lay almost on the boundary, the wood having since been truncated on this side. The wood comprises hornbeam, ash and hazel coppice, with some maple and sycamore, under scattered oak standards: but this vegetation survives only in a band *c*.15 metres wide around a central area which was grubbed out and replanted as an arboretum in the 1970s. Part of the southern ring of original vegetation is being managed by coppicing and has an understorey which features abundant dog's mercury, together with some primrose and wood anemone.

The wood was the subject of a legal dispute in 1675, but the associated documents provide no information about its extent or management (NRO WLS IV/6). In 1839 the wood covered nearly 30 hectares (NRO DA TN 143) but by 1884, to judge from the Ordnance Survey 25-inch, much of the northern section had been removed and the north-western boundary realigned, so that its area was reduced to *c*.23 hectares. Unusually, these changes created a more irregular boundary line than that which had formerly existed. Between 1892 and 1905 there were further alterations. The northern boundary was straightened and realigned and the eastern section of the wood, running up to Banyards Hall, was grubbed out. The wood has remained the same size – *c*.16 hectares – since this time.

The nineteenth-century northern and eastern boundaries of the wood have no banks or ditches at all. The south-western and north-western boundaries, however, are marked by substantial woodbanks with external ditches with a total width which varies from 6 to almost 8 metres. They are covered in rich growths of dog's mercury and, in places, carry large hornbeam and maple coppice stools as well as an oak pollard with a girth of 3 metres (at TM 1279292282). At the junction of the southern and western boundaries – at around TM 1275092061 – the boundary is formed by a double bank separated by a ditch, the whole more than 9 metres across. At one point this widens to form a pond, fed by a drain from the wood.

This is a medieval wood, possibly but not certainly primary, truncated in stages in the nineteenth century and damaged by replanting in the twentieth.

Dodd's Wood/Oliver's Wood, Rushall
TM 20508185

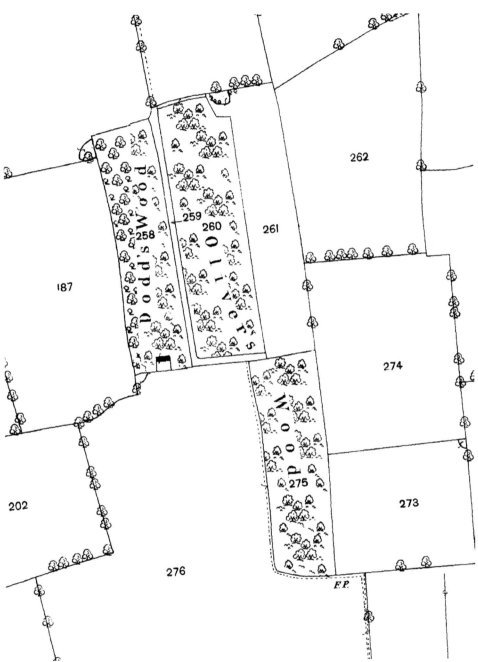

Figure 41 Dodd's Wood and Oliver's Wood, Rushall, as shown on the first edition Ordnance Survey 25-inch map of 1884.

Dodd's Wood and Oliver's Wood comprise a single area of woodland of around four hectares in the south of Rushall in south Norfolk, occupying Beccles Association soils on level or gently sloping ground. It has fairly straight boundaries and is shaped like an inverted 'L'. The first edition Ordnance Survey 25-inch map of 1884 shows that at this time the north-eastern portion of the wood did not yet exist, so that the wood then comprised two rectangles joined at their north-western and south-eastern corners, which were neatly nested within the surrounding field pattern (which itself displays a clear co-axial 'grain', being part of the so-called 'Scole–Dickleburgh field system' (above, p. 51)) (Figure 41). The division of the wood into two conjoined rectangles was not directly reflected in the nomenclature, for the name 'Dodd's Wood' was applied only to the western section of the northern rectangle, 'Oliver's Wood' to its eastern section *and* to the southern rectangle. A track – a public right of way – ran north–south through the centre of the northern rectangle of woodland and then east along its southern boundary, continuing south as a footpath along the western side of the southern rectangle. This still exists.

The vegetation of Dodd's Wood comprises outgrown hornbeam and some hazel coppice beneath young (*c*.50 years old) oak standards, with occasional examples of ash. In the northern section of Oliver's Wood there is more hazel, together with sporadic horse chestnut, ash and field maple, and some coppiced hornbeam; in the southern part there is a higher proportion of coppiced hornbeam, some hazel and scattered specimens of blackthorn, hawthorn and field maple. The newer, north-eastern section of the wood is mainly oak, without hornbeam coppice. The ground flora includes scattered examples of dog's mercury.

The boundaries of the wood are formed by ditches accompanied in places by slight banks. The central track is bounded by ditches flanked by banks less than 0.75 metres high, accompanied in places by what appear to be the remains of hedges: one carries a single oak pollard with a girth of *c*.2.8 metres. There are ponds in the north-western and south-western corners of Dodd's Wood, and in the north-east corner of Oliver's. A few metres to the east of the second of these is a rectangular depression with traces of brick footings, presumably the site of a shed or similar structure associated with pheasant rearing: a building and enclosure are shown here on the first edition Ordnance Survey six-inch map.

Although included in the *Ancient Woodland Inventory*, and containing hazel and hornbeam coppice and dog's mercury, there is no doubt that this is a relatively recent wood, planted within two small fields, probably in the early nineteenth century. It does not appear on Faden's map of 1797, but is shown on Bryant's map of 1826 and more clearly on the Rushall tithe award map of 1841. The banks and ditches within and around the wood clearly originated as field boundaries, the ponds as field ponds.

A recent wood of broadly 'pseudo-ancient' type.

Earsham Great Wood
TM 31169026

Earsham Great Wood occupies an area of around eight hectares on soils which, mapped as Newport 4 Association, in fact mainly comprise light clays of the Burlingham Series. The ground slopes gently from west to east, along the length of the wood, and falls more sharply at its western boundary. It is one of several local woods

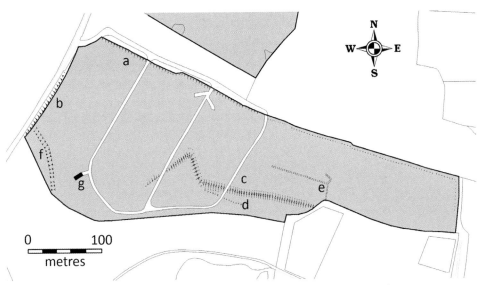

Figure 42 Earsham Great Wood: principal earthwork features (for key see text).

included on the *Ancient Woodland Inventory*, with Holly Grove lying some 70 metres to the south and America Wood less than 50 to the north.

Earsham Great Wood contains an understorey of coppiced hornbeam, with some hazel and ash and occasional maple and elm, under standards of oak and some ash, the latter mainly grown from coppice. The ground flora is dominated by extensive spreads of dog's mercury but other woodland species, such as primrose and water avens, are also present, and the County Wildlife Site citation also records the presence of enchanter's-nightshade (*Circaea lutetiana*). The western section of the wood has recently been recoppiced, and the density of the vegetation here made ground survey difficult.

The wood is bounded along the western section of its northern boundary by a low, spread bank ((a) on Figure 42), between 3 and 4 metres in width and 0.1–0.2 metres in height, with a functioning external ditch, the recutting of which – coupled with the construction of the concrete military road immediately to the north – has degraded it in places. It may be of medieval origin, but this is uncertain. Most of the wood's western boundary is marked by a steep lynchet, where the ground falls away to the public road (b). The wood's other boundaries, however, are defined by a ditch without a significant bank, although this is accompanied along the eastern side by a slight lynchet, and there is a slight inner bank – lying parallel to and some 6 metres in from the outer boundary – evident along the northern and parts of the eastern sides, a feature of uncertain significance. All these boundaries are evidently post-medieval.

The wood contains a number of internal earthworks, of which (c) is a massive bank flanked on its northern side by a ditch that appears too large to have been an internal subdivision and instead resembles a former external woodbank, suggesting that the medieval core of the wood lay to its south. The feature follows a highly irregular course through the centre of the wood: at the point where it turns abruptly to the east a slight, barely visible bank (d) diverges from it, taking a more southerly course through the wood before disappearing. (e) is a small complex of drainage ditches, the main north–

south component of which is accompanied by a slight bank to the west. (f) is a linear depression deeply buried in the undergrowth and perhaps not reliably plotted. It may be an earlier boundary to the wood but appears more like a hollow way.

The wood is shown with its current boundaries on an estate map of *c*.1770 (NRO 631/2), but when an earlier map was surveyed, in *c*.1720 (NRO 631/1), it was significantly smaller than today, and did not extend to the east of (e), the main north–south component of which probably represents, in origin, its eastern boundary. This late expansion of the wood explains the absence of woodbanks along most of its northern and the whole of its eastern boundaries, and along the southern boundary to the east of (e); but it does not explain the absence of a woodbank along the western section of this boundary, as, allowing for deficiencies in cartography, this appears today to follow the same general line as it did in 1720. This said, minor differences in the way the 1720 map depicts the western end of this boundary may account for feature (e) (i.e., the boundary here may have been changed slightly since the early eighteenth century, leaving an original boundary feature lying within the wood).

The early history of the wood cannot now be reconstructed with any confidence. As noted, the character of feature (c) suggests that it originally formed the northern boundary of a wood which mainly lay to the south, and which was subsequently truncated in this direction (hence the absence of a southern woodbank) and extended to the north. While the wood thus clearly has medieval origins, and is almost certainly in part primary in character, its boundaries have evidently undergone a number of significant changes over the centuries, of which expansion to the east in the course of the eighteenth century was only the last. There is little obvious sign of this complex history in the wood's vegetation. The coppiced structure appears much the same everywhere and both dog's mercury and primrose appear as common in the post-medieval eastern extension to the wood as in the older western section.

During the Second World War the wood was used, along with others on the Earsham estate, to store bombs for a number of local USAAF airfields (see above, p. 142). The pattern of concrete rides and aprons laid out at this time survives in reasonable condition but of the various military buildings shown on contemporary plans of the wood (TNA AIR 29/1558, plans 3040/52, 3041/52, 3042/52) only one (g) survived when the wood was surveyed, and even this has now been removed.

East Wood, Denton
TM 2918780

East Wood, Denton, extends over an area of around 14 hectares, mainly on soils of the Beccles 1 Association, although the southern and western sections occupy slightly lighter soils, where the ground begins to fall away towards a tributary of the river Waveney. The northern section of the wood lies on a north-facing slope, where the ground falls towards another minor stream. The understorey of the wood consists almost entirely of outgrown coppiced hornbeam with sporadic stools of maple and ash, the latter more prominent towards the south, together with some hazel and occasional examples of holly and elder. There are a number of oak standards but many of these are now beginning to be shaded out by the outgrown hornbeam canopy. The ground flora is dominated by dog's mercury, but with a wide range of other herbs including wood sorrel, wood sanicle (*Sanicula europaea*), wood melick (*Melica uniflora*) and

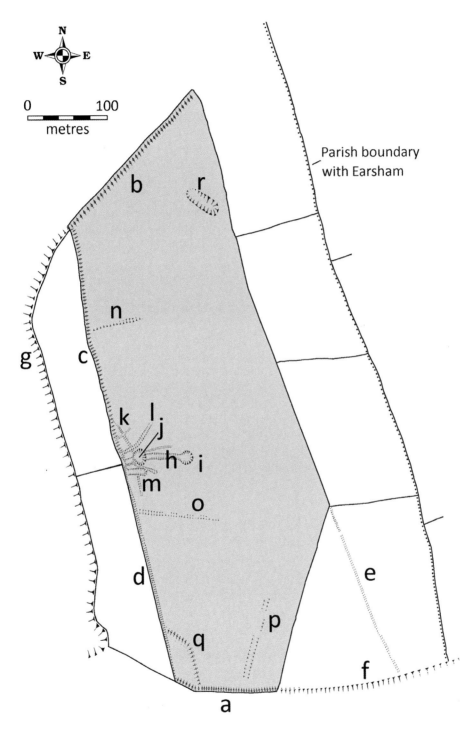

Figure 43 East Wood, Denton: principal earthwork features (for key see text). Field boundaries as shown on the first edition Ordnance Survey six inches: one mile map of 1885.

herb Paris (*Paris quadrifolia*). In the damper areas hairy woodrush (*Luzula pilosa*), great wood rush (*L. Sylvatica*) and remote sedge (*Carex remota*) occur. The wood lies close to, but not on, the eastern boundary of Denton parish, being separated from it in the nineteenth century by a strip of relatively narrow fields.

The southern boundary ((a) on Figure 43) comprises a substantial woodbank rising in places nearly 1 metre above the woodland floor and *c*.2.5 metres above the base of the flanking ditch: bank and ditch together are around 7 metres across. The northern boundary (b) is similar, except that the place of the ditch is here taken by the stream, down to which the ground slopes steeply: a number of large hornbeam pollards grow on the bank here. The northern section of the western boundary (c) is also marked by a substantial bank, although not as large as those just described – around 5 to 6 metres across and with a bank rising *c*.1.5 metres above the flanking ditch (except at its northern end, where the boundary runs down towards the stream: here it is rather higher). The other boundaries, however, are relatively minor in character and much straighter in plan. The southern part of the western boundary (d) has a slight external bank with a shallow inner ditch. The other boundaries have a shallow ditch and remains of a hedge of hawthorn and blackthorn, with occasional ash and maple, but only slight traces of a bank. The northern section of the eastern boundary has, nevertheless, a number of old hornbeam and oak pollards growing along it.

The first edition Ordnance Survey six-inch map of 1885 shows, in the adjacent area of pasture, scattered trees 'ghosting' a lost south-eastern corner of the wood. Some of these, oak standards with girths of 4.4 and 3.8 metres, still survive, together with the earthworks of the former boundaries. These, interestingly, mimic the character of the surviving boundaries of which they form continuations. The former eastern boundary (e) is thus a slight ditch, the southern (f) a more substantial bank and south-facing lynchet. The fact that the former shape of the wood is so clearly preserved by the pattern of trees shown on the Ordnance Survey map suggests that it had been removed relatively recently, although evidently before 1839, the date of the tithe award map, which shows the wood with boundaries identical to those of today (NRO DN/TA 209).

This was evidently the last of a series of contractions in the wood's area. The lynchet marking the southern edge of the 'ghost' of the wood (f) continues eastwards all the way to the parish boundary with Earsham, which itself is marked by a substantial bank and ditch, carrying a hedge which contains large amounts of hornbeam. This fact, along with the slight and evidently post-medieval nature of the main eastern boundary of the wood and the pattern of narrow fields here, strongly suggests that the wood originally extended all the way to the parish boundary. There is equally compelling evidence that the wood's boundaries have been reduced on the western side. On the Ordnance Survey six-inch map the line of the substantial southern boundary of the wood is directly continued, to the west, as a field boundary. This terminated at a north–south field boundary which still exists, running roughly parallel with the present western boundary of the wood. This is associated with a massive lynchet (g), over-deepened as a quarry towards the south but otherwise around 2 metres high, rising to 3 metres as it heads north. As it does so it curves eastwards, to join the present northern boundary of the wood. The hedge carries a variety of woodland relict vegetation, including substantial coppice stools of hazel and maple and – towards the north – three substantial pollards (two hornbeam, one maple). This was clearly the original western boundary of the wood.

On this side, as on the eastern, the wood evidently contracted in two stages. The substantial nature of the northern section of the western boundary (c) suggests that the north-western corner of the wood was cleared in medieval times; the less substantial character of the southern section of this boundary (d) indicates more recent clearance of the south-western portion. It is noteworthy that the change in the character of this western boundary occurs at the point where the first edition Ordnance Survey map shows a field boundary (now lost) running west from the edge of the wood as far as the massive lynchet/former boundary (g). Taking all these probable reductions in its area into account, it would appear that in early medieval times the wood extended over an area of *c.*28 hectares, roughly twice its present size.

The earthworks within the wood are complex and their character uncertain. The most impressive are a series of banks, pits and hollow ways which are found around halfway down the western side of the wood, at the point where the character of the wood's western boundary changes (Figure 22, p. 74). A major hollow way (h) leads to a small yet deep pit (i) and is itself interrupted by a second pit (j). It has also been interrupted, at the point where it leaves the wood, by deliberate filling, leaving a marked scarp running across it a little way in from the wood's boundary. A slight bank with an internal ditch (k) runs sub-parallel with the wood's boundary as far as pit (j). It is crossed, and slighted, by one minor and one major (l) ditch, the latter almost a minor holloway. At first sight the line of (k) appears to be continued beyond pit (j), but the bank here (m), which continues for some distance to the south, is actually on a slightly different alignment. It is interrupted by another pit and ends shortly before it meets another ditch/hollow way running in from the boundary of the wood (o).

The age and purpose of these earthworks are unclear. The earliest feature is probably the hollow way (h), which seems too substantial to have been caused by carts accessing the relatively small pit (i), the purpose of which is itself uncertain. The minor ditches/hollow ways that fan out from the same general point at which (h) begins, on the edge of the wood, may simply have been for access to the wood. Both stretches of bank/ditch – (k) and (m) – are presumably later than hollow way (h), because they change alignment at it. The purpose of these banks is likewise obscure. The reasons why this strange collection of features should be found at precisely the point where the character of the wood's western boundary changes markedly is likewise uncertain, but this location does at least hint that all post-date the removal, presumably in the medieval period, of the north-western corner of the original wood.

The other earthworks within the wood are less marked and, if anything, more mysterious. Features (n), (o) and (p) are slight and indistinct. The first begins at the wood's western edge as a vague north-facing scarp but gradually becomes a ditch *c.*2 metres wide, the southern side more distinct than the northern. Features (o) and (p) are both slight, almost invisible, hollow way-like features. All three may have been created by medieval and post-medieval exploitation of the wood, but it is possible that they are prehistoric or Roman features. Feature (q) is more distinct. It is a west-facing scarp, sometimes becoming a bank and accompanied in places by a very slight ditch, which runs in two fairly straight sections cutting off the south-western corner of the wood. The fact that the longer of these sections, running north–south, lies approximately parallel to the western boundary of the wood might suggest that it is contemporary with the wood: it appears to be medieval but its purpose is obscure. Lastly, a deep pit in the north of the wood (r) appears to have been dug to extract clay or sand, presumably in medieval or post-medieval times.

Although much of its archaeology poses problems of interpretation it is clear that East Wood is largely or entirely 'primary' in character, although some of the earthworks within it may just possibly be of prehistoric or Roman origin. A combination of archaeological and topographic evidence suggests that, following the definition of its boundaries in the early Middle Ages, the wood contracted in stages during the later medieval and post-medieval periods.

Edgefield Little Wood
TG 10923410

Edgefield Little Wood lies close to, but not on, the parish boundary with Plumstead – which just clips its north-eastern corner – and also close to that with Little Barningham. It occupies 10.7 hectares on ground which slopes very gently, and in an uneven manner, from north-east to south-west. The subsoil is largely gravel, part of the glacial moraine of the Holt–Cromer Ridge: the soils are of the Wick 3 Association, and Faden's county map of 1797 shows that the wood – then significantly smaller than today – was bounded to the east by Plumstead Common and to the south by Edgefield Heath. 'Little Wood' is so named to distinguish it from the rather larger Edgefield Great Wood, which lay immediately to the north and which was grubbed out in the nineteenth century (between the time of the tithe award map (1845: DN/TA 912) and the making of the Ordnance Survey 25-inch (1886)).

The original 'core' of Little Wood is represented by areas (a1) and (a2) (Figure 44). This is bounded to the east, and along much of its northern and southern boundaries, by a substantial woodbank of typical medieval form which is *c*.6 metres wide and rises 1.0–1.5 metres above the ditch on the northern and southern side, slightly higher along the eastern. The ditch is, in places, particularly wide. On the western edge, and along the remainder of the northern and southern sides, the boundary becomes a substantial lynchet with no clear inner bank. On the top of the lynchet, and along a short stretch of the woodbank on the north and south sides, are the remains of an oak hedge with huge coppice stools, evidently an outgrown medieval feature. The absence of the hedge from the eastern edge of the wood may be because it has here been overshadowed and neglected following the eastward expansion of the wood during the post-medieval period. The oak stools are mainly, although not entirely, of sessile (*Quercus petraea*) rather than pedunculate oak (*Quercus robur*). There are no earthworks visible within the wood, although it is possible that some have been missed beneath the dense bracken.

The western third of this section (a1) was replanted in the second half of the twentieth century with a mixture of oak, rowan and hazel: this followed an earlier replanting with conifers apparent on the 1946 RAF vertical air photographs. The central and eastern sections (a2) comprise outgrown oak coppice (again, mainly *Quercus petraea*), accompanied to the north by large quantities of holly: the latter has grown more abundant in recent years. There are scattered examples of nineteenth-century Scots pine, and some oak and young birch standards.

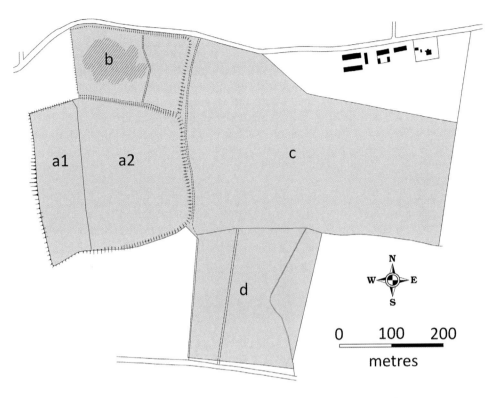

Figure 44 Edgefield Little Wood: principal earthwork features (for key see text).

The other parts of the wood are clearly additions to this original core. Area (b) is probably medieval in origin, as it is bounded to the east by a small but nevertheless significant woodbank, on the north by a degraded bank, ditched in places on both sides, and on much of the western side by a slight but noticeable lynchet, rising *c*.0.5– 0.7 metres above the surrounding field, with only traces of an internal bank. The interior of this portion of the wood is now composed of larch and Scots pine, planted in the twentieth century, with occasional birch and oak: there is little evidence of coppicing. Much of the ground surface is covered by small, amorphous pits (the area shaded in Figure 44), presumably for the extraction of gravel – and presumably before this section of the wood existed. The pits are shallow, sometimes single and sometimes merging with others; they are mainly *c*.5–10 metres wide but occasionally smaller. There are scattered spoil heaps between them. It is probable that the area once formed open heathland, only enclosed and added to the original wood fairly late in the Middle Ages.

The rest of the present wood is not included in the *Ancient Woodland Inventory* area; it appears to have been planted at the expense of the heathland in the period after 1816 (the additional areas are not shown on the Ordnance Survey two-inch drawings of that date (BM OSD 243)). Area (c) comprises mixed woodland containing large amounts of sweet chestnut coppice, birch, oak, rowan, scattered beech standards (especially towards the north) and areas of recent planting. The straight northern and eastern boundaries have traces of a ditch but no bank. The more irregular southern boundary has a faint bank. The eastern half of this area is shown as woodland on the tithe award map of 1845 (NRO DN/TA 912), the western as unplanted field. Area (d) is now a Scots pine plantation, with no obvious evidence for internal earthworks. Again, the tithe award map implies that it was then still open heathland. The straight, probably nineteenth-century western boundary has no accompanying earthwork, nor the similar eastern boundary, but the latter is the consequence of twentieth-century expansion and the earlier boundary (as marked on the first edition Ordnance Survey six-inch map) survives within the wood as an earthwork comprising a ditch, with a slight bank *c*.2–3 metres wide to the west. Scattered stools of birch along the top of the bank are the remains of a hedge; where the bank meets the road to the south there is a large small-leaved lime, at least 300 years old. This is clearly an old boundary, although of a field rather than a wood.

Edgefield Little Wood is a complex piece of landscape. Essentially, a small area of medieval woodland comprising oak coppice and surrounded by an oak hedge on a substantial bank and lynchet was expanded to the north (over common land?), probably in the late Middle Ages. Subsequent additions, mainly at the expense of heath, were made in the course of the eighteenth and nineteenth centuries.

Foxley Wood
TG 05452257

Foxley Wood, extending over some 124 hectares, is the largest area of ancient woodland in Norfolk, and is now owned and managed by the NWT. It occupies soils which, while mapped as falling within the Beccles Association, display much variation in terms of acidity and drainage. Parts of the wood were replanted in the twentieth century with commercial conifers but since the wood was acquired by the Trust in 1998 much of this has in turn been replanted with indigenous species. Those areas which have not been replanted comprise, on the more acidic soils, oak standards (*Quercus robur*) over an understorey of hazel coppice, some of which is actively managed, with varying proportions of downy birch and holly. Where the soils are less acidic ash accompanies hazel, while the damper areas – mainly towards the centre and north-east of the wood – have an understorey dominated by ash and maple, with less hazel and some alder. Small quantities of wild service, small-leaved lime and Midland hawthorn (*Crataegus laevigata*) also occur. The ground flora includes a wide range of 'ancient woodland indicators' – dog's mercury, bluebells, herb Paris, early purple orchid, greater butterfly orchid (*Platanthera chlorantha*), orpine (*Sedum telephium*), lily-of-the-valley (*Convallaria majalis*) and thin-spiked wood sedge (*Carex strigosa*). In spite of this range of species it is clear that in the early Middle Ages much of the wood's area was managed as a deer park and comprised grazed wood-pasture and probably areas of open launde, together with embanked coppices. Blomefield suggests that the park was established by 1282, but the earliest confirmed documentary reference dates from 1390, when a keeper of the park was appointed (Blomefield 1806, VIII, 210; CPR 1388–1392, 304). In 1391 John Lowyck was granted the underwood in the park 'on condition that of the said underwood sufficient cover be reserved for the king's deer within that park, that he suitably enclose at his own expense from time to time that coppices whereof he takes the underwood, and that the underwood is taken in season'. Following disparkment, probably in the fifteenth century, the entire area of the park was managed as coppice, and a map of 1815 – which even at this date still

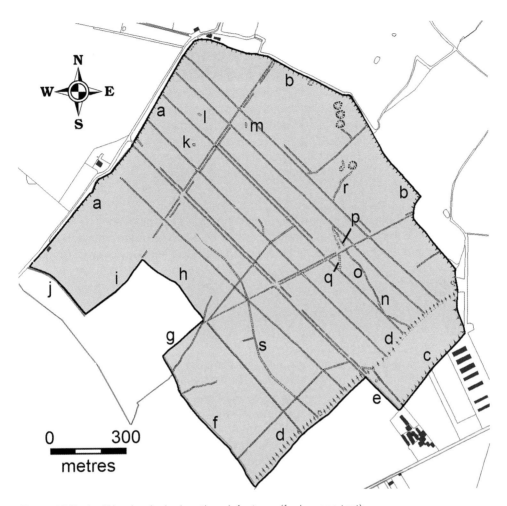

Figure 45 Foxley Wood: principal earthwork features (for key see text).

describes the wood as 'Foxley Park' – shows that it was divided into ten named 'fells', implying a coppice rotation of ten years, something confirmed by the tithe file of 1838, which describes the rotation as 'eight to ten years' (Figure 18) (NRO NRS 4087; TNA IR18/5928). The wood is shown with identical outlines on Faden's county map of 1797, on the 1815 map just referred to and on the tithe award map of 1840 (NRO DN/TA 308).

There are no obvious archaeological indications of the wood's origins as a deer park (Figure 45). Along its north-western (a) and north-eastern (b) sides it is bounded by a woodbank of normal medieval form, with an external rather than an internal ditch. This is much degraded in places, especially towards its southern end of (a). In the far northern corner this bank has a short (c.30-metre) stretch of internal ditch. The south-eastern boundary (c) is similar in character, but better preserved and more substantial, with a total width (including external ditch) of around 8 metres. This embraces what is evidently a medieval extension to the wood, for there is an even larger internal bank (d) running parallel to it. The latter is also followed by the line of the parish boundary between Bawdeswell and Foxley, but is clearly in origin an earlier

185

woodbank, rather than any other kind of boundary feature. It continues beyond the western end of the projection – which is described as 'Bawdeswell Fell' on the 1815 map – as the wood's external boundary, although today it runs a few metres in from the edge of the wood, which has expanded into the adjacent field. It is one of the largest woodbanks known in Norfolk, rising in places nearly 1 metre above the floor of the wood and reaching a total width, with ditch, of more than 9 metres. Faden's county map of 1797 shows that the wood was bordered on this south-eastern side by Bawdeswell Common, suggesting that – probably quite early in the medieval period – the wood was expanded in this direction at the expense of common grazing or heath. The wood seems to have subsequently contracted again, for (e), marking the south-western edge of the extension, is formed by a diminutive bank with an internal ditch, and is evidently post-medieval and perhaps seventeenth-century in date (the wood has expanded to the west of this feature, over a narrow field, since the late nineteenth century, so that the present boundary is a former field bank). Faden's map shows that a narrow strip of enclosed fields here separated the wood from Bawdeswell Common. The wood has also contracted, at some point before the late eighteenth century, along its south-western boundaries. Section (f) is thus marked by a sharp but narrow bank, around 1 metre high, above an external ditch, while (g), (h), (i) and (j) have no bank at all, suggesting that they are even more recent.

Internally the wood contains at least four sawpits of uncertain age; three lie quite close together in the north of the wood ((k), (l), (m)); the other (n), to the south-east, was rather curiously created by over-deepening an existing ditch. All have dimensions of *c*.5–6 by *c*.1.0–1.5 metres, and are now *c*.0.3–0.5 deep. The wood is dissected by a large number of shallow linear gripes or drainage ditches, some still functioning but others now abandoned. They are probably of late eighteenth- or early nineteenth-century date: they correspond to the pattern of 'fells' shown on the 1815 map. There may be other examples, buried in the undergrowth, which we have not recorded. There are, in addition, a number of short gripes, sometimes irregular or serpentine in form but sometimes straight. These appear to be additions to the original grid.

The wood contains a number of ponds and dry pits, all fairly shallow. Some are perhaps the result of excavating material but most are probably natural. Much of the damper ground within the centre-north-east of the wood is characterised by amorphous undulations of natural origin. In addition, there are several enigmatic earthworks. Feature (o) is a shallow ditch *c*.2 metres across, which follows an irregular course through the wood and has a sharper eastern side, becoming at times a simple scarp. At its southern end it has been deepened to form the saw pit (n), suggesting that it was not then a functioning drain. It may be continued by (p) – the junction between the two features has been obliterated by a ride – although for much of its length this is rather slighter, no more than a shallow, broad ditch. Feature (q) may likewise be early: it does not resemble the other drainage gripes in the wood, being both wider and vaguer in character. More obvious in the undergrowth is (r), which begins as a substantial south-facing bank with traces of a ditch to the south, both together around 3 metres wide. But after *c*.45 metres it becomes a bank, again with traces of a ditch to the south; and 10 metres further along develops into a slight ditch around 4 metres wide, continuing as such until it fades among the disturbed ground around a number of ponds. In the west of the wood feature (s), similar to (o) but with less evidence of a flanking bank, may also be early, but may be a post-medieval drain pre-dating the creation of the drainage 'grid': it could not be fully investigated owing to the density of the vegetation.

It is possible that (o), (p) and (r) originally formed a single feature, the boundary to an enclosure: perhaps one of the coppice compartments implied by the medieval documents. Feature (r) certainly has, in places, the appearance of a minor medieval woodbank. But otherwise no obvious evidence for medieval subdivisions was noted during survey, and the surviving medieval boundaries of the wood do not resemble those of a deer park. As in the case of Hockering (q.v.), there is thus nothing in the archaeological evidence to support the unequivocal documentary evidence that Foxley originated as a compartmentalised park. It seems unlikely that the wood, with its surviving external boundaries, represents the central section of a once more extensive park, not least because it was bounded to the north-west by a public road, apparently of some antiquity, and to the south-east by Bawdeswell Common.

Gawdyhall Big Wood
TM 25038501

Gawdyhall Big Wood, designated an SSSI, extends over more than 30 hectares on ground which is either level or slopes very gently towards the south, where the land falls towards the valley of a tributary of the river Waveney. It mainly occupies soils of the Beccles 1 Association, but small areas in the south extend onto Hanslope Association soils. The wood lies immediately to the south of the eighteenth-century landscape park associated with Gawdy Hall (demolished in 1939), the main drive to which runs roughly north–south through its centre. On the first edition Ordnance Survey six-inch map of 1885 particular names are given to subsections of the wood. The western area is labelled 'Horse Wood', the north-eastern 'Little Hawker's Wood' and the south-eastern 'Great Hawkers Wood': it is possible that only the central area was, historically, 'Gawdyhall Big Wood'. The wood is characterised by a mixture of outgrown hornbeam, ash and hazel coppice, often mixed, but with stands of pure hornbeam found towards the peripheries of the wood, especially in the west and north-west, and along the southern margins, while stands of pure ash occur in the north-eastern section (within 'Little Hawker's Wood'). There are scattered examples of other species, including old specimens of sweet chestnut and Norway spruce. Some areas of the wood have recently been recoppiced. The ground cover is sparse where the wood is shady, but elsewhere includes large amounts of dog's mercury and smaller concentrations of primrose and bluebell. The wood is shown with similar but not identical outlines on an estate map of 1789 (NRO MS 4567) and on the tithe award map of Redenhall-with-Harleston of 1839 (NRO DN/TA 222). The area it occupies is not, unfortunately, included on a map of the Gawdy estate surveyed in 1734 (NRO MS 4568).

The wood is enclosed around most of its perimeter by a substantial woodbank (a) with an external ditch (Figure 46). The wood has expanded beyond this to the south in relatively recent times, the additions being composed primarily of ash and sycamore; and to the north-east during the nineteenth century. Conversely, the south-western corner of the wood appears to have been removed at some point before 1789, perhaps when Lodge Farm was established in the sixteenth or seventeenth century, and here boundary sections (b) and (c) are defined by a ditch accompanied by only a slight bank, topped in places by the remains of a laid hedge. The main

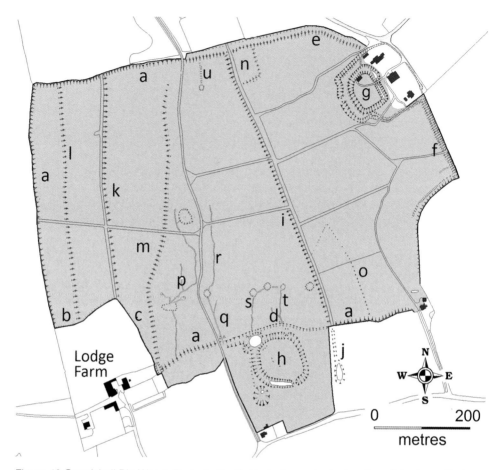

Figure 46 Gawdyhall Big Wood, Redenhall-with-Harleston: principal earthwork features (for key see text).

medieval woodbank (a) varies in character, but is generally a massive feature, around 7 metres wide including the accompanying external ditch. Along parts of the southern boundary (d), however, beside the moated site (h), it takes the form of a steep south-facing scarp flanked by a ditch, with little in the way of a bank; while on the eastern section of the northern boundary (e) there is a double bank, separated by *c.*6–8 metres, which marks where the wood has expanded over a road shown on the eighteenth-century maps. There is also a substantial ditch separating double banks along much of the eastern side of the wood (f), something perhaps associated with the fact that the 1734 map shows that the wood here bordered a small linear roadside common called 'Hawker's Green'.

The most striking archaeological features within the wood are the two substantial moats, one in the south and one in the north-east. Although now lying within the wood, both originally lay outside it. That to the north-east (g) is marked as 'Abbey Yards' on the first edition Ordnance Survey six-inch map; that to the south (h) as 'Site of Hawkers Hall'. There may be some confusion here, for not only are the names Great and Little Hawkers Wood associated with the *northern* rather than the *southern* site, but the 1734 map shows that the former then fronted on an area of common land called Hawkers Green. The manorial history of the area (part of the large parish of Redenhall-with-Harleston) is confused. Apart from the main manor of Redenhall-with-Harleston, Blomefield (1806, 5, 358–72) records the manor of Wortwell and five others (Reden-Hall, Coldham Hall, Holbrook or Gawdy Hall, Merks and Hawkers) which were, by the eighteenth century, united under single ownership. Gawdy Hall is represented by the moated site to the north of the wood, which surrounded the house of the same name until the 1930s, and Merks Hall lies *c.*1.5 kilometres to the north-east. If one of the moats in the wood represents Hawkers, then the other can perhaps be associated with Coldham Hall (the name 'Abbey Yards' is presumably an example of folkloric invention, for there do not appear to be any records of monastic landholding in the parish, although it was already being applied to the site in 1734 (NRO MS 4568)).

Both moats lay outside the wood until the twentieth century, and are shown as largely or entirely free of trees on the first edition Ordnance Survey six-inch map of 1886. The north-eastern moat (g) comprises a sub-rectangular ditch, still largely water-filled, which surrounds a central island. This is slightly raised above the surrounding ground level and its surface displays some amorphous disturbances. A wide outer ditch serves to separate the moat from the main body of the wood. The southern moat is more massive, comprising a huge sub-oval ditch only partly water-filled when surveyed. The central island is, again, rather disturbed in places but any coherent earthworks here have probably been levelled by later ploughing – the island was under cultivation at the time the tithe award map was surveyed (NRO DN/TA 222) – and perhaps by recent replanting of the area, as the NHER reports the presence, in 1982, of a substantial linear mound along the north-eastern edge which is now only faintly visible (NHER 11100).

There are four internal woodbanks, all orientated roughly north–south. The largest (i) is a massive feature – larger than most sections of the wood's external woodbank – and is accompanied to the east by a still functioning ditch. It is noteworthy that its line is continued beyond the margins of the wood, to the south, as a wide linear depression, partly water-filled and wrongly labelled as 'moat' by the Ordnance Survey six-inch map (j). Within the wood, this feature appears to have marked the combined western boundary of Little Hawkers Wood and Great Hawkers Wood; but, as explained below, it is possible that these are secondary, and that (i) originally formed the boundary between Gawdy Hall Big Wood (to the west) and farmland associated with the moated site (g) (to the east). The other internal banks, which all lie in the western half of the wood, are less substantial. One (k) has, like (i), been reused and recut as a modern drainage ditch. It may mark the eastern boundary of Horse Wood. The others (l and m) are less massive, although still substantial features.

The eastern side of the wood – i.e., the area to the east of the major north–south bank (i) – contains two other earthworks. In the north there is a small (*c.*0.15 hectares) enclosure (n) defined by a bank and ditch of uncertain date. The ditch looks like a recent drainage ditch but the character of the accompanying bank suggests a medieval origin. In the south there is a slight scarp/bank (o), ranged roughly north–south and lying more or less parallel to (i). Towards the north it gradually fades and is difficult to trace in the undergrowth but can, with the eye of faith, be seen gradually turning, and then bending sharply and running south-west to join (i). The character of both features is unclear but, coupled with the uncomfortable manner in which the 'Abbey Yard' was squeezed between the wood and Hawker's Green, and the substantial size of bank (i), probably suggests that the area of the wood to the east of the latter (i.e., Great and Little Hawkers) is secondary, an addition to a primary 'core' lying to the west. A change in the character of the southern boundary of the wood at the point where it meets feature (i) is also noteworthy in this context.

The wood also contains a number of serpentine, irregular drainage ditches, many of which run into internal and apparently natural ponds. Prominent examples are plotted ((p), (q), (r), (s), (t) and (u)); others exist but were not mapped. There are also several amorphous undulations, apparently natural in character. All these features appear to be concentrated in the area to the west of (i), supporting the idea that this section is primary and that the area to the east of (i) – which seems on the whole to consist of level ground – is secondary, occupying former farmland.

An interesting and archaeologically complex wood which has expanded across adjacent manorial sites in relatively recent times and which has been truncated to the south-west in the post-medieval period. It is likely that the western section is primary and the eastern secondary, and presumably of late medieval origin.

Hales Wood
TM 37289521

Hales Wood extends over an area of 6.7 hectares in the south of Hales parish, separated by only a narrow pasture field from the parish boundary with Kirby Cane to the south, which here runs along the watershed between the rivers Waveney and Chet. The wood is shown, with identical boundaries to those of today, on the Hales tithe award map of 1839 (DN/TA 157). The wood occupies a level site on soils of the Beccles Association. The understorey comprises neglected hazel, maple and ash coppice under oak standards, with scattered examples of goat willow near the principal ponds and ditches: the south-eastern portion was replanted in the later twentieth century with ash, oak and cherry. The ground flora is limited, owing to the extent of shading, but includes much dog's mercury, together with enchanter's-nightshade, bluebell, early purple orchid, primrose and barren strawberry in the less shaded areas.

The wood is bounded to the north by a substantial woodbank rising *c*.0.3–0.5 metres above the woodland floor, with a functioning external ditch: it is around 8 metres wide in all ((a) on Figure 47). The bank has been partly levelled towards its western end. The western and eastern boundaries (b) and (c)) have a less pronounced bank, *c*.0.2 metres in height and 4 metres wide, and are almost certainly of a later date: these sides of the wood are less sinuous in plan than the northern. The straight southern boundary (d) is marked by a ditch with, at most, a very slight bank, which carries the remains of a hedge: the wood has evidently been truncated in this direction in the post-medieval period. The most impressive internal earthwork is a substantial embanked enclosure (e) in the north of the wood. Its northern boundary, and the northern section of its western, are formed by the external woodbank, the others by banks of similar magnitude which run within the wood: the southern section of its western boundary has been partly levelled. The feature looks medieval but it appears to pre-date the woodbank, which meets its western side more or less at right angles, and which kinks slightly where it joins its north-eastern corner: that is, an earlier enclosure was incorporated within the wood's boundary when this was established,

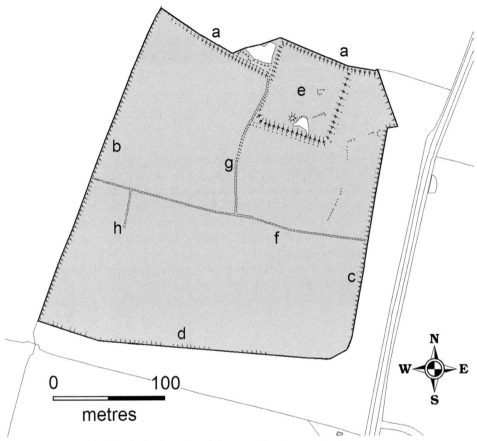

Figure 47 Hales Wood: principal earthwork features (for key see text).

presumably in the twelfth or thirteenth century. The enclosure may thus relate to earlier pastoral use of the area before the wood itself was enclosed and embanked, although it may have continued in use after this date. Two ponds – one within the enclosure, and one more substantial in character occupying the angle between the woodbank and its western boundary – are reminiscent of the fishponds associated with the probable demesne enclosure in Hethel Wood (q.v.), although less regular in character. There are a number of other slight, amorphous scarps within the enclosure.

The only other earthworks noted were a number of surface drains ((f), (g), (h)), which are fairly straight and probably of nineteenth-century date, and slight, scarcely visible scarps in the east of the wood which are probably related to rides shown on the Ordnance Survey six-inch map. In the south-eastern section LIDAR, at 1-metre resolution, appears to show a pattern of parallel ridges ranged roughly north–south, superficially resembling ridge and furrow. These were not observed on the ground in the dense vegetation of the newly planted trees here, with which they are almost certainly associated.

Probably a wood of 'primary' character, apparently truncated in stages in the late medieval and post-medieval periods, which incorporates within its boundaries an earlier enclosure.

Hedenham Wood
TM 31349460

Hedenham Wood covers an area of *c.*23 hectares on ground which slopes gently from north to south. In addition, an intermittent stream runs roughly north–south through its centre, creating towards the south a shallow valley. The northern and western sections of the wood occupy soils mapped as Beccles 1 Association by the Soil Survey; the southern section overlies soils of the Burlingham Association. The wood has been discussed briefly by Rackham (1986b), and is designated an SSSI. It mostly comprises standards of oak over an understorey of hornbeam, with some hazel, ash and maple; but the wetter areas, beside the stream, contain more extensive stands of ash, maple and elm. The coppice has not been cut for several decades, except in a small area in the south-east of the wood. This has been much damaged by grazing deer. There are scattered examples of goat willow, aspen, spindle, guelder rose and dogwood, while the south-centre of the wood, the former site of a high-status late medieval house and associated enclosures, originally featured much suckering elm, although this was largely replanted with ash and oak standards in the later twentieth century following Dutch elm disease. There are other areas of replanting, again featuring indigenous hardwoods (mainly ash and oak), in the north-east of the wood. Nevertheless, the dominance of hornbeam is the wood's most striking feature.

The ground flora is limited over much of the wood, owing to the heavy shade cast by the hornbeam, but features dog's mercury, enchanter's-nightshade, ramsons (*Allium ursinum*) and bluebell, with smaller quantities of other woodland species, including greater butterfly orchid, herb Paris, stinking hellebore (*Helleborus foetidus*) and wood anemone. The wide ride running east–west through the centre of the wood has a particularly rich flora, including pendulous sedge (*Carex pendula*), wood sedge and meadowsweet. The south-western and south-eastern sections of the wood contain large patches of nettles.

A map of the demesne lands of Hedenham manor, surveyed in 1617 by Thomas Waterman (NRO MC 1761/2), shows that the wood then extended much further to the west than today, as far as the public road from Hedenham to Seething, covering an area of around 33 hectares (Figure 48). Faden's county map of 1797, surveyed in the early 1790s, likewise shows the wood extending as far as the road; so too, although less clearly, do the enclosure map of 1816 and Bryant's county map of 1826. By 1838, however, when the tithe award map for Hedenham (NRO DN/TA 133) was surveyed, the western area of the wood had been grubbed out and converted to straight-sided arable fields. The new western boundary to the wood (a) (Figure 49) is defined by a slight bank and ditch accompanied by the remains of a hawthorn hedge.

In the middle of the southern half of the wood Waterman's map shows an open clearing marked 'Hell Yards', which is approached from the east by a road or track bounded on both sides. The section of wood to the north of the latter is shown without trees, although explicitly described as 'wood', because it was in separate ownership: while the bulk of the wood was owned by Phillip Bedingfield, the manorial lord, this section belonged to one Robert Rachmen. The two sections remained in separate ownership until the parliamentary enclosure of 1816, when John Irby, by then the owner of the Rachmen portion, exchanged it with James Bedingfield for land elsewhere in the parish (NRO C/Sca 2/100). To the south of the road leading to 'Hell Yards' the area forming the south-eastern corner of the wood is described on the map as 'Pytle' (from

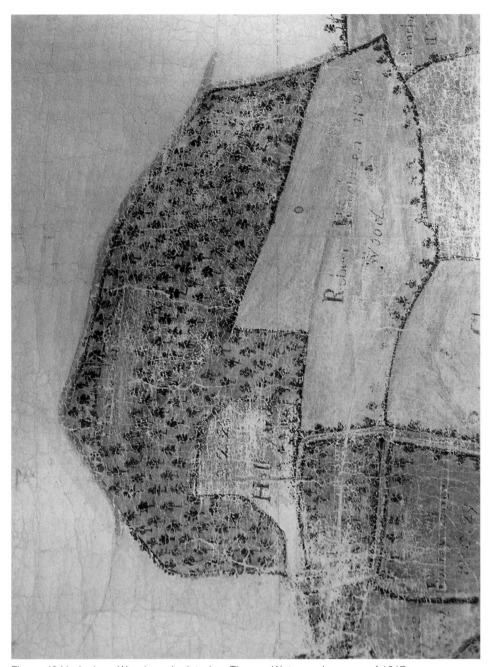

Figure 48 Hedenham Wood, as depicted on Thomas Waterman's survey of 1617.

'pightle', the local term for a small field), presumably indicating that it had been added to the area of the wood relatively recently. The eastern and much of the southern and northern boundaries of the wood shown on the map are much as they are today, with the exception of the north-eastern corner, which appears more angular in character: the character of the woodbank here, which appears to be of medieval form, suggests that this is the result of cartographic error.

The wood is bounded on its northern and along the northern section of its eastern boundary by a substantial woodbank with a functioning external ditch, generally around 7 metres in width, of normal medieval form (b) (Figure 49). In addition, the wood is bisected from east to west by another substantial bank (c), with a ditch to its south, of similar if not identical character. To the north of this bank the wood contains no significant earthworks other than a straight, rather minor, west-facing scarp accompanied to the east by an intermittent ditch (d). This appears to be of post-medieval date, and corresponds with the line of subdivision shown on Waterman's map between the portions of the wood owned by Rachmen and Bedingfield. To the south of bank (c), in contrast, there are a large number of archaeological features. The most striking is (e), a deep, seasonally water-filled linear depression partly flanked to the east by a large bank. The Ordnance Survey describe this as a 'moat', but the enclosure to the west (now largely occupied by pheasant pens) is defined by ditches ((f) and (g)) which partly run uphill, and can therefore never have been entirely water-filled (although some sections of (f) do hold standing water, these are largely where it has been widened and deepened by later quarrying/extraction). Feature (h) is of uncertain origin but may be an earlier hollow way, one end of which was perhaps widened and deepened to form feature (g).

This whole area (i.e., the enclosure defined by (f), (g) and (h)) corresponds roughly with the open clearing in the south of the wood shown by Waterman and marked as 'Hell Yards' – presumably a corruption of 'Hall Yards'. The complex is the site of a late medieval high-status residence featuring a large semi-ornamental fishpond. Indeed, certain features of the site suggest a measure of conscious landscape design, most notably the straight, wide approach to the south (i), which seems to have been created by extensive levelling. It leads directly to an ancient hedged lane running south through the fields in the rough direction of Hedenham church.

As already noted, the map shows a road approaching 'Hell Yards' from the east. This survives today as two parallel banks (j). In addition, to the south-west of the probable hall site are a number of substantial banks and ditches ((k)–(m)) which define a complex of small enclosures. This area was completely wooded by 1617, but had evidently once been open, and had comprised a number of small closes in the vicinity of the hall. It is noteworthy that there are large areas of nettles here, suggesting that the soil is rich in phosphates and nitrates, perhaps from animal manure, and thus implying that these small closes were used for keeping stock.

The new southern boundaries to the wood, established after the manorial site and associated closes had been abandoned, vary in character. The southern boundary and the southern section of the eastern boundary are marked by wide, low (c.0.2 metres) and rather diffuse banks with functioning external ditches ((n) and (o)): the latter is less substantial than the former, and in places has no real bank at all. The southern section of the new eastern boundary (p) is similarly diffuse but the northern section (q) – beyond the junction with the former lane (j) – is noticeably more massive

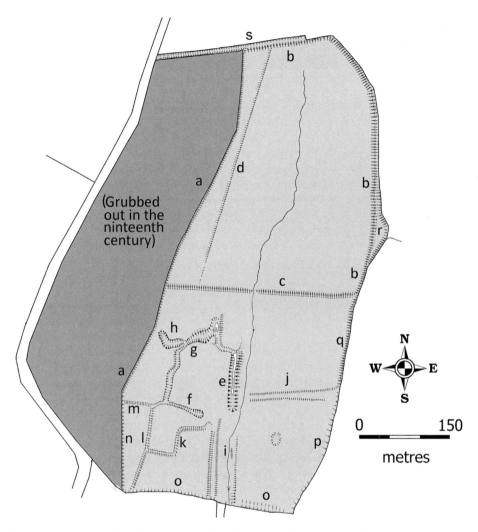

Figure 49 Hedenham Wood: principal earthwork features (for key see text).

and little different in character from the boundaries defining the original 'core' of the wood. The eastern section of the southern boundary has a double bank, the inner probably a field boundary pre-dating the wood.

There are a number of other minor features of interest in the wood, including (r), where a very minor addition has at some point been made to the eastern boundary of the wood, and a new woodbank – as massive as the original – constructed. Quite why such an effort was made, to add a rather small area to the original wood, is uncertain, but the addition is evidently medieval and was certainly in place by 1617. Much of the northern boundary comprises, beyond the medieval woodbank, a hollow way marking the line of a road shown on Waterman's map that was abandoned only in the twentieth century (s).

The northern part of Hedenham Wood, covering some 13 hectares, thus appears to be 'primary' in character. The section to the south of (c), in contrast, is clearly secondary, growing over an abandoned house site, roads and small fields. Some of the latter were probably under arable cultivation, as towards the eastern end of (c) the ground level to the north of the old external woodbank appears to be higher than to the south, suggesting some plough erosion. The high-status site within the wood represents the main manor of Hedenham, held by the Bedingfield family since the sixteenth century. The house was probably abandoned in the fifteenth or early sixteenth centuries: the Bedingfields were residing at Ditchingham Hall, in the adjoining parish of Ditchingham, by 1543, for Philip Bedingfield Esquire, who died in that year, is described in his will as 'of Ditchingham' (NRO Will Register Atmere 375). Nevertheless, the southern expansion of Hedenham Wood across its site and associated enclosures was evidently gradual. As noted, 'Hall Yards' and the road approaching it from the east were still open when mapped by Waterman in 1617, and the fact that 'The Pightle' was separately named suggests that this field, at least, had only recently become colonised by trees.

The wood was still being managed on traditional lines in the 1890s, when the new owner William Carr described in his estate notebook how men were paid £4 5d an acre for coppicing it. But it had evidently been somewhat neglected under the last of the Bedingfields. Coppicing had not taken place for twelve years, and as a result the cut material was deemed 'too coarse and strong for hurdle making', perhaps implying that hazel was then more prominent than hornbeam within the wood. There had been no planting for three decades, and 'all timber of commercial value had been cut and sold'. Carr undertook some replanting, both of hazel understorey and oak standards, although the young oaks acquired from the nursery for this purpose had poorly developed root systems and many died soon after transplanting (NRO MC 166/238).

Hedenham thus has a complex history, first expanding to the south in the sixteenth and seventeenth century, then contracting on its western side. It is noteworthy that there is little if any difference in the vegetation (both in terms of stand type and herb layer) in the surviving 'primary' (northern) and 'secondary' (southern) sections of the wood, other than that the western section of the latter contains more nettles, presumably signifying its prior use as farmland. It is also noteworthy that while hornbeam is now dominant over large areas of the wood, beside the main rides and on the edge of the wood, the understorey is more mixed, as it is in areas recently recoppiced. It is possible that the present dominance of hornbeam is the consequence of relatively recent changes: of the decline in management in the course of the twentieth century, the growth of the hornbeam coppice to canopy level, and the consequent shading out of understorey shrubs such as hazel or maple.

Hethel Wood
TG 15980078

Hethel Wood covers an area of *c.*25 hectares on heavy clay soils of the Beccles Association: much of the wood is very poorly draining. Unusually, the central ride crossing the wood from west to east is followed by a public footpath. From the eighteenth century until the Second World War the wood stood on the western margins of Hethel Park, Hethel Hall itself lying some 300 metres to the north-east. In the Second World War Hethel airfield, originally built for the RAF but transferred to the USAAF Eighth Air Force in 1942, was constructed immediately to the west (Freeman 2001,

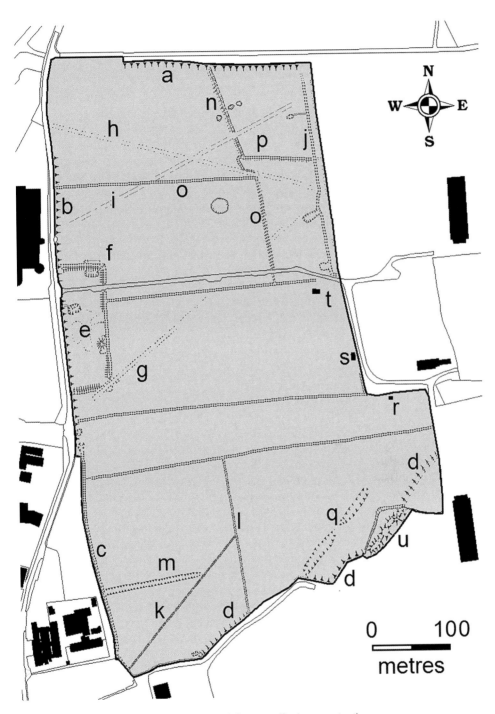

Figure 50 Hethel Wood: principal earthwork features (for key see text).

285, 308). A range of communal services and accommodation were located within the wood, with technical facilities and headquarters buildings on its western edge. The north-western area of the wood was partly cleared of trees to provide space for buildings. Hethel Hall was demolished in the middle decades of the twentieth century and the wood is now flanked by farmland to the north, south and east, and by the Lotus car factory – occupying the site of the former airfield – to the west.

The wood comprises sparse oak standards over outgrown ash and neglected hazel and hornbeam coppice, with some hawthorn and field maple. Birch, willow and alder also occur: the former species is common where areas were cleared during the war, and the two latter species dominate the damper sections of the wood. There are also scattered examples of dogwood and holly. The ground flora includes much bramble but also extensive areas of dog's mercury, remote sedge, primrose, wood sanicle, barren strawberry and yellow archangel.

The wood is first depicted on an undated early eighteenth-century estate map (NRO RQG 127, 488X5) with the same boundaries as today, except to the north-east, where it extended further to the east. It had been truncated to its present limits by the middle of the nineteenth century (NRO DN/TA 597) (Figure 27). The eighteenth-century map also shows that the wood was dissected by a network of six rides, evidently at least partly aesthetic in character, as two were focused on the hall to the north-east, one of which is continued across the intervening parkland as an avenue. This pattern of rides is also shown on another undated eighteenth-century map, in private ownership, but with two further rides added; and this arrangement survived intact into the twentieth century and in fragmentary form as late as 1946.

The wood has a substantial perimeter bank and ditch of normal medieval form along the central and eastern sections of the northern boundary (a) and along the central section of the western boundary (b), varying in width from 6 to 8 metres, including external ditch (Figure 50). The northern end of the western boundary and the western end of the northern have been levelled by wartime activity. The southern section of the western boundary (c) is defined by a wide and partly water-filled ditch, possibly medieval; the south-eastern boundary (beyond which the wood has expanded in the far south-eastern corner) is mainly defined by a woodbank rather smaller than that to the north and west (d), although evidently of medieval date; this has been damaged or removed in places. The eastern margins of the wood are defined by a ditch without a bank, indicating where the wood has been truncated since the eighteenth century.

The wood contains a number of earthworks, although their character is not always clear, in part because of subsequent reuse and adaptation. In addition, the overgrown and waterlogged character of the southern sections of the wood, in particular, presented problems of surveying and measurement. The most important feature is the enclosure (e) on the western edge of the wood. It is defined on its northern, eastern and southern side by a massive bank and ditch as much as 9 metres across in places; its western boundary is defined by the external woodbank. The northern section of the enclosure contains a large rectangular pond (f), while to the south lie a large mound, a smaller, more irregular pond and amorphous undulations. The character of the enclosure is unclear but it evidently post-dates the establishment of the wood's western boundary and the form of its perimeter banks indicates a medieval date. The large pond may be a fishpond, the mound possibly the base for a dovehouse and the whole complex perhaps a demesne enclosure containing woodward's accommodation.

The south-eastern corner of the enclosure has been slighted by one of the rides shown on the eighteenth-century map (g), the faint earthworks of which comprise shallow parallel ditches. Faint traces of some of the other rides can be detected in places as very slight ditches or cambers ((h), (i)), while the line of one is perpetuated by the central east–west footpath/ride. The edges of others appear to be perpetuated by the alignment of nineteenth-century (?) drainage ditches ((j), (k), (l)), but other examples of the latter within the wood do not correspond with any of the early rides (in the south of the wood the network is probably incompletely surveyed owing to the poor conditions). Most of the drainage ditches are around 2 metres wide but one (m) is nearly three times this width. Some in the north-eastern section ((n), (o), (p)) are also different in character: accompanied by slight banks, they may have been adapted from earlier subdivisions of the wood, although this is by no means certain.

The wood contains a number of ponds, including the long, conjoined linear feature (q), possibly in origin a hollow way but more probably natural: curiously, this appears to continue the alignment of a section of the external boundary of the wood. The wartime use of the wood has left relatively few archaeological traces. There are three small brick-built buildings standing close to the eastern margins of the wood ((r), (s), (t)) and complex, amorphous undulations mark the sites of others in the wood's north-western corner; large piles of concrete from demolished buildings, originally lying outside the wood, occupy part of the south-eastern boundary (u); and the ride/footpath running east–west through the middle of the wood is concreted.

Hethel Wood is evidently 'primary' in character, a reflection of the damp nature of the site and its heavy soils. There is no evidence of earlier use of its area, and the relationship of the medieval western enclosure to the woodbank leaves little doubt that the former post-dates the latter.

Hockering Wood
TG 07201444

Hockering Wood is (after Foxley, and the largely replanted Haveringland Great Wood) the third largest genuinely ancient wood in Norfolk, extending over an area of 89 hectares and containing the most extensive area of small-leaved lime woodland in the county. It occupies land which is level to the north, but which slopes in the south towards the river Tud, a tributary of which has its source in the wood. The soils within the wood are mapped by the Soil Survey as falling within the Beccles Association, except in the extreme south-eastern corner, where Burlingham soils occur; but in fact they appear very variable in character, in some places sandy, elsewhere heavy and poorly draining; sometimes acidic, sometimes calcareous.

Today much of the northern half of the wood is occupied by conifer plantations but elsewhere it principally comprises lime standards, singled in the second half of the twentieth century from coppice, over lime and hazel coppice. There are also scattered oak standards, while a wide variety of other timber, including exotic oaks and beech, is thinly scattered through the wood. There are also areas of birch, largely occurring where land was cleared during the Second World War. The ground flora is sometimes sparse, or dominated by bracken or – in replanted areas especially – by bramble. But a wide range of ancient woodland indicators can be found throughout the wood, including dog's mercury, bluebell, wood anemone, herb Robert (*Geranium robertianum*), water avens, herb Paris and pendulous sedge. There are localised spreads of lily-of-the-valley, especially in the vicinity of the moated site in the eastern part of the wood.

The history of the wood is not well documented. It is shown, with almost the same outline as today, on Faden's map of 1797, on a map of 1805 (NRO 21428 Box F) and on the Hockering tithe award map of 1839 (NRO DN/TA 63). An extent of the manor of Hockering drawn up in 1316 refers to the 'capital messuage, a park, a wood called Swynehagh and a little wood' (Blomefield 1811, X, 229). Faden shows 'Swinnow Wood' as a separate area of woodland, to the north, which had disappeared by the nineteenth century. However, the 1805 map explicitly labels 'Hockering or Swinnow Wood', so it was clearly an alternative name for Hockering Wood itself.

The situation is further confused by the fact that in 1360 two deer parks of 100 acres (*c*.40 hectares) are recorded in Hockering (CIPM, Vol. 10, 501). The shape of one of these could, before the late twentieth century, be picked out in the pattern of field boundaries to the east of the wood, in the area around Park Grove and Park Farm, but Robert Liddiard has plausibly suggested that the other is represented by Hockering Wood, which has the suggestively named Lodge Farm on its southern boundary. This second park was still being mentioned in documents as late as 1581 (Liddiard 2010, 26). It is interesting that the three other unquestionably ancient woods in the county which extend over an area of more than 60 hectares – Foxley, Haveringland Great Wood and Hevingham Park – likewise originated as deer parks. It is also noteworthy that Faden's map shows that the wood formed one of several areas of unploughed land in the neighbourhood, with Siphons Green adjoining it to the south-west, Hockering Heath lying to the north-east, 'Swinnow Wood' to the north and other areas of woodland to the east: with the other deer park in the parish, this evidently represents the remains of a once continuous tract of once wooded ground on the interfluves between the rivers Tud (to the south) and the Wensum (to the north).

By the eighteenth century the wood formed part of the Berney estate, centred on Morton Hall, and was leased by John Berney to John Curson for 15 years in 1740 and for 11 years in 1744 (NRO BER 336 291/7–8). The document associated with the former event implies that the wood was coppiced on a 14-year cycle, and the 1805 map likewise shows the wood divided into 14 fells, suggesting again a 14-year cycle of cutting, as does an agreement for 1828 (NRO BER 336). The tithe files of *c*.1837, however, suggest an 8- to 10-year cycle (TNA 18/6005). The latter source also describes how the underwood was 'used for sheep hurdles and thatching and daubing materials', perhaps suggesting the prominence of hazel in the underwood. On the break-up of the Berney estate in 1923 the wood was sold (for £12,050, a substantial sum), the sales catalogues describing how it contained oak, larch, Scots pine, Douglas fir, 'mixed timber' and a 'quantity of underwood, some of which is fit to be cut'. Much of the timber was removed by the new owner, and limited replanting took place featuring oak, Turkey oak, red oak and various conifers ((Natural England archives, Peterborough). As described in the main text (above, pp. 140–2), during the Second World War the wood was used as a Forward Ammunition Dump. Many of the rides were concreted and large numbers of bomb storage areas created. In 1956 the wood was acquired by Captain Hutton. Around two-thirds of the wood still retained mixed coppice of small-leaved lime and hazel, and over large areas he singled the lime stools, which soon overtopped the hazel and suppressed their growth.

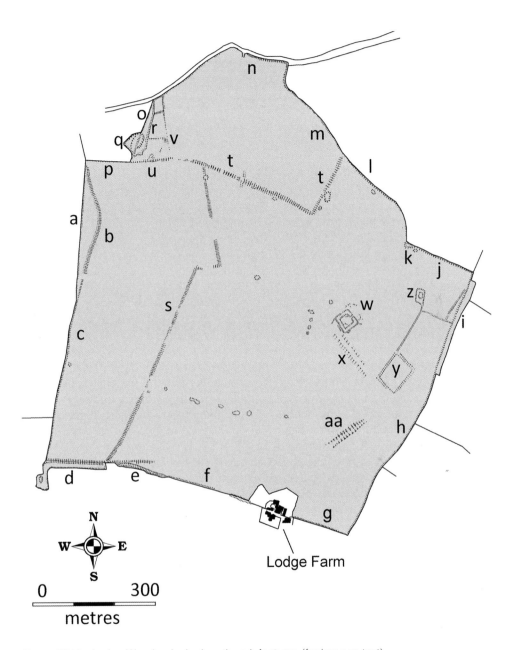

Figure 51 Hockering Wood: principal earthwork features (for key see text).

The wood has a complex archaeology, which includes numerous rectangular earthworks used to store munitions during the war: although of considerable archaeological interest, these are omitted from Figure 51 (although one example is illustrated in Figure 32). A Nissen hut, relocated, stands by the present entrance on the north side of the wood and the ruins of the other lie in the far south. The principal rides within the wood all carry their wartime surfacing, and a number of additional roads, laid out at this time, remain.

The outer boundaries of the wood are complex and variable. On the northern section of the western side a narrow addition has been made to the wood, probably in the eighteenth or early nineteenth century (and certainly before 1839: NRO DN/ TA 63), and the straight outer boundary has a small bank which carries the remains of a hedge and is flanked by a deep external ditch (a). The original woodbank swings eastwards into the wood, and then westwards again, in a smooth curve (b): it is around 7 metres wide, including ditch, and rises around 0.7 metres above the woodland floor. Further to the south this bank becomes once more the external boundary of the wood (c), but is here less well preserved, its outer edge truncated by modern recutting of the external ditch, and it gradually becomes less well defined and lower, disappearing altogether for a short section. The southern boundary is more complex. At its western end the wood has again been slightly extended, as a narrow strip (d), at some point in the past: the extension is bounded by a straight, diminutive hedgebank, although this carries some large oaks, with girths of up to 4.7 metres, so is presumably of some antiquity. The original woodbank is here a substantial feature, and carries three pollard oaks (at *c*. TG 0673313936; 0673413936; and 0673513936); and a pollarded lime. Moving eastwards, beyond the end of this extension, the ditch flanking this bank gradually widens to form a linear pond (e) which diverges gradually from the bank itself, the latter continuing on a slightly different alignment before fading out. The boundary of the wood is here formed by the pond and then, further to the east, by a low, rather diffuse and perhaps post-medieval woodbank (f) with a sharp field ditch on the outside. This widens into another linear pond (recently widened as an ornamental feature by the owners of Lodge Farm). The boundary has been largely obliterated around Lodge Farm but beyond it is marked by a better defined, sharper bank, around 0.8 metres high on the inside but only *c*.3 metres across, which drops into a substantial external functioning ditch (g).

The eastern boundary of the wood is defined by a more substantial bank of more usual medieval form (h) *c*.0.3 metres high and *c*.6–7 metres wide, including the functioning external ditch. In places it carries close-packed stools of small-leaved lime resembling the remains of a hedge. At the northern end another narrow strip has been added to the original wood (i), and here the bank is particularly well preserved although, curiously, without a clear outer ditch.

The north-eastern boundary (j) is narrower, only *c*.4 metres in width, and falls steeply into a functioning external ditch. Another pond, enclosed by a subsidiary outer bank, occurs where the boundary changes direction (k), beyond which the woodbank is wider and lower for a short stretch (l) before becoming more substantial once again, although degraded in places (m). Interestingly, the northern boundary, which runs along the side of a public road (n), is more massive – 6 metres or more across – and carries a number of close-set pollarded limes. It has, however, been largely levelled beside the current main entrance to the wood. The final stretch of the external boundary, along the north-western side of the wood, is defined by two straight alignments: one (o) is marked by a sharp, narrow bank, the other (p) by a ditch, accompanied in places by a low, amorphous and spread bank. The former is a recent feature, cutting through a deep pit (q) which was established between 1839 and 1886; the earlier boundary to the wood, more sinuous and substantial, lies a little to the east of both (r).

The wood contains a number of linear banks and ditches that are difficult to interpret owing in part to the fact that certain crucial sections have been levelled by wartime activity or by replanting. A relatively straight east-facing bank/ditch (s) runs north–south through the western half of the wood. It has been badly damaged in places by conifer planting, and even where this has not occurred it is sometimes more shallow ditch than bank, but its central section comprises a substantial bank and ditch nearly 7 metres across, with the bank rising *c*.0.6 metres above the base of the ditch. It kinks in an unusual manner midway along its length and terminates at a junction with another bank running east–west (t). This latter feature starts about halfway along the wood's north-eastern boundary and runs south-westwards for about 170 metres, passing very close to two pits/ponds. At around 7 metres in width, including the ditch to the east, it is a fairly substantial feature. At *c*. TG 0739714585 it makes a right-angle bend and then runs west through the wood, the ditch now to the south, passing near or beside further ponds. Around TG 0705014720 it disappears, apparently destroyed by the construction of Nissen huts (the bases of which survive) and when it reappears it is different in character (u), now being a substantial *north*-facing scarp with traces of a flanking bank to the south, which continues – gradually becoming less prominent – to the corner of the wood, where it becomes the external woodbank (p) already described. It is possible, however, that (t) in fact turns north and that (u) is really a distinct feature, for traces of a low bank with a ditch to the east are just visible as (v). To the west of this, and to the north of (u), a network of banks and ditches in the north-western corner of the wood appears to mark where it has expanded over agricultural land.

The wood contains a number of other significant earthworks. (w) is a small moated site, the inner island measuring only 30 metres square and the outer ditch 42 metres by 42 metres. The island is accessed by an apparently later causeway from the north-east, where there are traces of an outer enclosure. There are remains of early post-medieval brickwork in the south-western corner. To the south of the moat is a very diffuse bank (x), mapped as a feature on Figure 51 but possibly natural; LIDAR shows it continuing further to both the north-west and the south-east, but this was not noted during ground survey. To the south-east is a trapezoidal enclosure of uncertain date or purpose (y) defined by a slight bank and ditch. It is noteworthy that moat and enclosure share the same orientation as the diffuse bank (x). To the north of (y), and connected to it by a drainage ditch, is a small pond with a central island (z), again of uncertain purpose but probably relatively recent and perhaps associated with the management of the wood for shooting. Of more interest is (aa), to the south, a linear feature which runs up the sloping ground. Superficially resembling a hollow way and *c*.12–14 metres in width, it is flanked to the north-west by a substantial spread bank *c*.6 metres wide, and thus appears more like a linear earthwork, possibly of pre-medieval date. In addition, the wood contains a number of ponds, some arranged in rough lines but nevertheless probably of natural origin.

Hockering Wood presents many problems of interpretation. As with Foxley (q.v.), the wood's outer boundaries appear to be those of a coppiced wood – a bank with an external ditch – rather than the remains of a park pale with an *internal* one. Here, however, the small moat – located in a commanding position, with wide views to the south especially – would be consistent with the site of a lodge (although it is curious that 'Lodge Farm' lies on the wood's present southern boundary). The various internal banks may have functioned as the boundaries of coppiced areas within a compartmentalised park, although precisely how features (t), (u) and (p) are related is unclear. It is possible that all once formed the northern boundary of the park, with the area to the north a later addition, made at the expense of common land. Alternatively, this northern area may always have formed a separate area of coppiced woodland. In this context, we should note that the recorded area of *both* the Hockering parks (100 acres, or *c*.40 hectares) is considerably less than the current area of the wood, and that boundary (t) has a ditch to the south and east – i.e., on the 'correct' side for a deer park to the south. If this northern section was woodland, and the southern comprised the deer park, then feature (s) might represent the boundary of an area of compartmentalised coppice within the latter. The north-western corner of the wood appears to be a late medieval addition made at the expense of enclosed fields; there are a number of minor post-medieval additions around the margins of the wood; and the wood may have been truncated to the south.

In addition to such complications and difficulties, the true date and character of the diffuse bank (x), enclosure (y) and the linear feature (aa) remain unclear. What does seem certain, however, is that with the exception of the north-western corner (and the various minor additions) Hockering Wood is 'primary' in character, in the sense that it has never been divided into fields and ploughed. Its probable history as a deer park, however, indicates that large areas must have comprised grazed wood pasture, and perhaps open launde, in the past. Features (y) and (aa) may be associated with early pastoral exploitation of the area.

Holland's Wood, North Lopham
TM 05028219

Holland's Wood occupies Beccles 1 Association soils on level clayland in the south Norfolk parish of North Lopham. It covers just over four hectares and, like Lopham Grove (qv.), originally formed part of the medieval Lopham Park (above, p. 105). It mainly comprises outgrown hornbeam coppice with scattered oak standards, but there are some areas (mostly towards the edge of the wood) where the coppice is more mixed, with field maple and hazel, and some ash and hawthorn. Over much of the wood the ground flora is almost non-existent, apart from scattered clumps of dog's mercury.

A map of 1612 in the Arundel archives, surveyed by Thomas Waterman (Arundel Castle Archives P5/1), shows that at this time the wood formed part of a much larger area of woodland within Lopham Park called 'Poule Chimbroke', continuing to the north as 'Little Chimbrooke'. Only the western and north-western boundaries of the present wood, the former coinciding with that of the deer park itself, were then in existence. A map of 1720, in contrast, made after the park had been disparked, shows all the boundaries of the wood in place, but the area they enclosed was completely unwooded, and described as 'Smith's Close' (Arundel archives H3 18). The rest of the former Chimbrooke woods had, likewise, been converted to farmland, the parcel to the south of 'Smith's Close' being described on the map as 'Barn meadow'. The area occupied today by Holland's Wood was still shown as open pasture on another map in the Arundel archives, surveyed in 1812 (albeit with six tree symbols in the far north suggesting a measure of tree cover); but, rather curiously, the meadow to the south was now detailed as woodland. The wood had evidently been planted by 1847, when it is shown on the North Lopham tithe award map (NRO DN/TA 871).

The southern boundary of the present wood is very straight and marked by a small bank and ditch, with a low outer bank in places, giving a total width of only 4 metres: it is evidently post-medieval. The western boundary, already in place by 1612, is more substantial, comprising a bank and ditch with an overall width reaching 5 metres in places. The western stretch of the north-eastern boundary, likewise in place by 1612, is similar, but slightly narrower; the eastern section of this boundary has a more substantial bank with outer ditch, totalling 7 metres in width, and appears medieval in character. The eastern boundary comprises two sections with slightly different orientations: the northern has a woodbank similar to that just described, suggesting that it may have originated as a medieval subdivision of the Chimbrooke Woods; the southern section, however, has a ditch with a slight external bank and an even slighter internal one, suggesting post-medieval realignment. There are no obvious earthworks within the wood, which has a number of apparently natural dips and undulations. There is a small pit, probably of no great antiquity, towards the south-eastern corner (*c.* TM 0503982142) and a pond in the north-western, bounded to north and west by the woodbank and to the south and east by other, lower banks.

A wood with an uncertain history. While it clearly occupies an area which was wooded in 1612, the map evidence leaves no doubt that – like Lopham Wood, on the far side of Lopham Park – it had become open pasture by the early eighteenth century, before being replanted as coppice some time in the nineteenth.

Holly or Holy Grove, Earsham
TM 31288997

Holy Grove, one of several *Inventory* woods on the Earsham estate, occupies 5.3 hectares of ground which slopes slightly towards the south and east on soils which vary from light clay loams of the Burlingham Series to gravels of the Newport 4 Series (towards the lower ground). The *Inventory* area of the wood comprises degraded hazel coppice with some ash among much sycamore, and with areas of outgrown game cover (snowberry, laurel etc.), all under scattered oak (and some ash and sycamore) standards. There are areas of elm, especially within the wood's irregular, south-western projection. The ground is almost entirely covered in dog's mercury, and scattered examples of water avens and primrose have also been recorded, according to the County Wildlife Site citation. Much of the long south-eastern boundary of the wood is marked by a substantial lynchet and the south-western boundary takes the form of a low woodbank, around 7 metres across including external ditch. Elsewhere, the boundary comprises a wide ditch, reaching over 3 metres in places, without a significant bank. Much of the north-eastern section of the wood is occupied by former extraction pits dug (presumably for gravel) into the sloping ground. The only other earthworks noted were a number of drainage ditches; some diffuse linear banks; and, within the south-western projection, a short, curving stretch of hollow way.

In spite of its evocative name, south-western woodbank, south-eastern lynchet, coppiced understorey and 'ancient woodland indicators', Holy Grove did not exist when a map of the estate was surveyed in *c.*1720 (NRO MEA 3/362) (Figure 28). Its area was then occupied by hedged fields, probably under pasture, one of which (within the northern part of the present wood) contained a number of scattered free-standing trees. This part of the wood had been planted up as a wood by *c.*1770, when a second estate map was surveyed (NRO MEA 3/631), but the majority of the *Inventory* area became wooded only after this date, in the later eighteenth or early nineteenth century: the wood is shown with its present limits on the tithe award map of 1840 (NRO DN/TA 564). A dozen or so large oak pollards survive within the northern section of the wood, mostly growing in lines and some associated with the diffuse banks which are evidently former field boundaries.

A wood of broadly 'pseudo-ancient' type.

Honeypot Wood
TF 93281438

Honeypot Wood covers an area of *c.*9.5 hectares on level ground characterised by soils of the Beccles 1 Association: the parish boundary between Wendling and Longham forms its northern boundary. It comprises mixed ash and field maple coppice, with areas of hazel, some goat willow and scattered examples of dogwood, blackthorn and hawthorn, under oak standards. The rich ground vegetation includes dog's mercury, water avens, herb Paris, primrose and wood anemone, as well as the greater butterfly orchid, broad-leafed helleborine (*Epipactis helleborine*) and twayblade (*Listera ovate*). Since 1980 the wood has been managed as a nature reserve by the Norfolk Wildlife Trust.

The wood is shown with the same size and shape as today on the 1815 Wendling enclosure map (NRO C/Sca 2/323) and the 1842 tithe award map (NRO DN/TA 543), with the exception of minor changes in the southern boundary which were effected between 1842 and 1884, when the first edition Ordnance Survey six-inch map was made. Documentary evidence relating to the wood is sparse, although an indenture of 1835 between the owner, Edward Lombe of Great Melton, and James Coleman describes how the wood was divided into a number of separate fells which were cut at intervals of only seven years or less (the cutting was not to begin before 14 October or continue after 25 March). The use of the coppice for making hurdles, hoops and poles is also mentioned. Twenty *standils* of oak were to be left in each acre felled. The standards were not included in the lease (NRO EVL 650/6).

The wood is largely enclosed by a medieval woodbank and external ditch, varying in width from *c.*5 to *c.*6.5 metres (Figure 52). This is a rather low feature along the western section of the northern boundary of the wood (a); has been removed along the eastern section of the southern boundary; and has been damaged along most of the western boundary by the construction of a concrete road during the war (a new ditch, on the inside of the remains of the bank, is present here) (b). Along much of the southern (c) and eastern (d) sides it is well preserved: its absence from the eastern end of the southern boundary is probably the result of nineteenth-century realignment, indicated by slight differences in the way it is depicted on the tithe award map of 1842 and the Ordnance Survey map of 1884. Two oak pollards, with girths of 2.7 and 3.5 metres, grow on the surviving section of the southern woodbank, where there is a pond just outside the wood's boundary, apparently a recent feature as it is absent from both the tithe award map and the first edition Ordnance Survey six-inch. Another oak pollard, with a girth of 3.8 metres, stands on the western boundary.

The wood lies on what was the south-eastern edge of Wendling airfield, which was built for the RAF but taken over by the USAAF in 1942 (Freeman 2001, 285, 313), and

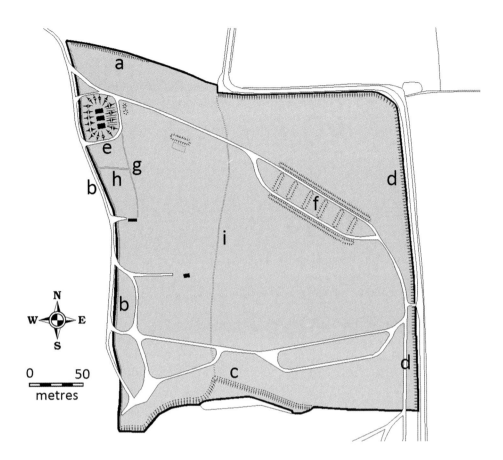

Figure 52 Honeypot Wood, Wendling: principal earthwork features (for key see text).

was used for storing munitions. It contains a number of structures and earthworks relating to this phase of its history. These include concrete roads; a number of brick-built storage buildings, some of them (for storing pyrotechnics and incendiary bombs) placed within high blast banks (e); and a bomb storage area surrounded by substantial earthwork banks which were arranged in such a way that the bombs could be rolled from the lorries, down ramps and into the storage bays, on the other side of which another concrete road provided access for the trolleys which took them to the planes (f). The remains of further storage facilities exist outside and to the south of the wood. The speed with which these remains have become colonised by dog's mercury, primrose and other 'indicator species' is noteworthy.

The only other earthworks located within the wood are three shallow ditches c.2 metres wide and accompanied by slight banks. Of these, (g) and (h) are associated with wartime storage buildings and were probably dug during the war; (i), however, which has a slightly more noticeable bank (to the west), and which runs the full width of the wood, is probably an earlier drain or, just possibly, the denuded remains of a medieval bank subdividing the wood.

A medieval wood, probably 'primary' in character, with important archaeological remains of military use in the Second World War.

Hook Wood, Morley St Peter
TM 05569809

Hook Wood covers an area of 3.1 hectares in the south-west of the parish of Morley St Peter, on Beccles 1 Association soils. No documents relating to the wood have been recovered, but it is clearly shown on a map of Morley surveyed by Thomas Waterman in 1629, where it has the same outline as today (NRO PD3/108). The wood is there named 'Park Wood' and a field to the north as 'Park Meadow', and the outline of a small deer park (covering some 26 hectares) can be picked out in the pattern of surrounding field boundaries. This oval shape was bounded to the south by the extensive Garsing Common, from which it may in part have been enclosed. On its northern edge the manor of Morley Hall, the main manor in Morley St Peter, stood on a moated site (NHER 9118). The origins of the park are uncertain. Its close association with the hall suggests a late medieval origin, but its position on the parish boundary between Morley St Peter and Attleborough, and the fact that it was contiguous with the common, may suggest that it was created in the twelfth or thirteenth century.

The wood, now relatively unmanaged and principally used as game cover, has a relatively open canopy, especially towards the east, which comprises standards of oak and ash, the latter outgrown from coppice. The understorey mainly consists of stools of field maple and hazel, the former dominant in the west and the latter in the east. There are also scattered stools of hornbeam and some hawthorn, spindle, holly, crab apple and white willow. Some elm grows on the margins of the wood. The ground vegetation includes bluebell, dog's mercury, wood melick and yellow archangel, as well as abundant ground ivy and rough meadow-grass (*Poa trivialis*). Ryegrass, soft rush and creeping bent occur in the more open rides and creeping thistle and nettle in those more shaded.

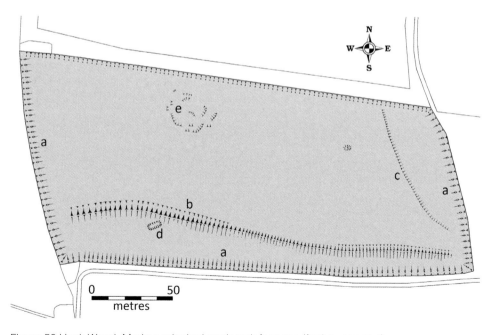

Figure 53 Hook Wood, Morley: principal earthwork features (for key see text).

The wood is surrounded to south, east and west by a fairly small woodbank between 4 and 5 metres across including ditch, and with a height above the woodland floor of around 0.5 metres ((a) on Figure 53). The north side is bounded by simple ditch around 2 metres across with only slight traces of an internal bank. Unlike the other three boundaries, this is more or less dead straight. The wood has evidently been truncated in this direction, but before 1629 to judge from Waterman's map, which, as noted, shows the wood with the same dimensions as today. Interestingly, the field immediately to the north is described on the map as 'Stub'd Wood'. The three older boundaries, while clearly earlier, may not be very much older – perhaps late medieval in date – for a very substantial bank and ditch, running sinuously east–west through the wood a little to the north of the southern boundary, appears to be an earlier woodbank (b). It is, including ditch, between 7 and 10 metres across, with the bank rising as much as 1 metre above the ditch. It appears to have been obliterated to east and west by the construction of the present woodbanks. If this is indeed an earlier boundary, then it relates either to a wood which existed before the park was created *or* to an area of enclosed coppice within the park, the boundaries of which were altered either when the park was still in existence or after it had ceased to exist. Either way, together with the fact that the wood has been truncated to the north, its presence emphasises the dynamic rather than the static character of ancient woodland boundaries.

The wood contains another, more enigmatic earthwork. A very slight east-facing scarp, apparently a lynchet and seldom more than 0.3 metres in height, curves through the eastern section of the wood (c). There is no accompanying ditch. Although the wood occupies heavy Beccles 1 Association soils the ground falls gently to the east towards soils mapped by the Soil Survey as Burlingham 1, the boundary of which lies some 200 metres away. The feature appears to be evidence of arable use of this section of the wood at some time in the remote past, possibly in the Roman or later prehistoric rather than medieval periods. No other comparable earthworks were noted within the wood, although much of its area is fairly overgrown, and the only other feature of note is a probable saw pit (d), which is rectangular and dug into the putative former woodbank. Lastly, in the north-centre of the wood is an extensive area of slight, amorphous disturbance, of uncertain date or significance but probably modern (e).

Horningtoft Great Wood
TF 94852376

Horningtoft Great Wood occupies an area of 7.8 hectares on level ground: the soils within the wood are mapped as Beccles 1 Association. The wood is a small fragment of a much larger area of woodland covering some 70 hectares, which formerly extended to the south and to the west as far as what is now the main road from Dereham to Fakenham. It was reduced in area some time between 1817, when the Ordnance Survey draft drawings were made (BL OSD 239), and 1826, when Bryant's map of Norfolk was published. The western periphery of the remaining area of woodland had been truncated by a further hectare and incorporated into the adjacent pasture field by the time the first edition Ordnance Survey six-inch map was surveyed in the 1880s. This field remains under grass, and traces of the southern boundary of the present wood can still be seen continuing west and then

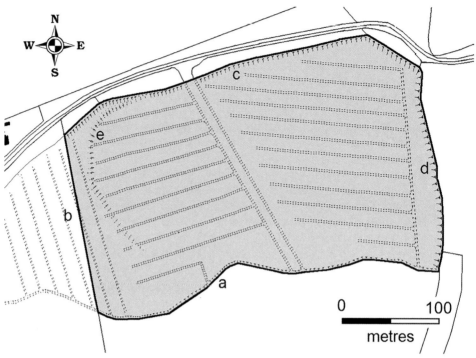

Figure 54 Horningtoft Great Wood: principal earthwork features (for key see text).

turning north and running as far as the road. When the main body of the wood was stubbed in the early nineteenth century a partly moated enclosure and associated closes were revealed on its western periphery (see pp. 57–8; Cushion and Davison 2003, 110–11).

The surviving area of woodland remains in good condition. The coppice – last fully felled in the 1930s, but in small areas cut again in the 1990s – comprises ash, maple and hazel, with some small-leaved lime, beneath standards of ash and oak. It is noticeable that ash is more abundant in areas which were not recoppiced in the late twentieth century. Some examples of beech have been planted, and other shrub and tree species present include aspen, elder, dogwood, rowan, blackthorn, hawthorn, crab and both sallow and goat willow. Holly has, as in a number of other Norfolk woods, increased its representation in recent years. The ground flora includes dog's mercury, especially where the soils are wetter; primrose; wood sorrel; bluebell; lily-of-the-valley; herb Paris; crested cow-wheat (*Melampyrum cristatum*); bird's nest orchid (*Neottia nidus-avis*); broad-leafed helleborine (*Epipactis helleborine*); and greater butterfly orchid.

The southern boundary of the wood ((a) on Figure 54) comprises a diminutive woodbank which follows a slightly irregular course and continues as an earthwork, as noted, into the pasture field to the west. It varies in size but reaches in places a total width (including outer ditch) of nearly 6 metres and a height of *c.*0.3 metres above the woodland floor. Before the wood was truncated in the early nineteenth century its boundary lay some way to the south of this line: the earthwork presumably represents an internal subdivision reused as a convenient outer boundary for the rump of the wood. The western boundary of the present wood (b), created a few decades later, is completely different in character, being ruler-straight and without any bank or ditch. The northern and western boundaries of the wood ((c) and (d)) preserve its original, pre-nineteenth-century limits and are marked by a woodbank and ditch *c*.5–6 metres in width, accompanied on the eastern side by a slight outer bank. Towards the western end of the northern boundary of the wood a slighter inner bank diverges gradually from the external woodbank (e), curving south and then south-east before gradually fading. Its purpose is unclear: it may mark an internal subdivision of the wood, but it could mark the remains of an early enclosure of medieval or earlier date.

The interior of the wood is covered in a dense network of open drains, spaced at intervals of around 18 metres, ruler-straight and arranged in three main blocks. Traces of this system extend into the eastern end of the pasture field to the west, where the wood was (as noted) truncated in the middle decades of the nineteenth century: they do not, however, here extend to the south of the earthwork traces of the former southern boundary of the wood, clearly indicating that they were installed *after* the main area of the wood was stubbed before 1826.

This surviving portion of Horningtoft Great Wood appears 'primary' in character.

Horningtoft Little Wood
TF 93952386

Horningtoft Little Wood covers an area of just over 2 hectares. It occupies a gently sloping site on soils of the Burlingham Association and comprises oak and some ash standards (the latter mainly outgrown coppice stools) over a shrub layer of sparse hazel coppice and much bramble. The ground flora is diverse, including large quantities of bluebell and wood anemone and with extensive spreads of dog's mercury, especially to the north. Wood melick and wood millet are also present. Faden's survey of 1797, the Ordnance survey drawings of 1815 and the enclosure map of 1812 (NRO C/Sca 2/325) all show a rather larger wood, long and thin, extending further both to the east (as far as the Fakenham road) and to the west, and covering around 6.5 hectares. By the time the first edition Ordnance Survey six-inch map was surveyed in 1890 the wood had lost its western end and covered *c*.4.4 hectares. It had been truncated to its present limits by 1905, to judge from the second edition of the six-inch map. Not surprisingly, there is no bank (or even ditch) on the eastern side of the wood, but the other boundaries are, likewise, recent looking. The southern is marked by a sharp bank 2 metres wide and 1 metre high, with an outer ditch; the western by a similar bank without a ditch; and the northern by a low bank, 2 metres across, accompanied by a wide outer ditch. The wood as shown on the earliest maps was thus probably already the rump of a larger medieval wood that had extended further to the north and south.

The western end of the wood contains a substantial quarry pit. The only other earthworks are a number of puzzling straight shallow ditches around 1 metre wide, which are presumably for drainage although ranged at a variety of angles, and not in a manner that makes the best use of the contours.

The rump of a larger medieval wood, possibly but not certainly 'primary' in character, truncated in at least two stages.

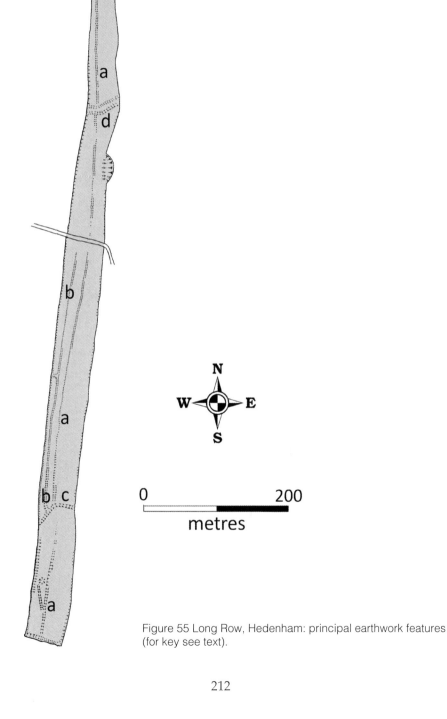

Figure 55 Long Row, Hedenham: principal earthwork features (for key see text).

Long Row, Hedenham
TM 31839377

Long Row is one of three neighbouring woods in the north of Hedenham parish, the others being Round Grove and Hedenham Wood (q.v.), *c.*160 metres and *c.*360 metres to the west respectively. Tindall Wood in Ditchingham lies *c.*520 metres to the east. All four woods are now owned by the Ditchingham estate. The northern part of Long Row lies on level ground and occupies soils of the Beccles 1 Association; the southern occupies sloping ground on Burlingham 1 Association soils, running down towards the Broome Beck, a tributary of the Waveney. The wood mainly comprises outgrown coppice of ash, hazel and maple, with some hornbeam; there are scattered oak standards. There are abundant growths of dog's mercury and some primrose. The wood has a highly unusual shape, without parallel in Norfolk, taking the form of a long, narrow rectangle orientated north–south, with the parish boundary between Hedenham and Ditchingham running lengthways through its centre. It covers an area of 6.2 hectares but is 1.1 kilometres in length, and an estate map of 1617, surveyed by Thomas Waterman, shows that it was then even longer, extending for nearly half a kilometre further to the north (NRO MC 1761/2). It forms a major axis in the degraded co-axial field pattern which characterises the surrounding landscape (see above, p. 53).

The earthworks within the wood comprise two linear ditches/banks running lengthways down the wood (Figure 55: (a) and (b)), together what appears to be a transverse boundary (c) and the remains of an old track or road crossing the wood from east to west (d). The parish boundary probably coincides with feature (a); the latter, together with (b), seems to define an early lane which, to judge from its relationship with the local topography, originated as a droveway – of early medieval or, perhaps, earlier date – providing access to wood-pastures on the clay plateau from the lighter land to the south. The lane was evidently abandoned and invaded by woodland which subsequently spread into the adjacent fields and was then enclosed within slightly wider boundaries and managed by coppicing, something which had evidently occurred before 1617. The western boundary bank of the wood, although not large (*c.*5 metres across) is probably medieval; the eastern boundary has only a small bank, or none at all, and is probably post-medieval, presumably a realignment of an earlier boundary.

A secondary wood, of unusual form, apparently preserving the remains of an ancient lane or drove way.

Lopham Grove
TM 06248380

Lopham Grove lies in the far north of Lopham parish and occupies soils of the Beccles 1 Association. It lies within what was, until the eighteenth century, part of Lopham Park (Arundel Castle Archives P5/1). The wood covers an area of 8.8 hectares and contains a typical ash–hazel–field maple understorey, formerly coppiced, with scattered examples of hornbeam. Towards the south and west, however, hornbeam becomes dominant, while towards the south hawthorn increases in prominence. The majority of standards are oaks, but there is also much ash, some sweet chestnut and, in the south-west, hornbeam, presumably singled from the neighbouring coppice, although this is not certain. The floor is carpeted with dog's mercury, except in places under

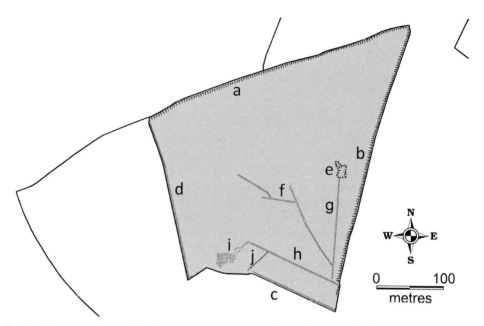

Figure 56 Lopham Grove, South Lopham: principal earthwork features (for key see text).

hornbeam, where the ground is bare, and in sections where grasses predominate. Spurge laurel occurs towards the south-west, and there are large quantities of wood spurge (*Euphorbia amygdaloides*), wood sedge, primrose, bluebell and early purple orchid. A 20-metre swathe running north–south in the western half of the wood appears to have been clear-felled within the last 20 years and this is dominated by naturally regenerating ash, with some evidence of deliberate planting, also of ash. There are occasional patches of sycamore, and laurel has been established in places along the western boundary. All these features would be consistent with an area of ancient semi-natural woodland modified for shooting in the nineteenth and twentieth centuries.

The north-western and eastern sides of the wood ((a) and (b) on Figure 56) are marked by a fairly diffuse but substantial bank 4–5 metres wide including the flanking ditch and 0.5–0.75 metres high. The southern margin (c) has a much sharper, more distinct, bank of post-medieval appearance 3 metres wide, including the ditch to the south, and *c*.0.7 high. This has, nevertheless, a substantial (2.9 metres) hornbeam pollard growing on it, suggesting perhaps a seventeenth-century date. The bank ends where the direction of the boundary changes: a section here has no bank or ditch. The western boundary (d) has no bank at all, just a field ditch, and is evidently quite recent. Internally there are few earthworks: a large, irregular pit towards the eastern side (e); and straight drainage ditches forming a rough herringbone pattern, probably of nineteenth-century date ((f) and (g)). Another ditch (h), 1.5 metres wide and flanked to its north by a bank just over 1.0 metre wide and *c*.0.2 metres high, runs parallel to the southern boundary of the wood, turning to the south-west at its western end and then becoming obscured by amorphous disturbances (i). A further ditch (j), just over 1.0 metre wide, runs between this and the southern woodbank.

The second edition Ordnance Survey six-inch map of 1907 shows that at this stage the bank and ditch (c) did not form the southern boundary of the wood, which was then marked by the bank and ditch (h), but was instead the edge of a strip of orchard, separated by ditch (j) from the garden around a house – 'Wood House' – whose site corresponds with the area of amorphous disturbance (and some rubble) (i). Both (c) and (h), and also (j), have lines of shrubs or trees associated with them, evidently the remains of hedges: in the case of (j), outgrown ash; in that of the others, maple, ash, hawthorn and spindle. The orchard, although now absorbed into the wood, contains no hazel or hornbeam coppice, but instead is filled with ash and some oak, mainly with girths of a metre or less (although one ash is 1.7 metres): Turkey oak, a pear and one or two crab apples also occur. Nevertheless, it is noteworthy that dog's mercury has invaded much of this area, albeit interspersed with nettles and other coarse vegetation. It is also interesting that while, within the main area of the wood, young hornbeam seedlings fail to thrive, their roots presumably unable to reach the mineral soil beneath the leaf litter, in the former orchard a large number of young plants have successfully grown from seeds dropped from the pollard in bank (c), around which they are clustered.

The main area of Lopham Grove appears to be a 'genuine' ancient wood, the differences in the character of its boundaries perhaps marking several stages of contraction: boundaries (a) and (b) seem to represent original medieval boundaries, the others the consequence of grubbing out much of the wood – perhaps in the eighteenth or nineteenth centuries – to create Wood Farm. In reality, the 'woodbanks' (a) and (b) represent earthworks raised to mark the parish boundary between Lopham and Fersfield, with which these sides of the wood coincide, and a map of 1720 shows the entire site as completely unwooded (Arundel Castle Archives H3 18) (Figure 29), although a small area of probable wood-pasture existed in the middle of the field lying to the west. Its area was, however, apparently wooded in 1612, to judge from the map of Lopham Park made by Thomas Waterman (Arundel Castle Archives P5/1). The present wood had evidently been planted by 1847, when the North Lopham tithe award map was surveyed (NRO DN/TA 871). This is a classic example of woodland coming and going from the landscape, with woodland relict vegetation presumably surviving in hedges following clearance and returning when woodland became re-established on the site.

Lopham Grove is one of the most striking examples of a 'pseudo-ancient wood' in Norfolk, with oak standards, mixed coppice and no fewer than six 'ancient woodland indicators'.

Middle Wood or Thorpe Wood, Thorpe Abbots
TM 18358023

Thorpe Wood lies on Beccles 1 Association soils, but on sloping ground on the edge of the Waveney valley, and close to areas of deep, sandy Newport 3 Association soils. It extends over an area of just under 7 hectares and mainly comprises outgrown hornbeam coppice below oak standards: birch and field maple occur sporadically, with hazel and elder concentrated towards the edges of the wood. Parts of the north-eastern sections have been replanted with ash, Scots pine, oak and Norway spruce; smaller areas of replanting occur elsewhere. The ground flora largely comprises ivy and nettle, although three ancient woodland indicators – dog's mercury, barren strawberry and primrose – also occur. Since 1945 the wood has expanded across the

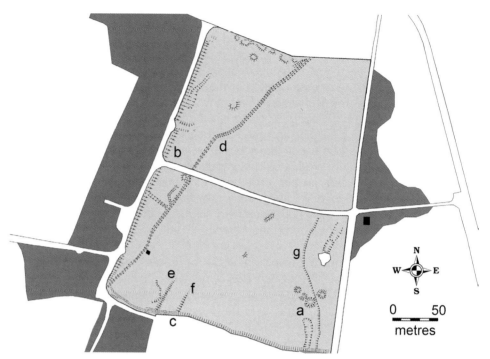

Figure 57 Middle Wood or Thorpe Wood, Thorpe Abbots: principal earthwork features (for key see text).

fields to both east and west (darker grey areas on Figure 57). The wood is shown, with the same boundaries as in 1946, on the tithe award map of 1840 (NRO DN//TA 513). It is crossed from north-east to south-west by a stream contained within a deep ditch ((d) on Figure 57), and the parish boundary between Thorpe Abbots and Billingford runs along its western boundary. Like Billingford Wood (q.v.), which lies some 400 metres to the west, Thorpe Wood was used to house facilities for the nearby Thorpe Abbots airfield, an RAF base transferred to the USAAF in 1942 (Freeman 2001, 283). The wartime remains are fewer here, however, limited to amorphous undulations and piles of rubble, especially on the northern edge of the wood; a single small building towards the south-western corner; and another lying in secondary woodland just to the east of the wood proper. It is possible that the enigmatic series of four pits (a), some with outer banks, in the south-eastern section of the wood may also relate to this phase of the wood's history.

Along the western sides of the wood runs a medieval woodbank (b), *c.*6 metres wide including outer ditch, which is broken in places where roads associated with wartime use have cut across it. The southern boundary (c) is marked by a ditch flanked by diminutive banks on either side towards the west, but unaccompanied towards the east, suggesting that the wood has been truncated on this side in the early post-medieval period. No woodbanks exist along the northern and eastern boundaries, which are both very straight, as are the road immediately to the east and the boundaries of the fields beyond this, beside Wood Farm. The wood may have been truncated on these sides relatively recently to create new farm land, possibly in the later eighteenth century.

There are a number of hollows and pits within the wood which probably pre-date the Second World War. The most important earthworks, however, are three apparent lynchets, each *c.*0.1–0.2 metres in height. Two, parallel and ranged south-west–north-east, are relatively short (*c.*25 metres: (e) and (f)). The third (g) meanders for over 100 metres through the wood. Each is around 0.6–0.3 metres high and faces west. They appear to indicate arable use of the site, although at what date is uncertain. While (e) and (f) could well be medieval, this seems less likely of (g), with its strangely irregular course.

A medieval wood, apparently secondary in whole or part, which has probably been reduced in size in stages in the course of the post-medieval period before expanding again, at the expense of adjoining fields, in relatively recent times.

North Elmham Great Wood
TF 97251980

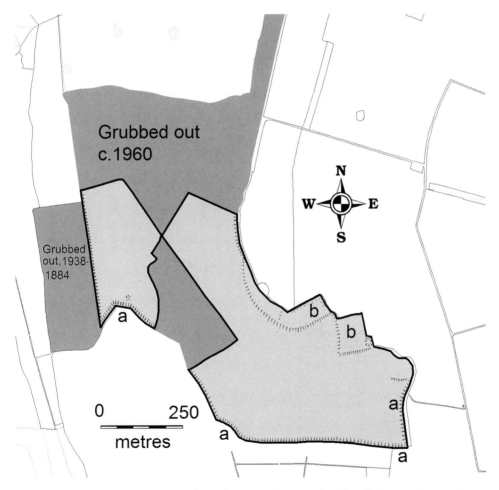

Figure 58 North Elmham Great Wood, as shown on the second edition Ordnance Survey six-inch map (1906). Shaded areas: grubbed out since that date.

North Elmham Great Wood covers an area of 40 hectares on fairly acid Burlingham Association soils, on ground which slopes west towards the Panford Beck and south towards the Blackwater. The southern sections of the wood comprise hazel coppice under oak and ash standards; some field maple, bird cherry and hawthorn and sweet chestnut are also present. Towards the north there are more standards, including large numbers of sycamore. Much of the south of the wood, and the central part of its northern section, have been replanted with commercial broadleafs and conifers. The ground flora is poor over large parts of the wood, with much bramble, but includes dog's mercury and bluebell, together with wood dock (*Rumex sanguineus*) and primrose.

In the Middle Ages the wood formed part of the holdings of the bishop of Norwich, which included the deer park to the north, first mentioned in 1205 (Liddiard 2010, 33): it may be the wood described as 'Burgrave' in 1382 (CPR, 1381–5, 167). Faden's map of 1797 and the tithe award map of 1838 (NRO DN/TA 364) show that the wood then covered around 168 acres (*c*.68 hectares). In the middle decades of the nineteenth century the western and northern sections of the wood were grubbed out, reducing its area to 56 hectares. A further section to the west was stubbed in the middle decades of the twentieth century, reducing the wood to its present area and form – effectively two separate woods, joined at the corner.

The medieval boundary bank, which varies in width but is generally around 6 metres across, with outer ditch, survives along the southern boundary and parts of the western and eastern boundaries (a) (Figure 58). It also survives on the north-eastern side (b), although here it lies in part within the wood, which has expanded – some time before 1790 – across a number of small fields, covering *c*.3 hectares. The other existing boundaries are the result of the various reductions in the wood's area in the course of the nineteenth and twentieth centuries. There are no other internal earthworks, with the exception of a single small pit.

Evidently a primary wood, with a complicated history of both expansion and contraction.

Old Grove and Primrose Grove, Gillingham
TM 41179400

Old Grove and Primrose Grove are conjoined areas of woodland covering 7 hectares on Beccles Association soils in the north of the parish of Gillingham; the northern end of the latter wood touches the parish boundary with Raveningham. The *Ancient Woodland Inventory* area also includes a narrow strip of woodland, covering less than a hectare, lying to the west of the main wood and separated from it by a north–south public road which leads from Gillingham to Raveningham. This small western section has recently been recoppiced. It comprises mixed hazel, maple, elm and ash coppice under relatively young oak and ash standards. There are extensive spreads of dog's mercury and some primrose. The wood lies at a slightly lower level than the adjoining road to the east, from which it is separated by a rather diffuse bank *c*.3 metres wide, without a ditch; its northern, southern and eastern boundaries are defined by relatively narrow (*c*.2 metres) banks with external ditches. The main body of the wood, to the east of the road, also lies slightly below its level. It has been replanted in places with ash and oak, Lombardy poplar and Sitka spruce. Where replanting has not occurred, however, the southern section of the wood comprises a canopy of sparse oak standards, outgrown ash coppice and remnant hazel coppice, with some maple and hawthorn and patches of elm, while the northern consists of oak standards over outgrown hornbeam coppice. In the northern section the ground cover is sparse, but elsewhere there are extensive patches of dog's mercury and, in the more open areas, early purple orchid and remote sedge occur. Towards the margins of the wood primrose, hard shield fern (*Polystichum aculeatum*) and wood speedwell (*Veronica montana*) are found. The western boundary, beside the road, is marked in part by a ditch without a bank, and – further to the north – by a diminutive woodbank generally around 3 metres wide and 0.3 metres in height. The northern boundary, which also runs beside a road, is a similar but better defined and slightly higher bank. The other boundaries are marked by rather sharper banks around 2–3 metres wide, with external ditches.

In spite of its coppice structure and array of ancient woodland 'indicators', the wood is not very old. When the Gillingham tithe award map was surveyed in 1839 (NRO DN/TA 829) it did not exist, with the exception of the narrow strip lying to the west of the road (Figure 30). The only internal earthworks are banks and ditches – in part reused as a drainage system – which can be correlated with field boundaries shown on the tithe award map. The roadside banks are evidently the remains of substantial field hedges. Even the small strip of woodland lying to the west of the road, which *was* in existence by 1839, is unlikely to be of any great antiquity given the nature of its boundaries and its shape, which clearly indicate that it was enclosed piecemeal from the open fields at some point in the post-medieval period.

Evidently, this is wholly or very largely a 'pseudo-ancient' wood.

Old Pollard Wood, Holt
TG 07684006

Old Pollard Wood occupies an area of acid gravels, part of the Holt–Cromer ridge, and the soils are poor and thin, falling within the Newport 4 Association. It occupies in part a level plateau, but to the west the ground is dissected, falling precipitously, and the wood here extends down steeply sloping ground. It is now in divided ownership. The northern section has been largely replanted in the second half of the twentieth century, in part with conifers and in part with deciduous species, although some of the earlier vegetation, mainly oak coppice, still remains. The southern section of the original wood now forms the grounds of Holt Hall, which was built within it in *c*.1860 by Walter Hamilton Pemberton. The house was subsequently sold to John Rogers, who spent £2,000 enlarging it, and remained in the hands of the Rogers family until sold to Norfolk County Council in 1945. The 1839 tithe award map (NRO DN/TA 345) shows the wood extending, uninterrupted, southwards across what is now the site of the house: its park, gardens, clumps and belts were thus, as it were, sculpted from a once continuous area of woodland. In the course of the twentieth century much of the open ground then created, especially to the west of the hall, became invaded with scrub and woodland again, filling in many of the spaces between what had, in the later nineteenth century, been discrete blocks of woodland.

The surviving northern section of the wood, lying at a distance from the house, preserves in part the boundaries shown on the tithe award map, but these appear to be the result of post-medieval truncation: neither the north-western nor the north-eastern sides are marked by significant banks, and only the lynchet on the curving western side, generally between 1 and 2 metres in height, might represent the medieval limits. The wood contains a single internal earthwork comprising a 2-metre-wide bank accompanied by a 3-metre-wide ditch, which follows a meandering course through the wood and which is still marked as a boundary on the modern Ordnance Survey. Outgrown oaks on the bank may be the remains of a hedge. The ditch changes sides, from north to south of the bank, roughly half way along the feature's length. It probably represents an internal subdivision of medieval or early post-medieval date. No other earthworks were found: the area of the wood appears to have always been uncultivated.

The outer boundaries of the southern section of the wood, in contrast, have been radically altered since 1839, truncated to the east and given a scalloped form, following the contours, to the west, presumably at the time the new hall was built. The new boundaries are marked by diminutive banks, and a number of similar banks exist on the edges of the present, rather extended, areas of woodland, and also in places running through them. They are between 3.5 and 4 metres in width and generally around 0.5 metres in height, occasionally reaching *c.*0.8 metres, and lack accompanying ditches. In spite of their size, and the fact that they boast the asymmetrical profiles typical of medieval woodbanks, all can be correlated with the boundaries of open and wooded areas created in the 1860s.

This southern section of the wood has been less extensively replanted than the north, and mainly comprises outgrown oak coppice, many of the stools being massive and some coppiced high, at around 1 metre. There are also a few equally massive stools of sweet chestnut; scattered nineteenth-century planting of beech and sweet chestnut; sporadic patches of holly; and much rhododendron. In the largest of the open areas cut from the wood in the nineteenth century, however, to the north of the hall at *c.* TG 0792439982, there is a single oak pollard (girth *c.*4.3 metres), possibly hinting, along with the name 'Old Pollard Wood', that parts at least of this extensive wood were once managed as wood-pasture.

An area of primary ancient woodland, truncated in stages in the post-medieval period.

Rawhall Wood, Beetley
TF 94401850

Rawhall Wood covers nearly 9 hectares on soils which, mapped as Beccles Association, are in fact varied, and include both freely draining Burlingham and poorly draining Beccles Series. The ground generally slopes from the east to the west, down to where the wood is bounded by an area of low-lying meadow land. Most of the wood was clear-felled and replanted in the 1970s or 1980s with Scots pine, Douglas fir and Norway spruce, so that only small areas, towards the north, still retain the original vegetation. This comprises outgrown ash and hazel coppice, with scattered examples of hornbeam, maple, hawthorn and crab. Some beech trees have been planted in the later twentieth century beside the principal rides. The ground flora varies in response to the soils but includes, principally in the non-replanted areas, dog's mercury, bluebell, barren strawberry, wood melick (*Melica uniflora*), herb Paris and yellow archangel. The wood is shown with the same outline as today on the Beetley

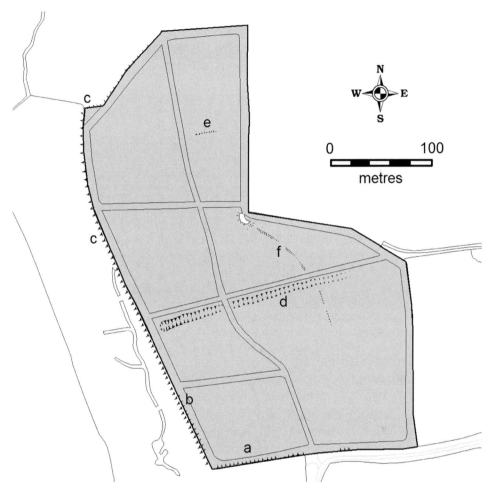

Figure 59 Rawhall Wood: principal earthwork features (for key see text).

tithe award map of 1844 (NRO DN/TA 833), but both Faden's map of 1797 and the Ordnance Survey drawings of 1815 (BL OSD 239) show a roughly rectangle wood covering around 12 hectares, indicating that the north-eastern corner of the wood was removed in the early nineteenth century.

There are no woodbanks and only a narrow ditch on the boundaries created when the wood was truncated (Figure 59). Traces of a low (*c.*0.3–0.4 metres high) woodbank around 7 metres across, including the wide external ditch, survive along the western stretch of the southern boundary (a) and also in places along the southern section of the western boundary (b). Most of the western side of the wood (c) is marked by a pronounced lynchet, generally between 0.6 and 1.0 metres above the level of the adjoining meadow. Elsewhere along the southern and western boundaries, and along the northern boundary, occasional vestiges suggest that a continuous woodbank was removed when the present, rather unusual, pattern of perimeter rides was put in place in the later twentieth century – apparently when the wood was coniferised. Much earth-movement appears to have taken place generally at this time, and the inner margins of the perimeter rides, and the sides of many of the internal ones, are accompanied by low, irregular banks of soil which have not been plotted on Figure 59.

In spite of all this, a marked hollow way (d) way survives within the coniferised sections, crossing the wood from east to west and running close to, and roughly parallel with, the central ride. It is around 7 metres wide, deepening as it progresses downhill towards the west. In addition, within the unreplanted areas of the wood there are two very slight earthworks. (e) is a short, north-facing scarp, possibly accompanied in places by slight traces of a wide ditch. (f) is a very slight feature, variously a depression and a south- and west-facing scarp, which begins close to the pond in the corner of the wood and can be traced with the eye of faith into the coniferised area to the south of the main east–west ride. These features hint at earlier agricultural use of some at least of the wood's area. In this context, attention should be drawn to the pronounced lynchet marking the western boundary of the wood: as the land to the west is now, was at the time of the tithe award and has probably (given its damp and low-lying character) always been under grass, it is difficult to see how this was formed, unless the area of the wood was itself once under cultivation. The hollow way lacks flanking banks, but whether this indicates that it ran through an area of unenclosed open fields or simply that any such banks were levelled when the wood was replanted remains uncertain.

Probably, but by no means certainly, a late medieval secondary wood.

Ringer's Grove, Shotesham
TM 25829680

Ringer's Grove covers an area of *c*.2.5 hectares on soils of the Beccles 1 Association. Approximately rectangular in shape, and with corners orientated roughly towards the cardinal points, it is bounded on its north-western side by a public road and on its south-western by a narrow roadside green. Most of its south-eastern edge coincides with the parish boundary between Shotesham St Mary and Shotesham All Saints. The wood's vegetation comprises young oak standards over a mixed coppice dominated by outgrown ash, but with varying quantities of maple and hazel, the latter becoming more prominent towards the south-east. There are scattered examples of hawthorn and crab apple, some elm and occasional standards of hornbeam, possibly grown from singled coppice. The ground flora is dominated by dog's mercury, except in places towards the south, where there is much bracken and nettles.

The north-western boundary of the wood, beside the road, comprises a bank between 2 and 2.5 metres in width with a much recut external ditch. The bank is seldom more than 0.2 metres in height above the woodland floor, and in places disappears altogether. The south-eastern boundary is defined by a more substantial, rather sharp bank, around 0.6–0.8 metres in height and 4 metres wide, with an external ditch. The south-western boundary is unusual. It comprises a well-defined bank, flanked on the inside by a shallow and on the outside by a deeper, functioning ditch, the whole between 6 and 7 metres across: the inner ditch fades towards the west. This arrangement may be related to the fact that the wood here abuts, as already noted, a narrow strip of common land. The north-eastern boundary is marked by a wide functioning ditch; in places the inside edge appears slightly raised, but there is no true bank. The few internal earthworks include a substantial, partly water-filled pit towards the eastern corner of the wood, probably an extraction pit as it has a curving hollowed entrance to the north; two other ponds, both much shallower, near the northern and western corners; and several drainage ditches, fairly straight and without banks, presumably of nineteenth-century date.

With its coppiced structure, abundant dog's mercury, substantial boundary earthworks on its south-eastern and south-western sides and location on a parish boundary, it is not surprising that Ringer's Grove is included in the *Ancient Woodland Inventory*. But a map of 1650 (NRO FEL 1077) shows that it did not then exist: its area comprised two fields, 'Pressmore Wonge als Lath Close' and 'Blacksmith's Croft'. The large boundary bank along the south-western boundary marks the edge of the small roadside green called 'Lath Green' on the map; the bank on the south-eastern boundary of the wood marks the line of the parish boundary.

A classic example of a 'pseudo-ancient' wood.

Round Grove, Hedenham
TM 31599403

Round Grove is one of four ancient woods on the Ditchingham estate, lying between Hedenham Wood – 170 metres to the north-west – and Long Row – 160 metres to the east. Unlike the others, however, it is not included in the *Ancient Woodland Inventory*. This is in spite of the fact that, until relatively recently, it seems to have displayed a typical coppice-with-standards structure (traces of which remain), has a ground flora which includes dog's mercury and primrose and is depicted on the map of

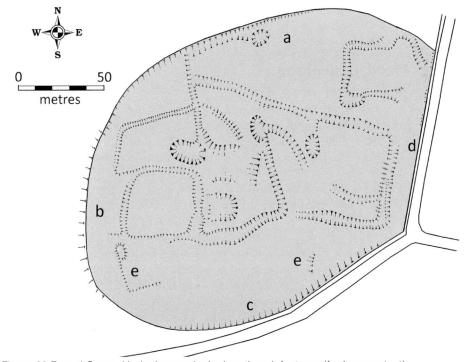

Figure 60 Round Grove, Hedenham: principal earthwork features (for key see text).

Hedenham made by Thomas Waterman in 1617 (NRO 1761/1). The wood occupies 2.7 hectares on sloping ground on the edge of the clay plateau, looking down towards the valley of the Broome Beck, mainly on soils of the Burlingham Association. It has been comprehensively replanted with indigenous species in relatively recent times, following Dutch elm disease and the 1987 gales. Remnants of the original coppiced vegetation on the margins of the wood include hornbeam, hazel and elm.

The wood is bounded on its northern (a) and southern (c) sides by a diminutive woodbank, around 3 metres wide, with an external ditch: on the western side (b) there is little in the way of a bank but instead a marked lynchet, the wood standing *c*.0.8 metres above the adjacent arable field (Figure 60). There is no bank on the straight eastern boundary (d), which was realigned some time between the making of the tithe award map in 1839 (NRO DN/TA 133) and of the Ordnance Survey six-inch map in the 1880s. The most striking feature of the wood is the fact that its entire area is covered with a complex system of earthworks – hollow ways, banks and ditches. There are a number of pits, some partly water-filled, to which some of the linear depressions appear to lead. This is evidently a complicated and probably multi-period site, perhaps in origin a set of interconnected settlement enclosures of medieval date which was later overlain with a number of trackways, some perhaps providing access to the ponds. There are slight signs of an earlier, pre-settlement phase in the form of probable plough lynchets (e). While Round Grove is evidently 'ancient' in the terms of the *Inventory*, it is thus clearly secondary in character. It was presumably planted, or grew up spontaneously, here because the earthworks made the site difficult to plough. Assuming that the settlement was abandoned in the later fourteenth or fifteenth centuries, like many other small sites on the south Norfolk claylands, the wood may have been little more than a century old when Waterman's map was surveyed in 1617.

A secondary, late medieval area of ancient woodland.

Sexton's Wood, Hedenham
TM 29849151

Sexton's Wood lies in the south-west of Hedenham, on the parish boundary with Denton, which runs along its western edge. It was one of the woods held by the Bigod earls of Norfolk and in 1270 was described as 'le Sexting', and as covering 86½ acres (35 hectares). There are records of tenants repairing the woodbank at one of the Hedenham woods, possibly this one but possibly Tindalls (q.v.), in 1272 (Rackham 1986b, 166–7). At this stage the wood was apparently coppiced on a long cycle of as much as 16 years. By the post-medieval period Sexton's Wood was no longer under the same ownership as the other woods in Hedenham (to the north of the Broome Beck) and as a result was not, like them, mapped in the early seventeenth century by Thomas Waterman. It is shown, with almost identical boundaries to today, on the 1816 enclosure map (NRO C/Sca 2/100) and the 1839 tithe award (NRO DN/TA 133). The wood covers an area of *c*.39 hectares of level ground on soils of the Beccles 1 Association, although in detail they are varied and the wood contains some very sandy areas. It is largely composed of hornbeam, mixed to varying extents with hazel, ash and maple, and with sallow in the damper areas: hornbeam appears to be less prominent in those relatively limited parts of the wood which are still subject to regular coppicing. It is also less prominent on the damper ground, beside the minor stream

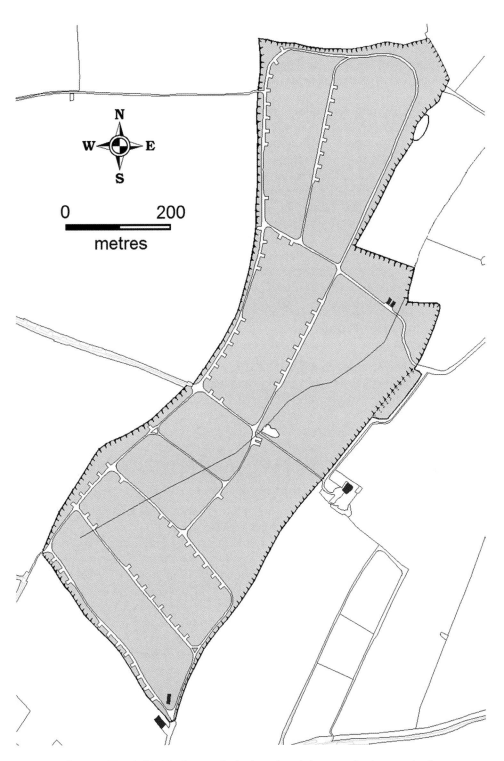

Figure 61 Sextons Wood, Ditchingham: principal earthwork features (for key see text).

flowing through the centre of the wood. The ground vegetation is sparse because of the dense shade but includes areas of dog's mercury and scattered wood sage (*Teucrium scorodonia*); herb Paris has also been recorded here.

The wood is bounded on all sides by a substantial medieval woodbank and external ditch, averaging in all around 6 metres across; this has been partly levelled along the southern boundary and damaged in places along the western (Figure 61). The wood had expanded, as a short and narrow strip, beyond the woodbank on its south-eastern side at some stage before 1816, adding *c*.0.25 hectares to its area. There are oak and hornbeam pollards on the northern parts of the eastern and western, and along the northern, boundaries. There are no internal earthworks, clearly indicating that the wood is 'primary' in character, although a network of concrete tracks, laid out along the pre-existing rides, testifies to the wood's use in the Second World War. It was one of the storage areas created around Earsham park for the United States Airforce (together with Great Wood in Earsham and America Wood – both areas of ancient woodland – and the more recent Beech Wood, Parks Wood and New Plantation) (TNA AIR 29/1558, plans 3040/52, 3041/52, 3042/52).

A primary medieval wood, still contained within its thirteenth-century boundaries.

Shotesham Little Wood
TM 25309745

Shotesham Little Wood lies to the south of the village of Shotesham on the old parish boundary between Shotesham St Mary and Shotesham All Saints, which follows the wood's northern, eastern and southern edges. Its name distinguishes it from Shotesham Great Wood, which still survives some 200 metres to the north-west, although now largely coniferised. Little Wood is shown on a map of *c*.1650 (FEL 1076) in the NRO, where its north-eastern section is described as 'Piggotts als Palmers Wood' and its south-western as 'Hallett Wood'. It had almost the same boundaries as today, but to the north-west – across the parish boundary in Shotesham All Saints – it then adjoined another area of woodland, in separate ownership, which has since disappeared, which was also called Hallett Wood, while to the south it abutted on a small wood called 'Catesgrove', which has likewise gone.

Little Wood, in contrast to these, survives in excellent condition. The south-west of the wood occupies a level plateau site but the ground falls away to the north-east. The character of the soils changes correspondingly, with heavy clay soils (Beccles Series) on the higher level ground and sandier clays (Burlingham Series) on the slope. Most of the wood is dominated by hornbeam coppice under oak standards, but the understorey becomes more diverse towards the north-east, with more hazel and ash; hazel also dominates the extreme south-western section of the wood.

The wood covers, in all, some 18.8 hectares. Just under 17.5 hectares of this comprises what appears to be the medieval 'core' of the wood, an irregularly shaped area defined to north, south and east by a continuous woodbank (a), much of it followed by the parish boundary (Figure 62). This is generally around 6 metres across, including ditch, and stands *c*.0.5–0.6 metres above the ground level of the interior of the wood. It has been rather damaged in places, especially along the southern boundary, partly through recent recutting. Area (b) lies outside and to the north of the medieval core, has no external bank, and is a recent (twentieth-century) extension.

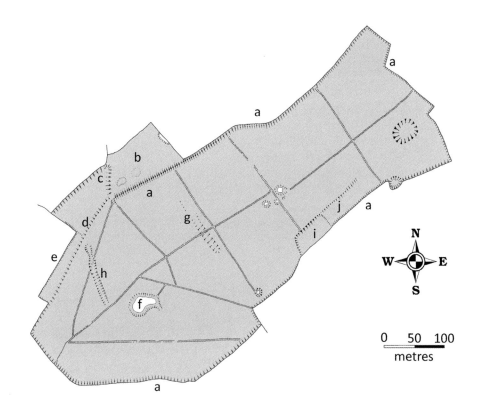

Figure 62 Shotesham Little Wood: principal earthwork features (for key see text).

The western end of the wood also lies outside the original 'core' and evidently has a complex history. Although woodbank (c) appears to be similar in character to the main external woodbank (a), the line of the latter is more directly continued by the rather smaller scarp/bank (d). It is thus possible that this was the original western boundary of the wood; that the area defined by (c) represents a subsequent extension; and that this in turn was partly grubbed out in the post-medieval period (but evidently before c.1650), and a new, much smaller woodbank (e) raised to define the wood's new western boundary. Such an interpretation does not, however, explain why (d) (a scarp with little trace of a ditch) is so different in character to (a), a woodbank of normal medieval form. Clearly, some measure of expansion and contraction has occurred at this end of the wood, and it is striking how this area is today characterised by stands of almost pure hazel.

Within the wood there are a number of earthworks. Feature (f) is a pond, set in a pit, with a hollow-way entrance to the south-east: whether this was to facilitate extraction of excavated material or to provide access for cattle remains unclear. There are also smaller ponds and pits scattered through the wood. Features (g) and (h), which lie more or less parallel with each other in the western half of the wood, resemble hollow ways. Both run across more or less level ground; neither is orientated with the overall direction of slope, from south-west to north-east. Their date and function is unclear, although they are evidently man-made. Features (i) and (j) appear to be two enclosures set into the southern boundary of the wood. The first is defined by the main external woodbank (a), which turns in from the present outer boundary of the wood, runs parallel to it for *c.*60 metres, and then runs back to it again. The second, in contrast, is defined by a quite separate bank, a continuation of the recessed line of (a). Feature (i) is shown as part of the adjacent open fields on the 1650 map, across which the wood subsequently expanded: feature (j) may mark where earlier, medieval, expansion has taken place. It is noteworthy that the parish boundary follows the present edge of the wood rather than its boundary in 1650, showing that it has been realigned since the seventeenth century. Lastly, the wood is dissected by a network of straight drainage ditches, laid out to intercept a number of the (presumably pre-existing) ponds). Like those found in other woods in the county, these are probably of nineteenth-century date.

A medieval wood, mainly primary, with possible indications of early pastoral use (the holloways (g) and (h)) and evidence for minor, piecemeal expansion, partly at the expense of open-field arable.

Shropham Grove
TL 98069245

Shropham Grove occupies sandy, acid soils of the Worlington Association on the margins of Breckland. In 1839, to judge from the tithe award map (NRO DN/TA 421), it covered an area of around 17 hectares; by the 1880s, to judge from the first edition Ordnance Survey six-inch map, it had been truncated on its western side, now extending over some 14 hectares; and in the second half of the twentieth century it was further reduced in area, in part through further contraction on the west, in part through the creation of a poultry farm on its eastern side, so that it now extends over *c.*5.6 hectares. The surviving portion of the wood largely comprises outgrown hornbeam and sweet chestnut coppice, and some hazel, under oak and occasional hornbeam standards (one with a girth of 3.4 metres). It also contains blocks of relatively young oak, sweet chestnut, beech and ash plantation, as well as scattered areas of young birch, maple, oak, sweet chestnut and bird cherry. Large amounts of sycamore occur in the south-western section. There are a few large oak coppice stools, some possibly regenerating from felled standards, some of which appear to have been cut at around 1 metre above the ground, possibly suggesting some quasi-wood-pasture phase in the wood's history. The eastern boundary, beside the public road, is defined by a woodbank of variable character but apparently medieval origins which is around 6 metres wide, including the shallow external ditch. Much of it has been destroyed to make space for the poultry farm, although its line is still marked by a single oak pollard with a girth of 3.9 metres (at TL 9825592490). The eastern *c.*100 metres of the southern boundary is likewise medieval, and marked by a substantial bank. At the eastern end this is over 7 metres wide, excluding a largely levelled ditch, but towards the west it narrows appreciably to *c.*5 metres. It carries an oak pollard with a girth of 4.5 metres (TL 9809392350). The western boundary of the wood, although modern, is in part marked by another substantial bank, around 5 metres wide, which was originally (before the removal of the western side of the wood) an internal bank: it can be seen, running through the middle of the wood, on the 1946 RAF vertical photographs. The straight northern boundary is post-medieval. No internal earthworks were noted, although the wood was much overgrown with brambles and bracken when investigated.

A medieval wood, probably primary, much reduced and damaged in the nineteenth and twentieth centuries, originally subdivided by an internal bank. The unusual form of the oak coppice may suggest that it was grazed in the past.

The Shrubbery, Tivetshall St Mary
TM 16198556

The Shrubbery covers 2.15 hectares and, despite its name, is evidently an ancient and, in large part, probably primary wood. It lies on Beccles 1 Association soils on level or gently sloping ground close to the parish boundary with Gissing, from which it is separated by a narrow field no more than 15 metres wide in places. The wood comprises hazel and hornbeam coppice, with some ash, under scattered oak standards. There is some hawthorn and elder, and quantities of field maple occur towards the east. The ground flora includes ground ivy, rough meadow grass and dog's mercury, with bramble, nettle and fern in places.

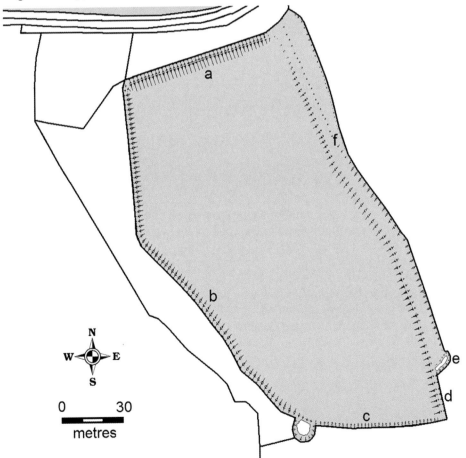

Figure 63 The Shrubbery, Tivetshall: principal earthwork features (for key see text).

The wood is bounded to the north by a low bank with massive ditch, in all around 8 metres across (a); and on the west by a slightly higher but narrower bank, the northern section of which still carries the remains of a hedge of maple, ash and hornbeam (b) (Figure 63). Here the narrow field to the west lies around 1 metre below the level of the woodland floor, suggesting that it has been ploughed in the past. The southern boundary of the wood (c) has only a weak bank and ditch. The eastern boundary is complex. The first *c.*25 metres (d), as far as the pond (e), is marked by a pronounced woodbank nearly 7 metres wide. To the north of the pond, the woodbank lies some way back from the present boundary: the wood has here evidently expanded across a roadway (f) and, further to the north, apparently beyond it. The wood contains no other earthworks. The wood is shown with the same boundaries as today on the Tivetshall St Mary tithe award map of 1839 (NRO DN/TA 95) and on Faden's 1797 map of Norfolk There are no earlier maps of the parish.

A medieval wood, probably primary, which has expanded eastwards over an abandoned roadway, presumably in the later Middle Ages. It provides a striking contrast with Tivetshall Wood (qv.), entirely secondary, which lies immediately to the north.

Sporle Wood
TF 86041176

Sporle Wood extends over some 20 hectares on soils mapped by the Soil Survey as belonging to the Burlingham Association, although the interior of the wood is very poorly draining in places, featuring large areas of Beccles Series soils. The wood's eastern boundary coincides with the parish boundary between Sporle and Necton, and its northern with the boundary between South Greenhoe and Launditch Hundreds. The vegetation comprises neglected coppice of maple, ash and hazel under oak standards, together with much wych elm, hawthorn and scattered dogwood and spindle. The ground flora includes dog's mercury, bluebell, primrose, wood anemone, pignut, barren strawberry and yellow archangel.

The wood is shown on a schematic map of *c.*1750 (NRO MS20888) and, with identical boundaries to today, on the tithe award map of 1838 (DN/TA 378). The former shows an area of six irregular fields to the south of the wood, all called 'Sporle Wood Close', together with a further area of woodland – Breakey Wood – covering 22 acres (*c.*9 hectares), suggesting that the wood may once have extended much further in this direction. A marriage settlement of 1697 between the lord of the manor, Matthew Holworthy, and one Elizabeth Disbrow estimates the area of the wood at 100 acres (*c.*40 hectares), but a lease agreement of 1745 gives its area as only 47 acres (*c.*19 hectares), so contraction may have occurred in the first half of the eighteenth century (CRO NRA 8790).

In the fifteenth century the wood was the property of the Paston family and it is mentioned a number of times in their extensive correspondence. In 1450 the hedge surrounding the wood was in poor condition and the coppice damaged by straying livestock; in 1472 there was discussion of the best way to sell the underwood; and in the same year a survey of the timber was made which suggests that, whereas the main part of the wood had a density of around 6.9 standards per acre (17 per hectare), a perimeter belt twelve feet (3.66 metres) wide had as many as 116 per acre (286 per hectare) (Gairdner 1904, V, 167). There are records of wood sales in 1472 and 1475.

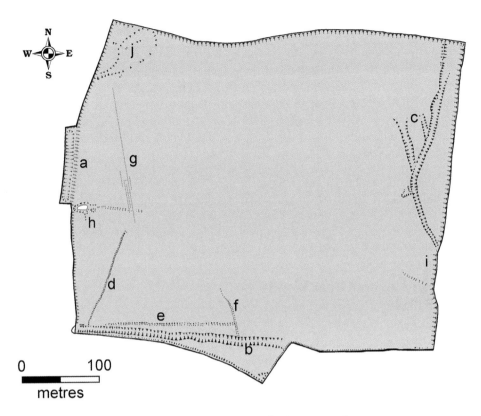

Figure 64 Sporle Wood: principal earthwork features (for key see text).

There are also references to the wood in post-medieval documents. In 1735 there was a dispute over terms of a lease relating to the wood and problems were recorded with cattle grazing the underwood (NRO 20888). In 1750 the wood was divided into nine compartments or 'fells', and had around 65 standards an acre (NRO 20888). In the twentieth century some of the wood was planted with larch, but this has now been replaced with oak, maple and hazel; parts of the wood are now being coppiced again.

The wood is bounded on the north, east and west by woodbanks of normal medieval form, that on the northern boundary slightly more substantial than the others (Figure 64). The woodbank along the western section of the south boundary is less substantial; along the eastern section there is little in the way of a bank at all, merely a ditch. These differences perhaps support the idea that the wood has contracted on its southern side, the form of the boundary here being consistent with a post-medieval rather than medieval date. Within the wood there are a number of earthworks. (a) is a deep rectangular pit, of uncertain age and purpose, which is dug into a narrow later extension of the wood (the original woodbank is continuous to the east). It may be a clay extraction pit dug into a former open-field strip, although the *c*.1750 map does not appear to show it and also suggests that by this date the wood was flanked on this side by enclosed fields. (b) is a substantial hollow way which runs east–west, close to the southern boundary of the wood. It does not appear to have ever been bounded by banks, suggesting that it originally ran through an area of undivided

231

common land or wood-pasture. (c) is a more complex collection of branching hollow ways, some occupied by seasonal watercourses and probably in part natural. Again, there are no traces of associated hedge banks. (d), (e) and (f) are narrow ditches, flanked in places by slight banks of uncertain age or purpose. (d) and (e) might be early attempts at drainage but this cannot explain (e), which runs parallel to the contours. (g) is a complex of straight, shallow ditches, typical of nineteenth-century woodland drainage. It may be more extensive than mapped, but the wood is densely overgrown in this area. (h) is a pond; (i) is a slight linear depression; (j) an area of amorphous disturbance.

This is evidently a primary wood, although perhaps containing (in the form of the hollow ways) evidence for early pastoral use. The wood probably once extended much further to the south, halving in area in the first half of the eighteenth century. The fifteenth- and eighteenth-century documents noted above contain some important information about the wood's management, and have been drawn upon on a number of occasions in the main text.

Swanton Novers Great Wood
TG 01513129

Swanton Novers Great Wood is, together with Little Wood to the west, Barney Wood to the north-west and Guybons Wood to the north, designated an SSSI; it is also a National Nature Reserve. It covers 51.5 hectares in the south-west of the parish of Swanton Novers, its southern edge coincident with the parish boundary, and occupies soils mapped as Beccles 2 Association, although in fact they are very diverse in character. The wood, which is largely surrounded by more recent plantations (light grey on Figure 65), occupies a plateau of acid glacial sands and gravels overlying calcareous boulder clay, and the latter reaches the ground surface in a number of places. The vegetation is varied. Across much of the wood it comprises sessile oak (*Quercus petraea*) standards over a mixed coppice of hazel, lime (*Tilia cordata*), birch, ash, maple, willow and rowan, the precise composition varying with the diverse soils. In damper areas the understorey consists of alder, bird cherry and hazel; and across parts of the wood it is largely or entirely oak. There are small areas of recent conifer planting and patches of holly, a species which has increased its representation here over recent decades. Where the oak is dense the ground flora is impoverished and dominated by bracken. Elsewhere, especially where lime occurs, there is much dog's mercury and bluebell. The flora is extraordinarily diverse, including other 'indicator' species such as great woodrush (*Luzula sylvatica*) and rarities such as May lily (*Maianthemum bifolium*).

The wood is depicted much as it is today on the Swanton Novers enclosure map of 1813 (NRO C/Sca 2/152) and on the tithe award map of 1838 (NRO DN/TA 109). The former, together with Faden's county map of 1797, shows that before enclosure the wood was flanked on all sides except the north by common land – Stock Heath and its extension, Swanton Common – and had clearly been cut out of a wider area of common 'waste' at some point in the remote past. Stock Heath itself appears to have retained some tree cover well into the post-medieval period: Faden shows scattered trees in places, and where a portion of the Heath – in the far north – was planted up as a plantation following enclosure (Middle Heath Plantation) a large number of old oak pollards still survive among much later trees (see above, p. 92).

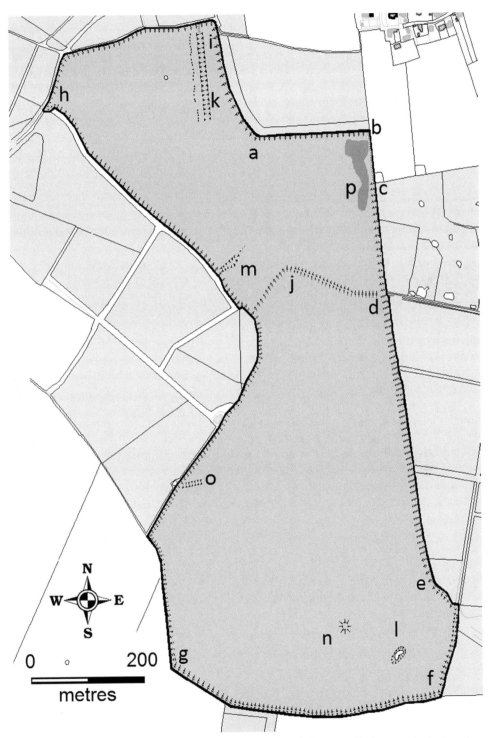

Figure 65 Swanton Novers Great Wood: principal earthwork features (for key see text: size of earthworks slightly exaggerated for clarity).

The wood is surrounded by a woodbank of variable character (Figure 65). From (a) to (b) it is around 1 metre high and 3 metres wide, without a flanking ditch; and from (b) to (c) only 1 metre wide and the same in height, again without a ditch, although there is a substantial lynchet on the field side, the ground falling by around 1.5 metres. Between (c) and (d) there is again a 3-metre-wide bank, flanked for some of its length by a ditch; and from (d) to (e) a substantial double bank, with an inner bank nearly 0.5 metres high and 3 metres wide, and an outer bank some 2 metres wide, separated by a ditch some 6 metres in width. The boundaries so far discussed are all rather straight and sharp and look post-medieval, or at least late medieval, in form. The wood was bounded on this side, until the enclosure of 1813, by Swanton Common, and there is no evidence of an inner, medieval woodbank, clearly indicating that these boundaries must have been created by the truncation, rather than the expansion, of a medieval 'core'. The wood, that is, must have contracted to make way for the expansion of the adjacent common, unless only first sundered from it relatively late in the Middle Ages, both rather unusual circumstances.

From (e) to (f) there is again a single bank, around 4 metres wide, flanked by a ditch 6 metres wide. This appears more typically medieval in appearance, as does the entire length of the southern boundary (f) to (g), which is marked by a well-defined bank some 4–5 metres in width and 0.3–0.4 metres high flanked by an outer ditch 3 metres wide. The western boundary of the wood is smaller, with a bank around 3 metres in width and around 0.3 metres high (g to h). The northern boundary (h to i) consists of a bank around 4 metres wide and as much as 0.5 metres in height without a flanking ditch. The final section – the north-eastern boundary (i to a) – is similar, but with a flanking ditch.

There are a number of internal earthworks. (j) is a curving bank 3 metres wide and 0.4 metres high, with a ditch to the south: it appears medieval and is presumably a subdivision of management or ownership. (k) is a deep linear depression with a spread bank to the west: it is nearly 10 metres wide and resembles a hollow way, although its purpose is unclear. (l) is a depression containing a pond; (m) a pit, perhaps a pond in wet weather, accessed by a linear depression: it may be a stock watering pond, although the woodbank now cuts across it, preventing access. (n) is a low, flat-topped mound about 20 metres in diameter and 0.5 metres high, which Cushion suggests may be a barrow (Cushion 2004, 56): it has no apparent ditch, however. (o) is a linear depression leading in from the edge of the wood. In the north-eastern corner of the wood there are a number of shallow depressions and irregular undulations (p), possibly marking where clay has been extracted. A number of small, apparently natural ponds/depressions occur elsewhere within the wood (not mapped in Figure 65).

The wood was surveyed by Brian Cushion with customary accuracy (our plan differs from his in only minor details). As part of his investigation, Peter Murphy augered the base of feature (k). Only a thin layer of organic material (less than 0.3 metres) was encountered above sandy till: this, 'given the input of leaf litter that this feature must receive ... is surprising' (Cushion 2004, 58).

Swanton Novers Great Wood is evidently 'primary' in character, although the fact that it was clearly cut out of Stock Heath is a powerful reminder of how – like other woods – it must once have been some kind of grazed wood-pasture, a circumstance which might partly explain the thinness of the organic deposits noted by Murphy. In addition, the possible barrow site in the south (n) may suggest that parts, at least, once comprised a more open environment. The straight eastern boundary seems to indicate that the wood has contracted, giving way to common heath/wood-pasture, some time in the early post-medieval period.

Tindall Wood, Ditchingham
TM 32719352

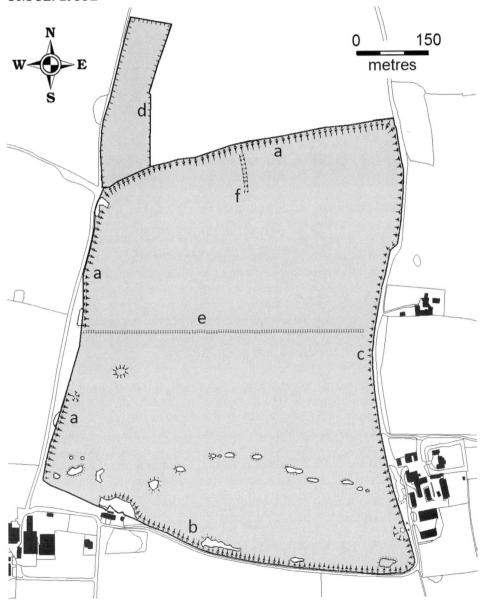

Figure 66 Tindall Wood, Ditchingham: principal earthwork features (for key see text : size of earthworks slightly exaggerated for clarity).

Tindall Wood, an SSSI, is one of a group of woods lying in Hedenham and Ditchingham, to the north of the Broome Beck: the others – Long Row, Round Grove and Hedenham Wood – lie *c*.700, *c*.900, and *c*.1,000 metres to the west, respectively. The wood is the largest of the group and one of the most extensive in Norfolk, covering some 44 hectares, including an extension to the north known as Cooper's Grove which covers around 5 hectares. It lies on poorly draining level or gently sloping ground on the margins of the boulder clay plateau, on soils mainly of the Beccles Series, although there are patches of sand within the wood, and the clay soils are generally lighter towards the south, where the land begins to fall away towards the valley of the Broom Beck. Tindall Wood was, like other woods in the district, part of the Bigod's Ditchingham estates and its area was estimated in 1270 at 104½ acres (42 hectares); the same survey suggests that 5 acres were felled each year, i.e., the wood was cut on a very long rotation, of 16 years, although the following year over half the underwood was felled at one go. There are references to making faggots; to the felling of standards to build a barn; to the income derived from bark; and, in 1280, to the employment of a woodward (Rackham 1986b, 166–7). The wood is shown with identical outlines on the enclosure map of 1816 (NRO C/Sca 2/100) and on the tithe award map of 1841 (NRO DN/TA 361). Its southern boundary is also depicted, again as it is today, on an estate map of 1615 surveyed by Thomas Waterman (NRO NRO 1761/2).

The wood comprises oak and some ash standards over outgrown hornbeam coppice, with areas of hazel and field maple and scattered examples of spindle, guelder rose and hawthorn. There is alder coppice in some of the wetter areas, and some patches of invasive elm. In places, especially in the north-east, the wood has been replanted with indigenous species and some of the coppice structure has been lost. The ground cover is rich and varied in parts of the wood, with areas of dog's mercury and an abundance of enchanter's-nightshade and primrose, together with wood melick, herb Paris, ramsons, greater butterfly orchid and wood sorrel. Where the soils are acid, however, the flora is more impoverished and dominated by bramble and bracken. The wide rides have a particularly rich flora.

The wood is enclosed on its northern and along much of its western sides by a substantial woodbank with external ditch, the whole in places up to 9 metres in width (a) (Figure 66). The southern (b) and eastern (c) boundaries are less massive, around 7 metres across with flanking ditches and in places hardly rising above the woodland floor. The northern extension of the wood, Cooper's Grove, is bounded by a minor bank of apparent post-medieval date (d). A ditch, accompanied by a low bank around 1 metre wide and *c*.0.25 metres in height, runs the width of the wood (e): it is dead straight, associated with an east–west ride, and evidently post-medieval. A slight linear depression runs back for a short distance from the middle of the northern boundary (f). The moated site of Tindall Hall adjoins the eastern side of the wood.

There are a number of ponds associated with the wood's perimeter ditch and bank. In most cases these lie outside the bank, and are formed by a widening of the ditch, but some on the southern boundary lie within the bank and are partly cut into it. There are also a number of pits and depressions within the wood, many water-filled and apparently natural, mostly concentrated in a curving arc across the south of its area.

Tindall is evidently a primary wood, enclosed directly from the wastes at some point before the later thirteenth century. It has apparently remained within its original boundaries ever since, with the exception of the addition of Cooper's Grove to the north at some point in the post-medieval period.

Tivetshall Wood
TM 16198580

Tivetshall Wood, also known as Brick Kiln Wood, extends over an area of *c*.3 hectares on soils of the Beccles 1 Association. It lies immediately to the north of the wood called The Shrubbery (q.v.), from which it is separated by a minor public road, and is bisected by the parish boundary between Tivetshall (to the east) and Gissing (to the west). It is shown, with identical outlines to those of today, on the Tivetshall St Mary tithe award map of 1839 (NRO DN/TA 95). Most of the wood is dominated by hazel and hornbeam coppice, much of it still actively managed, with scattered oak standards, but in areas near the centre of the wood the understorey is dominated by mixed hazel and maple. The ground flora is often sparse but includes a number of 'ancient woodland indicators' – dog's mercury, thin-spiked wood sedge, wood millet (*Milium effusum*) and wood melick – along with a variety of less indicative herbs. Large patches of nettle and bramble also occur.

In spite of the presence of locally rare indicators such as *C. strigosa*, the wood is largely if not entirely secondary in character, for it is filled with a mass of earthworks (Figure 67). Their character is uncertain: some of the more amorphous undulations may relate to the industrial use of the site suggested by the wood's alternative name; one (a) marks the line of the parish boundary; but others appear to be hollow ways and field boundaries, the latter defining areas so small that they may represent closes associated with a small abandoned medieval settlement. One of the hollow ways (b)

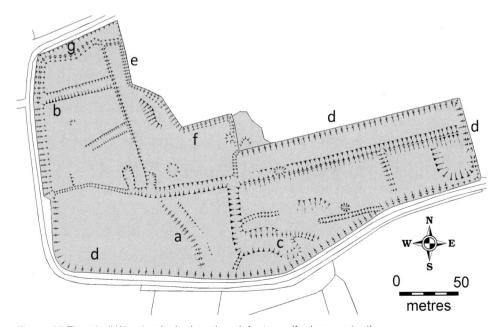

Figure 67 Tivetshall Wood: principal earthwork features (for key see text).

directly continues the line of an existing road, to the west of the wood, which was seemingly diverted around its margins. The line of the road to the north of the wood may also be continued by some of the earthworks within it, while feature (c) may represent a continuation of the hollow way which runs down the eastern side of The Shrubbery (q.v.) to the south. Without excavation it is hard to unravel this complex palimpsest, but there is no doubt that Tivetshall Wood is an area of secondary woodland. On the other hand, it is evidently medieval in origin, to judge from the size of the woodbanks which survive along its southern, eastern, and much of its northern and western sides (d); the smaller banks and ditches along parts of the north and west boundaries ((e) and (f)) suggest that the wood has been truncated in these directions some time in the early post-medieval period. The configuration of banks also, however, suggests that the wood has expanded slightly to the north in area (g), perhaps at the expense of a small roadside green.

An ancient secondary woodland, planted or regenerating in the later Middle Ages.

Toombers Wood
TF 65200680

Toombers Wood lies at the point where the parish boundaries of Stradsett, Stow Bardolph and Shouldham Thorpe meet, although most of its area is within Shouldham Thorpe. It occupies an area of light clay soils of the Burlingham Association. It was not included on the *Ancient Woodland Inventory* when this was compiled in 1981, although its name – which preserves that of a lost Domesday vill – and peripheral location suggest an ancient origin, as do aspects of its structure and vegetation. The wood, which covers *c*.23 hectares, was throughout most of the post-medieval period part of the Stow Bardolph estate.

Most of the south-eastern section of the wood has been replanted with Scots pine, Norway spruce, Sitka spruce and oak; and parts of the north-east with oak and ash. The western sides retain their earlier vegetation, albeit with scattered modern planting, mainly comprising hazel coppice beneath oak and some ash standards, with scattered specimens of sycamore and occasional holly, dwarf gorse, goat willow and wych elm. The ground flora includes a variety of ferns (to the south), replaced by much bracken to the north. Violets, bugle, cranesbill, enchanter's-nightshade and wood dock all occur, with meadowsweet, creeping cinquefoil (*Potentilla reptans*) and silverweed (*Argentina anserina*) in the rides. There are at least two 'ancient woodland indicators', remote sedge and primrose. A substantial and apparently medieval woodbank survives along the somewhat irregular southern stretch of the western boundary, its width varying from 6.5 to 8.0 metres, including the wide flanking (and recut) ditch (a). Its alignment appears to have been changed at some point in the past, increasing the area of the wood slightly (b). A more diminutive, dead straight and probably early post-medieval bank, between 4 and 5 metres wide including external ditch, runs along the western section of the southern boundary (c). The other boundaries, however, which are all ruler-straight, have either no bank at all or a very small one, and relatively slight ditches. Traces of hedges survive in places.

The tithe award maps for Shouldham Thorpe (1846: DE/TA 23), Stow Bardolph (1840: DE/TA 26) and Stradsett (1840: DN/TA 285) show the present boundaries of the wood already in place. The overall impression is thus of a medieval wood, the

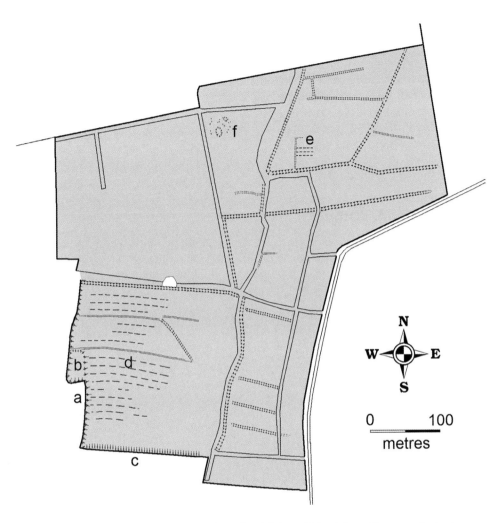

Figure 68 Toombers Wood in Stradsett, Stow Bardolph and Shouldham Thorpe: principal earthwork features (for key see text).

boundaries of which have been truncated in stages in the course of the post-medieval period, beginning with that on the south-western side. The wood is, however, largely, and probably entirely, secondary. An area of ridge and furrow, rare in Norfolk except in this western district on the edge of the Fens, occupies the south-western section of the wood (d); and what is probably the remains of another area occurs in the north-east (e) (Figure 68). Both have, in part, been incorporated into the wood's nineteenth-century drainage system. The absence of ridge and furrow from elsewhere in the unreplanted sections of the wood may in part be due to the fact that it is hidden by the abundant bracken: it is certainly unlikely to imply that part of the wood is 'primary' in character, for no internal banks, which might represent earlier boundaries, exist. Whether the surviving ridge and furrow represents areas enclosed directly from open fields or whether it was preserved under pasture prior to the wood's establishment remains unclear.

There are some slight amorphous pits and hollows in the north of the wood (f), and two phases of drainage ditches. One is probably of nineteenth-century date and comprises a numbers of shallow ditches, mainly 1–2 metres wide and *c*.0.3 metres deep, which in places have been slotted into the ridge and furrow; the other consists of a network of much wider and deeper ditches, mainly occupying the replanted eastern sections of the wood and evidently of twentieth-century date. Some ditches fall in between these two categories, perhaps because they originated in the first phase but were recut in the second.

A medieval secondary wood, truncated in stages in the post-medieval period and partly damaged by modern replanting.

Wayland Wood, Watton
TL 92539960

Wayland Wood lies just over a kilometre to the south of the town of Watton, on the parish boundary with Merton and Thompson, and occupies an area of *c*.34 hectares on soils which, mapped by the Soil Survey as falling within the Ollerton Association, are in fact largely clayey in character, overlying till – mainly soils of the Burlingham and Beccles Series. The wood is referred to and described in a number of documents in the Walsingham (de Grey) archive in the NRO, and is shown on an estate map of 1723 (NRO WLS XVII/9 410X6). The fact that the wood shares the name of Wayland Hundred indicates that it was the meeting place of the latter, and the historian Blomefield described how 'the Sheriff's turn ... was always kept at a certain place in this wood' (Blomefield 1805, II, 312–19). The second element of the wood's name is Scandinavian *lundr*, 'a grove, a sacred grove', perhaps suggesting that the wood – or a more extensive, less intensively managed area of woodland in this area – had a more ancient ceremonial role (Rackham 1986b, 164). The wood was the original setting for the 'Babes in the Wood' story, first appearing in the form of a printed ballad in 1595 (Opie and Opie 1983, 387), and it is just possible that this retains some dim memory of ancient ritual use.

The later history of the wood is confusing and complex, not least because it appears to have been divided from an early date into three separate ownerships. The main part of the wood, Wayland, was in origin probably demesne of the main manor of Watton but it was given to Thetford Priory in the Middle Ages, passing to the duke of Norfolk at the Dissolution and eventually – by the 1580s – to the de Grey family of nearby Merton. The eastern side of the wood was divided into two sections, Mounteney's Wood and the Nab. The former was originally part of the demesne of Mounteney's manor in the parish of Threxton, which lay to the west of Watton, and remained in separate ownership in 1593, when a Commission investigating mismanagement of the wood describes it as the property of Edward Goose of Threxton: it was acquired by the de Greys some time before 1674 (NRO WLS IV/6). The Nab, also known as College Wood (NRO WLS 11/7, 407X3), was a relatively small area, covering only 4 acres (1.6 hectares), and was in the Middle Ages the property of Thompson College in the adjoining parish of Thompson, to the south. It was acquired by the de Greys after the Dissolution (it was owned by them in 1593) but was subsequently sold, apparently after 1674 (it is mentioned in the lease of Wayland of that date), and repurchased in 1724 (NRO WLS XXX/7). It may have been managed as wood-pasture into the

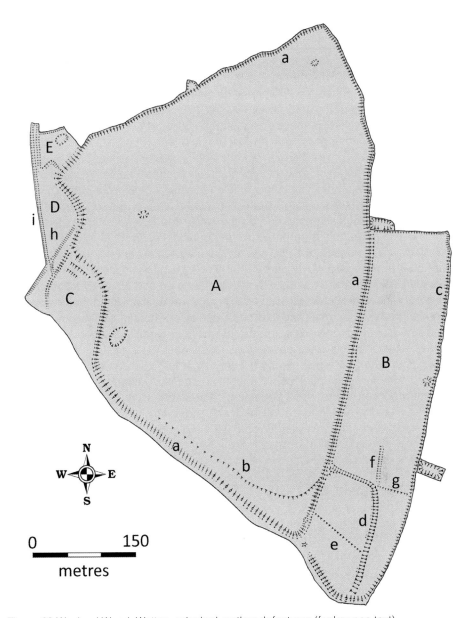

Figure 69 Wayland Wood, Watton: principal earthwork features (for key see text).

sixteenth century, for the 1593 depositions refer to it as the 'wood or pasture inclosed called the Nab', although by 1724 it was being described as 'all that coppice or piece of wood known as Threxton Nabbe'.

In the seventeenth century the wood was cut on a ten-year rotation, to judge from a lease agreement of 1674 (NRO WLS LXIX 25), and by implication was still being so managed in the nineteenth century (NRO WLS VIII/7/1). In the depositions relating to the 1593 dispute (NRO WLS IV/6) there are references to the underwood being used for making hurdles, spars, hop poles and charcoal: part of the underwood was being sold 'by the acre'. A detailed account of the uses to which the underwood was put was published in the *Irish Farmer's Gazette* in 1851 (see above, p. 117) (NRO WLS VIII/7/1). As early as 1768 efforts were being made to preserve pheasants within the wood (NRP WLS XL VI/15), and the use of the wood as a game covert is described in 1893 in Lord Walsingham and Ralph Payne-Gallwey's famous *Shooting – field and covert* (Walsingham and Payne-Gallwey 1893, 221–2). The wood was acquired by the Norfolk Wildlife Trust in 1975 and is designated an SSSI.

The vegetation comprises oak and some ash and birch standards over an understorey of hazel, bird cherry (*Padus padus*), sallow, ash and hornbeam. It contains a good range of ancient woodland indicators, including water avens, bluebell, early purple orchid, wood anemone and yellow archangel; it is the only place in Norfolk where the Yellow Star of Bethlehem (*Gagea lutea*) grows. Large areas of the wood are now regularly coppiced by the NWT, and in places the underwood is very dense: it is nevertheless probable that the principal earthworks have been noted and plotted. The main feature is the substantial medieval woodbank (a) defining the original core of the wood (A) (Figure 69). This has a bank and ditch which are, in all, between 7 and 9 metres across: the bank stands around 0.5–0.75 metres above the interior of the wood. A low, diffuse scarp (b) which runs a little to the north of the southern boundary may mark the line of an earlier woodbank, but may have other explanations (see below). A number of extensions to the area of the wood were made after the main woodbank was constructed. The largest (B) is to the east, where an area of *c*.8.5 hectares is enclosed by a bank (c) which is less substantial than that associated with the original wood, although apparently likewise of medieval date. This eastern section of the wood equates to 'Mounteney's Wood' and 'The Nab': in 1593 these were both said to be 'divided with a greate ditch and distinctly known from the said wood called Wayland Wood' (NRO WLS IV/6). The northern section of the enclosing woodbank, with ditch and bank less than 6 metres across, is low and diffuse; the eastern boundary becomes more substantial, reaching *c*.0.7 metres in height in places. There is a single oak pollard in this section, at TL 9282099532. The vegetation within (B) differs noticeably from that in the main wood, the understorey containing much larger amounts of hornbeam. In the southern part of this extension is a complex of earthworks ((d), (e), (f) and (g)). The first of these, to judge from a map of 1723, defines the area of 'The Nab' which, as noted, formed a detached portion of the neighbouring parish of Threxton. The function and date of the others is uncertain. The low scarp (e), dead straight and perhaps early post-medieval in date, is clearly a subdivision of the Nab. The others, interestingly, seem to form extensions of the two main sections of (d), apparently implying that the Nab enclosure was formed from pre-existing features of some kind. (f) is a narrow hollow way which gradually fades out towards the north; (g) is a well-defined, south-facing scarp, probably a lynchet. Both seem to relate to a farmed landscape which existed before this part of the wood came into existence, perhaps in the late Middle Ages.

A third extension (C), was made to the west of the main body of the wood, probably in the post-medieval period as it lacks a proper perimeter bank, although evidently before 1723, when the map of that date shows it as wooded. Two low scarps here may be associated with previous cultivation of the area. Area (D), to the north, was added to the wood after 1723, but before the early nineteenth century. In 1723 it was under arable cultivation, partly as two open-field strips and partly as a narrow enclosure, 'The

Lord's Ground', the northern boundary of which appears to correspond to bank (h). A straight ditch, rather than a woodbank (i), marks the western edge of this addition to the wood. It extends further north than the land mapped on the 1723 map, forming the western boundary of another small addition to the wood (E), which had again been made before the early nineteenth century. This is defined to the south by a ditched boundary that in plan describes a curious, inverted-v shape; this turns north at its western end and continues, parallel with (i). The northern boundary of (E) is formed by a slight scarp and ditch, which becomes a ditch alone further to the east. The layout of the boundaries of area (E) suggests that it was added to the wood at the same time as, or after, area (D). There are a number of ponds/pits within the wood, and three – quite deep – on its periphery.

The main body of the wood – Wayland Wood proper, within its massive woodbank – would thus appear to be 'primary' in character; the adjacent woods of Mounteneys and The Nab in contrast are secondary, and probably late medieval in date, while the smaller additions to the west of the wood are later still. But numerous finds from within the main area of the wood made in 2001–7 suggest that it did not develop directly from the 'wildwood', but rather went through a period of at least partial deforestation. These finds include sherds of Neolithic and Iron Age pottery, prehistoric flints, a late Neolithic/early Bronze Age flint scraper, a Neolithic polished flint axe, a possible early Saxon iron spearhead and an unusual Iron Age whetstone/pounder (NHER3363). It is possible that the low scarp/bank in the south of the wood (b) represents the remains of a prehistoric enclosure. This might explain the wood's role as an early medieval meeting place and the hints at early ritual use.

West Bradenham Great Wood
TF 91411024

West Bradenham Great Wood covers an area of *c*.24 hectares. The northern two-thirds of the wood occupies soils of the Beccles Association, the southern section those of the Burlingham Association. The wood lies in the north-west of the parish of West Bradenham, its north-western edge coinciding with the parish boundary with Little Fransham, and it is ranged roughly south-west–north-east. The north-eastern section is much wider than the south-western. The wood's boundaries lie conformably with the dominant grain of the neighbouring field boundaries, which display a vaguely sub-parallel 'coaxial' pattern, running with the main direction of slope north-eastwards towards the watershed (between the Wissey to the south and the Blackwater to the north). The northern and western sections of the wood were replanted in the late twentieth century with standards of oak and ash: area (A) is in fact shown as a field on the first edition Ordnance Survey 25-inch map of 1884, but this was a short-term reduction in the wood's area, as the tithe award map (NRO DN/TA 65) shows it as wooded, as does the Ordnance Survey six-inch map from 1929.

In the replanted areas only traces of the original vegetation remain. Elsewhere the wood comprises oak standards, many quite young, above an understorey of formerly coppiced hazel, accompanied by varying mixtures of ash and maple: there are some large ash stools, especially in the central sections. Towards the south and east there are also concentrations of hornbeam, again including some massive stools (up to *c*.6 metres in circumference). There are also sporadic examples of apple, birch, goat

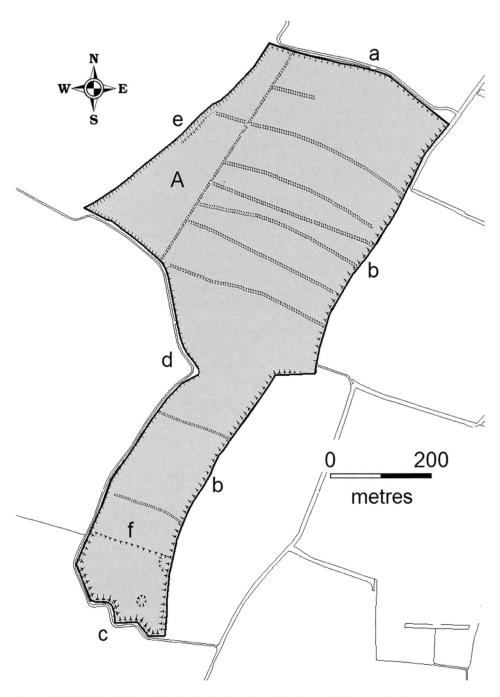

Figure 70 West Bradenham Wood: principal earthwork features (for key see text).

willow and elm. In the far south there are a few specimens of small-leaved lime, some growing on the woodbank. The ground flora includes dog's mercury, primrose and, in places, bluebells; there are scattered examples of wood anemone, lily-of-the-valley and wood sorrel.

The wood is surrounded on most sides by a woodbank and accompanying ditch of varying character (Figure 70). Along the northern boundary (a) this is around 0.5 metres in height and, including outer ditch, around 4–5 metres across: it may have been damaged during the replanting of the adjacent areas. The eastern boundary (b), in contrast, has a substantial bank and ditch between 5 and 7 metres wide and between 0.6 and 0.8 metres in height. The bank on the southern boundary (c), which follows a curving, irregular line, is even larger. There are massive maple stools in places along both sections which may represent the remains of a hedge. The western boundary of the wood (d) is rather different. To the south it is a low bank, varying from 3 to 4 metres across but scarcely 0.2 metres in height, with an external ditch; but moving north it gradually changes to a rather sharper bank around 3 metres wide and 0.7 metres high. The north-western boundary (e) comprises a much sharper bank, around 2 metres across and around 0.7 metres high, with an external ditch around 2 metres wide. The edge of the wood here coincides with the parish boundary, and this may explain the presence along one section of a parallel internal bank, around 10 metres into the wood, of similar width but lower height. The southern, eastern and northern boundaries of the wood are apparently medieval; the western possibly so; but the diminutive character of the north-western bank is difficult to explain. Given that the boundary coincides with the parish boundary it is unlikely to result from post-medieval truncation.

The wood was very overgrown when visited, and it is possible that some earthworks may have been missed. The most obvious internal features are a number of drainage ditches, mostly recent adaptations of nineteenth-century features. They form a roughly parallel network, ranged east–west and denser in the central sections of the wood than to the south, where the ground is lighter. Some of the ditches are straight but others gently curving, perhaps suggesting different ages. Those in the central section of the wood appear to have been truncated when area (A) became a field in the late nineteenth century. The most interesting earthwork is in the southern section of the wood, where there is a slight but very clear scarp running west to east, from TF 91106 to TF 91245 (f). This is about 0.2–0.3 metres in height and around 3–4 metres across. At its eastern end it forms the northern edge of a pit which has evidently been dug up against it. There is no accompanying ditch: the feature resembles a lynchet created by ploughing up against a hedge or fence, soil accumulating to the north and eroding to the south. It does not appear to be a subdivision of the wood or a former boundary. No other banks were detected within the wood, to the south, so it does not seem to be associated with the late medieval expansion of the wood over arable land. The strong implication is that it pre-dates the wood as a whole. It is noteworthy that it lies within the section of the wood overlying Burlingham rather than Beccles soils. Other than this, the wood is largely devoid of earthworks, except for a small irregular pit in the far south.

West Bradenham is one of the only woods in Norfolk for which we appear to have a date for the construction of the perimeter bank: a document of 1226 describes how the lord of the manor of Bradenham had 'about the wood … raised one earthwork for the livestock, lest they eat up the younger wood' (Rackham 1986b, 168). This may supply a *terminus ante quem* for the possible lynchet bank (f).

245

Winter's Grove, Woodton
TM 26719430

This small complex of woods lies on Beccles Association soils within the parish of Woodton, but close to the boundary with Hempnall. The area labelled Winter's Grove on the Ordnance Survey maps, and included in the *Ancient Woodland Inventory*, covers *c*.9 hectares and comprises two distinct but conjoined sections: a large, roughly rectangular northern and eastern block, covering *c*.6 hectares (a); and a narrower, more tapering area to the south, covering around 3 hectares (b) (Figure 71). In addition, separated from the latter by a narrow field, is a small rectangular block of woodland that is not included in the *Inventory* area. This is unnamed on all surviving maps and covers around a hectare (c).

(a) consists largely of outgrown coppiced hornbeam, with some hazel, ash and maple and with scattered oak standards (*Quercus robur*). Some wych elm also occurs in the south-east corner. In some places the ground flora is dominated by bramble but elsewhere bluebell, dog's mercury and wood sorrel occur. This section of the wood is completely surrounded by a substantial woodbank of typical medieval form: a bank, rising *c*.0.7 metres above the internal ground level, falls sharply *c*.1.4 metres to the base of an external ditch: the total width of bank and ditch is around 6 or 7 metres. Four pollards grow on the southern boundary bank (i.e., on the division between (a) and (b)): two maple (girths of 2.5 and 1.8 metres) and two hornbeam (3.5 and 3.7 metres). Although the interior of the wood was carefully inspected, no earthworks of any kind were found: the ground surface was completely level, without undulations, pits or ditches of any kind.

(b) is more mixed in its vegetation, with more oak, less hornbeam, more ash and maple and some thorn – in general, it is more scrubby in character. There is no woodbank, only a ditch similar to any other field ditch. Again there is some dog's mercury and bluebell, but no internal earthworks, except a number of dry pits to the east within an area shown as largely open ground on the first edition Ordnance Survey six-inch map of the 1880s.

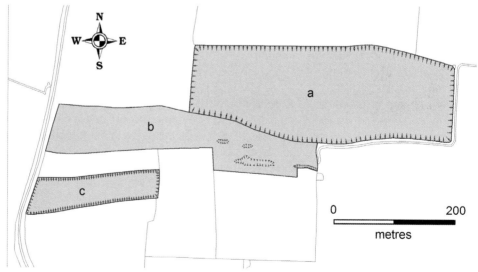

Figure 71 Winters Grove, Woodton: principal earthwork features (for key see text).

(c) displays more signs of past management. It comprises *c.*80 per cent coppiced hornbeam; *c.*2.5 per cent each of ash and hazel; and 15 per cent field maple. There are large amounts of dog's mercury. There is a slight but significant perimeter bank, 0.3 metres high internally, falling 0.5 metres into an external ditch (absent in places along the north boundary). There are around 15 oak standards aged about 150 years.

(c) does not appear on the Woodton tithe award map of 1841 (NRO DN/TA 476) and was evidently created, at the expense of a small field, in the mid-nineteenth century. The origins of (b) are unclear, but it is evidently a post-medieval, possibly early nineteenth-century, area of coppiced woodland. (a) is almost certainly medieval, but probably not primary. It sits neatly within the pattern of field boundaries, itself largely the result of late medieval/early post-medieval piecemeal enclosure.

Woodrising Woods: Woodrising Wood, Shepherd's Fell and Hazel Hurn

These three areas of ancient woodland lie on boulder clay soils and on relatively high ground in the area to the south of Shipdham in mid-Norfolk (Figure 72). Woodrising Wood mainly occupies soils mapped as Burlingham Association; the others lie entirely on soils of the Beccles Association. The first edition Ordnance Survey six-inch map of 1883 shows the woods with similar boundaries to those of today, as does the 1839 tithe award map (NRO DN/TA 71). The draft Ordnance Survey drawings of 1817, however, show a single continuous area of woodland labelled Woodrising Wood, as does (more schematically) Faden's county map of 1797. While it is possible that the three woods were separated from each other by the expansion of farmland in the early nineteenth century, it is noticeable that the first edition Ordnance Survey six-inch map shows the areas between them as pasture fields, densely scattered with trees, which may suggest that originally a large single block of woodland was divided into parcels which were partly managed as coppice and partly as wood-pasture. In 1817 the trees in the latter were perhaps dense enough to be considered 'woodland' by the Ordnance Survey's surveyors, but by the 1880s these areas had become more open in character. In the second half of the twentieth century the pasture area between Woodrising Wood and Shepherd's Fell was planted with trees (shaded grey on Figure 72); the remaining portion, lying between the three woods, was ploughed up.

Shepherd's Fell and Hazel Hurn butt up against the boundary between Mitford and Wayland Hundreds, which follows the watershed between the Blackwater (to the north) and the Wissey (to the south). The field patterns running up to this boundary, on both sides, have a loosely co-axial layout. The woods have suffered from extensive replanting in the post-war period.

Woodrising Wood
TF 97680338

Woodrising Wood (16.7 hectares) was extensively replanted with commercial conifers in the 1960s but some of the coppice understorey – stools of hazel, ash and some maple – still remain, together with much dog's mercury. As noted, the replanting extended the area of the wood to the south-west, across the area of well-timbered pasture shown on the Ordnance Survey six-inch maps and on the 1946 RAF aerial

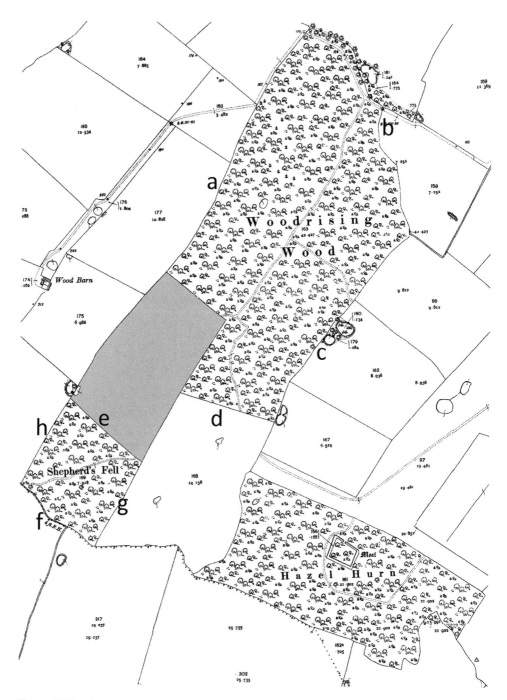

Figure 72 The three woods at Woodrising – Woodrising Wood, Hazel Hurn and Shepherd's Fell – as depicted on the Ordnance Survey 25-inch map of 1910: area planted with woodland in the late twentieth century shaded grey.

248

photos. The western boundary of the wood (a) comprises a ditch, accompanied by a woodbank towards the north, which is probably medieval but is in a poor state of preservation; this is flanked by a broad (c.7 metres wide) ridge to the east, the whole perhaps the remains of a trackway which was adapted as a boundary when the wood was first enclosed in the early Middle Ages. The north-eastern boundary of the wood (b) is formed by a large and well-preserved woodbank with external ditch, around 6 metres across in all. The eastern boundary (c) is a bank c.5 metres wide with functioning external ditch. The southern boundary (d) is a straight, evidently post-medieval ditch, accompanied in places by a bank: this was originally the division between the wood and the area of pasture to the south (separating the wood from Hazel Hurn to the south-east).

The wood is bisected from end to end by a long, sinuous bank around 3 metres wide and 0.5 metres high that is flanked to the west by a functioning ditch which runs a little to the west of the ride shown on the Ordnance Survey map (Figure 72). This originally continued to the south as the boundary between the wood and a wood-pasture area to the west, and then as the boundary between the two wood-pasture areas. It is noteworthy that this boundary, and the main perimeter boundaries of the wood, fit in with the surrounding, vaguely co-axial field pattern. The wood contains a number of amorphous, probably natural, depressions, some of which lie within the former pasture area, and two rather better-defined examples, which may represent saw pits.

Shepherd's Fell
TF 97320304

This has been replanted with oak and conifer nurses but the remnant vegetation includes hazel, maple and some crab and bird cherry, as well as one or two alder stools in damp areas. There are patches of dog's mercury and bluebells. The north-eastern boundary ((e) on Figure 72) has a low bank c.3.0 metres by 0.5 metres, with a ditch to the north; this looks late medieval or early post-medieval, and has what appears to be the remnants of a hazel hedge growing along it. The south-western boundary (f) – which is also the hundred boundary – is a low but substantial feature, around 0.3–0.4 metres high but in places 4 metres across, falling to a functioning ditch. The south-eastern boundary (g) is smaller, c.2 metres wide and 0.3 metres high; the north-western boundary (h) is even slighter. There is only a single earthwork feature of note: a slightly curving linear hollow which runs for c.10 metres in from the western edge of the wood, beginning at a point c.15 metres north of the latter's junction with the wood's southern boundary.

Hazel Hurn
TF 97790286

This is the most archaeologically interesting of the three woods (Figure 73), and also the only one where there are significant remnants of the original vegetation. This survives intact in the central section and in an area at the eastern end, and consists of oak standards above an understorey of hazel and ash, with some maple and wych elm and occasional bird cherry. There are large areas of bluebells, dog's mercury and

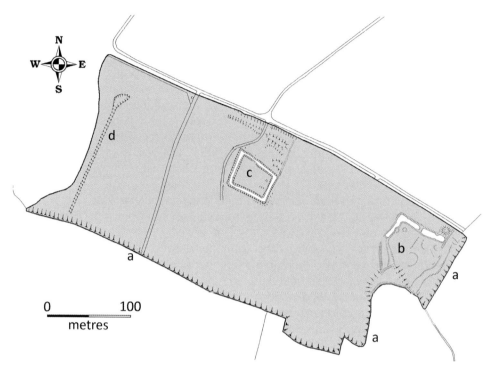

Figure 73 Hazel Hurn Wood, Woodrising: principal earthwork features (for key see text; see also Figure 17).

wild garlic, and extensive patches of yellow archangel (*Lamiastrum galeobdolon*). The County Wildlife Sites citations also record wood speedwell (*Veronica Montana*), wood sedge (*Carex sylvatica*), wood sorrel, remote sedge (*Carex remota*) and wood melick.

The southern and south-eastern boundaries of the wood have large and apparently medieval woodbanks ((a) on Figure 73), but the northern and western sides are marked by relatively insubstantial banks/ditches that are evidently post-medieval. There are a number of internal earthworks. At the eastern end of the wood (b) there is a complex area of pits, linear features and ponds described as a 'fishpond complex' by the NHER, but which looks more like the remains of a medieval, partly moated enclosure (Figure 17). Towards the centre of the wood is a moated site (c) with an outer enclosure to the north comprising a linear east–west bank which actually continues for some way to the west, parallel with and a little to the south of the north boundary of the wood. These features, it should be emphasised, are not associated with a lost landscape of enclosed fields and, if not constructed within coppiced woodland, presumably originally stood within areas of open pasture or wood-pasture. In the west of the wood there is an enigmatic hollow way (d) that runs from a large pond close to the north-western boundary in a south-westerly direction, parallel with the boundary of the wood.

Of some note is the way in which the boundaries of the various woods and pasture areas form a co-axial plan; the enigmatic 'hollow ways' and the arms of the moat in Hazel Hurn are also aligned with this pattern. It is hard, in the absence of early maps or documents, to reconstruct the development of these woods but the available evidence suggests three main phases. Until perhaps the thirteenth century the area probably comprised woodland pasture accessed by a roughly co-axial pattern of tracks from the lower ground to the north, and perhaps exploited by the moated site and partly moated enclosure in Hazel Hurn. Subsequently the area formed by the three woods and the intervening areas of pasture shown on the earliest maps was enclosed as a single block, with boundaries in part decided by the existing, roughly co-axial framework of tracks. It is possible that this area was subdivided from the start into coppiced and wood-pasture areas, but given the apparently post-medieval character of most of the surviving boundaries between these (i.e., the northern boundary of Shepherd's Fell ((e) on Figure 72), the western boundary of Hazel Hurn and the southern boundary of Woodrising Wood (d)) this division may have occurred only during the late medieval or post-medieval period. By the late nineteenth century the grazed areas had become relatively open, tree-covered pasture.

In spite of the presence of moated enclosures and hollow ways, there is no evidence that the areas occupied by the three woods have ever been cultivated. In this sense, all are 'primary' in character.

Bibliography

Addington, S., 'Landscape and settlements in south Norfolk', *Norfolk Archaeology*, 38 (1982), pp. 97–139.

Air Ministry, *The Royal Air Force builds for war: a history of design and construction in the RAF 1935–1945* (London, 1954).

Albert, W., *The turnpike road system in England 1663–1840* (Cambridge, 1972).

Alder, A. 'Trees beyond the woods – big moor shadow woodlands', in I. Rotherham, C. Handley, M. Agnolettis and T. Samojlik (eds), *Trees beyond the wood: an exploration of concepts of woods, forests and trees* (Sheffield, 2013), pp. 17–39.

Aldous, J.R., 'Broadleaves in Britain – policy, practice and potential', in G.C. Barnes (ed.), *Forestry at the BA*, Forestry Commission Occasional Paper No. 16 (1988), pp. 38–42.

Allen, R., *The British industrial revolution in global perspective* (Cambridge, 2009).

Allison, K.J., 'The sheep-corn husbandry of Norfolk in the sixteenth and seventeenth centuries', *Agricultural History Review*, 5 (1957), pp. 12–30.

Amyot, T.E., 'The Winfarthing Oak', *Transactions of the Norfolk and Norwich Naturalists' Society*, 2 (1874), pp. 12–18.

Ardron, P. 'In search of *Silva obscurus*: relict and lost wooded landscapes', in I. Rotherham, C. Handley, M. Agnolettis and T. Samojlik (eds), *Trees beyond the wood: an exploration of concepts of woods, forests and trees* (Sheffield, 2013), pp. 359–68.

Armstrong, M.J., *History and antiquities of the county of Norfolk*, 10 volumes (Norwich, 1781).

Ashwin, T., 'Excavation of an Iron Age site at Silfield, Wymondham, Norfolk 1992–3', *Norfolk Archaeology*, 42 (1996), pp. 241–82.

Avery, B.W., *Soil classification for England and Wales (higher categories)*, Soil Survey Technical Monograph 14 (Harpenden, 1980).

Bacon, K., 'Landholding and enclosure in the hundreds of East Flegg, West Flegg and Happing in Norfolk, 1695–1832', PhD thesis (University of East Anglia, 2003).

Bailey, M., *A marginal economy? East Anglian Breckland in the later Middle Ages* (Cambridge, 1989).

Bannister, N.R., *Woodland archaeology in Surrey: its recognition and importance* (Guildford, 1996).

Barnes, G. and Williamson, T., *Hedgerow history: ecology, history and landscape character* (Oxford, 2006).

Barnes, G. and Williamson, T., *Ancient trees in the Landscape: Norfolk's arboreal heritage* (Oxford, 2011).

Barnes, G., Dallas, P., Thompson, H., Whyte, N. and Williamson, T., 'Heathland and wood pasture in Norfolk: ecology and landscape history', *British Wildlife*, 18 (2007), pp. 395–403.

Barnes, G.C., 'Woodland in Norfolk: a landscape history', unpublished PhD thesis, University of East Anglia (Norwich, 2003).

Barnes, P., *Norfolk landowners since 1880* (Norwich, 1993).

Barrett-Lennard, T., 'Two hundred years of estate management at Horsford during the 17th and 18th centuries', *Norfolk Archaeology*, 20 (1921), pp. 57–139.

Barringer, C., 'Tanners and tanning', in T. Ashwin and A. Davison (eds), *An historical atlas of Norfolk*, 3rd edn (Chichester, 2005), pp. 160–1.

Barrow, E. and Hulme, M., 'Describing the surface climate of the British Isles', in M. Hulme and E. Barrow (eds), *Climates of the British Isles, past, present and future* (London, 1997), pp. 33–61.

Bateman, J. *The great landowners of England and Wales* (London, 1873).

Bathe, G., Lennon, B. and Soencer, J., 'Continuity and change: fluctuations in woodland cover, arable and pasture in prehistoric and modern times. Cycles of land-use and abandonment', *Landscape Archaeology and Ecology*, 9 (2011), pp. 54–75.

Beckett, G., 'The fate of woodland plants: a critical look at the survival and travel of our woodland plants', *Transactions of the Norfolk and Norwich Naturalists' Society*, 42/1 (2009), pp. 51–3.

Beckett, J., *The aristocracy in England 1660–1914* (Oxford, 1986).

Beevor, H.E., 'Norfolk woodlands, from the evidence of contemporary chronicles', *Transactions of the Norfolk and Norwich Naturalists' Society*, 11 (1924), pp. 448–508.

Bennett, K.D., 'Devensian Late Glacial and Flandrian vegetational history at Hockham Mere, Norfolk, England 1. Pollen percentages and concentrations', *New Phytologist*, 95 (1983), pp. 457–87.

Bennett, K.D., 'Competetive interactions among forest tree populations in Norfolk, England, during the last 10,000 years', *New Phytologist*, 103 (1986), pp. 603–20.

Bennett, K.D., 'Holocene pollen stratigraphy of central East Anglia and comparison of pollen zones across the British Isles', *New Phytologist*, 109 (1988), pp. 237–53.

Birks, H.B., 'Mind the gap: how open were European primeval forests?', *Trends in Ecology and Evolution*, 20 (2005), pp. 152–6.

Birrell, J., 'Deer and deer farming in medieval England', *Agricultural History Review*, 40 (1993), pp. 112–26.

Birtles, S., '"A green space beyond self interest": the evolution of common land in Norfolk c.750–2003', PhD thesis (University of East Anglia, 2003).

Blomefield, F., *An essay towards a topographical history of the county of Norfolk*, 11 volumes, 2nd edn (London, 1805–1811).

Boardman, E.T., 'The development of a Broadland estate at How Hill, Ludham', *Transactions of the Norfolk and Norwich Naturalists' Society*, 15 (1939), pp. 14–15.

Boulton, G.S., Cox, F., Hart, J. and Thornton, M., 'The glacial geology of Norfolk', *Bulletin of the Geological Society of Norfolk*, 34 (1984), pp. 103–22.

Bowyer, M.J., *Action stations: wartime military airfields of East Anglia* (Cambridge, 1979).

Boyes, J. and Russel, R., *The canals of eastern England* (Newton Abbot, 1977).

Brenchley, W.E. and Adam, H., 'Recolonization of cultivated land allowed to revert to natural conditions', *Journal of Ecology*, 3 (1915), pp. 193–210.

Briton Brush Co. Ltd, *Brochure* (Wymondham, Norfolk 1935).

Brown, J., *The forester* (London, 1861).

Brown, J., *Agriculture in England: a survey of farming, 1870–1947* (Manchester, 1987).

Brown, T. and Foard, G., 'The Saxon landscape: a regional perspective', in P. Everson and T. Williamson (eds), *The archaeology of landscape* (Manchester, 1998), pp. 67–94.

Brunet, J. and Von Oheimb, G., 'Migration of vascular plants to secondary woodlands in southern Sweden', *Journal of Ecology*, 86 (1998), pp. 429–38.

Bryant, S., Perry, B. and Williamson, T., 'A "relict landscape" in south-east Hertfordshire: archaeological and topographic investigations in the Wormley area', *Landscape History*, 27 (2005), pp. 5–15.

Butcher, R.W., *The land of Britain: Suffolk* (London, 1941).

Buxton, S., *Fishing and shooting* (London, 1902).

Campbell, B.M.S., 'The extent and layout of common fields in eastern Norfolk', *Norfolk Archaeology*, 28 (1981), pp. 5–32.

Campbell, B.M.S., *English seigniorial agriculture* (Cambridge, 2000).

Campbell, B.M.S., 'Medieval land use and land values', in T. Ashwin and A. Davison (eds), *An historical atlas of Norfolk*, 3rd edn (Chichester, 2005), pp. 48–9.

Carter, S.P., 'Habitat change and bird populations', *British Wildlife*, 1 (1990), pp. 324–34.

Carthew, G.A., *A history of the hundred of Launditch and the Deanery of Brisley* (Norwich, 1877).

Carus-Wilson, E.M., *Essays in economic history*, Vol. 2 (London, 1962).

Chapman, N. and Whitta, R., 'The history of the deer of Thetford Forest', in P. Ratcliffe and J. Claridge (eds), *Thetford Forest Park: the ecology of a pine forest* (Alice Holt, 1996), pp. 141–9.

Chard, R., 'The Thetford Fire Plan', *Journal of the Forestry Commission*, 28 (1959), pp. 154–89.

Chatwin, C.P., *British regional geology: East Anglia and adjoining areas* (London, 1961).

Chevenix Trench, C., *A history of marksmanship* (London, 1972).

Clark, C., *A brush with heritage: the history of Hamilton Acorn, Norfolk brushmakers since 1746* (Norwich, 1996).

Clarke, W.G., 'A list of vertebrate animals found in the vicinity of Thetford', *Transactions of the Norfolk and Norwich Naturalists' Society*, 6 (1897), pp. 300–6.

Clarke, W.G., 'Some Breckland characteristics', *Transactions of the Norfolk and Norwich Naturalists' Society*, 8 (1908), pp. 555–78.

Clarke, W.G., 'The natural history of Norfolk commons', *Transactions of the Norfolk and Norwich Naturalists' Society*, 10 (1918), pp. 294–318.

Clayden, B. and Hollis, J.M., *Criteria for differentiating soil series*, Soil Survey Technical Monograph 17, Soils Survey of England and Wales (Harpenden, 1984).

Clemenson, H., *English country houses and landed estates* (London, 1982).

Clements, F.E., *Plant succession: an analysis of the development of vegetation* (Washington, 1916).

Colebourn, P.H., 'Discovering ancient woods', *British Wildlife*, 1 (1989), pp. 61–75.

Collins, E.J.T., 'The coppice and underwood trades', in G.E. Mingay (ed.), *The agrarian history of England and Wales Vol. 6, 1750–1850* (Cambridge, 1989), pp. 484–501.

Collins, E.J.T., 'The wood-fuel economy of eighteenth-century England', in S. Cavaciocchi (ed.), *L'uomo e la Foresta Secc. XIII–XVIII* (1996), pp. 1097–121.

Comey, P.M., Smithers, R.J., Kirby, J.S., Peterken, G.F., Le Duc, M.G. and Marrs, R.H., 'Impacts of nearby development on the ecology of ancient woodland', Woodland Trust (2008).

Connell, J. and Slatyer, R., 'Mechanisms of succession in natural communities and their role in community stability and organisation', *The American Naturalist*, 111 (1977), pp. 119–1144.

Council for British Archaeology, 'Letter to the Prime Minister: biodiversity off-setting and the archaeological significance of ancient and historic woodlands', 2014 <http://new.archaeologyuk. org/Content/downloads/2896_CBA%20letter%20to%20the%20Prime%20Minister%20(bio-diversity%20off-setting%20and%20Ancient%20Woodland).pdf> accessed 8 May 2015.

Couvreur, M., Bart, C., Verheyen, K. and Hermy, M., 'Large herbivores as mobile links between isolated nature reserves through adhesive seed dispersal', *Applied Vegetation Science*, 7 (2004), pp. 229–36.

Curtis, C.E., *Practical forestry: its bearing on the improvement of estates* (London, 1890).

Cushion, B., 'Norfolk's ancient woodland: historic environment rapid identification survey', unpublished report for Norfolk Landscape Archaeology (Dereham, 2004).

Cushion, B. and Davison, A., *Earthworks of Norfolk*, East Anglian Archaeology 104 (Dereham, 2003).

Dallas, P., 'Sustainable environments: common wood-pastures in Norfolk', *Landscape History*, 31/1 (2010), pp. 23–36.

Daniels, S., 'The political iconography of woodland in later eighteenth-century England', in D. Cosgrove and S. Daniels (eds), *The iconography of landscape* (Cambridge, 1988), pp. 51–72.

Davenport, F.G., *The economic development of a Norfolk manor, 1086–1565* (Cambridge, 1906).

Davison, A., *The evolution of settlement in three parishes in south east Norfolk*, East Anglian Archaeology 49 (Dereham, 1990).

Davison, A., 'Inland waterways', in T. Ashwin and A. Davison (eds), *An historical atlas of Norfolk*, 3rd edn (Chichester, 2005), pp. 156–7.

Day, S.A., 'Woodland origin and ancient woodland indicators: a case study from Sidling's Copse, Oxfordshire, UK', *The Holocene*, 3 (1993), pp. 45–53.

DEFRA, *Biodiversity offsetting in England*, Green Paper (London, 2013a).

DEFRA, *Government forestry and woodlands policy statement. incorporating the Government's response to the Independent Panel on Forestry's Final Report* (London, 2013b).

Delabere Blaine, P., *An encyclopaedia of rural sports: or a complete account of … hunting, shooting, racing &c* (London, 1838).

Department for Communities and Local Government, *National Planning Policy Framework* (2012).

Dimbleby, G.W., *The development of British heathlands and their soils* (Oxford, 1962).

Dodwell, B. (ed.), *The charters of Norwich Cathedral Priory Pt. 1* (London, 1974).

Dolman, P., Fuller, R., Gill, R., Hooton, D. and Tabor, R., 'Escalating ecological impact of deer in lowland woodland', *British Wildlife*, 21 (2010), pp. 242–54.

Drury, P. and Rodwell, W., 'Settlement in the later Iron Age and Roman periods', in D.G. Buckley (ed.), *The archaeology of Essex to AD 1500* (London, 1980), pp. 59–75.

Dye, J., 'Change in the Norfolk landscape: the decline of the deer park', MA dissertation (University of East Anglia, 1990).

Dymond, D., *The Norfolk landscape* (London, 1990).

Dzwonko, Z., 'Migration of vascular plant species to a recent wood adjoining ancient woodland', *Acta Societas Botanicorum Poloniae*, 70 (2001), pp. 701–77.

Edlin, H.L., *Trees, woods and man* (London, 1956).

Evans, D., *A history of nature conservation in Britain* (London, 1992).

Evelyn, J., *Sylva* (London, 1664).

Everitt, A., 'River and wold: reflections on the historical origins of regions and pays', *Journal of Historical Geography*, 3 (1977), pp. 1–19.

Falconer, J., *Bomber Command Handbook 1939–1945* (Stroud, 1998).

Fleming, A., *The Dartmoor reaves* (London, 1988).

Fletcher, J., *Gardens of earthly delight: the history of deer parks* (Oxford, 2011).

Forestry Commission, *Tenth Annual Report of the Forestry Commission, year ending September 30th 1929* (London, 1930).

Forestry Commission, *Thirtieth annual report of the forestry commissioners for the year ending September 30th 1949* (London, 1949).

Forestry Commission, *Woodland wealth appraisal* (London, 2010).

Forestry Commission and Natural England, *Standing advice for ancient woodland and veteran trees* (London, 2014).

Forsyth, A., 'Game preservation and fences', *Journal of the Horticultural Society*, 1 (1946), pp. 244–56.

Fowler, P., *Farming in the first millennium AD* (Cambridge, 2002).

Freeman, R., *The Mighty Eighth: war manual*, 2nd edn (London, 2001).

French, C., Lewis, H., Allen, M., Green, M., Scaife, R. and Gardiner, J., *Prehistoric landscape development and human impact in the Upper Allen Valley, Cranbourne Chase* (Cambridge, 2007).

Fryer, V., Murphy, P. and Wiltshire, P., 'Vegetational history and early farming', in T. Ashwin and A. Davison (eds), *An historical atlas of Norfolk*, 3rd edn (Chichester, 2005), pp. 10–11.

Fuller, R.J., 'Searching for biodiversity gains through woodfuel and forest management', *Journal of Applied Ecology* (2013), pp. 1–16.

Fuller, R.J. and Green, G.H., 'Effects of woodland structure on breeding bird populations in stands of coppiced lime (Tilia cordata) in western England over a 10-year period', *Forestry*, 71 (1988), pp. 199–215.

Funnell, B., 'Recent geology', in P. Wade-Martins (ed.), *An historical atlas of Norfolk* (Norwich, 1993), pp. 16–17.

Funnell, B., 'Geological background', in T. Ashwin and A. Davison (eds), *An historical atlas of Norfolk*, 3rd edn (Chichester, 2005), pp. 4–5.

Gairdner, J., *The Paston Letters, AD 1422–1509*, 6 vols (London, 1904).

Gay, C.E., 'The Norfolk Naturalists Trust', *Transactions of the Norfolk and Norwich Naturalists' Society*, 16 (1944), pp. 3–13.

Godwin, H., 'Studies in the post-glacial history of British vegetation 15. Organic deposits of Old Buckenham Mere, Norfolk', *New Phytologist*, 67 (1968), pp. 95–107.

Goldberg, E., Peterken, G. and Kirby, K., 'Origin and evolution of the ancient woodland inventory', *British Wildlife*, 23 (2011), pp. 90–6.

Goodfellow, S. and Peterken, G., 'A method for survey and assessment of woodlands for nature conservation using maps and species lists: the example of Norfolk woodlands', *Biological Conservation*, 21 (1981), pp. 177–95.

Grigor, J., *The eastern arboretum, or a register of remarkable trees, seats, gardens &c in the county of Norfolk* (London, 1841).

Grigson, G. (ed.), *Thomas Tusser; the five hundred points of good husbandry* (Oxford, 1984).

Grime, J.P., *Plant strategies, vegetation processes and ecosystem properties*, 2nd edn (Chichester, 2001).

Gurney, D., 'Roman Norfolk (*c*. AD 43–410)', in T. Ashwin and A. Davison (eds), *An historical atlas of Norfolk*, 3rd edn (Chichester, 2005), pp. 28–9.

Hale, T., *A compleat body of husbandry* (London, 1756).

Halstead, P., 'Ask the fellows who lop the hay: leaf fodder in the mountains of north-west Greece', *Rural History: economy, society, culture*, 9 (1998), pp. 211–35.

Hanbury, W., *An essay on planting* (London, 1758).

Harrison, S., 'Open fields and earlier landscapes: six parishes in south-east Cambridgeshire', *Landscapes*, 3 (2002), pp. 35–54.

Harrison, S., 'A history of evolution and interaction: man, roads and the landscape to c.1850', PhD thesis (University of East Anglia, 2005).

Harvey, N., *The industrial archaeology of farming in England and Wales* (London, 1980).

Helliwell, R., 'The development of ancient woodland vegetation', *Quarterly Journal of Forestry*, 100 (2006), pp. 133–41.

Hermy, L., Honnay, P., Firbank, L., Grashof-Bokdam, C. and Lawesson, J.E., 'An ecological comparison between ancient and other forest plant species of Europe, and the implications for forest conservation', *Biological Conservation*, 91 (1999), pp. 9–22.

Hesse, M., 'Fields, tracks and boundaries in the Creakes, South Norfolk', *Norfolk Archaeology*, 41 (1992), pp. 305–24.

Higham, N., 'Forests, woodland and settlement in medieval Cheshire: a note', *Annual Report of the Medieval Settlement Research Group*, 4 (1989), pp. 24–5.

Hill, D. and Robertson, P., *The pheasant: ecology, management and conservation* (Oxford, 1988).

Hinton, D., 'The "Scole–Dickleburgh field system" examined', *Landscape History* 19 (1997), pp. 5–13.

Hodder, K., Buckland, P., Kirby, K. and Bullock, J., 'Can the pre-Neolithic provide suitable models for re-wilding the landscape in Britain', *British Wildlife*, 20/5 (special supplement) (2009), pp. 4–15.

Hodge, C.A.H., Burton, R.G.O., Corbett, W.M., Evans, R. and Searle, R.S., *Soils and their use in eastern England*, Soil Survey of England and Wales (Harpenden, 1984).

Hodge, S.J. and Harmer, R., 'Woody colonization on unmanaged urban and ex-industrial sites', *Forestry*, 69/3 (1996), pp. 245–61.

Hooke, D., *Trees in Anglo-Saxon England* (Woodbridge, 2010).

Hooke, D., 'The woodland landscape of early medieval England', in N. Higham and M.J. Ryan (eds), *Place-names, language and the Anglo-Saxon landscape* (Woodbridge, 2011), pp. 143–74.

Hopkins, H., *The long affray* (London, 1985).

Jacques, D., *Georgian gardens: the reign of nature* (London, 1983).

Jacques, D. and Van der Horst, A., *The gardens of William and Mary* (London, 1988).

Jessop, A., *Arcady: for better, for worse* (London, 1887).

Johnson, W., 'Hedges: a review of some early literature', *Local Historian*, 13 (1978), pp. 195–204.

Kent, N., *General view of the agriculture of the county of Norfolk* (London, 1796).

Kenworthy-Browne, J., Reid, P., Sayer, M. and Watkin, D., *Burke's and Savills guide to country houses, Vol. 3: East Anglia* (London, 1981).

Kirby, K.J., Smart, S.M., Black, H.I.J., Bunce, R.G.H., Corney, P.M. and Smithers, R.J., 'Long term ecological change in British woodland (1971–2001): a re-survey and analysis of change based on the 103 sites in the Nature Conservancy "Bunce 1971" woodland survey', English Nature Research Report 653 (Peterborough, 2005).

Kirby, K.J., Pyatt, D.G. and Rodwell, J., 'Charaterisation of the woodland flora and woodland communities in Britain using Ellenberg values and Functional Analysis', in I. Rotherham, M. Jones and C. Hadley (eds), *Working and walking in the footsteps of ghosts vol. 1., the wooded landscape* (Sheffield, 2012), pp. 66–86.

Langford, P., *Polite and commercial people: England, 1727–1783* (Oxford, 1989).

Langley, B., *New principles of gardening* (London, 1728).

Lawes, J.B., *The Rothamsted experiments* (London, 1895).

Lennard, R., 'The destruction of woodland in the eastern counties under William the Conqueror', *English Historical Review*, 15 (1945), pp. 36–43.

Liddiard, R., *'Landscapes of lordship': Norman castles and the countryside in medieval Norfolk 1066–1220*, British Archaeological Reports British Series 309 (Oxford, 2000).

Liddiard, R., 'The deer parks of Domesday Book', *Landscapes*, 4 (2003), pp. 4–23.

Liddiard, R. (ed.), *The medieval park: new perspectives* (Macclesfield, 2007).

Liddiard, R., 'The Norfolk Deer Parks Project: report for the Norfolk Biodiversity Partnership', 2010 <http://www.norfolkbiodiversity.org/pdf/reportsandpublications/Norfolk%20Deer%20Parks%20_Rob%20Liddiard_.pdf> accessed January 2015.

Loudon, J.C., *Arboretum et fruticetum britanicum, or, the trees and shrubs of Britain …* (London, 1838).

McCamley, N.J., *Disasters underground* (Sheffield, 2004).

McKernan, P. and Goldberg, E., 'A review of the revision of the *Ancient Woodland Inventory* in the South East', Natural England Research Report NERR042 (Peterborough, 2011).

Macnair, A.D.M. and Williamson, T., *William Faden and Norfolk's eighteenth-century landscape* (Oxford, 2010).

Macphail, R.I., *Soil report on the turf stack and buried soil in barrow excavations in Norfolk. 1950–1982*, East Anglian Archaeology 29 (Dereham, 1986).

Malster, R., 'Shipbuilders of Yarmouth', *Norfolk Sailor*, 8 (1964), pp. 2–8.

Manning, C.R., 'Earthworks at the Castle Hill, Darrow Wood, Denton', *Norfolk Archaeology*, 9 (1884), pp. 335–42.

Marshall, W., *The rural economy of Norfolk* (London, 1787).

Marshall, W., *Planting and rural ornament* (London, 1796).

Marshall, W., *The review and abstract of the county reports to the Board of Agriculture. Vol. 3. Eastern Department* (London, 1818).

Martin, E. and Satchell, M., *Wheare most inclosures be. East Anglian fields, history, morphology and management*, East Anglian Archaeology 124 (Ipswich, 2008).

Miche, C.Y., *The practice of forestry* (London, 1888).

Mileson, S., *Parks in medieval England* (Oxford, 2009).

Miller, P., *The gardener's dictionary* (London, 1731).

Mitchell, A., *Trees of Britain and northern Europe*, 2nd edn (London, 1974).

Mitchell, F.G., 'How open were European primeval forests? Hypothesis testing using palaeoecological data', *Journal of Ecology*, 93 (2005), pp. 168–77.

Mitchell, F.G.J. and Kirby, K.J., 'The impact of large herbivores on the conservation of semi-natural woods in the British uplands', *Forestry*, 63 (1990), pp. 333–53.

Moreton, C. and Rutledge, P. (eds), 'Skayman's Book. 1516–1518', in *Farming and gardening in late medieval Norfolk*, Norfolk Record Society 56 (Norwich, 1997), pp. 95–155.

Morley, K., 'The origins and development of common land in the boulder clay region of Norfolk', MA dissertation (University of East Anglia, 2003).

Morris, M. and Wainwright, A., 'Iron Age and Romano-British settlement and economy in the Upper Bulbourne Valley, Hertfordshire', in R. Holgate (ed.), *Chiltern archaeology: recent work* (Dunstable, 1995), pp. 68–75.

Mosby, J.E.G., *The land of Britain: Norfolk* (London, 1938).

Moss, C., Rankin, W.M. and Tansley, A.G., 'The woodlands of England', *New Phytologist*, 9 (1910), pp. 113–49.

Munsche, P.B., *Gentlemen and poachers: the English game laws 1671–1831* (Cambridge, 1981).

Murphy, P., 'Pre-Norman vegetational change and woodland clearance', in P. Wade-Martins (ed.), *An historical atlas of Norfolk* (Norwich, 1993), pp. 20–1.

Nature Conservancy Council, *Inventory of ancient woodland* (Peterborough, 1981).

Nef, J.U., *The rise of the British coal industry* (London, 1932).

Norfolk Federation of Women's Institutes, *The Norfolk village book* (Norwich, 1999).

Norgate, F., 'Notes on Norfolk mammalia', *Transactions of the Norfolk and Norwich Naturalists' Society*, 2 (1878), pp. 458–70.

Oosthuizen, S., 'Prehistoric fields into medieval furlongs? Evidence from Caxton, South Cambridgeshire', *Proceedings of the Cambridgeshire Antiquarian Society*, 86 (1998), pp. 145–52.

Oosthuizen, S., 'The roots of common fields: linking prehistoric and medieval field systems in west Cambridgeshire', *Landscapes*, 4 (2003), pp. 145–52.

Opie, I. and Opie, P. (eds), *The Oxford book of narrative verse* (Oxford, 1983).

Owen, D.M., *The making of Kings Lynn*, British Academy Records of Social and Economic History, New Series 9 (London, 1984).

Palmer, C.J., *Manships history of Great Yarmouth* (London, 1856).

Palmer, C.J., *The perlustration of Great Yarmouth* (Great Yarmouth, 1872).

Parry, J., *Heathland* (London, 2003).

Peglar, S., Fritz, S. and Birks, H., 'Vegetation and land use history at Diss, Norfolk', *Journal of Ecology* 77 (1989), pp. 203–22.

Perry, J., *British farming in the Great Depression: an historical geography* (Newton Abbot, 1974).

Peterken, G.F., *Woodland conservation and management* (Cambridge, 1981).

Peterken, G.F., *Natural woodland: ecology and conservation in northern temperate regions* (Cambridge, 1996).

Peterken, G.F. and Game, M., 'Historical factors affecting the number and distribution of vascular plant species in the woodlands of central Lincolnshire', *Journal of Ecology*, 72 (1984), pp. 155–82.

Pevsner, N. and Cherry, B., *The buildings of England: Hertfordshire* (London, 1977).

Pevsner, N. and Wilson, B., *The buildings of England, Norfolk I: Norwich and north-east* (London, 2002).

Phillips, A.D.M., *The underdraining of farmland in England during the nineteenth century* (Cambridge, 1989).

Phillips, A.D.M., 'Arable land drainage in the nineteenth century', in H. Cook and T. Williamson (eds), *Water management in the English landscape: field, marsh and meadow* (Edinburgh, 1999), pp. 53–72.

Phythian Adams, C., *Re-thinking English local history* (Leicester, 1987).

Pollard, E., 'Hedges, VII. Woodland relic hedges in Huntingdonshire and Peterborough, *Journal of Ecology*, 61 (1973), pp. 343–52.

Pollard, E., Hooper, M.D. and Moore, N.W., *Hedges* (London, 1974).

Postgate, M.R., 'The field systems of Breckland', *Agricultural History Review*, 10 (1962), pp. 80–101.

Postgate, M.R., 'Field systems of East Anglia', in A.R.H. Baker and R.A. Butlin (eds), *Studies of field systems in the British Isles* (Cambridge, 1973), pp. 281–324.

Prince, H., 'The origins of pits and depressions in Norfolk', *Geography*, 49 (1964), pp. 15–32.

Prince, H., 'The changing rural landscape', in G. Mingay (ed.), *The Cambridge agrarian history of England and Wales*, Vol. 6 (Cambridge, 1987), pp. 7–83.

Quamme, B., 'Kings Lynn: Medieval Trade with Norway', *Norseman*, 7 (1949), pp. 89–94.

Rackham, O., *Trees and woodland in the British landscape* (London, 1976).

Rackham, O., *Ancient woodland* (London, 1980).

Rackham, O., *The history of the countryside* (London, 1986a).

Rackham, O., 'The ancient woods of Norfolk', *Transactions of the Norfolk and Norwich Naturalists' Society*, 27 (1986b), pp. 161–77.

Rackham, O., 'Pre-existing trees and woods in country-house parks', *Landscapes*, 5/2 (2004), pp. 1–15.

Rackham, O., *Woodlands* (London, 2006).

Rawding, C., 'Society and place in nineteenth-century north Lincolnshire', *Rural History: economy, society, culture*, 3/1 (1992), pp. 59–85.

Read, H.J., *Veteran trees: a guide to good management* (Peterborough, 2000).

Read, H.J., 'Pollards and pollarding in Europe', *British Wildlife*, 19 (2008), pp. 250–9.

Read, H.J. and Frater, M., *Woodland habitats* (London, 1999).

Redstone, L.J., Cozens-Hardy, B. and Campling, S. (eds), *Blakeney Maritime Trade 1587–1590* (Norwich, 1936).

Reid, C., *The origins of the British flora* (London, 1899).

Richens, R.H., *Elm* (London, 1983).

Rider Haggard, H., *Rural England*, 2 vols (London, 1902).

Rider Haggard, L. and Williamson, H., *Norfolk life* (London, 1943).

Rippon, S., Smart, C. and Pears, B., *The fields of Britannia: continuity and change in the late Roma and early medieval landscape* (Oxford, in press).

Rodwell, J.S., *British plant communities 1: woodlands and scrub* (Cambridge, 1991).

Rodwell, W., 'Relict landscapes in Essex', in H.C. Bowen and P.J. Fowler (eds), *Early land allotment*, British Archaeological Reports British Series 48 (Oxford, 1978), pp. 89–98.

Rogerson, A., 'Fransham: an archaeological and historical study of a parish on the Norfolk boulder clay', PhD thesis (University of East Anglia, 1995).

Rogerson, A., 'Middle Saxon Norfolk', in T. Ashwin and A. Davison (eds), *An historical atlas of Norfolk*, 3rd edn (Chichester, 2005), pp. 32–3.

Rogerson, A., Davison, A., Pritchard, D. and Silvester, R., *Barton Bendish and Caldecote: fieldwork in south-west Norfolk*, East Anglian Archaeology 80 (Dereham, 1997).

Rose, F., 'Indicators of ancient woodland: the use of vascular plants in evaluating ancient woods for nature conservation', *British Wildlife*, 10 (1999), pp. 41–251.

Rotherham, I.D., 'A landscape history approach to the assessment of ancient woodlands', in E.B. Wallace (ed.), *Woodlands: ecology, management and conservation* (New York, 2011a), pp. 163–84.

Rotherham, I.D., *Peat and peat cutting* (Princes Risborough, 2011b).

Rotherham, I.D., 'Searching for shadows and ghosts', in I.D. Rotherham, C. Handley, M. Agnoletti and T. Somojlik (eds), *Trees beyond the wood: an exploration of concepts of woods, forests and trees* (Sheffield, 2012), pp. 1–16.

Rotherham, I.D. and Ardron, P.A., 'The archaeology of woodland landscapes: issues for managers based on the case-study of Sheffield, England and four thousand years of human impact', *Arboricultural Journal*, 29/4 (2006), pp. 229–43.

Rotherham, I.D. and Wright, B., 'Assessing woodland history and management using vascular plant indicators', *Aspects of Applied Biology*, 108 (2011), pp. 105–12.

Rotherham, I.D., Jones, M., Smith, L. and Handley, C. (eds), *The woodland heritage manual: a guide to investigating woodland landscapes* (Sheffield, 2008).

Rowe, A., 'Pollards: living archaeology', in K. Lockyer (ed.), *Hertfordshire archaeology: recent research, a festschrift for Tony Rook* (Hertford, in press).

Rowe, A. and Williamson, T., *The origins of Hertfordshire* (Hertford, 2013).

Rowley, T., *The English landscape in the twentieth century* (London, 2006).

Rutledge, P., 'Colkirk: a north Norfolk settlement pattern', *Norfolk Archaeology*, 40 (1989), pp. 15–34.

Ryan, Luci and the Woodland Trust, *The impacts of development on ancient woodland – addendum* (Grantham, 2012).

Ryle, G., *Forest service: the first forty-five years of the Forestry Commission in Great Britain* (Newton Abbot, 1969).

Salzman, L.F., *Building in England down to 1540* (Oxford, 1952).

Schlich, W., 'Forestry and the war', *Quarterly Journal of Forestry*, 9 (1915), pp. 1–7.

Sheail, J., *An environmental history of twentieth-century Britain* (London, 2002).

Shoard, M., *The theft of the countryside* (London, 1980).

Short, B., Watkins, C. and Martin, J. (eds), *The front line of freedom: British farming in the Second World War*, Agricultural History Review Supplement Series 4 (Exeter, 2007).

Shrubb, M., *Birds, scythes and combines: a history of birds and agricultural change* (Cambridge, 2003).

Silvester, R., *The fenland project, 3: marshland and the Nar valley, Norfolk*, East Anglian Archaeology 45 (Dereham, 1988).

Simmons, I., *The environmental impact of late Mesolithic cultures* (Edinburgh, 1996).

Simmons, I., *An environmental history of Great Britain: from 10,000 years ago to the present* (Edinburgh, 2001).

Simpson, J., *British woods and their owners* (London, 1909).

Sims, R., 'The anthropogenic factor in East Anglian vegetational history: an approach using A[bsolute] P[ollen] F[requency] techniques', in H. Birks and R. West (eds), *Quaternary plant ecology* (Oxford, 1973), pp. 223–36.

Sims, R., 'Man and vegetation in Norfolk', in S. Limbrey and J.G. Evans (eds), *The effect of man on the landscape: the lowland zone*, CBA Research Report 21 (London, 1978), pp. 57–62.

Skipper, K. and Williamson, T., *Thetford Forest: making a landscape, 1922–1997* (Norwich, 1997).

Slotte, H., 'Harvesting of leaf-hay shaped the Swedish landscape', *Landscape Ecology*, 16 (2001), pp. 691–702.

Smith, A. Hassell, Baker, G. and Kenny, R.W. (eds), *The papers of Nathaniel Bacon of Stiffkey vol. 1* (Norwich, 1979).

Smith, A. Hassell and Baker, G. (eds), *The papers of Nathaniel Bacon of Stiffkey vol. 2* (Norwich, 1983).

Spencer, J., 'Indications of antiquity: some observations on the nature of plants associated with ancient woodland', *British Wildlife*, 2 (1990), pp. 90–102.

Spencer, J. and Kirby, K., 'An inventory of ancient woodland for England and Wales', *Biological Conservation*, 62 (1992), pp. 77–93.

Spooner, S. (ed.), *Sail and storm: the Aylsham navigation* (Aylsham, 2012).

Stevenson, H., *The birds of Norfolk* (London, 1870).

Stone, A. and Williamson, T., 'Pseudo-ancient woodland and the *Ancient Woodland Inventory*', *Landscapes*, 14 (2013), pp. 141–54.

Stroud, D., *Capability Brown* (London, 1965).

Switzer, S., *Ichnographica rustica* (London, 1718).

Taigel, A. and Williamson, T., 'Some early geometric gardens in Norfolk', *Journal of Garden History*, 11 (1991), Vols 1 and 2, pp. 1–111.

Tallant, F., 'Underwood: planting, growth, conversion and sale thereof', *Journal of the Royal Agricultural Society of England*, 16 (1880), pp. 114–20.

Tansley, A.G., *The British Islands and their vegetation*, Vol. 1 (Cambridge, 1949).

Tapper, S., *Game heritage* (Fordingbridge, 1992).

Taylor, C., 'Roman settlements in the Nene Valley: the impact of recent archaeological work', in P.J. Fowler (ed.), *Recent work in rural archaeology* (Bradford-on-Avon, 1975), pp. 109–20.

Tennyson, J., *Suffolk scene: a book of description and adventure* (London, 1939).

Thompson, F.M.L., *English landed society in the nineteenth century* (London, 1963).

Thompson, R.J., Butcher, W.G., Williams, P. and Warren, M., 'The use of vascular plants as indicators of ancient woodland in Somerset: the development of a county-specific list', *Somerset Archaeology and Natural History*, 147 (2003), pp. 247–56.

Tsouvalis, J., *A critical geography of Britain's state forests* (Oxford, 2000).

Turner, M., 'Parliamentary enclosure', in T. Ashwin and A. Davison (eds), *An historical atlas of Norfolk*, 3rd edn (Chichester, 2005), pp. 130–2.

Turner, R., *Capability Brown and the eighteenth-century English landscape* (London, 1985).

Twiddle, C.L., 'Pollen analysis: not just a quantative tool', in L. Clarke and J. Neild (eds), *Geomorphological techniques* (London, 2012) <http://www.geomorphology.org.uk/sites/default/files/geom_tech_chapters/4.1.4_PollenAnalysis.pdf> accessed January 2015.

Upcher, H., 'Norfolk farming', *Norfolk and Norwich Naturalists' Society*, 16 (1946), pp. 97–105.

Valverde, T. and Silvertown, J., 'Variations in the demography of a woodland understorey herb (*Primula vulgaris*) along the forest regeneration cycle: projection matrix analysis', *Journal of Ecology*, 86 (1997), pp. 545–62.

Vera, F., *Grazing ecology and forest history* (Wallingford, 2002a).

Vera, F., 'The dynamic European forest', *Arboricultural Journal*, 26 (2002b), pp. 179–211.

Wade, E., *A proposal for improving and adorning the island of Great Britain; for the maintenance of our navy and shipping* (London, 1755).

Wade, K., 'The early Anglo-Saxon period', in A.J. Lawson (ed.), *The archaeology of Witton near North Walsham, Norfolk*, East Anglian Archaeology 18 (Dereham, 1983), pp. 50–69.

Wade-Martins, P., *Village sites in the Launditch hundred*, East Anglian Archaeology 10 (Dereham, 1980).

Wade Martins, S. and Williamson, T., *The farming journal of Randall Burroughes of Wymondham (1794–1799)*, Norfolk Record Society 58 (Norwich, 1995).

Wade Martins, S. and Williamson, T., *Roots of change: farming and the landscape in East Anglia, c.1700–1870*, Agricultural History Society supplementary series 2 (Exeter, 1999).

Wade Martins, S. and Williamson, T., *The countryside of East Anglia: changing landscapes, 1870–1950* (Woodbridge, 2008).

Wager, S., *Woods, wolds and groves: the woodland of medieval Warwickshire*, British Archaeological Reports British Series 269 (Oxford, 1998).

Walsingham, Lord and Payne-Gallwey, R., *Shooting: field and covert* (London, 1893).

Warde, P., *Energy consumption in England and Wales 1560–2000* (Rome, 2006).

Warde, P. and Williamson, T., 'Fuel supply and agriculture in post-medieval England', *Agricultural History Review*, 62 (2014), pp. 61–82.

Warner, P., *Greens, commons and clayland colonization* (Leicester, 1987).

Warren, C.H., *This land is yours* (London, 1943).

Warren, M., 'European butterflies on the brink', *British Wildlife*, 1 (1989), pp. 185–96.

Watkins, C., 'The idea of ancient woodland in Britain from 1800', in F. Sabitano (ed.), *Human influence on forest ecosystem development in Europe* (Bologna, 1988), pp. 237–96.

Webb, N., *Heathlands* (London, 1986).

Wheeler, J., *The modern druid* (London, 1747).

White, J., 'What is a veteran tree and where are they all?', *Quarterly Journal of Forestry*, 91/3 (1997), pp. 222–6.

White, J., 'Estimating the age of large and veteran trees in Britain', Forestry Commission Information Note 250 (Alice Holt, 1998).

White, P., *The Arrow Valley, Herefordshire: archaeology, landscape change and conservation* (Hereford, 2003).

Wilkinson, R.G., 'The English industrial revolution', in D. Worster (ed.), *The ends of the earth: perspectives on modern environmental history* (Cambridge, 1988), pp. 80–99.

William, H. and Nisbet-Drury, I.C., 'Succession', *Journal of the Arnold Arboretum*, 54 (1973), pp. 331–68.

Williamson, H., *The story of a Norfolk farm* (London, 1940).

Williamson, T., 'Early co-axial field systems on the East Anglian boulder clays', *Proceedings of the Prehistoric Society*, 53 (1987), pp. 419–31.

Williamson, T., *The origins of Norfolk* (Manchester, 1993).

Williamson, T., *The Norfolk Broads: a landscape history* (Manchester, 1997).

Williamson, T., 'The "Scole-Dickleburgh field system" revisited', *Landscape History*, 20 (1998a), pp. 19–28.

Williamson, T., *The archaeology of the landscape park: landscape design in Norfolk, England 1680–1840*, British Archaeological Reports British Series 268 (Oxford, 1998b).

Williamson, T., *The transformation of rural England: farming and the landscape 1700–1870* (Exeter, 2002).

Williamson, T., 'Archaeological perspectives on landed estates: research agendas', in J. Finch and K. Giles (eds), *Estate landscapes: design, improvement and power in the post-medieval landscape* (Woodbridge, 2007), pp. 1–18.

Williamson, T., *Environment, society and landscape in early medieval England: time and topography* (Woodbridge, 2013).

Wiltshire, P. and Murphy, P., 'Current knowledge of the Iron Age environment and agrarian economy of Norfolk and adjacent areas', in J. Davies and T. Williamson (eds), *Land of the Iceni: the Iron Age in northern East Anglia* (Norwich, 1999), pp. 132–61.

Witney, K.P., 'The woodland economy of Kent, 1066–1348', *Agricultural History Review*, 38 (1998), pp. 20–39.

Woodbridge, J., Fyfe, R., Roberts, N., Downey, S., Edinborough, K. and Shennan, S., 'The impact of the Neolithic agricultural transition in Britain: a comparison of pollen-based land-cover and archaeological C14 date-inferred population change', *Journal of Archaeological Science*, 30 (2012), pp. 1–9.

Worster, D., *The wealth of nature: environmental history and the ecological imagination* (Oxford, 1993).

Wrigley, E.A.W., *Continuity, chance and change: the character of the industrial revolution in England* (Cambridge, 1988).

Wulf, M., 'Plant species as indicators of ancient woodland in north-western Germany', *Journal of Vegetation Science*, 8 (1997), pp. 635–42.

Yaxley, D., 'Medieval deer parks', in T. Ashwin and A. Davison (eds), *An historical atlas of Norfolk*, 3rd edn (Chichester, 2005), pp 56–7

Young, A., *General view of the agriculture of the county of Norfolk* (London, 1804).

Index

Entries in *italic* refer to illustrations